I0091945

Current Issues Facing Men and Boys

This important book offers an accessible overview and timely examination of the unique challenges faced by men and boys in contemporary society.

It covers a wide range of topics, including the male mental health crisis, the impact of media and popular culture on male identity, and issues related to body image, as well as education, work, sexual behavior, relationships, and the evolving roles of fatherhood. Additionally, it addresses the prevalence of violence, homelessness, substance misuse, and specific issues faced by men in institutional settings like the military and prison. Written in a user-friendly style, each chapter contains summary action points and signposts to further resources where relevant. The book takes an intersectional approach throughout, which continually considers the role of gender, ethnicity, religion, culture, class, and sexuality in the lives of men and boys. It therefore serves as an inclusive and comprehensive resource for promoting a more compassionate society, highlighting the need for evidence-based interventions and strategies to foster meaningful change that supports the well-being of men and boys.

Emphasizing that addressing men's issues complements and reinforces the broader fight for gender equality, this practical book is highly relevant for mental health professionals, educators, and other practitioners who are interested in understanding the unique challenges that men and boys face. It will also be useful reading for students of psychology, gender studies, sociology, health and social care, and many other subjects.

Benjamin A. Hine is Professor of Applied Psychology at the University of West London, UK. He is co-founder of the Men and Boys Coalition, a network that aims to raise awareness of the issues facing men and boys in the UK. He is also currently Chair of the Male Psychology Section of the British Psychological Society and is a researcher, speaker, and activist across a number of topics affecting men and boys, including reading attainment, experiences of family separation, and domestic violence. Find out more at www.drbenhine.co.uk.

Current Issues Facing Men and Boys

A Case for Urgent Change

Benjamin A. Hine

Routledge
Taylor & Francis Group

LONDON AND NEW YORK

Designed cover image: frimages via Getty Images

First published 2025
by Routledge
4 Park Square, Milton Park, Abingdon, Oxon OX14 4RN

and by Routledge
605 Third Avenue, New York, NY 10158

Routledge is an imprint of the Taylor & Francis Group, an informa business

© 2025 Benjamin A. Hine

The right of Benjamin A. Hine to be identified as author of this work has
been asserted in accordance with sections 77 and 78 of the Copyright,
Designs and Patents Act 1988.

All rights reserved. No part of this book may be reprinted or reproduced or
utilised in any form or by any electronic, mechanical, or other means, now
known or hereafter invented, including photocopying and recording, or in
any information storage or retrieval system, without permission in writing
from the publishers.

Trademark notice: Product or corporate names may be trademarks or
registered trademarks, and are used only for identification and explanation
without intent to infringe.

British Library Cataloguing-in-Publication Data
A catalogue record for this book is available from the British Library

Library of Congress Cataloging-in-Publication Data
Names: Hine, Benjamin A., author.
Title: Current issues facing men and boys : a case for urgent change / Benjamin A. Hine.
Description: Abingdon, Oxon ; New York, NY : Routledge, 2025. |
    Includes bibliographical references and index. |
Identifiers: LCCN 2024031556 (print) | LCCN 2024031557 (ebook) |
    ISBN 9781032709338 (hardback) | ISBN 9781032709321 (paperback) |
    ISBN 9781032709369 (ebook)
Subjects: LCSH: Men—Social conditions. | Men—Psychology. |
    Boys—Social conditions. | Boys—Psychology.
Classification: LCC HQ1090 .H555 2025 (print) | LCC HQ1090 (ebook) |
    DDC 305.31—dc23/eng/20241019
LC record available at https://lccn.loc.gov/2024031556
LC ebook record available at https://lccn.loc.gov/2024031557

ISBN: 978-1-032-70933-8 (hbk)
ISBN: 978-1-032-70932-1 (pbk)
ISBN: 978-1-032-70936-9 (ebk)

DOI: 10.4324/9781032709369

Typeset in Optima
by Apex CoVantage, LLC

This book is dedicated to the four most important men in my life – my father Ian, my brother Fraser, my son Theodore, and my best friend Nick.

Contents

Acknowledgments

As ever, I would first like to acknowledge my wife, Gemma, for her contribution not just to this book but to my life. She is my rock, and I love her to pieces.

Second, to my children, Theodore and Ottilie, not only for the love and joy they bring to me every day, but also for their patience when I am holed away, writing and ignoring bath time!

Third, I would like to thank the University of West London, and specifically my head of school, Dr. Jen Mayer, for supporting this project and giving me the time and space to complete this work.

Fourth, to all the many men and the organizations supporting men and boys that have reached out to support this text and give examples of the amazing work already happening in the men and boys sector – may this only grow.

Fifth, and finally, to all men and boys. We see you, and we love you.

Preface

When I was 11 years old, I saw the film *Billy Elliot* for the first time. I was absolutely captivated, not only by the epic movement (you know that scene where he just cuts loose and dances down the cobbles? Brilliant!), but also by the fact that I was seeing a boy that, in his words, didn't want to be a boxer – he wanted to be a ballet dancer. This rejection of the stereotypical desires of his father and everyone else around him was exactly the same rejection I felt for those same norms, and all of a sudden, my dream was to be a ballet dancer too. And I had the figure for it, with the right training. I was tall and extremely skinny, with (I think?) good rhythm (for a middle-class White boy in Hampshire, at least).

But my dream was simply not to be. When I approached my parents about my newfound passion, their answer was, "I don't think so. You've got enough problems as it is." (Don't worry, we have discussed this since!)

What were they referring to exactly? Probably the things I was being bullied for in my first years of secondary school. A "bouncy walk," a love of the Spice Girls, and just generally quite camp tendencies. Exactly the same things that make me think twice now, aged 35, when I go to order a cocktail at the pub instead of a good old-fashioned manly beer. Luckily, I am now confident enough in my own skin to do that, because it makes *me* happy, and it is what *I* want to drink – so a big whatever to anyone else! But that confidence has only come after (1) some healing conversations with family, (2) a supportive and loving relationship and marriage, and (3) a whole lot of therapy.

And let's be clear, my suffering is small fry in relation to some of the issues that men and boys face all over the world, including, but not limited to, their experiences as victims of sexual violence, their overwhelming overrepresentation in homeless and prison populations, and serious issues relating to everything from mental health to education and work. But those and my issues are all linked by the same fundamental questions: What is it to be a man? And why does no one seem to care about them?

And *I* was one of those uncaring people. I started out as a researcher solely focused on women's issues – see my early work on police investigation of rape and sexual assault. Indeed, at that time, I also had not really recognized or explored my own personal issues and experiences with gender and masculinity either, because no one had ever indicated that they were something that might have been unfair or unjustified. However, over the past ten years, I have been on quite the journey, both in my personal life, and in my career, toward an inescapable fact: men are missing from the conversation, and we need to do something about that, and fast.

And so that has led me to an interest in men's issues in a variety of domains and settings. It is why I am currently chair of the male psychology section of the British Psychological Society, the academic lead for the evidence-based domestic abuse research network (EBDARN), a trustee for the Mankind Initiative, and a cofounder and former trustee for the Men and Boys Coalition. It is also why I am a governor for my children's school, keeping a keen eye on boys' achievement metrics; a school reading volunteer, working with reluctant male readers in Key Stage 2; and a scout leader, working to help develop our scouts into well-rounded boys and teenagers (and the girls, too, of course).

It is also why I have written this book. I have seen that we are maybe, finally, beginning to realize that men and boys **do have** issues, just like women and girls (who knew?), and so, I thought it would be nice to get all these issues in one place, to give us a jumping-off point for the conversations that must follow.

And granted, these problems vary in size, scope, and severity, but they are nonetheless hugely worthy of our attention. Moreover, as discussed very shortly in Chapter 1, most of the issues outlined for men on "one side" are actually closely linked to issues for women on "the other," and part of the problem is that we have been separating them so rigidly, without appreciating that until we bring men into the conversation properly, we will not get anywhere with true gender equality.

I am not really doing all this for me personally, as my dreams are already mostly realized. No, not with an offer to join the Royal Ballet as a late bloomer, but because I have hopefully become for my son the person I needed when I was a boy. I already know my daughter, aged 3, will do anything she wants to do, and that is because she is both a second child who has no issue with asserting herself, but also because she is a girl being raised (rightfully) with the message that she can be anything, and I am there shouting that from the rooftops too. But I am *also* there shouting loudly that my son can be anything he wants to be, and he knows it, maybe too much. #KeenDad.

However, unlike my daughter, *he* is growing up in a society that has **not** been having the same type of conversations about boys and men as she is hearing about girls and women. Just to be clear, this is not a statement that women and girls are fine, and that I declare feminism to be over! Far from it. It is also not a rejection of the idea that there are patriarchal systems as well as intersectional systems of privilege that exist to bestow power to (some) men in most societies today. **But** I have noticed time and again, with my own son, and in speaking to other boys, men, parents, professionals, providers, and policymakers, that the norms and stereotypes for boys and men are still extremely restrictive, and we are simply not having enough conversations about how these are then shaping their experiences and informing the myriad issues I will outline in this book. Indeed, as I have already said, in some areas, we are not even aware there is a problem – and that needs to change. Pronto.

And so, what is my hope for you, dearest gentle reader?[1]

Basically, let's talk. Let's chat. And let's have some of those critical conversations about the issues currently facing men and boys and, importantly, how to fix them, to the benefit of everyone.

NOTE

1 That is for the *Bridgerton* fans, by the way.

Section 1

INTRODUCTION

1

INTRODUCTION

1.1 WHY DO WE NEED THIS BOOK?

In today's rapidly shifting societal landscape, where the discourse around gender equality has gained significant momentum, the unique set of challenges faced by men and boys frequently goes unnoticed or is overshadowed. This oversight not only undermines a holistic understanding of gender issues but also neglects the specific needs and vulnerabilities of half the population. And so, as we push forward in the quest for a more equitable society, it becomes imperative to broaden our perspective, ensuring that the conversation includes and addresses the complexities faced by men and boys.

This introductory chapter sets the stage for a comprehensive exploration of these challenges across this book.

1.2 IMPORTANT CONSIDERATIONS

But, before we begin, it's important we set the right tone with a number of considerations.

1.2.1 Being Constructive

Throughout this book, I will emphasize the need for constructive dialogue and proactive collaboration to support the well-being of men and boys.

DOI: 10.4324/9781032709369-2

Throughout, I will be calling on policymakers, educators, mental health pro-fessionals, and communities to work together in developing and implement-ing strategies that address the diverse needs of this group.

It is the hope, then, that this text will facilitate a journey of exploration aimed at uncovering the often-overlooked aspects of men's and boys' expe-riences. To do this, however, I invite readers to approach these issues with an open mind and a commitment to deep understanding, to then inspire actions that create a more inclusive, equitable, and compassionate society.

Put simply, constructive dialogue is fundamental to any discussion we are going to have about men's issues. We must therefore commit to having open, honest conversations that challenge stereotypes and the status quo and which incorporate diverse perspectives from men, women, and individuals of various gender identities. Such a dialogue should then foster a deeper understanding of the impact of traditional gender roles and societal expecta-tions on everyone, and to everyone's benefit.

And any resulting concerted action should complement this dialogue and involve collaborative efforts that not only raise awareness but also drive tan-gible changes. By uniting different community leaders and stakeholders, this book will advocate for systemic reforms, educational initiatives that chal-lenge outdated norms, mental health support that is accessible and stigma-free, and community programs that provide safe spaces for expression and support, all anchored on the principle of wanting to change society for the better.

Ultimately, fostering constructive dialogue and taking decisive action lay the groundwork for a society that values and supports the well-being of **all** its members, and for promoting a culture that rejects harmful norms and embraces diversity, empathy, and solidarity.

1.2.2   Recognizing Men as Human Beings

As part of this constructive dialogue, it is essential to approach the subject of men's issues without automatically framing men as "**the problem**." Men, like all individuals, are complex human beings with their own unique struggles, vulnerabilities, and challenges. Acknowledging this humanity is therefore crucial for fostering a compassionate and effective dialogue about the issues they face.

Historically, societal narratives have often oversimplified men's roles, sometimes casting them predominantly as the source of problems rather than as individuals who can also be deeply affected by societal pressures and expectations. This binary framing not only undermines constructive dia-logue but also overlooks the genuine difficulties that many men encounter. It is thus vital to recognize that men, too, can be victims of societal norms, mental health struggles, economic pressures, and more.

By reframing our approach to include an understanding of men's prob-lems and issues, we also open the door to more holistic and inclusive solutions. This is because this perspective encourages empathy and support for men as they navigate their personal and societal challenges and helps in dismantling harmful stereotypes that can prevent men from seeking help or expressing their vulnerabilities.

In promoting a more balanced view, this book advocates for addressing men's issues with the same seriousness and compassion that we extend to any other group. This includes acknowledging the diversity within the male experience, understanding that men from different backgrounds face distinct challenges, and providing tailored support that meets their varied needs.

1.2.3   The Right Focus

As you can see from the title, this book explicitly and unapologetically focuses on issues predominantly or uniquely affecting men and boys, either through their majority participation, prevalence or victimization, or distinct gendered experiences. It is important to clarify that this emphasis does not imply that women do not encounter similar issues or face them in unique ways themselves. However, the scope of this text is specifically tailored to explore the nuances of male experiences, and to recognize and address the often overlooked or misunderstood challenges that affect this demographic.

Wherever meaningful and necessary, comparisons with the experiences of women and girls will be made to provide context and deepen understanding. These comparisons will specifically aim to enrich the discussion, offering a balanced perspective while maintaining the book's primary focus on men's and boys' specific needs and situations. This approach ensures that the book serves as a dedicated resource for illuminating the experiences of men and boys within the broader gender discourse.

1.2.4   The Importance of an Intersectional Approach

Throughout this book, and particularly later in Chapter 23, I will consistently and loudly champion an intersectional approach in examining the lives of men and boys, recognizing that each person's experience is shaped by multiple, overlapping identities. This perspective will provide a nuanced understanding of their challenges and acknowledge that these experiences are diverse and influenced by factors like gender, ethnicity, religion, culture, class, and sexuality. Indeed, such diversity means that the experiences of men and boys cannot be viewed as uniform and, therefore, will not be treated as such.

The value of an intersectional approach lies in its ability to reveal how various aspects of identity interact, resulting in unique experiences of privilege and oppression. For example, the societal expectations for a Black heterosexual man can be significantly different from those of a White gay man, demonstrating that masculinity is shaped by various social factors and above and beyond sex and gender alone.

Furthermore, an intersectional lens helps us move past the broad general-izations that often dominate gender discussions. It enables a more effective address of the specific needs of different groups within the male population, ensuring that policies, programs, and interventions are comprehensive and beneficial to all, not just a few.

Additionally, adopting an intersectional viewpoint enhances empathy and solidarity among different groups, fostering a greater understanding of how discrimination and privilege intersect. This comprehensive awareness is crucial for creating supportive networks and alliances that can tackle the complex challenges faced by men and boys in a holistic and empathetic manner. That does not mean that you won't hear some references to "men" as a group, because there are some experiences that do universally shape male experiences and can be recognized as such. Moreover, not every study will have, or have been able to, explore men's experiences in an intersec-tional manner. However, where possible, I will seek to provide this insight and that's a promise.

1.2.5   Cross-Cultural Perspectives

While this book largely centers on issues affecting men and boys in the Western world, it is essential to acknowledge that this unavoidable focus is primarily a function of where most of the research is conducted and the progression of gender dialogue in these countries.

However, the issues facing men and boys are, of course, not confined to the Western world alone. Indeed, there is a pressing need for more cross-cultural research to understand how these challenges manifest globally, rec-ognizing that cultural, economic, and social contexts significantly influence these experiences. Wherever possible, this book will attempt to highlight global patterns and differences, providing a broader perspective on the issues at hand.

In this way, and by acknowledging the limitations of current research and emphasizing the importance of cross-cultural studies, this text aims to con-tribute to a more inclusive and comprehensive understanding of men's and boys' issues worldwide wherever possible. This approach not only enriches the discourse but also ensures that solutions are sensitive to diverse cultural contexts, ultimately fostering a more equitable and compassionate global society.

1.3   WHAT THIS BOOK WILL COVER

This book is structured to offer a comprehensive examination of issues men and boys face today, organized into thematic sections that collectively paint a clear picture of the landscape in this area. The content of these sections is given in the following:

1.3.1   Section 1: Introduction

This section lays the foundational understanding needed to grasp the complex dynamics at play in this area. After this introduction, Chapter 2 delves into "the impact of traditional gender roles," unpacking how these roles have historically shaped and continue to influence the lives of men and boys, setting the stage for the discussions that follow.

1.3.2   Section 2: Men, Mental Health, and the Media

Focusing on the critical intersection of mental health and media, this section addresses the escalating mental health crisis (Chapter 3) and the tragically high rates of suicide among men and boys (Chapter 4). It further explores how media and pop culture contribute to shaping male identity (Chapter 5) and the emerging concerns around screen time and gaming addiction (Chapter 6).

1.3.3   Section 3: The Body and Sexual Behavior

Chapters 7 through 11 examine the issues of body image, the pressures and risks associated with gym and steroid addiction, the controversial practice of circumcision, the complexities of sexual behavior and consent, and the impact of pornography. These chapters highlight the profound effects of societal standards and expectations on the physical and sexual well-being of men and boys.

1.3.4   Section 4: Education and Work

The challenges unique to male education are scrutinized (Chapter 12), along with the disparity in higher education enrollment (Chapter 13). Chapter 14 discusses the shifting landscape of employment, emphasizing the changing demands of the workforce and the impact on men's roles and identities, with Chapter 15 exploring how this affects work–life balance for men.

1.3.5   Section 5: Relationships and Fatherhood

This section delves into the realms of personal relationships, examining friendship and romance (Chapter 16), the evolving role of fathers (Chapter 17), and the impact of family breakdown, separation, and divorce (Chapter 18).

1.3.6   Section 6: Vulnerable Men

Exploring the vulnerabilities unique to men and boys, this section addresses their experiences with violence (Chapter 19), homelessness (Chapter 20), life in institutional settings like the army, prison, and the police (Chapter 21), and struggles with substance misuse and alcoholism (Chapter 22).

1.3.7   Section 7: Intersectionality and Intervention

The final section adopts an intersectional lens (Chapter 23) to understand the layered experiences of men and boys across different identities, concluding with a discussion on effective interventions and strategies for change (Chapter 24). Chapter 25, the conclusion, reiterates the call for urgent societal change to better support the well-being and empowerment of men and boys.

Each chapter contributes to a broader narrative that not only elucidates the challenges but also emphasizes the urgent need for inclusive, sensitive approaches to support men and boys from diverse backgrounds. By fostering an understanding of these issues and advocating for societal change, this book aims to inspire action and promote a more equitable, compassionate society for all.

1.4   HOW I WROTE THIS BOOK AND HOW TO USE IT

This book is intentionally crafted not as a dense academic textbook but as an introductory guide suitable for the public, practitioners, and policymakers. It is thus designed to be **accessible**, avoiding a heavy reliance on prolific academic references, which can often be barriers to understanding for those new to the subject. Instead, it provides a clear, straightforward narrative that supports key points with empirical evidence where necessary.

However, comprehensive academic citations are still utilized, and the book does not forgo rigor. Instead, it offers empirical support at critical junctures to reinforce the arguments made, ideally from research that has been conducted in the past ten years. Moreover, to aid those interested in delving deeper into specific topics, each chapter also includes signposts to further reading and recommended websites. These resources have been carefully selected to enhance understanding and provide gateways to more detailed studies and data for those inclined to explore beyond the scope of this book. This approach ensures that the content is both credible and digestible.

Out of respect for the depth and diversity of expertise in each field discussed, this text humbly acknowledges the contributions of numerous scholars and experts whose works have informed its contents. This deference is crucial, as it positions the book as a *starting* point for engagement with the issues facing men and boys, rather than a definitive expert manifesto. In fact, whilst researching this book, I was made aware of several texts that delve into some of the topics included. This book could never match the same level of detail across such a broad array of topics, and therein lies its unique benefit – putting all these issues in one place. Thus, rather than a book to end all books, this text is instead an invitation to learn, question, and contribute to an ongoing dialogue, one that enriches our collective understanding and fosters a more inclusive approach to addressing these critical topics.

1.5   LET US BEGIN

This chapter has set the foundation for understanding the multifaceted challenges within this demographic, emphasizing the necessity of a dialogue that incorporates diverse perspectives and experiences.

This book is intended not just as a collection of topics but as a conversation starter – a tool for education and change. It invites readers to engage actively with the content, question preconceived notions, and participate in broader societal discussions. With this text, I am hoping to ignite a commitment among all stakeholders – policymakers, educators, community leaders, and the general public – to foster a society that genuinely supports and understands the diverse needs of men and boys.

So then, let us begin.

2

MASCULINITY AND GENDER ROLES

2.1 INTRODUCTION

In human society, traditional gender roles have long dictated the behaviors, responsibilities, and expectations placed upon individuals based on their sex. Historically, masculinity has been framed around attributes of strength, stoicism, and dominance, while femininity has been associated with nurturing, emotional expressiveness, and submissiveness.[1] These roles, deeply ingrained through cultural norms, religious teachings, and societal expectations, are perpetuated from generation to generation, shaping the identities and experiences of men and boys in profound ways.

This chapter delves into the heart of how these long-standing norms influence the lives of men and boys, whilst also considering the other potential influences on gendered behavior (i.e., evolutionary and biological factors). It aims to unravel the complex web of expectations surrounding masculinity and to explore the myriad ways these expectations manifest in mental health challenges, educational and occupational disparities, and difficulties within personal relationships. By examining the roots and ramifications of traditional gender roles, the chapter seeks not only to illuminate the challenges they pose but also to highlight the urgent need for further discourse on what these terms mean for us all.

The goals of this exploration are multifold. Firstly, to bring to light the often-unspoken pressures men and boys face in conforming to outdated

DOI: 10.4324/9781032709369-3

models of masculinity. Secondly, to underscore the tangible impacts these pressures have on their well-being and societal participation. And finally, to advocate for a more fluid and inclusive understanding of masculinity – one that allows men and boys to live fuller, healthier lives, unencumbered by restrictive norms.

As we navigate through this discussion, it is crucial to remember that challenging and redefining traditional gender roles does not undermine the importance of recognizing and valuing the diversity of experiences among all genders. Moreover, it does not mean subscribing to an automatic assumption that masculinity and masculine traits are inherently *bad*. Instead, it contributes to a broader, more inclusive dialogue that seeks to uplift every individual, enabling them to thrive in a society that respects and celebrates their unique identities and contributions.

2.2   THE HISTORICAL CONTEXT OF MASCULINITY NORMS

The concept of masculinity has evolved significantly over time, shaped by a confluence of historical events, societal shifts, and cultural influences.[2,3,4] To understand the current perceptions of masculinity and the traditional gender roles associated with it, it is essential to examine its evolution and the factors that have influenced its development across different cultures and historical periods.

2.2.1   Hunter-Gatherers

In the early hunter-gatherer societies of the Stone Age, the roles of men and boys were deeply rooted in biological and environmental pressures.[5] Survival necessitated a clear division of labor based on physical attributes and practical needs. Men's greater physical strength and endurance made them the primary hunters and protectors of their communities. Hunting large game required coordination, strength, and bravery, traits that became synonymous with *masculinity*. Men's responsibilities also included defending their tribes from predators and rival groups, reinforcing the association between masculinity and physical prowess. This era laid the foundational concept of men as providers and protectors, roles that were essential for the survival of early human societies.

2.2.2   Ancient Civilizations

As human societies evolved into more complex structures during the rise of ancient civilizations, the roles of men continued to be shaped by both biological imperatives and emerging social hierarchies.[6] In civilizations such as Mesopotamia, Egypt, Greece, and Rome, men were expected to be warriors, leaders, and providers. Physical strength and the ability to fight were still crucial, but new dimensions of masculinity emerged, including leadership, governance, and intellectual achievement. Men held positions of power and authority, from kings and pharaohs to senators and philosophers. The construction of large-scale projects, such as pyramids and aqueducts, also relied on male labor, reinforcing the notion of men as builders and sustainers of society. These ancient civilizations institutionalized roles that valorized male strength, courage, and intellectual capability, further entrenching traditional notions of masculinity.

2.2.3   Non-Western Contexts

It is important to note that, beyond the well-documented histories of Western civilizations, numerous cultures around the world were developing more nuanced conceptions of masculinity. For instance, in many African tribes, masculinity is closely tied to roles within the community and rites of passage.[7] Among the Maasai of East Africa, young men undergo a series of ceremonies and challenges, including lion hunting (historically), to prove their bravery and transition into manhood.[8] Similarly, in Indigenous cultures across the Americas, masculinity often involves a deep connection to the land, spiritual responsibilities, and communal roles. The Navajo concept of "Hózhó" emphasizes harmony and balance, integrating masculine and feminine qualities within each individual.[9]

2.2.4   Medieval Times

During the medieval period, the roles of men continued to be shaped by both biological imperatives and environmental demands, albeit within the increasingly complex structures of feudal societies.[10] Men were expected to be warriors, defending their lands and lords, as well as providers, working the fields to sustain their families. The feudal system itself reinforced these roles, with knights and soldiers embodying the ideal of masculine strength and honor. Chivalry emerged as a code that dictated male behavior, combining martial skill with a sense of duty and protection toward women and the weak. This era solidified the connection between masculinity and the capacity for violence, honor, and loyalty.

2.2.5   The Renaissance

The Renaissance brought significant shifts in cultural and intellectual life, yet traditional gender roles remained strongly influenced by earlier patterns.[11] Men were still expected to be the primary providers and protectors, but the focus on humanism and individual achievement added new dimensions to masculinity. The ideal man was not only strong and brave but also cultured, educated, and skilled in the arts. This period saw the rise of the "Renaissance man" archetype, exemplified by figures like Leonardo da Vinci, who combined physical capability with intellectual and artistic prowess. However, economic and social structures still largely confined women to domestic spheres, perpetuating a clear division of gender roles.

2.2.6   The Industrial Revolution

The Industrial Revolution marked a profound transformation in societal structures and gender roles.[12] As economies shifted from agrarian bases to industrialized cities, men's roles as providers were again redefined. Men left the home to work in factories, mines, and other industrial settings, reinforcing the separation between the public sphere of work and the private sphere of homelife. This era saw the advent of the "breadwinner" model of masculinity, where economic success and the ability to financially support one's family became paramount. Physical strength was still valued, particularly in labor-intensive jobs, but new forms of masculinity emerged that emphasized economic power and professional achievement.

2.2.7   Modernity

The 20th and 21st centuries have brought rapid changes to traditional gender roles, driven by world wars, economic upheavals, and significant social movements. The two world wars in particular required men to take on roles as soldiers and defenders on an unprecedented scale but also saw women entering the workforce en masse to fill the gaps left by men.[13] Postwar periods often saw a return to traditional roles, but the seeds of change had been planted.

The feminist movements of the 1960s and 1970s were pivotal in challenging rigid gender norms, advocating for equal rights and opportunities for women in all spheres of life.[14] These movements also encouraged men to reconsider traditional notions of masculinity. Economic crises and the evolving job market further disrupted traditional roles, as more women became primary breadwinners and men took on greater responsibilities at home. Today, there is a growing acceptance of diverse expressions of masculinity, with an increasing recognition that emotional intelligence, caregiving, and domestic responsibilities are not antithetical to being a man.

In the modern context, the traditional roles of men are continually being redefined.[15] While some vestiges of historical gender roles persist, there is a broadening understanding of masculinity that includes vulnerability, emotional openness, and shared domestic responsibilities. This evolution reflects ongoing societal shifts toward gender equality and the dismantling of long-standing stereotypes that have defined men's roles for centuries.

2.2.8   Persistence of Traditional Tribes

It is important to acknowledge that many native tribes still exist today, maintaining their traditional ways of life and conceptions of masculinity. These tribes provide a living testament to the diverse expressions of masculinity across cultures and history. For example, the Aboriginal communities in Australia, the Inuit of the Arctic, and the numerous Indigenous tribes across the Amazon rainforest each have unique cultural practices and beliefs surrounding masculinity. These practices often emphasize a deep connection to nature, community responsibilities, and spiritual rituals, showcasing the rich diversity of masculine identities beyond the Western paradigm.

2.3   EXPLANATIONS OF MASCULINITY

The fact that our conceptualizations of masculinity have changed over time suggests that multiple factors inform the conceptualization and then performance of masculine traits. However, understanding the origins of masculinity requires an acknowledgment and exploration that considers biological, cognitive, and social factors and their influence on each other. Indeed, entire volumes have been written on this topic, reflecting its complexity and the interplay between various influences. This section aims to briefly highlight the intricate relationship between sex and gender, acknowledging that while some aspects of masculinity may be rooted in biology, the environment plays a crucial role in shaping these traits.

2.3.1   Biological Factors

From a biological perspective, differences between males and females in terms of physical strength, reproductive roles, and hormonal influences have historically contributed to the development of distinct gender roles.[16,17] Testosterone, for example, is often associated with aggression and competitiveness and has thus been linked to traditionally masculine behaviors. Evolutionary theories suggest that in early human societies, men's roles as hunters and protectors were influenced by their physical attributes, which were advantageous for survival and reproduction.[18] However, it is extremely difficult to accurately determine the true relationship between biological factors and gendered behavior, for several reasons (e.g., methodological challenges, causality issues, etc.). They are, therefore, only part of the picture and do not fully account for the complexities of modern masculinity.

2.3.2   Societal and Cultural Factors

If not biology, then we must turn to the environment. The process of socializing gendered identities is multifaceted and involves various actors, including peers, parents, teachers, schools, and the media.[19] These influencers play pivotal roles in shaping our understanding and expectations of gender from a young age. Parents often model and reinforce gender roles through their interactions and expectations, while teachers and school environments further contribute by promoting certain behaviors and norms. Peers also exert significant pressure, particularly during adolescence, as they validate or challenge each other's gender expressions. Meanwhile, the media provides a broader cultural backdrop, offering powerful narratives and images that shape societal norms and ideals regarding masculinity and femininity.

This traditional framework of gender socialization is now being supplemented by new influences, particularly through the advent of social media. Platforms like Instagram, TikTok, and YouTube have become spaces where gender norms are both reinforced and challenged.[20] Online communities provide a stage for expressing and exploring diverse masculinities, facilitating discussions around mental health, gender equality, and the deconstruction of traditional gender roles. This digital age has allowed for greater cross-cultural exchanges, exposing individuals to a variety of masculine ideals and practices that transcend national and cultural boundaries.

However, it is important to recognize that, just like with biological factors, the environment does not fully explain the development of gender identities and expressions. There is significant variation both across and within cultures, including the experiences of transgender and nonbinary individuals. These variations highlight that while environmental factors heavily influence gender expectations and behaviors, they do not dictate them entirely. Each individual's experience of gender is thus unique and shaped by a complex interplay of social, cultural, and personal factors, underscoring the need for a nuanced and inclusive understanding of masculinity and gender identity.

2.3.3   Cognitive and Psychological Factors

Cognitive and psychological approaches to masculinity explore how individuals internalize and perform gender roles. As outlined in the previous section, from a young age, boys and girls are socialized differently, with expectations and norms communicated through family, education, and the media. Cognitive development theories suggest that children learn about gender roles through observation and imitation of adults and peers.[21] Psychological perspectives emphasize the importance of identity formation and the pressures to conform to societal norms, which can shape behaviors, attitudes, and self-perception. These internalized norms can reinforce traditional notions of masculinity, such as emotional stoicism and the pursuit of success. However, as earlier stated, if children simply internalized what they saw in the environment, this would not account for the huge amount of variation we see in gendered expression and identity. So again, this is not the whole picture.

The relationship between sex and gender is thus clearly complex, with masculinity shaped by a combination of biological, cognitive, and social factors. If we were to try and formalize some kind of model, we might say that while biological influences may provide a foundation, the environment also plays a crucial role in defining and redefining what it means to be masculine, which may then be internalized and cognitively organized appropriately. Regardless of the exact relationships, society continues to evolve, and so too does our understanding of masculinity; ultimately moving toward a more inclusive and dynamic conception that embraces diversity, challenges traditional norms, and further complicates our ability to determine where these characteristics emerge from. Above all, this ongoing evolution underscores the importance of considering multiple perspectives and influences in any discussion of gender roles.

2.4   MASCULINITIES

As mentioned earlier, masculinity, as a social construct, paradoxically varies dramatically and shows some homogeneity across different cultures and societies, shaping the identities and experiences of men and boys in profound ways.[22,23] These varying conceptions of masculinity influence not just how men are perceived by others but how they view themselves and their roles within their communities. In some cultures, masculinity is closely tied to the ideals of strength, stoicism, and provision, while in others, emotional expressiveness and communal responsibilities define what it means to be a man. The diversity in these conceptions underscores the fluidity of masculinity, challenging the notion that there are universal traits that all men must embody to be considered masculine.

Despite this diversity, certain themes do still tend to link masculinity across cultures. These include notions of physical strength, dominance, and emotional restraint, which are often valued and reinforced through socialization processes. The expectation for men to act as providers and protectors is another common thread, reflecting broader societal structures and economic roles historically assigned to men. While the specific expressions of these traits can differ, the underlying ideals often promote a form of masculinity that emphasizes control, self-sufficiency, and a duty toward family and community. These shared elements highlight the pervasive influence of traditional gender roles, even as the specific cultural contexts shape their manifestation.

This variability in understanding masculinity also reflects the dynamic nature of gender norms, which evolve over time and are influenced by a myriad of factors, including economic conditions, political ideologies, and social movements. For boys growing up in these different contexts, their socialization into manhood involves navigating these complex and often conflicting messages about what is expected of them as men, which can have a lasting impact on their development and sense of self.

The concept of **hegemonic masculinity**, introduced by sociologist R. W. Connell, provides a framework for understanding these patterns.[24] *Hegemonic masculinity* refers to the dominant form of masculinity that is culturally exalted above other forms and is characterized by authority, heterosexuality, and the subordination of women and marginalized masculinities. This theory helps explain how certain traits become idealized and how men who embody these traits gain social power and legitimacy. However, hegemonic masculinity also perpetuates gender inequalities and pressures men to conform to narrow ideals, often at the expense of their well-being. Understanding this concept is crucial for challenging the structures that uphold harmful gender norms and for promoting more inclusive and diverse expressions of masculinity.

Michael Kimmel's concept of "masculinity as homophobia" further expands on the pressures of conforming to hegemonic masculinity.[25] Kimmel argues that men are often driven by a fear of being perceived as not masculine enough, which is frequently associated with being labeled as homosexual, regardless of their actual sexual orientation. This fear drives men to engage in hypermasculine behaviors and to distance themselves from anything deemed feminine or weak. Kimmel's work highlights how homophobia is deeply intertwined with the construction of masculinity, reinforcing rigid gender norms and perpetuating a culture of exclusion and violence against those who do not conform to traditional masculine ideals. This concept underscores the importance of addressing homophobia in efforts to redefine and broaden the understanding of masculinity.

Judith Butler's theory of gender performativity provides another critical perspective on masculinity, and ultimately one that posits more control over how we might shape gendered behavior.[26,27] Butler posits that gender is not an inherent identity but rather a series of actions and behaviors that individuals perform based on societal expectations. According to Butler, these performances are repetitive and socially regulated, creating the illusion of a stable gender identity. In the context of masculinity, this means that what is considered "masculine" is continuously enacted through behaviors and attitudes that align with cultural norms. Butler's theory challenges the notion of fixed gender identities and opens up possibilities for more fluid and diverse expressions of gender. By understanding gender as performative, it becomes possible to deconstruct traditional notions of masculinity and encourage more inclusive and varied ways of being male.

As societal norms and cultural understandings continue to evolve, so too does the concept of masculinity. Recent academic work and social movements have introduced newer concepts such as "inclusive masculinity" which offer a broader and more progressive perspective on how masculinity can be understood and expressed. Introduced by sociologist Eric Anderson, the concept of "inclusive masculinity" challenges the traditional, rigid frameworks of hegemonic masculinity, and suggests that in less-homophobic and more accepting environments, men are able to express a wider range of emotions and behaviors that were previously stigmatized.[28] This shift allows for the inclusion of traits traditionally deemed as feminine, such as emotional openness and nurturing behaviors, without the fear of being perceived as less masculine. Inclusive masculinity also posits that multiple forms of masculinity can coexist without a hierarchical structure. This means that the traditional, dominant form of masculinity is not the only accepted way to be a man and in settings where inclusive masculinity thrives, men can form deeper, more meaningful relationships, express vulnerability, and engage in behaviors that promote equality and empathy.

These theoretical frameworks provide valuable tools for analyzing and understanding the complex ways in which masculinity is constructed, experienced, and enforced. If we accept that at least a large proportion of masculine behavior is socially determined – and I think we should – they also highlight the need for ongoing critical reflection and dialogue to foster healthier, more inclusive forms of masculinity that allow all individuals to express their identities authentically and without fear of retribution.

2.4.1   A Word on the Concept of "Toxic Masculinity"

As part of the ongoing discourse on masculinities, the term "toxic masculinity" has also emerged as a way to describe certain cultural norms associated with masculinity that can be harmful to both men and society at large.[29] Originating from the men's movement of the late 20th century, particularly from discussions in psychology and gender studies, the phrase highlights behaviors and attitudes such as emotional suppression, dominance, and aggression that are often socially rewarded but detrimental to mental health and social harmony. However, toxic masculinity is often misunderstood as a blanket condemnation of all men or all aspects of masculinity, which is not the case. Instead, it targets specific, harmful behaviors and cultural expectations that restrict men's emotional expression and encourage damaging behaviors. Understanding this distinction is essential in promoting healthier, more inclusive conceptions of masculinity that allow men to express a full range of emotions and behaviors without fear of stigma or repercussion. Some have argued against the phrase altogether as deeply unhelpful,[30] and such arguments are compelling.

2.5   REDEFINING MASCULINITY?

Instead of "toxic masculinity," there are increasing calls to redefine masculinity altogether, which arises from the recognition that traditional gender roles often impose restrictive norms on men and boys, limiting their potential and adversely affecting their well-being, but also recognizes the positive value of some masculine traits (and not wanting to "throw the baby out with the bathwater" as it were). It is argued that challenging and redefining male roles is not merely a theoretical exercise but a necessary step toward fostering a more inclusive, equitable, and healthy society. This section outlines the arguments for redefining masculinity and highlights initiatives and movements that already contribute to a healthier understanding of what it means to be a man.

2.5.1   Arguments for Redefining Masculinity

The adherence to rigid gender norms and expectations places a significant burden on men and boys, impacting their mental health, behavior, and the way they interact with the world around them. The pressure to conform to a narrow set of masculine ideals can lead to a range of adverse outcomes, outlined broadly in the chapters that will follow including:

- *Mental health.* Traditional masculinity, with its emphasis on stoicism and self-reliance, discourages men and boys from expressing vulnerability or seeking help. This has significant implications for mental health, contributing to higher rates of depression, substance abuse, and suicide among men. Redefining masculinity to include emotional expressiveness and vulnerability can help break down these barriers, encouraging men to seek support and fostering better mental health outcomes. For instance, campaigns like "Movember" and organizations like "Man Therapy" are working to raise awareness about men's mental health issues and to promote healthier ways for men to cope with stress and emotional challenges.

- *Educational and occupational outcomes.* Traditional views on masculinity can steer boys away from pursuing interests and careers perceived as feminine, limiting their educational and occupational prospects. A more inclusive understanding of masculinity would allow boys and men to explore a wider range of interests and vocations without fear of stigma, leading to more diverse and fulfilling career paths. Initiatives like the "My Brother's Keeper Alliance" seek to broaden the horizons for young men of color, encouraging them to pursue a variety of educational and career opportunities.[31]

- *Relationships and social connections.* Rigid gender roles often hinder men's ability to form deep, emotionally supportive relationships with both women and other men. By challenging these norms, men can develop richer, more fulfilling connections, improving their social support networks and overall well-being. Programs like "The ManKind Project" provide spaces for men to connect on a deeper level, fostering emotional intelligence and supportive peer networks.[32]

- *Violence and aggression.* The association of masculinity with dominance and aggression contributes to higher incidences of violence, both interpersonal and in broader societal contexts. Redefining masculinity to prioritize empathy, cooperation, and nonviolence can lead to safer communities and healthier relationships. Organizations such as "A Call to Men" work to educate men and boys about healthy, respectful manhood, aiming to reduce violence against women and promote gender equity.[33]

2.5.2   Arguments for Understanding Rather Than Redefining Masculinity

However, while there are compelling arguments for redefining masculinity, some advocate for a more nuanced approach that emphasizes *understanding* traditional masculinity rather than demonizing it. This perspective suggests that instead of fully abandoning traditional masculine traits, society should strive to contextualize and integrate them in healthier ways, by focusing on the following:

1. *Valuing positive masculine traits.* Traits traditionally associated with masculinity, such as strength, courage, and independence, can be valuable and should not be dismissed outright. The challenge lies in framing these traits in ways that are constructive rather than harmful. For example, courage can be redefined to include the bravery to seek help and show vulnerability, and strength can encompass emotional resilience as well as physical prowess.
2. *Cultural sensitivity.* Masculinity is expressed differently across cultures, and efforts to redefine it must be sensitive to these variations. What is considered a positive redefinition in one cultural context might not resonate in another. Engaging in cross-cultural dialogue and understanding diverse expressions of masculinity can lead to more effective and inclusive approaches.
3. *Avoiding overcorrection.* There is a concern that in the rush to redefine masculinity, there may be an overcorrection that pathologizes traditional male behaviors and identities. Advocates for understanding masculinity argue for a balanced approach that recognizes the positive aspects of traditional masculinity while addressing its negative impacts. This involves promoting a more flexible and inclusive definition of masculinity that allows for a range of expressions and identities.
4. *Encouraging male engagement.* To successfully address the issues associated with traditional masculinity, it is crucial to involve men in the conversation. Efforts to redefine masculinity should aim to be inclusive and engaging for men, rather than alienating or accusatory. Programs that encourage male participation, such as "MenEngage" and "HeForShe," highlight the importance of collaborative efforts in promoting gender equality and healthy masculinity.[34,35]

The debate over redefining masculinity clearly reflects a broader conversation about gender roles and equality in modern society. While there are strong arguments for challenging traditional norms to promote mental health, educational and occupational opportunities, relationships, and non-violence, it is equally important to approach this redefinition with sensitivity and balance. Understanding masculinity in its various cultural and contextual forms can help create a more inclusive and constructive vision of what it means to be a man, fostering a society where all individuals can thrive.

2.6 THE RISE OF RIGHT-WING RADICALIZATION AMONG YOUNG MEN

Discussions around masculinity feed into a broader conversation amongst men, particularly young men, around politics and worldviews. Specifically, in recent years, there has been a noticeable trend of young men becoming increasingly radicalized toward right-wing and conservative ideologies.[36] This shift is concerning due to its potential to foster division, intolerance, and violence within societies and its implications for progressive conversations around gender. Understanding the reasons behind this phenomenon and addressing the underlying issues are crucial for creating a more inclusive and cohesive society. There are, I believe, several issues:

1. *Disconnection from gender conversations.* Many young men feel excluded from or alienated by contemporary discussions on *gender*, which often focus on issues facing women and marginalized groups (as outlined earlier). This exclusion can create a sense of resentment and lead some men to seek out communities that validate their feelings of disenfranchisement.
2. *Economic and social uncertainty.* Economic instability, job insecurity, and social changes can leave young men feeling uncertain about their future (explored further in Chapter 14). Right-wing movements often exploit these fears, offering simplistic solutions and scapegoating particular groups as the cause of these problems.
3. *Identity and belonging.* Traditional notions of masculinity are being challenged, and some young men struggle to find a place in a rapidly changing society. Right-wing ideologies often provide a sense of identity, belonging, and purpose that they feel is lacking in mainstream culture.
4. *Perceived threats to masculinity.* The rise of gender equality and changing gender roles can be perceived as a threat to traditional masculinity. Right-wing groups often capitalize on these fears, framing their ideology as a defense of traditional masculine values and roles.
5. *Online radicalization.* The internet and social media platforms play a significant role in radicalizing young men (explored further in Chapter 6). Online communities and echo chambers can reinforce extremist views, providing a space where these ideologies can thrive without challenge.
6. *Lack of productive conversations.* Society often fails to engage young men in meaningful and productive conversations about gender, identity, and their place in the world. This lack of engagement can push

them toward radical ideologies that promise to address their concerns in a more direct, albeit divisive, manner (hence why this book came about).

2.6.1 Strategies for Addressing Right-Wing Radicalization

To counter the trend of right-wing radicalization among young men, it is essential to implement strategies that address the root causes and provide healthier alternatives for expressing their identities and concerns, including:

1. *Inclusive gender conversations.* Encourage inclusive discussions on gender that actively involve men and address their concerns. These conversations should validate the experiences of men while promoting gender equality and dismantling harmful stereotypes.
2. *Economic and social support.* Provide robust economic and social support systems that address the insecurities and uncertainties young men face. Job training programs, educational opportunities, and mental health services can help alleviate some of the pressures that drive radicalization.
3. *Positive male role models and mentorship.* Promote positive male role models who exemplify inclusive and progressive masculinities. Mentorship programs can provide young men with guidance and support, helping them navigate the complexities of modern identity without resorting to extremism.
4. *Challenging extremist narratives online.* Develop initiatives to counteract online radicalization, such as digital literacy programs that teach young men to critically evaluate the information they encounter online. Creating online spaces that promote positive, inclusive messages can also help dilute the influence of extremist ideologies.
5. *Community engagement and support.* Foster community programs that engage young men in positive, constructive activities. Sports, arts, volunteer work, and other communal activities can provide a sense of purpose and belonging, reducing the appeal of radical ideologies.
6. *Education on diversity and inclusion.* Integrate education on diversity, inclusion, and the harmful effects of extremism into school curriculums. Teaching young men about different cultures, perspectives, and the value of inclusivity can help build resilience against radicalization.
7. *Support for emotional and mental health.* Provide access to mental health services that address the emotional and psychological needs of young men. Programs that promote emotional intelligence, resilience, and healthy coping mechanisms are vital for preventing the kind of disillusionment that can lead to radicalization.

2.7   INITIATIVES AND MOVEMENTS PROMOTING A HEALTHIER MASCULINITY

Several organizations are already having productive conversations about men and masculinity worldwide.

- *The Good Men Project (USA)*. An online platform that offers stories, insights, and discussions about what it means to be a good man in the 21st century. It challenges stereotypes and encourages men to explore new models of masculinity that are inclusive and emotionally intelligent. Website: https://goodmenproject.com.
- *MenEngage Alliance (global)*. A global network of organizations and individuals committed to engaging men and boys in gender equality and positive masculinity. Through advocacy, education, and community programs, MenEngage works to transform harmful gender norms and promote a more equitable society. Website: https://menengage.org.
- *Equimundo (formerly Promundo) (global)*. An international organization focused on promoting gender justice and preventing violence by engaging men and boys in partnership with women and girls. Equimundo develops research, policies, and educational programs that challenge traditional gender roles and encourage positive, healthy masculinities. Website: www.equimundo.org.
- *A Call to Men (USA)*. A nonprofit organization that educates men all over the world on healthy, respectful manhood. Embracing and promoting a new masculinity, the organization works to create a world where all men and boys are loving and respectful and all women, girls, and those at the margins are valued and safe. Website: www.acalltomen.org.
- *The Representation Project (USA)*. Uses film and media as catalysts for cultural transformation. Their films, including *The Mask You Live In*, address how traditional masculinity harms men and boys. The project encourages individuals to challenge and overcome limiting stereotypes through their campaigns and educational programs. Website: https://therepresentationproject.org.
- *Men's Sheds (Australia and global)*. Community-based nonprofit organizations that provide a space where men can come together to work on meaningful projects, socialize, and share skills. The initiative aims to improve men's health and well-being by reducing social isolation and promoting mental health. Website: https://mensshed.org.
- *White Ribbon Campaign (Canada and global)*. A global movement of men and boys working to end male violence against women and girls. It encourages men to take a stand against violence and to promote gender equality and healthy, respectful relationships. Website: www.whiteribbon.ca.
- *MenCare (global)*. A global fatherhood campaign that promotes men's involvement as equitable, nonviolent caregivers. By advocating for

parental leave, caregiving policies, and positive parenting, MenCare works to redefine caregiving roles and challenge traditional gender norms. Website: https://men-care.org.

- *Sonke Gender Justice (South Africa)*. An organization that works to promote gender equality and prevent gender-based violence in South Africa and beyond. They engage men and boys in initiatives that challenge harmful gender norms and promote healthy, equitable relationships. Website: https://genderjustice.org.za.
- *HeForShe (global)*. A solidarity movement for gender equality initiated by UN Women. It invites men and boys to join the fight for gender equality and work alongside women to create a gender-equal world. Website: www.heforshe.org.
- *Mankind Project (global)*. Offers training and support for men to help them lead lives of integrity, authenticity, and service. Through workshops and group meetings, the project aims to promote emotional literacy and personal growth. Website: https://mankindproject.org.
- *Breakthrough (India and USA)*. A human rights organization working to make violence and discrimination against women and girls unacceptable. They use media, arts, and technology to challenge and transform gender norms and engage men and boys in promoting gender equality. Website: https://inbreakthrough.org.
- *MÄN (Sweden)*. Works to engage men in preventing violence and promoting gender equality. They focus on transforming destructive masculinities and supporting men to develop more equitable, empathetic relationships. Website: https://mfj.se.
- *Men Against Violence and Abuse (MAVA) (India)*. Works with men and boys in India to prevent gender-based violence and promote gender equality. Through workshops, campaigns, and community outreach, MAVA challenges harmful gender norms and supports positive masculinity. Website: www.mavaindia.org.
- *FutureMen (UK)*. Focused on supporting boys and men to become dynamic and confident individuals. The organization provides a range of services, including mentoring, fatherhood support programs, and community outreach. Their initiatives aim to help men develop the skills and confidence needed to navigate key life transitions and contribute positively to society. FutureMen offers specific programs for new and expectant fathers, providing practical and emotional support to help them thrive in their roles. Website: https://futuremen.org/.
- *What Makes a Man*. An initiative that aims to redefine and support modern masculinity. It provides resources, workshops, and a community platform for men to discuss and embrace healthier expressions of manhood. The organization tackles topics such as mental health, relationships, and societal expectations, encouraging men to break free from traditional stereotypes and develop a more inclusive and supportive approach to masculinity. For more information, visit What Makes a Man.

These examples represent just a fraction of the growing number of initiatives worldwide dedicated to redefining masculinity. Through education, advocacy, and community engagement, these movements are laying the groundwork for a future where men and boys are free to express their full humanity without the constraints of outdated gender norms.

2.8   MASCULINITY IN THIS BOOK

Theories of masculinity are pivotal in framing the discussions and analyses across the various chapters of this book. By leveraging these theories, the book aims to dissect the multifaceted experiences of men and boys, exploring how societal norms and expectations shape their lives, influence their behavior, and impact their mental health. Here is an overview of how masculinity theory will be raised across the book's chapters.

2.8.1   Section 2: Men, Mental Health, and the Media

- *Men's and boys' mental health crisis and suicide: the silent killer.* These chapters will examine how traditional masculinity norms contribute to mental health issues and high suicide rates among men and boys. Theories of masculinity will help explain the societal pressures that discourage men from expressing vulnerability and seeking help.
- *The role of media and pop culture in shaping male identity and screen time and gaming addiction.* Here, masculinity theory will be used to explore how media representations of men reinforce certain ideals of masculinity, impacting men's self-perception and contributing to issues like gaming addiction as a form of escape from societal pressures.

2.8.2   Section 3: The Body and Sexual Behavior

- *Body image issues and gym/steroid addiction.* Masculinity theories will provide a lens through which to understand how societal expectations around physical appearance drive unhealthy behaviors and body image issues among men.
- *Circumcision, sexual behavior and consent, and pornography.* These chapters will discuss how constructs of masculinity influence sexual behavior, perceptions of consent, and the consumption of pornography, impacting men's sexual health and relationships.

2.8.3   Section 4: Education and Work

- *Challenges in male education, the higher education issue, the changing world of employment.* By applying theories of masculinity, these chapters will delve into how gender expectations affect educational outcomes for boys and the challenges men face in the evolving job market, highlighting the need for interventions that counteract these trends.

2.8.4   Section 5: Relationships and Fatherhood

- *Friendship and romance; the changing landscape of fatherhood, family breakdown, separation, and divorce (FBSD); the struggle for work–life balance.* Through the lens of masculinity theory, these sections will explore how traditional roles and expectations impact men's relationships, their involvement in parenting, and their struggle to achieve work–life balance.

2.8.5   Section 6: Vulnerable Men

- *Men, boys, and violence: victims and perpetrators; male homelessness: a neglected crisis; men in institutional settings: the army, prison, and the police; substance misuse and alcoholism.* Theories of masculinity will be critical in analyzing how societal norms contribute to violence, homelessness, challenges in institutional settings, and substance abuse among men and boys, emphasizing the need for supportive systems that address these issues.

2.8.6   Section 7: Intersectionality and Intervention

- *Intersectional approaches to men and boys: gender, ethnicity, religion, culture, class, and sexuality; effective interventions and strategies for change.* These concluding chapters will highlight how an intersectional understanding of masculinity – considering factors like ethnicity, class, and sexuality – is essential for developing effective, inclusive interventions and strategies that support men and boys across diverse backgrounds.

By weaving theories of masculinity throughout the book, I aim to provide a comprehensive understanding of the challenges and pressures unique to men and boys in contemporary society. This theoretical framework will underscore the importance of redefining masculinity and fostering environments that support healthier, more inclusive expressions of male identity.

2.9   CONCLUSION

Through examining the development of masculinity over the course of history, we have engaged in a thorough exploration of the profound impact of traditional gender roles on men and boys, and have uncovered the multifaceted ways in which societal expectations and norms shape identities and influence a broad spectrum of life experiences. From mental health struggles to educational and occupational disparities, and from relationship difficulties to deep-seated feelings of inadequacy, the shadow cast by rigid constructs of masculinity is both wide and deep. These insights underscore the urgent need for a societal shift in how masculinity is perceived and lived.

Furthermore, we now have an appreciation as to the complicated origins of masculinity and the competing influence of biological, social, and cognitive factors. With an acceptance of the large role of socialization, we have also the influence of various actors, including peers, parents, teachers, schools, and the media, in shaping our understanding and expectations of gender from a young age. In recent times, the advent of social media has also introduced new dimensions to this socialization process, offering spaces for the expression and exploration of diverse masculinities. Moreover, significant variation exists both across and within cultures, including the experiences of trans and nonbinary individuals, underscoring that each individual's experience of gender is unique.

As we conclude, it is clear that the task of challenging and redefining masculinity is not merely an academic exercise but a societal imperative. The health and well-being of men and boys, and indeed the broader fabric of society, depend on our collective ability to foster an understanding of masculinity that embraces vulnerability, values emotional literacy, and celebrates diversity. However, we must make sure that any such discourse is balanced and fair and acknowledges the positives of men and masculinities.

As we move forward, keep the theories of masculinity outlined in this chapter in your mind so that we may fully understand men's experiences across a range of different areas.

NOTES

1 Donnelly, K., & Twenge, J. M. (2017). Masculine and feminine traits on the Bem Sex-Role Inventory, 1993–2012: A cross-temporal meta-analysis. *Sex Roles, 76,* 556–565.

2 Kimmel, M. S. (2018). The contemporary "crisis" of masculinity in historical perspective. In *The Making of Masculinities (Routledge Revivals)* (pp. 121–153). Routledge.

3 Jablonka, I. (2022). *A history of masculinity: From patriarchy to gender justice.* Penguin UK.

4 Edley, N. (2017). *Men and masculinity: The basics.* Routledge.

5 Fuentes, A. (2021). Searching for the "roots" of masculinity in primates and the human evolutionary past. *Current Anthropology, 62*(S23), S13–S25.

6 Zsolnay, I. (Ed.). (2016). *Being a man: Negotiating ancient constructs of masculinity.* Routledge.

7 Mfecane, S. (2018). Towards African-centred theories of masculinity. *Social Dynamics, 44*(2), 291–305.

8 https://maasai-association.org/ceremonies.html

9 Kahn-John, M., Badger, T., McEwen, M. M., Koithan, M., Arnault, D. S., & Chico-Jarillo, T. M. (2021). The Diné (Navajo) Hózhó lifeway: A focused ethnography on

intergenerational understanding of American Indian cultural wisdom. *Journal of Transcultural Nursing, 32*(3), 256–265.

10 Hadley, D. (2015). *Masculinity in medieval Europe*. Routledge.

11 McCall, T. (2024). *Making the renaissance man: Masculinity in the courts of renaissance Italy*. Reaktion Books.

12 Tosh, J. (2005). Masculinities in an industrializing society: Britain, 1800–1914. *Journal of British Studies, 44*(2), 330–342.

13 Roper, M. (2005). Between manliness and masculinity: The "war generation" and the psychology of fear in Britain, 1914–1950. *Journal of British Studies, 44*(2), 343–362.

14 Howson, R. (2006). *Challenging hegemonic masculinity*. Routledge.

15 Plummer, D. (2016). *One of the boys: Masculinity, homophobia, and modern manhood*. Routledge.

16 Lippa, R. A. (2016). Biological influences on masculinity. In Y. J. Wong & S. R. Wester (Eds.), *APA handbook of men and masculinities* (pp. 187–209). American Psychological Association. https://doi.org/10.1037/14594-009.

17 Reeves, R. V. (2022). *Of boys and men: Why the modern male is struggling, why it matters, and what to do about it*. Brookings Institution Press.

18 Fuentes, Searching for the "roots" of masculinity in primates and the human evolutionary past, S13–S25.

19 Blakemore, J. E. O., Berenbaum, S. A., & Liben, L. S. (2013). *Gender development*. Psychology Press.

20 Alvermann, D., Wynne, E., & Wright, W. (2021). Tales from TikTok: Gender and cultural intersectionalities. In *Genders, cultures, and literacies* (pp. 198–211). Routledge.

21 Starr, C. R., & Zurbriggen, E. L. (2017). Sandra Bem's gender schema theory after 34 years: A review of its reach and impact. *Sex Roles, 76*, 566–578.

22 Franklin II, C. W. (2012). *The changing definition of masculinity*. Springer Science & Business Media.

23 Connell, R. W. (2020). *Masculinities*. Routledge.

24 Connell, R. W., & Messerschmidt, J. W. (2005). Hegemonic masculinity: Rethinking the concept. *Gender & Society, 19*(6), 829–859.

25 Kimmel, M. S. (2016). 6 Masculinity as Homophobia. In *Race, class, and gender in the United States: An integrated study*, 59.

26 Butler, J. (2004). *Undoing gender*. Routledge.

27 Butler, J. (2020). Performative acts and gender constitution: An essay in phenomenology and feminist theory. In *Feminist theory reader* (pp. 353–361). Routledge.

28 Anderson, E. (2010). *Inclusive masculinity: The changing nature of masculinities*. Routledge.

29 Harrington, C. (2021). What is "toxic masculinity" and why does it matter? *Men and Masculinities, 24*(2), 345–352.

30 https://inside-man.co.uk/2018/08/21/masculinity-isnt-toxic-debate/

31 www.obama.org/programs/my-brothers-keeper-alliance/

32 https://mankindprojectuki.org/

33 www.acalltomen.org/

34 https://menengage.org/

35 www.heforshe.org/en

36 www.americansurveycenter.org/newsletter/are-young-men-becoming-conservative/

Section 2

MEN, MENTAL HEALTH, AND THE MEDIA

3

MALE MENTAL HEALTH

3.1 INTRODUCTION

The mental health of men and boys has emerged as a critical concern in recent times, and alarmingly, the incidence of mental health issues such as depression, anxiety, and suicide among this demographic is on the rise. Historically, mental health challenges in men and boys have often been overlooked or under addressed, partly due to societal expectations and stigma surrounding the expression of emotional vulnerability in males (as discussed in Chapter 2). However, the escalating severity and frequency of these issues underscore the urgency of addressing this crisis.

However, it is important to note here that any approach to the mental health issues faced by men and boys must be made without resorting to victim-blaming or attributing their struggles to personal failings.[1] Societal narratives around men and masculinity often contribute to a misunderstanding of the underlying factors that influence mental health, such as socioeconomic pressures, cultural expectations, and lack of appropriate support mechanisms. By adopting a more empathetic and analytical approach that seeks to understand these contributing factors, we can inform more effective interventions and support systems that address the root causes and not just the symptoms of mental distress in men and boys. This perspective is crucial in cultivating a compassionate society where men are encouraged and supported to seek help without judgment or stigma.

DOI: 10.4324/9781032709369-5

Crucially, acknowledging and tackling the mental health struggles of men and boys are not just a matter of individual well-being; it is a societal imperative that impacts families, communities, and the broader health system. This chapter therefore aims to delve into the complexities of this issue, exploring its multifaceted nature, as well as proposing strategies for improvement and support.

3.2   THE SCALE OF THE PROBLEM

The increasing prevalence of mental health issues among men and boys is highlighted by alarming statistics. For example, reviews indicate that a significant number of men and boys suffer from depression[2] and anxiety,[3] but also that these conditions are frequently underdiagnosed.[4] Moreover, suicide rates in this demographic are notably high, standing out as a leading cause of death, especially in younger men.[5] When compared with other groups, figures suggest that men and boys are facing a *unique* set of challenges in this area,[6] particularly in relation to suicide.[7] For instance, men are significantly less likely than women to seek help for mental health issues, a reluctancy again underpinned by restrictive masculine stereotypes, which can exacerbate the severity of their conditions.

And so, we clearly have a serious issue with men and mental health, and we are rapidly beginning to understand the scale of the problem. But we still need to understand more about how certain issues might uniquely affect boys and men and their experiences with mental ill health, before we can begin to address the underlying causes and work toward more effective solutions.

3.3   CONTRIBUTING FACTORS

So, what are some of the factors which influence the prevalence of mental health issues in men and boys and their responses to these issues? It is already clear that societal expectations play a significant role, where traditional norms about masculinity often discourage emotional expression and seeking help.[8,9] This leads to a pervasive stigma around mental health, particularly in male populations, making it challenging for many to acknowledge and address their struggles. Specifically, embarrassment about help-seeking, negative attitudes toward emotional expression, a need for independence/control, and not seeing oneself as susceptible to disease were all found to be linked to men's willingness to approach services.

The impact of digital media is another critical factor, as constant connectivity and the pressures of social media can exacerbate feelings of inadequacy and depression.[10] Additionally, economic stressors, such as job insecurity and financial burdens, contribute to the mental health crisis. These stressors can be particularly acute for men, who often face societal pressure to be the primary earners in their families. This was no more so the case than during the recent COVID-19 pandemic, where men's mental health was closely related to deterioration in economic status.[11] Indeed, the crisis brought about unprecedented stressors around job loss, financial strain, social isolation, and health anxieties, all of which have contributed to increased rates of depression, anxiety, and other mental health issues in this group. Moreover, many men found themselves facing new roles or responsibilities, heightened stress levels, and limited access to traditional support systems, at the same time as more limited access to mental health services – a recipe for disaster.

In addition to these factors, genetic and biological factors can also play a role in mental health issues. Certain genetic predispositions can make individuals more susceptible to conditions like depression and anxiety, and hormonal differences and changes, particularly in testosterone levels, can also impact mood and mental health in men.[12]

The impact of childhood trauma and abuse also cannot be overlooked in either male or female mental health. Experiences of physical, emotional, or sexual abuse during childhood can have long-lasting effects on mental health, leading to conditions such as PTSD, depression, and anxiety in adulthood.[13] These traumatic experiences can also influence how men cope with stress and seek help, but again, are sometimes overlooked as men themselves seek to "bottle up" their experiences, and society reinforces this approach.

Environmental factors such as urbanization and pollution also contribute to the mental health challenges faced by men and boys. For example, living in densely populated urban areas can increase stress levels due to noise, overcrowding, and limited access to green spaces.[14] Indeed, pollution, both air and noise, has been linked to increased rates of mental health disorders, though none of these effects are exclusive to men.

Together, these factors create a complex web of challenges that need to be understood and addressed to effectively combat the mental health crisis among men and boys.

3.4   THE AGE FACTOR: ADOLESCENTS VS. ADULTS

The mental health challenges faced by adolescent boys and adult men, though similar in some ways, also evolve and differ significantly with age. In adolescent boys, issues often manifest in the form of behavioral problems, academic struggles, and social withdrawal, influenced heavily by the physical and emotional changes of puberty.[15] Adult men, on the other hand, tend to face mental health challenges in the context of workplace stress, relationship issues, and societal expectations to be providers and caretakers, as discussed earlier. The coping mechanisms and expressions of distress also differ; while younger boys might exhibit more outwardly aggressive or defiant behaviors, adult men might internalize their struggles, leading to issues like substance abuse or chronic depression. Younger men may also experience greater issues with help-seeking, as masculinity norms heighten in adolescence and boys struggle to understand their teenage experiences.[16] Understanding these age-related differences is again crucial for developing age-appropriate interventions and support systems.

3.5   INTERSECTIONALITY IN MEN'S MENTAL HEALTH

The intersectionality of factors such as race, socioeconomic status, and sexuality also play a critical role in the mental health of men and boys.[17] For instance, men of color might face additional stressors related to racial discrimination, impacting their mental health uniquely.[18] Indeed, it is widely understood that the stigma associated with mental health issues is greater in certain cultures and ethnic backgrounds and will "layer" onto gendered expectations to particularly limit these men. For instance, in many Western societies, there is an emerging shift toward recognizing and discussing mental health openly, yet traditional norms about stoicism and self-reliance often persist, impacting men's willingness to seek help. In contrast, in parts of Africa, mental health issues themselves are often stigmatized and misunderstood, or attributed to spiritual or supernatural causes, which can hinder both women and men from seeking appropriate care and add to already gendered expectations.

Socioeconomic status also influences access to mental health resources, with those in lower-income brackets often facing greater barriers.[19] Additionally, men who identify as part of the LGBTQ+ community encounter specific challenges, including societal stigma and discrimination, which can exacerbate mental health issues and limit support and access to resources.[20,21]

This indicates that if we want to effectively intervene in men's mental health, any intervention must be inclusive and accessible and acknowledge and understand how these intersecting factors influence men's experiences.

3.6   SEEKING HELP: CHALLENGES AND SOLUTIONS

As already noted, men and boys often face significant barriers in seeking mental health support. These include societal stigma associated with expressing vulnerability, a lack of awareness about mental health issues, and the perception that seeking help is a sign of weakness. Additionally, there can be practical barriers, such as limited access to mental health resources and services.

To make mental health services more appealing and accessible to men, a multifaceted approach is needed that considers the unique barriers and cultural factors affecting men's help-seeking behaviors,[22] including:

1.   *Tailored communication and outreach.* Services should be marketed in a way that resonates with men, emphasizing strength and resilience rather than vulnerability. This includes using language that reflects

self-improvement, control over one's life, and positive masculinity. Marketing strategies could and should also utilize channels and spaces that men frequently use, such as sports clubs, gyms, and online platforms where they are likely to engage.

2. *Accessible service formats.* Providing flexible service options, such as online counselling or therapy apps, can help overcome the stigma associated with visiting mental health clinics. Men may prefer these discreet options that they can access from the privacy of their homes. These digital tools can also offer resources like stress management tutorials, chatbots for instant emotional support, and connections to peer support networks.

3. *Incorporation into male-dominated environments.* Integrating mental health resources and services into workplaces, especially in male-dominated industries, can normalize help-seeking behaviors among men. Workshops and training sessions that focus on mental resilience and stress management as part of professional development can be effective.

4. *Focus on practical problem-solving.* Programs that emphasize practical skills for managing symptoms of stress, anxiety, and depression can be particularly appealing, without completely forgoing the equally important emotional needs of men. This can include teaching strategies for emotional regulation, conflict resolution, and assertive communication, which provide men with tangible tools to improve their mental health. Though it is important to do this in a way that doesn't ignore or minimize the emotional side of support and men's needs.

5. *Male-specific support groups and programs.* Developing support groups or treatment programs targeted specifically at men can provide the space needed for men to express their emotions and struggles in a supportive, male-only environment. This could include mentorship programs that connect younger men with older peers who have navigated similar challenges or designing spaces and activities that allow men to "open up" in ways they feel comfortable.

6. *Emphasizing confidentiality and anonymity.* Ensuring that services are confidential, and that men's privacy is protected, can help mitigate fears about the consequences of seeking help. Clear communication about these policies can encourage more men to take the first step toward accessing support.

7. *Community and peer involvement.* Encouraging community sports teams, local clubs, and other male-oriented communities to promote mental health awareness and support can foster a more supportive environment. Peer-led interventions, where men are trained to provide basic support and guidance to their peers, can also be effective.

By addressing the specific needs and preferences of men and boys through these targeted approaches, mental health services can become more engaging and effective for this demographic, ultimately leading to better mental health outcomes.[23] However, in doing so, we should also take care to not inadvertently reinforce the same stereotypes we are attempting to cater to. So above all, we need to treat men as the human beings they are and afford them the empathy and care they need that befits that acknowledgment.

3.7   KEY STAKEHOLDERS

Let's take a look at some of the key groups that must be involved in the drive for change.

3.7.1   The Role of Education and Awareness

Any support mechanisms need to be underpinned by much broader mental health education and awareness, as these are also vital tools in addressing the mental health crisis among men and boys and increasing help-seeking. Indeed, educational programs play a crucial role in destigmatizing mental health issues more broadly and in promoting a better understanding of these conditions. By increasing awareness amongst and about men and boys issues specifically, we can hopefully encourage early intervention, which is often key in preventing more severe mental health problems. These awareness campaigns could also challenge the harmful societal norms and expectations around masculinity that often discourage men and boys from seeking help, without compromising the importance that many masculine traits have for men and boys.

The vision is that in schools, workplaces, and communities, these programs can create environments that are more supportive and understanding of mental health challenges, fostering a culture where seeking help is seen as a strength, not a weakness.

3.7.2   The Role of Health-Care Providers

Health-care providers themselves obviously also play a crucial role in delivering this change, as they are the ones identifying and treating mental health issues in men and boys, and often as the first point of contact for individuals experiencing mental health problems. However, the challenge here lies in the fact that many men are reluctant to discuss mental health issues in the first instance due to stigma or a lack of awareness, and that professionals may bring their own prejudices to their practice. Best practices for health-care providers thus involve creating a nonjudgmental space for discussions, using gender-sensitive approaches, and being proactive in screening for mental health issues during regular health checkups.

In doing so, health-care providers need to be aware of the myriad influential factors outlined in this chapter and adopt the subsequent best practices, such as employing male-friendly communication strategies; offering a range of treatment options, including talk therapy, medication, and lifestyle advice; and involving family members when appropriate. Training in gender-specific mental health issues is thus essential for health-care providers to effectively support this demographic.

3.7.3   Social Networks

The role of support systems, such as family, friends, and community networks, is crucial in aiding men and boys with mental health issues. These support systems can provide emotional support, reduce feelings of isolation, and encourage individuals to seek professional help. Family members and friends can play a key role in noticing early signs of mental distress and offering a nonjudgmental space for discussion, and this role is particularly important, considering that men and boys may struggle to identify these signs themselves or acknowledge their vulnerability. Community networks, including peer support groups and men's health initiatives, can offer a sense of belonging and understanding, which is especially important for those who might feel alienated from traditional mental health services. Building strong, supportive communities where men and boys feel comfortable discussing and addressing their mental health is essential for their well-being. Some examples of these initiatives are provided here:

3.7.3.1   *United Kingdom*

Men's Sheds. Originating from Australia, Men's Sheds has become popular in the UK. These community spaces provide men with a place to engage in practical activities like woodworking, metalworking, and repair tasks. More importantly, they serve as a social hub where men can find companionship and support, reducing isolation and promoting mental well-being. Website: https://menssheds.org.uk/.

Andy's Man Club. This is a peer-to-peer support group for men, providing a network of clubs across the UK where men over 18 can meet to discuss their mental health and personal problems openly and without judgment. Website: http://andysmanclub.co.uk/.

ManUp! An initiative designed to tackle the stigma around men's mental health and encourage men to open up about their emotions. It provides a platform for men to share their stories, access resources, and engage in discussions about mental health and well-being. The organization aims to create a supportive community where men feel empowered to speak out and seek help when needed. Website: www.manup.how/.

HIS (Help Information Support) Charity. Dedicated to bridging the gap in mental health services for men and young lads from key stage 3 to adulthood. Founded in memory of a friend who took his life in 2019,

HIS provides comprehensive support through a buddy system, weekly counseling, and holistic therapies such as yoga, tai chi, mindfulness, massage, osteopathy, and acupuncture. The charity operates across London and Kent, focusing on preventing male suicide and promoting mental well-being. Website: https://hischarity.org.uk/.

Men's Health Unlocked (MHU). A collaborative network dedicated to improving the health and well-being of men and boys in Leeds. The initiative brings together multiple organizations, including Forum Central, Touchstone, Space 2, and Barca-Leeds, to tackle health inequalities specific to men through a joined-up and gendered approach. MHU's activities include connecting men to vital services, raising awareness of men's health issues, and delivering health awareness sessions. The network also supports strategic systems change and advocacy efforts to better men's health outcomes citywide. MHU has been instrumental in delivering innovative projects funded by the National Lottery Community Fund and has supported over 2,000 men in Leeds in the past 18 months. Website: www.barca-leeds.org/services/mhu.

3.7.3.2   United States

Movember Foundation. While originally focused on raising awareness for prostate cancer, Movember has expanded to address men's mental health. This global organization runs events to encourage men to become aware of their health issues, with a strong focus on mental health and preventing suicide among men. Website: https://us.movember.com/mens-health/mental-health.

Man Therapy. This is an online resource targeting men's mental health. It uses humor and a relatable tone to engage men in topics around mental health and therapy, offering tools, resources, and information to combat depression, anxiety, and suicide. Website: www.mantherapy.org/.

3.7.3.3   Canada

Men's Health Initiative. This initiative offers various services specifically tailored to men's health needs, including mental health support. It aims to provide accessible and effective solutions for men seeking help and guidance. Website: https://menshealthfoundation.ca/.

Heads Up Guys. Based in Canada but also serving men in the United States, this initiative provides resources and support specifically for men battling depression. The platform offers practical tips and information about how men can manage symptoms of depression and maintain mental well-being. Website: https://headsupguys.org/

3.7.3.4   Australia

Black Dog Institute. Dedicated to understanding, preventing, and treating mental illness, the Black Dog Institute has a strong focus on education and public resources that promote mental health, particularly among men. They offer a range of resources and programs designed to support men's mental health. Website: www.blackdoginstitute.org.au/.

3.7.3.5   South Africa

Men's Clinic International. Originally focusing on sexual health, this clinic also addresses broader health concerns, including mental health. They provide services aimed at improving men's overall well-being in a confidential and professional environment. Website: www.menshealth.co.za/.

3.7.3.6   India

Men Against Violence and Abuse (MAVA). This unique organization focuses on engaging men to fight gender-based violence, which is closely linked to mental health issues among men. They provide support and education on masculinity and mental health. Website: https://mavaindia.org/.

3.7.3.7   Ireland

Men's Health Forum in Ireland. This organization aims to enhance the health of men and boys through research, advocacy, and awareness campaigns. They address various health issues, including mental health, by promoting better practices and policies. Website: www.mhfi.org/.

3.7.4   Policy and Advocacy

A critical review of existing policies related to men's mental health reveals gaps and areas for improvement which require urgent rectification. Many current policies do not sufficiently address the unique challenges faced by men and boys in accessing mental health care. Advocacy efforts are thus needed to promote policies that include targeted mental health initiatives for men, funding for research on men's mental health, and the integration of mental health education in schools and workplaces. Additionally, there is a need for policies that encourage culturally competent care and address the barriers that prevent men and boys from seeking help. By advocating for these changes, we can work toward a more inclusive and effective mental health-care system that better serves the needs of men and boys.

Australia has been at the forefront of developing several notable policy initiatives aimed at improving mental health care for men, reflecting an understanding of the specific challenges this group faces. Here are some examples:

1.   *National Male Health Policy.* Australia's National Male Health Policy is one of the key frameworks aimed at improving the health of all males and addressing the disparities between different population groups of men and boys. This policy focuses on a capability approach, which encourages men to take charge of their health, and a determinants framework, which addresses social factors affecting men's health.
2.   *Beyond Blue's Men's Program.* Beyond Blue, an Australian mental health organization, has initiatives specifically targeted at men's mental health. This includes programs to increase awareness, reduce stigma, and provide tools and resources tailored to men's mental health needs. They also work on promoting mental health in workplaces, which is a critical setting for engaging men.
3.   *Movember Foundation's Mental Health Initiatives.* Although not a government policy, the Movember Foundation's work in Australia focuses on men's mental health and suicide prevention. They fund projects aimed at improving social connections, as well as research into effective treatment and prevention strategies specifically for men.
4.   *Headspace Projects.* Headspace, Australia's National Youth Mental Health Foundation, provides tailored services for young men particularly dealing with mental health issues. They offer a holistic approach, including support for physical health, mental health, work support, and substance use.
5.   *Australian Men's Shed Association.* While primarily a community-based initiative, Men's Sheds has been supported by Australian government policies as they provide a space for men to engage in meaningful projects, contributing to their mental and physical health in a supportive environment.

These initiatives demonstrate a broad and integrated approach to men's mental health, seeking to address both the clinical and social aspects of care, encourage community and workplace support, and reduce stigma around seeking help.

3.8   MEN'S PHYSICAL HEALTH AND LOWER LIFE EXPECTANCY

The physical health of men and boys is a critical concern that mirrors the issues discussed regarding mental health. Men generally have a lower life expectancy than women, influenced by factors such as biological differences, behavioral tendencies, and societal expectations. Conditions like heart disease, cancer (especially prostate cancer[24,25]), and diabetes are more prevalent among men, who are also more likely to engage in risky behaviors, such as smoking and excessive alcohol consumption. Next are a few brief sections that demonstrate how most of the issues and solutions provided more mental health in this chapter are mirrored for physical health.

3.8.1   Contributing Factors

Apart from perhaps behavioral factors, many of the societal and cultural influences outlined for mental health are relevant to physical health also. Here are the key factors involved in men's physical health:

- *Biological factors.* Genetic predispositions and hormonal influences, particularly testosterone, can affect the incidence and progression of diseases.
- *Behavioral factors.* Lifestyle choices, including diet, exercise, smoking, and alcohol use, play a significant role in men's health outcomes.
- *Societal and cultural influences.* Traditional norms around masculinity often discourage men from seeking medical help, leading to delayed diagnosis and treatment.[26,27,28]

3.8.2   Parallels With Mental Health Issues

And as we can see here more explicitly, many of the same stressors are present for men in relation to physical health:

- *Stigma and societal expectations.* Just as societal expectations can prevent men from seeking mental health support, they can also deter men from seeking medical care for physical health issues.
- *Economic and employment stress.* Economic pressures and job insecurity contribute to both mental and physical health problems.
- *Access to health services.* Limited access to health-care affects both mental and physical health, with men less likely to engage in regular health checkups and preventive screenings.

3.8.3   Addressing the Physical Health Crisis

And, similarly, we need to focus on education, prevention, and increased access to services to solve the problem:

- *Health education and awareness.* Increasing awareness about the importance of regular health screenings and a healthy lifestyle.
- *Preventive health measures.* Encouraging regular physical activity, balanced nutrition, smoking cessation, and moderate alcohol consumption.

- *Access and utilization of health-care services.* Developing policies to make health care more accessible and appealing to men, and providing services in settings men frequent, such as workplaces.
- *Supportive environments.* Creating supportive environments that encourage men to seek help and maintain healthy lifestyles, involving family, friends, and communities in promoting men's health awareness and support.

Addressing men's physical health is clearly as crucial as tackling their mental health issues. And, by understanding and addressing the interconnected factors influencing both areas, we can improve the overall health and life expectancy of men and boys, leading to a healthier society.

3.9   CONCLUSION

This chapter underscores the urgent need for action in addressing the mental health crisis among men and boys. It is clear that a multifaceted approach is required, encompassing education, policy reform, and enhanced community support. Further research is also essential to understand the unique challenges faced by this demographic and to develop effective interventions. Above all, there must be a collective effort to shift societal perceptions, reduce stigma, and create an environment where seeking help is normalized and encouraged.

The well-being of men and boys is not just an individual concern but a societal one, impacting families, communities, and the broader health system. As such, it demands our immediate attention and concerted action.

NOTES

1 Whitley, R. (2018). Men's mental health: Beyond victim-blaming. *The Canadian Journal of Psychiatry, 63*(9), 577–580.
2 Moreno-Agostino, D., Wu, Y. T., Daskalopoulou, C., Hasan, M. T., Huisman, M., & Prina, M. (2021). Global trends in the prevalence and incidence of depression: A systematic review and meta-analysis. *Journal of Affective Disorders, 281*, 235–243.
3 Fisher, K., Seidler, Z. E., King, K., Oliffe, J. L., & Rice, S. M. (2021). Men's anxiety: A systematic review. *Journal of Affective Disorders, 295*, 688–702.
4 Shi, P., Yang, A., Zhao, Q., Chen, Z., Ren, X., & Dai, Q. (2021). A hypothesis of gender differences in self-reporting symptom of depression: Implications to solve under-diagnosis and under-treatment of depression in males. *Frontiers in Psychiatry, 12*, 589687.
5 www.samaritans.org/about-samaritans/research-policy/suicide-facts-and-figures/latest-suicide-data/
6 Otten, D., Tibubos, A. N., Schomerus, G., Brähler, E., Binder, H., Kruse, J., . . . & Beutel, M. E. (2021). Similarities and differences of mental health in women and men: A systematic review of findings in three large German cohorts. *Frontiers in Public Health, 9*, 553071.

7   Richardson, C., Robb, K. A., & O'Connor, R. C. (2021). A systematic review of suicidal behaviour in men: A narrative synthesis of risk factors. *Social Science & Medicine, 276,* 113831.

8   Yousaf, O., Grunfeld, E. A., & Hunter, M. S. (2015). A systematic review of the factors associated with delays in medical and psychological help-seeking among men. *Health Psychology Review, 9*(2), 264–276.

9   Seidler, Z. E., Dawes, A. J., Rice, S. M., Oliffe, J. L., & Dhillon, H. M. (2016). The role of masculinity in men's help-seeking for depression: A systematic review. *Clinical Psychology Review, 49,* 106–118.

10 Parent, M. C., Gobble, T. D., & Rochlen, A. (2019). Social media behavior, toxic masculinity, and depression. *Psychology of Men & Masculinities, 20*(3), 277.

11 Hadar-Shoval, D., Alon-Tirosh, M., Asraf, K., Tannous-Haddad, L., & Tzischinsky, O. (2022). The association between men's mental health during COVID-19 and deterioration in economic status. *American Journal of Men's Health, 16*(2), 1557 9883221082427.

12 Walther, A., Breidenstein, J., & Miller, R. (2019). Association of testosterone treatment with alleviation of depressive symptoms in men: A systematic review and meta-analysis. *JAMA Psychiatry, 76*(1), 31–40.

13 Hoeve, M., Colins, O. F., Mulder, E. A., Loeber, R., Stams, G. J. J., & Vermeiren, R. R. (2015). Trauma and mental health problems in adolescent males: Differences between childhood-onset and adolescent-onset offenders. *Criminal Justice and Behavior, 42*(7), 685–702.

14 Sundquist, K., Frank, G., & Sundquist, J. A. N. (2004). Urbanisation and incidence of psychosis and depression: Follow-up study of 4.4 million women and men in Sweden. *The British Journal of Psychiatry, 184*(4), 293–298.

15 Rice, S. M., Purcell, R., & McGorry, P. D. (2018). Adolescent and young adult male mental health: Transforming system failures into proactive models of engagement. *Journal of Adolescent Health, 62*(3), S9–S17.

16 Lynch, L., Long, M., & Moorhead, A. (2018). Young men, help-seeking, and mental health services: Exploring barriers and solutions. *American Journal of Men's Health, 12*(1), 138–149.

17 Parent, M. C., Hammer, J. H., Bradstreet, T. C., Schwartz, E. N., & Jobe, T. (2018). Men's mental health help-seeking behaviors: An intersectional analysis. *American Journal of Men's Health, 12*(1), 64–73.

18 Cadaret, M. C., & Speight, S. L. (2018). An exploratory study of attitudes toward psychological help seeking among African American men. *Journal of Black Psychology, 44*(4), 347–370.

19 Seidler et al., The role of masculinity in men's help-seeking for depression, 106–118.

20 Pachankis, J. E., Sullivan, T. J., Feinstein, B. A., & Newcomb, M. E. (2018). Young adult gay and bisexual men's stigma experiences and mental health: An 8-year longitudinal study. *Developmental Psychology, 54*(7), 1381.

21 Russell, S. T., & Fish, J. N. (2016). Mental health in lesbian, gay, bisexual, and transgender (LGBT) youth. *Annual Review of Clinical Psychology, 12,* 465–487.

22 Seidler, Z. E., Rice, S. M., River, J., Oliffe, J. L., & Dhillon, H. M. (2018). Men's mental health services: The case for a masculinities model. *The Journal of Men's Studies, 26*(1), 92–104.

23 Sharp, P., Bottorff, J. L., Rice, S., Oliffe, J. L., Schulenkorf, N., Impellizzeri, F., & Caperchione, C. M. (2022). "People say men don't talk, well that's bullshit":

A focus group study exploring challenges and opportunities for men's mental health promotion. *PLoS One, 17*(1), e0261997.

24 Mardani, A., Farahani, M. A., Khachian, A., & Vaismoradi, M. (2023). Fear of cancer recurrence and coping strategies among prostate cancer survivors: A qualitative study. *Current Oncology, 30*(7), 6720–6733.

25 Langelier, D. M., Jackson, C., Bridel, W., Grant, C., & Culos-Reed, S. N. (2021). Coping strategies in active and inactive men with prostate cancer: A qualitative study. *Journal of Cancer Survivorship*, 1–11.

26 Wall, D., & Kristjanson, L. (2005). Men, culture and hegemonic masculinity: Understanding the experience of prostate cancer. *Nursing Inquiry, 12*(2), 87–97.

27 Bowie, J., Brunckhorst, O., Stewart, R., Dasgupta, P., & Ahmed, K. (2022). Body image, self-esteem, and sense of masculinity in patients with prostate cancer: A qualitative meta-synthesis. *Journal of Cancer Survivorship, 16*(1), 95–110.

28 Salifu, Y., Almack, K., & Caswell, G. (2023). 'Out of the frying pan into the fire': A qualitative study of the impact on masculinity for men living with advanced prostate cancer. *Palliative Care and Social Practice, 17*, 26323524231176829.

4

SUICIDE

4.1 INTRODUCTION

Suicide among men and boys presents a critical public health crisis that demands urgent and effective responses. Alarming statistics reveal that suicide rates in this demographic are significantly higher than in women, identifying it as one of the leading causes of death, especially among young men. This alarming trend not only reflects the urgent need for comprehensive mental health support but also highlights broader societal issues that contribute to the prevalence of suicide.

Building on the insights from Chapter 3, this chapter will delve deeper into the specific factors leading to high suicide rates among men and boys, exploring both the personal and societal influences. By understanding these dynamics, it is possible to then outline targeted strategies that can mitigate these risks and foster a supportive environment that encourages men and boys to seek help before reaching a crisis point. Through a blend of awareness, community support, and informed policy interventions, this chapter seeks to address the complexities of suicide prevention and care within this vulnerable group, ultimately aiming to save lives and improve mental health outcomes.

DOI: 10.4324/9781032709369-6

4.2   UNDERSTANDING THE STATISTICS: UK AND AROUND THE WORLD

An in-depth analysis of suicide rates highlights alarming trends that vary significantly across different demographics, with men showing particularly high rates both in the UK and globally. In the UK, suicide is the single biggest killer of men under the age of 45, and The Office for National Statistics (ONS) reports that the suicide rate among men is three times higher than that of women.[1] This discrepancy points to a deeply entrenched issue that transcends mere individual struggles and speaks to broader societal failures in addressing male mental health.

Globally, the trends are similarly disturbing. According to the World Health Organization (WHO), nearly 800,000 people die due to suicide every year, and men are significantly more likely than women to take their own lives in almost every country in the world. In high-income countries, the male-to-female ratio of suicide can be as high as 4:1, underscoring a universal crisis.[2] Indeed, several large reviews have revealed elevated risks for men of both serious suicide attempt[3] and completion.[4]

These statistics not only reflect the severity of the crisis but also underscore the need for gender-specific approaches to mental health and suicide prevention. The higher rates of suicide among young and middle-aged men suggest that these groups are particularly vulnerable and may benefit from targeted interventions. Geographical differences also play a role, with some regions reporting higher rates and differences, often influenced by socioeconomic, employment-related, and cultural factors, which could be addressed through localized strategies.

4.3   CONTRIBUTING FACTORS

Expanding upon the insights from Chapter 3, it is evident that male socialization and entrenched societal expectations significantly elevate the risk of suicide among men.[5,6] Traditional masculine norms, which often discourage emotional expression and vulnerability, play a critical role. These norms promote stoicism and self-reliance, pushing men to internalize stress and conceal their mental health struggles. This lack of emotional openness and reluctance to seek help are a significant barrier that can lead men to view suicide as a solitary solution to their problems. Moreover, it is important to note the influence of *multiple* masculinities in understanding why men often do not seek the necessary support.[7,8]

Masculine stereotypes also enforce the notion that seeking help is a sign of weakness, which can prevent men from accessing the mental health support they need. This is compounded by societal expectations that men must always be strong and in control, further isolating those who struggle with mental health issues.[9] The impact of these stereotypes is profound, often leaving men with few options other than to continue suffering in silence or consider more drastic measures. This is compounded by challenges within the current mental health provision system, such as limited male-focused mental health services and resources, which further hinder men's access to appropriate care. These systemic and societal barriers require urgent attention to improve mental health outcomes for men.

Moreover, the methods by which men typically approach suicide contribute to higher completion rates compared to women. Studies have shown that men are more likely to use lethal means in their suicide attempts, which leads to a higher rate of fatality. This choice of methods is influenced by the same masculine ideals that equate gun ownership or the choice of violent methods with strength and decisiveness, inadvertently increasing the lethality of suicide attempts.[10]

Finally, other contextual factors, such as the experience of separation and divorce, along with the resulting custody proceedings, can significantly impact men's mental health and increase suicide ideation. Men often face emotional distress and a sense of failure during these times, exacerbated by the loss of daily contact with their children and perceived biases in custody decisions. The feelings of isolation and helplessness that arise from these experiences are critical factors contributing to suicidal thoughts. This issue will be explored in greater detail in Chapter 18, which examines the specific challenges men encounter in navigating family breakdowns and the importance of support systems in mitigating these risks.

4.4   PREVENTION AND INTERVENTION STRATEGIES

To combat the high rates of suicide among men and boys, effective strategies must prioritize early intervention and education, tailored to address the unique challenges this group faces. Awareness programs are crucial in dismantling the stigmas around mental health and encouraging open discussions about emotional struggles.[11] These programs should be implemented in environments frequented by men and boys, such as schools, universities, and workplaces, and should utilize relatable language and culturally resonant themes. Here are some suggestions on what this might look like:

1. *Educational programs and campaigns.* Initiatives should focus on educating men about mental health from a young age. This can include integrating mental health education into school curricula and offering workshops that focus not only on the signs of mental distress but also on practical coping mechanisms and the importance of seeking help. By changing perceptions from the ground up, these educational efforts can significantly alter the long-term outlook for mental health among men.

2. *Community-based approaches.* Engaging local communities in suicide prevention is critical. This involves training community leaders and

influencers in mental health first aid, enabling them to identify at-risk individuals in their communities and to provide immediate support or direct them to professional help. Community centers, places of worship, and sports clubs can serve as platforms for these training sessions, making mental health support accessible and immediate.

3.   *Workplace mental health initiatives.* Workplaces must play an active role in mental health advocacy by creating environments that promote mental well-being. This includes establishing clear policies for mental health days, providing access to counselling services, and training management in mental health awareness. Such initiatives help normalize conversations about mental health in traditionally male-dominated spaces, reducing stigma and encouraging help-seeking behaviors.

4.   *Tailored communication and outreach.* Beyond traditional advertising, using digital platforms and social media can effectively reach men and boys where they are most active. Campaigns should highlight stories of recovery and support, featuring role models and influencers who have addressed their mental health challenges openly, thus providing relatable testimonials that resonate with a wide audience.

5.   *Enhanced access to crisis intervention.* Ensuring that men have immediate access to crisis intervention services, such as helplines and online chat supports that guarantee anonymity and confidentiality, is essential. These services should be widely publicized through all available media to ensure that men who are reluctant to seek face-to-face help can still find support in critical moments.

By integrating these approaches into a comprehensive suicide prevention strategy, the impact on reducing suicide rates among men and boys can be significant. Each element of the strategy works synergistically to build a supportive framework that not only addresses immediate risks but also works toward long-term cultural changes that validate emotional openness and help-seeking among men.

A fantastic example of such an intervention in the UK is CALM (Campaign Against Living Miserably). CALM is a leading organization that specifically targets men's mental health to prevent suicide. Their approach includes a helpline and a web chat service that operates every day of the year, providing immediate support to men in crisis. CALM focuses on tackling suicide by sparking conversation, running innovative campaigns, and supporting people who have been impacted by suicide. Website: www.thecalmzone. net/.

Another example is Men's Minds Matter, a UK-based charity dedicated to developing and delivering psychological interventions specifically for men who are suicidal. They focus on raising awareness and providing resources to help men navigate suicidal crises, aiming to reduce the disproportionately high rates of male suicide. Website: www.mensmindsmatter.org/.

4.5 THE IMPACT OF TECHNOLOGY AND SOCIAL MEDIA ON MEN'S MENTAL HEALTH

The role of technology and social media in shaping mental health, particularly among men and boys, has become a central topic of concern and study (more on this in the next two chapters). While these digital tools offer unparalleled opportunities for connection and engagement, their influence on mental health can be dual-edged, particularly for younger men who are frequent users. The pressures to maintain a certain online persona can amplify feelings of inadequacy, anxiety, and isolation, factors that are significantly linked to suicidal thoughts among men. However, there have also been promising uses of social media to help prevent suicide.[12] Let us explore some examples of positive digital influence further:

1. *Digital interventions for suicide prevention.* Research highlights promising strategies using digital platforms to reduce the stigma around mental health among specific groups, such as farming men in Australia. The "Ripple Effect" digital intervention, for instance, tailored its content to the cultural and professional context of farming men, using relatable testimonies and goal-setting activities to challenge stigma and improve mental health literacy.[13]
2. *Effectiveness of web-based interventions.* The Man Up project and website, linked to the Australian documentary, serve as exemplary models of how media and digital platforms can facilitate discussions about masculinity and suicide, encouraging help-seeking behaviors. The platform effectively utilized multimedia strategies to resonate with men, showing that well-crafted messages can lead to significant engagement and help-seeking actions online.[14]
3. *Man Therapy and online help-seeking.* The Man Therapy initiative demonstrates the potential of online interventions tailored for men, facilitating professional help-seeking among a demographic traditionally resistant to traditional mental health approaches. This initiative successfully leveraged humor and direct engagement to break down barriers to accessing mental health resources.[15]

These examples underscore the potential of tailored digital interventions in not only reaching men at risk of suicide but also in offering them viable, appealing options for support that respect their preferences for anonymity and convenience. Moving forward, it is crucial to continue exploring and expanding these strategies, ensuring they are integrated into broader suicide prevention frameworks to maximize their reach and effectiveness.

4.6 POSTVENTION STRATEGIES

Postvention, focusing on the aftermath of a suicide attempt, is particularly critical for men, given the unique challenges and societal pressures they face in relation to mental health.[16,17] This targeted support is vital not only for individual recovery but also for addressing broader issues that contribute to high suicide rates among men. Some key elements of postvention for men are highlighted here:

1. *Support networks.* Postvention for men benefits significantly from the involvement of support networks that understand and cater to male perspectives on mental health. This includes creating male-only support groups or services that focus on communication styles and engagement strategies that resonate with men. These groups provide a space where men can express their feelings and challenges without the constraints of traditional gender expectations.
2. *Role of health-care providers.* Health-care providers play a crucial role in postvention for men by identifying those at risk and ensuring they receive the necessary support. Training in gender-specific mental health issues is crucial for providers to effectively engage with men who may be reluctant to discuss or address their mental health needs.
3. *Monitoring and follow-up.* Consistent monitoring and follow-up are essential components of postvention, ensuring that men continue to engage with mental health services after a crisis. This ongoing engagement helps mitigate the risk of further crises and supports the long-term stability of the individual.
4. *Community and workplace involvement.* Integrating postvention strategies into workplaces and community settings can help reach men in environments they frequent. Programs that promote mental health awareness and suicide prevention within these spaces can reduce stigma and provide accessible support, making it easier for men to seek help.

4.6.1   Policy and Advocacy

Like comments made in the previous chapter in relation to policy, while current policies on suicide prevention include general mental health strategies, there is a noticeable deficiency in measures specifically targeting the unique needs of men and boys. This gap underlines the necessity for robust advocacy efforts to develop and implement policies that directly address these specific needs. Such advocacy should promote increased funding for men's mental health initiatives (as argued in Chapter 3) and support the creation of suicide prevention campaigns that are specifically designed for men. Additionally, ensuring that mental health services are accessible and appropriately tailored to the male demographic is crucial (again, as previously outlined).

4.7   INTERSECTIONALITY AND MALE SUICIDE

The concept of intersectionality is crucial in understanding the multifaceted nature of suicide risk among men and boys. Indeed, by exploring the intersection between gender and race, culture, sexuality, religion, socioeconomic status, and more, we can gain a deeper understanding of the specific factors that contribute to the elevated suicide risk in different demographic groups. The following sections provide a brief overview of risk factors for each group and suggestions for tailored intervention:

4.7.1 Race and Ethnicity

Men of color often face additional stressors related to racial discrimination and systemic inequality, which can significantly impact their mental health and risk of suicide.[18,19] These individuals may experience:

- *Racial discrimination.* Persistent exposure to racial discrimination can lead to chronic stress, anxiety, and depression, increasing suicide risk.
- *Cultural stigma.* Mental health issues may be more stigmatized in certain racial and ethnic communities, leading to reluctance in seeking help.
- *Economic disadvantages.* Men of color are more likely to face economic hardships, including unemployment and low-income jobs, which can exacerbate feelings of hopelessness and despair.

Tailored Interventions

- *Culturally competent care.* Mental health services should be culturally sensitive and staffed by professionals trained to understand and address the unique experiences of men of color.
- *Community-based programs.* Initiatives that engage trusted community leaders and utilize culturally relevant approaches can help reduce stigma and encourage help-seeking behaviors.
- *Economic support programs.* Providing economic assistance and job training programs can alleviate some of the stressors that contribute to mental health issues.

4.7.2 Socioeconomic Status

Men from lower socioeconomic backgrounds face numerous challenges that can increase their risk of suicide,[20] including:

- *Financial stress.* The inability to meet basic needs and financial instability can lead to chronic stress and feelings of worthlessness.
- *Limited access to health care.* Men in low-income brackets often have reduced access to mental health services and support.
- *Environmental stressors.* Living in high-stress environments, such as crime-ridden neighborhoods, can contribute to poor mental health.

Tailored Interventions

- *Affordable mental health services.* Expanding access to affordable or free mental health services for low-income individuals is essential.
- *Social support networks.* Strengthening community support systems, such as local support groups and outreach programs, can provide crucial assistance.
- *Policy interventions.* Advocacy for policies that address economic inequality and improve access to health care can have a significant impact on reducing suicide risk.

4.7.3   Sexual Orientation

Those who identify as part of the LGBTQ+ community, including GBTQ+ men, face unique challenges that can increase their risk of suicide,[21] including:

- *Social stigma and discrimination.* LGBTQ+ individuals often face significant societal stigma, discrimination, and rejection, which can lead to mental health issues.
- *Internalized homophobia.* Struggling with acceptance of their sexual orientation can lead to internal conflicts and severe emotional distress.
- *Isolation.* Lack of acceptance from family, friends, and the broader community can result in feelings of isolation and loneliness.

Tailored Interventions

- *Inclusive mental health services.* Mental health providers should offer services that are inclusive and affirming of LGBTQ+ identities.
- *Support groups.* Establishing support groups specifically for GBTQ+ men can provide a safe space for individuals to share their experiences and receive support.
- *Antidiscrimination policies.* Promoting and enforcing antidiscrimination policies in workplaces, schools, and communities can help create a more accepting environment.

By acknowledging and addressing the intersectionality of race, socioeconomic status, and sexual orientation with gender, we can develop more effective, targeted interventions to reduce the risk of suicide among men and boys. Understanding these unique challenges allows for a more comprehensive approach to mental health that considers the diverse experiences and needs of all individuals.

4.8   CONCLUSION

The high rates of suicide among men and boys constitute a public health crisis that demands urgent action. This chapter highlights the critical need for comprehensive strategies that address the unique mental health challenges faced by this demographic, with societal support, policy reform, and improved mental health services all essential in combating this issue. It is thus crucial to move beyond traditional approaches and develop targeted interventions that consider the specific needs and experiences of men and boys. And, by fostering a society that supports mental health and challenges outdated norms, we can create an environment where seeking help is not only accepted but also encouraged.

The time for action is now, to not only save lives, but to also improve the quality of life for men and boys struggling with mental health issues.

NOTES

1 www.ons.gov.uk/peoplepopulationandcommunity/birthsdeathsandmarriages/deaths/bulletins/suicidesintheunitedkingdom/2022registrations
2 www.who.int/data/gho/data/themes/mental-health/suicide-rates
3 Freeman, A., Mergl, R., Kohls, E., Székely, A., Gusmao, R., Arensman, E., . . . & Rummel-Kluge, C. (2017). A cross-national study on gender differences in suicide intent. *BMC Psychiatry, 17*, 1–11.
4 Miranda-Mendizabal, A., Castellví, P., Parés-Badell, O., Alayo, I., Almenara, J., Alonso, I., . . . & Alonso, J. (2019). Gender differences in suicidal behavior in adolescents and young adults: Systematic review and meta-analysis of longitudinal studies. *International Journal of Public Health, 64*, 265–283.
5 Pirkis, J., Spittal, M. J., Keogh, L., Mousaferiadis, T., & Currier, D. (2017). Masculinity and suicidal thinking. *Social Psychiatry and Psychiatric Epidemiology, 52*, 319–327.
6 Bennett, S., Robb, K. A., Zortea, T. C., Dickson, A., Richardson, C., & O'Connor, R. C. (2023). Male suicide risk and recovery factors: A systematic review and qualitative metasynthesis of two decades of research. *Psychological Bulletin, 149*(7–8), 371.
7 Vogel, D. L., & Heath, P. J. (2016). Men, masculinities, and help-seeking patterns. In Y. J. Wong & S. R. Wester (Eds.), *APA handbook of men and masculinities* (pp. 685–707). American Psychological Association. https://doi.org/10.1037/14594-031.
8 Rasmussen, M. L., Hjelmeland, H., & Dieserud, G. (2018). Barriers toward help-seeking among young men prior to suicide. *Death Studies, 42*(2), 96–103.
9 King, T. L., Shields, M., Sojo, V., Daraganova, G., Currier, D., O'Neil, A., . . . & Milner, A. (2020). Expressions of masculinity and associations with suicidal ideation among young males. *BMC Psychiatry, 20*, 1–10.
10 Mergl, R., Koburger, N., Heinrichs, K., Székely, A., Tóth, M. D., Coyne, J., . . . & Hegerl, U. (2015). What are reasons for the large gender differences in the lethality of suicidal acts? An epidemiological analysis in four European countries. *PLoS One, 10*(7), e0129062.
11 Pirkis, J., King, K., Rice, S., Seidler, Z., Leckning, B., Oliffe, J. L., . . . & Schlichthorst, M. (2023). Preventing suicide in boys and men. In *Suicide risk assessment and prevention* (pp. 483–494). Springer International Publishing.
12 Robinson, J., Cox, G., Bailey, E., Hetrick, S., Rodrigues, M., Fisher, S., & Herrman, H. (2016). Social media and suicide prevention: A systematic review. *Early Intervention in Psychiatry, 10*(2), 103–121.

13 Kennedy, A. J., Brumby, S. A., Versace, V. L., & Brumby-Rendell, T. (2020). The ripple effect: A digital intervention to reduce suicide stigma among farming men. *BMC Public Health*, *20*, 1–12.

14 King, K., Schlichthorst, M., Turnure, J., Phelps, A., Spittal, M. J., & Pirkis, J. (2019). Evaluating the effectiveness of a website about masculinity and suicide to prompt help-seeking. *Health Promotion Journal of Australia*, *30*(3), 381–389.

15 Gilgoff, J. N., Wagner, F., Frey, J. J., & Osteen, P. J. (2023). Help-seeking and man therapy: The impact of an online suicide intervention. *Suicide and Life-Threatening Behavior*, *53*(1), 154–162.

16 Oliffe, J. L., Ferlatte, O., Ogrodniczuk, J. S., Seidler, Z. E., Kealy, D., & Rice, S. M. (2021). How to save a life: Vital clues from men who have attempted suicide. *Qualitative Health Research*, *31*(3), 415–429.

17 Andriessen, K., Krysinska, K., Kõlves, K., & Reavley, N. (2019). Suicide postvention service models and guidelines 2014–2019: A systematic review. *Frontiers in Psychology*, *10*, 491007.

18 Kubrin, C. E., & Wadsworth, T. (2009). Explaining suicide among blacks and whites: How socioeconomic factors and gun availability affect race-specific suicide rates. *Social Science Quarterly*, *90*(5), 1203–1227.

19 Curtin, S. C., & Hedegaard, H. (2019). Suicide rates for females and males by race and ethnicity: United States, 1999 and 2017. *NCHS Health E-Stats*. https://stacks.cdc.gov/view/cdc/79168. Suicide rates for females and males by race and ethnicity: United States, 1999 and 2017.

20 Pirkis, J., Currier, D., Butterworth, P., Milner, A., Kavanagh, A., Tibble, H., . . . & Spittal, M. J. (2017). Socio-economic position and suicidal ideation in men. *International Journal of Environmental Research and Public Health*, *14*(4), 365.

21 Raifman, J., Charlton, B. M., Arrington-Sanders, R., Chan, P. A., Rusley, J., Mayer, K. H., . . . & McConnell, M. (2020). Sexual orientation and suicide attempt disparities among US adolescents: 2009–2017. *Pediatrics*, *145*(3).

5

MEDIA, POP CULTURE, AND MALE IDENTITY

5.1 INTRODUCTION

In today's world, various forms of media and popular culture are pivotal in shaping public perceptions and individual identities, including exerting a profound influence on the formation of male identity. From movies and television shows to advertisements and social media, the images and narratives propagated through these channels significantly impact how masculinity is perceived and expressed.

The portrayals of men in media often adhere to a narrow set of characteristics, emphasizing traits like physical strength, stoicism, and dominance. While these representations can sometimes be positive, they frequently paint a limited and sometimes harmful picture of what it means to be a man. This can lead to unrealistic expectations and pressures, affecting the self-esteem, mental health, and behavior of men and boys.

The significance of media portrayals in shaping societal perceptions of masculinity cannot be understated. They not only influence individual men's understanding of their identity but also affect how society at large perceives and interacts with men. These portrayals contribute to the social narrative about what is acceptable or expected in male behavior, often reinforcing stereotypes and inhibiting a more nuanced understanding of masculinity.[1,2]

DOI: 10.4324/9781032709369-7

In this chapter, we will delve into the complex ways in which media and pop culture shape male identity. We will examine the impacts of these portrayals on individual men and boys and discuss the broader implications for society. By understanding these dynamics, we can then begin to advocate for more diverse and realistic representations of men in media, promoting a healthier, more inclusive understanding of masculinity.

5.2 PORTRAYALS OF MASCULINITY IN TRADITIONAL MEDIA

Masculinity in movies, TV shows, and advertising is often characterized by a set of recurring themes.[3] These include the depiction of men as physically strong, emotionally reserved, and assertively dominant. Heroes in action movies, for instance, typically showcase bravery, toughness, and a propensity for violence as solutions to conflict. Similarly, advertisements often depict men as powerful, successful, and hypercompetitive. These portrayals reinforce a narrow conception of masculinity, emphasizing physical prowess and emotional stoicism as desirable or expected traits.

A significant issue in media representations of men is the lack of diversity. This lack encompasses various aspects, such as race, sexuality, body type, and more. Men of color, men from the LGBTQ+ community, and men who do not conform to traditional physical ideals are often underrepresented or portrayed in a stereotypical manner. This lack of diversity not only perpetuates stereotypes but also fails to provide role models for individuals from these groups, reinforcing a sense of exclusion and invisibility. For example, men of color are often typecast into specific roles that do not fully represent the breadth of their experiences and personalities. Similarly, portrayals of GBTQ+ men can often be limited to clichéd or tokenistic representations, which do not reflect the depth of their experiences. Moreover, the media's focus on idealized body types contributes to a culture where men feel pressured to achieve unattainable physical standards, impacting their self-esteem and body image.

5.2.1 Specific Examples

Different media genres portray masculinity in various ways, each reinforcing specific traits and stereotypes. Understanding these genre-specific trends can shed light on how different aspects of masculinity are emphasized or undermined across various forms of media. The following sections give some common tropes and proposed impact for each genre.

5.2.1.1 Action Films

Action films are one of the most influential genres in shaping perceptions of masculinity. Typically, these films emphasize physical strength, bravery, and dominance.[4] The protagonists in action movies are often portrayed as rugged, self-reliant heroes who use violence as a primary means of resolving conflicts. Classic examples include characters like James Bond, John McClane from *Die Hard*, and more recently, superheroes like those in the Marvel Cinematic Universe (MCU).

5.2.1.1.1 COMMON TROPES

- *Physical prowess*. Action heroes are usually depicted as exceptionally strong and capable fighters.
- *Emotional stoicism*. These characters often suppress their emotions, displaying little vulnerability.
- *Individualism*. The action hero typically works alone, highlighting self-reliance and independence.
- *Hypermasculinity*. Traits like aggression, fearlessness, and dominance over others are celebrated.

5.2.1.1.2 IMPACT

These portrayals can create unrealistic expectations for men and boys, suggesting that true masculinity is linked to physical dominance and emotional suppression. This can lead to pressure to conform to these ideals and a reluctance to seek help or show vulnerability.

5.2.1.2 Comedies

In contrast to action films, comedies often present a different aspect of masculinity, focusing on humor and social relationships.[5,6] However, they can also perpetuate stereotypes, sometimes reducing men to simplistic or exaggerated caricatures for comedic effect.

5.2.1.2.1 COMMON TROPES

- *The clumsy fool*. Characters like those played by Adam Sandler or Will Ferrell often depict men as inept, bumbling, and emotionally immature.
- *The womanizer*. Comedy often includes characters who are preoccupied with sexual conquest, reinforcing shallow and stereotypical views of male sexuality.
- *Bromance*. A more positive trend in modern comedies is the focus on deep male friendships, as seen in films like *Superbad* and *The 40-Year-Old Virgin*.

5.2.1.2.2 IMPACT

While comedic portrayals can humanize men by showing their vulnerabilities and flaws, they can also reinforce negative stereotypes. The emphasis on male incompetence and superficial relationships can undermine the complexity of male identity.

5.2.1.3 *Dramas*

Dramas offer a more nuanced exploration of masculinity, often focusing on character development and emotional depth.[7] These films and TV shows are more likely to portray men dealing with complex issues such as mental health, family dynamics, and personal struggles.

5.2.1.3.1 COMMON TROPES

- *The troubled hero.* Characters like Don Draper from *Mad Men* or Tony Soprano from *The Sopranos* struggle with inner demons, showing the darker side of masculinity.
- *The family man.* Dramas often explore the roles of men within their families, highlighting both strengths and weaknesses in these relationships.
- *Emotional complexity.* These characters display a wide range of emotions, breaking away from the stoic archetype.

5.2.1.3.2 IMPACT

By presenting more multifaceted portrayals of men, dramas can contribute to a broader understanding of masculinity. They show that men can be strong yet vulnerable, ambitious yet flawed, and loving yet conflicted. This can help normalize emotional expression and mental health issues among men.

5.2.1.4 *Reality TV*

Reality TV is a genre that often emphasizes dramatic and sensationalized aspects of life, and its portrayal of masculinity can be equally varied.[8] Shows like *The Bachelor* or *Survivor* often emphasize competitive and romantic aspects of male identity.

5.2.1.4.1 COMMON TROPES

- *The alpha male.* Reality TV often highlights men who exhibit dominant and competitive traits.
- *The romantic.* Shows focused on romance can perpetuate traditional notions of chivalry and male leadership in relationships.
- *The everyday man.* Some reality shows, like those focused on family life or personal improvement (e.g., *Queer Eye*), portray men in more relatable and diverse ways.

5.2.1.4.2 IMPACT

The diverse portrayals in reality TV can reinforce both positive and negative stereotypes. While some shows may perpetuate traditional and competitive views of masculinity, others offer a more varied and realistic depiction, showcasing men in everyday scenarios and highlighting personal growth and emotional openness.

5.2.1.5   Video Games

Although not a traditional film or TV genre, video games are a significant medium that shapes male identity.[9] Popular games often feature hypermasculine characters who embody physical strength and combat skills.

5.2.1.5.1   COMMON TROPES

- *The warrior.* Characters like those in "Call of Duty" or "God of War" emphasize physical power and combat abilities.
- *The lone hero.* Similar to action films, many video game protagonists are depicted as solitary figures overcoming massive odds.
- *The antihero.* Games like "Grand Theft Auto" feature morally ambiguous characters, challenging traditional notions of good and bad.

5.2.1.5.2   IMPACT

Video games can reinforce traditional masculine ideals of strength and dominance, but they also offer interactive narratives that can explore complex identities and moral choices. This dual nature makes video games a powerful tool for both perpetuating and challenging stereotypes.

5.2.1.6   Disney Movies

Disney movies have a significant impact on shaping the perceptions of masculinity among young audiences.[10,11,12] Over the years, Disney's portrayal of male characters has evolved, reflecting broader societal changes and influencing the way boys and men see themselves and their roles in society.

5.2.1.6.1   TRADITIONAL PORTRAYALS

Early Disney movies often featured male characters that embodied traditional, archetypal forms of masculinity. These characters were typically:

- *Heroic and brave.* Characters like Prince Charming in *Cinderella* and Prince Phillip in *Sleeping Beauty* are depicted as brave, chivalrous, and heroic, saving the damsel in distress and defeating evil forces.
- *Strong and independent.* Male protagonists in early Disney films often rely on their physical strength and individual prowess. Examples include Hercules in *Hercules*, who is literally a demigod with extraordinary physical power.

- *Emotionally reserved.* Many traditional Disney princes and heroes exhibit emotional stoicism, rarely showing vulnerability or expressing a wide range of emotions. This aligns with the stereotypical view that men should be strong and unemotional.

5.2.1.6.2 EVOLUTION OF MASCULINITY

In recent years, Disney has made conscious efforts to diversify its portrayal of male characters, presenting more complex and emotionally nuanced forms of masculinity. This shift is evident in several modern Disney movies:

- *Emotional depth and vulnerability.* Characters like Simba in *The Lion King* and Kristoff in *Frozen* showcase a broader emotional range. Simba struggles with guilt, fear, and responsibility, while Kristoff openly expresses his feelings and supports Anna in her quest.
- *Partnership and collaboration.* Modern Disney heroes often work along-side strong female characters as equals, promoting the idea of partnership rather than dominance. In *Tangled*, Flynn Rider collaborates with Rapunzel, showing respect for her abilities and agency.
- *Breaking stereotypes.* Films like *Moana* and *Frozen II* feature male characters who defy traditional masculine stereotypes. Maui in *Moana* has insecurities about his worth beyond his physical strength, and Kristoff in *Frozen II* sings about his feelings of love and uncertainty in a humorous and heartfelt ballad, "Lost in the Woods."

5.2.1.6.3 IMPACT

Disney movies play a crucial role in early childhood development, and the portrayal of masculinity in these films can significantly influence young boys' understanding of what it means to be a man. Positive impacts include:

- *Encouraging emotional expression.* By showing male characters who express vulnerability and emotions, Disney movies can help boys feel more comfortable with their own feelings.
- *Promoting equality and respect.* Modern portrayals that emphasize partnership and collaboration between male and female characters can teach boys the value of equality and mutual respect in relationships.
- *Diverse role models.* Introducing a variety of male characters with different strengths, weaknesses, and emotional landscapes can provide young viewers with diverse role models, helping them see that there are many ways to be a man.

5.3 MEDIA INFLUENCE ON MEN'S SELF-ESTEEM AND MENTAL HEALTH

Across various genres and media types, the influence of media on men's self-esteem and mental health is both profound and multifaceted (and this was briefly discussed in Chapter 3). Media images and narratives often set unrealistic standards for appearance, success, and behavior, and men and boys constantly exposed to these ideals may then feel compelled to strive for a level of perfection that is unattainable or irrelevant to their personal and cultural realities. This pressure can lead to a range of psychological issues, including low self-esteem, anxiety, and depression.

One of the most direct impacts of media on men's mental health is in the area of body image. The idealized male bodies – often muscular, tall, and lean – regularly portrayed in media can lead to dissatisfaction with one's own body, and to a similar level as women.[13,14] This dissatisfaction can manifest in unhealthy eating habits, excessive exercising, and in severe cases, body dysmorphic disorders. The constant comparison with media ideals can erode men's confidence and self-worth, contributing to a distorted perception of their bodies. More on this in Chapter 7.

Media narratives that equate masculinity with success, power, and control can also impact men's sense of self-worth. When personal achievements or life circumstances do not align with these portrayed ideals, it can result in feelings of inadequacy and failure.[15] This is particularly exacerbated in a media culture that often overlooks the emotional struggles of men, thereby limiting the representation of men's emotional resilience and adaptability.

5.4 THE MEDIA'S IMPACT ON MEN'S RELATIONSHIPS

Media portrayals also significantly influence men's approach to relationships, communication, and emotional expression. In many media narratives, men are often depicted as emotionally detached or inept, which can set a problematic precedent. This portrayal reinforces the idea that men should be stoic and reserved, potentially leading to difficulties in expressing vulnerability and emotional depth in their relationships.

In romantic relationships, media often idealizes certain stereotypes – the strong, silent type, the hero who saves the day, or the financially successful partner. These ideals can create a skewed expectation of what it means to be a good partner, often focusing more on superficial or materialistic aspects rather than emotional compatibility and mutual support. Men may feel pressured to conform to these unrealistic standards, which can lead to dissatisfaction and strain in relationships.[16] The media also often depict male communication as either overly assertive or humorously inept, particularly in romantic contexts. This can create unrealistic expectations for men about how they should communicate, potentially leading to issues in understanding and expressing emotions effectively. Such portrayals can discourage open and honest communication, which is essential for healthy relationships.

Similarly, in platonic relationships, media portrayals can influence how men interact with friends and colleagues. The glorification of competitiveness and lack of emotional bonding in male friendships as seen in media can discourage men from forming deep and supportive friendships. This can lead to a lack of a support network, which is crucial for mental well-being. However, it can be argued that this is changing with the increase in "bromances" being represented on screens.[17]

5.5 THE ROLE OF DIGITAL MEDIA AND ONLINE COMMUNITIES

Most of the recent research and inquiry on the relationship between the media, masculinity, and male identity have centered on newer digital platforms and technologies – principally social media. Indeed, the advent of digital media and the proliferation of online communities have significantly influenced male identity formation. Social media platforms, online gaming (see the next chapter), and forums offer new spaces for men and boys to express themselves, seek community, and form their identities. These digital spaces often allow for a level of anonymity or persona creation that can enable men to explore aspects of their identity they might not feel comfortable expressing in the physical world (more on this in Chapter 6).

5.5.1 Positive Aspects

Digital media can have several positive impacts on male identity. Online communities can provide support networks, spaces for sharing experiences, and information that might not be readily available elsewhere. They can also provide a forum for discussion and challenge around masculinity, and to engage in critical discourse.[18] For instance, forums and social media groups dedicated to men's mental health can offer valuable resources and a sense of solidarity. Online gaming communities can also provide spaces to foster teamwork, problem-solving skills, and social connections (see Chapter 6).[19]

5.5.2 Negative Aspects

However, there are also negative aspects to consider. Digital media can perpetuate harmful stereotypes and echo chambers, where extreme or one-sided viewpoints about masculinity are reinforced.[20] Social media, in particular, can create pressures to conform to idealized lifestyles or appearances, leading to issues with self-esteem and body image.[21,22] Moreover, the anonymity of online interactions can sometimes foster toxic behaviors, such as cyberbullying, trolling, or the spread of misogynistic attitudes (and which we will explore more in the next chapter).

5.6 CHALLENGING NARROW REPRESENTATIONS

To counter narrow representations, there is a need for a more inclusive portrayal of masculinity in the media. This diversity should encompass not only physical appearances and sexual orientations but also the wide range of emotions, vulnerabilities, and strengths that men exhibit. Such representations can offer a more realistic and relatable depiction of men, providing viewers with a broader understanding of what it means to be a man. So, how can we do this? And who needs to be involved?

5.6.1 Media Creators

Media creators play a pivotal role in shaping societal perceptions. To promote more diverse and realistic representations of men, they need to consciously move away from stereotypical portrayals and, instead, embrace the multitude of male experiences and identities. This can be achieved by:

1. *Incorporating diverse characters.* Introducing characters of various races, sexual orientations, body types, and backgrounds can provide a more accurate reflection of the real world.

2. *Developing multidimensional male characters.* Characters should be crafted with depth, showcasing a range of emotions and experiences that defy traditional masculine norms.

3. *Engaging with diverse writers and directors.* Bringing in creatives from diverse backgrounds can help in producing content that is more representative and authentic.

4. *Research and collaboration.* Collaborating with experts and communities to understand different perspectives and experiences can lead to more informed and respectful representations.

In recent years, there have been notable examples in media that aim to promote diverse and realistic representations of men, moving away from traditional stereotypes. Here are some key examples:

- *Ted Lasso* (TV Series, 2020–2023). This Apple TV+ series is praised for its portrayal of the title character, Ted Lasso, who embodies a nurturing and emotionally open form of masculinity that diverges from traditional stoic or aggressive male stereotypes. The show also emphasizes the importance of mental health and emotional well-being.
- *Moonlight* (Film, 2016). Although slightly earlier than your time frame, *Moonlight* remains a pivotal film for its exploration of masculinity. It presents a nuanced story of a young African American man grappling with his identity and sexuality. The film breaks away from conventional masculine norms by exploring vulnerability, identity, and the impact of nurturing versus toxic male influences.
- *This Is Us* (TV Series, 2016–2022). This series is notable for its deep, emotional exploration of its male characters, showing them in vulnerable,

caring, and complex roles that challenge traditional masculine stereotypes. The show deals with issues like mental health, fatherhood, and personal growth across different timelines and backgrounds.

- *Schitt's Creek* (TV Series, 2015–2020). *Schitt's Creek* features a diverse cast and has been commended for its portrayal of LGBTQ+ characters, particularly the pansexual character David Rose. The show promotes acceptance and love without adhering to typical gender norms, providing a fresh take on masculinity and relationships.
- *Atlanta* (TV Series, 2016–2022). Created by Donald Glover, *Atlanta* mixes surreal comedy and drama while addressing serious themes about race, economic disparity, and identity. The show features a predominantly Black cast and delves into the complexities of modern masculinity, portraying its male characters in varied and intricate ways.

These examples reflect a broader shift in media toward more inclusive and multidimensional portrayals of masculinity. By focusing on emotional depth, diversity, and realistic experiences, these media pieces contribute to reshaping societal perceptions of what it means to be a man in today's world.

5.6.2   Influencers and Celebrities

In the era of social media, influencers and celebrities have become central figures in shaping public perceptions, including ideas about masculinity. These individuals, often with millions of followers, wield significant influence, especially among younger audiences, who frequently turn to social media for trends, lifestyle cues, and role models. The ways in which these public figures portray masculinity can have a profound impact on their followers' understanding and expression of their own male identity.

Younger audiences, in particular, are highly impressionable and may look up to influencers and celebrities as benchmarks for their own behavior and appearance. When these public figures adhere to traditional or stereotypical portrayals of masculinity, it can reinforce narrow perceptions among their audience. Conversely, when they challenge these norms – for instance, by showing vulnerability, engaging in nontraditional activities, or advocating for mental health – they can play a pivotal role in broadening the understanding of what it means to be a man.

Given their significant influence, influencers and celebrities bear a certain level of responsibility in how they represent masculinity. There is thus a growing need for these figures to be mindful of their impact and to use their platforms to promote positive, diverse, and realistic images of men. This not only benefits their audience but also contributes to a broader cultural shift toward a more inclusive understanding of masculinity.

See some examples here of some particularly positive and negative influencers and celebrities.

5.6.2.1 *Positive Influencers*

5.6.2.1.1 TERRY CREWS

Crews has openly discussed his experiences with sexual assault, breaking the silence on a subject often considered taboo for men to discuss. His vulnerability and advocacy for survivors of sexual assault have challenged traditional masculinity norms.

5.6.2.1.2 THE ROCK (DWAYNE JOHNSON)

Known for his muscular physique and action roles, Johnson has also been vocal about his battles with depression. His openness about mental health issues defies the stereotype that men must always be emotionally resilient.

5.6.2.1.3 HARRY STYLES

Styles is recognized for challenging gender norms and stereotypes through his fashion choices and public statements. He often wears clothing that blurs traditional gender lines, encouraging a more fluid understanding of masculinity.

5.6.2.1.4 CHRIS MOSIER

An athlete and transgender rights activist, Mosier has used his platform to challenge traditional ideas about gender in sports and has been a visible advocate for the inclusion of trans individuals in athletics, discussing masculinity from a transgender perspective.

5.6.2.1.5 ZACKARY DRUCKER

As a transgender woman and an artist, Drucker works on platforms like Instagram to provide a narrative that often includes dialogues around masculinity, particularly challenging what it means to be male or female in a societal context.

5.6.2.2 *Negative Influencers*

5.6.2.2.1 DAN BILZERIAN

Bilzerian is often criticized for portraying a hypermasculine lifestyle on social media that includes guns, women portrayed as trophies, and extravagant displays of wealth. His portrayal of masculinity is often linked to material success and objectification.

5.6.2.2.2 ANDREW TATE

Tate has made various controversial statements regarding masculinity and gender roles, many of which have been criticized as reinforcing toxic masculinity norms. He promotes a very traditional and narrow view of how men should behave and has been called out for misogynistic rhetoric.

5.6.2.2.3 NIKOCADO AVOCADO

He is known for his "mukbang" videos, where he consumes large amounts of food. Critics have suggested that his content, which often includes emotional outbursts and unhealthy eating behaviors, can promote a harmful and negative portrayal of self-care and emotional expression.

It is essential to recognize the power of influence these public figures hold. When they challenge harmful norms and advocate for inclusivity, they contribute to a healthier societal understanding of masculinity. Conversely, when they perpetuate stereotypes, it can have a regressive effect. Therefore, the role of influencers and celebrities in shaping the discourse on masculinity is not to be underestimated.

5.6.3 Advocacy and Education

Advocacy and education are crucial in influencing media portrayals. Advocacy groups can:

1. *Raise awareness.* Campaigns that highlight the importance of diverse representations in media can educate both creators and consumers.

2. *Collaborate with media houses.* Partnering with media companies to provide guidelines or workshops on diversity and representation can lead to more informed content creation.

3. *Promote policy changes.* Advocating for policies that encourage diversity in media can help institutionalize these changes.

Several advocacy groups and initiatives have been influential in promoting diversity and more nuanced representations of masculinity in media. Here are some key examples that support these activities:

- *The Representation Project.* Founded by Jennifer Siebel Newsom following her documentary *The Mask You Live In*, which explores American masculinity's harmful stereotypes, the Representation Project uses film and media as tools to raise awareness. They launch various campaigns and educational programs aimed at challenging and overcoming limiting gender norms. Website: https://therepproject.org/.
- *GLAAD (Gay and Lesbian Alliance Against Defamation).* GLAAD has been particularly effective in advocating for LGBTQ+ representations

in media, which includes diverse portrayals of masculinity. They work directly with media companies and creators through workshops, consultations, and their annual "Where We Are on TV" report, which assesses inclusivity in television. Website: https://glaad.org/.

- *Common Sense Media.* This organization provides education and advocacy aimed at helping families navigate media and technology. While their focus is broad, they often highlight the importance of diverse and realistic portrayals of gender in media, offering resources and guides for both consumers and creators. Website: www.commonsensemedia.org/.

- *Geena Davis Institute on Gender in Media.* Founded by actress Geena Davis, the institute conducts research and collaborates with the entertainment industry to dramatically alter how girls and women are reflected in media. Their work also extends to the portrayals of men and boys, advocating for more varied and nonstereotypical representations. Website: https://seejane.org/.

- *MenCare.* This global fatherhood campaign promotes men's involvement as equitable, nonviolent fathers and caregivers to achieve family well-being and gender equality. MenCare works through advocacy and media campaigns to change public perceptions and behaviors regarding men's roles in parenting and caregiving. Website: www.mencare.org/.

These organizations and their efforts show a tangible impact on how media portrays masculinity, advocating for a shift toward more inclusive and realistic representations. By educating both the creators and the public, they contribute to ongoing cultural shifts in the portrayal of gender in media.

5.6.4 Consumers

Consumers also have the power to influence media portrayals through their choices and voices. They can:

1. *Support diverse media.* Actively seeking out and supporting media that portrays diverse representations of men can help shift market trends.

2. *Voice opinions.* Providing feedback to media creators and companies through social media or viewership ratings can influence future content production.

3. *Critical consumption.* Being aware and critical of media consumed can help individuals understand and challenge unrealistic portrayals.

5.7 CONCLUSION

Media and popular culture wield an extraordinary influence over male identity, deeply affecting men's self-esteem, mental health, relationships, and their very sense of self. This chapter has journeyed through the various dimensions of how masculinity is shaped by both traditional media and burgeoning digital platforms. We have seen that while media can entrench antiquated stereotypes, it also holds the potential to be a potent vehicle for good, championing diverse and authentic representations of masculinity.

The current media landscape is at a crossroads, often caught between perpetuating outdated narratives and fostering a richly diverse portrayal of male experiences. It is clear that for men and boys – and indeed, for society's collective well-being – embracing a wider spectrum of masculine identities is not only beneficial but also necessary. When media upholds a limited vision of what it means to be a man, it stifles the ability of individuals to live genuinely and fully.

Recognizing this, there is an urgent call for a shift toward inclusivity and diversity in media portrayals – a shift that demands a concerted effort from media creators, consumers, advocacy groups, and educators. We must encourage media that represents a fuller range of male experiences and identities, moving beyond clichés to capture the complexity and truth of people's lives. Consumers have the power to drive this change by seeking out and endorsing media that reflect realistic images of men, and by critically engaging with the content they consume. Advocacy and education are fundamental in illuminating the effects of media representations and cultivating a media audience that is both critical and discerning.

By fostering more inclusive and diverse representations of men, media can serve as a formidable ally in shaping a more affirmative and comprehensive understanding of masculinity. It can support the creation of a culture where men are liberated to express all aspects of their identity, unbounded by reductive stereotypes. This endeavor promotes healthier, more rewarding lives for men and boys. In essence, this transformation is not solely an industry challenge but a societal imperative – a call to action for each of us to help forge a more empathetic and inclusive world.

NOTES

1 Giaccardi, S., Ward, L. M., Seabrook, R. C., Manago, A., & Lippman, J. (2016). Media and modern manhood: Testing associations between media consumption and young men's acceptance of traditional gender ideologies. *Sex Roles, 75,* 151–163.

2 Waling, A. (2017). "We are so pumped full of shit by the media" masculinity, magazines, and the lack of self-identification. *Men and Masculinities, 20*(4), 427–452.

3 Kareithi, P. J. (2014). Hegemonic masculinity in media. *Media and Gender: A Scholarly Agenda for the Global Alliance on Media and Gender, 30,* 27–29.

4 Tasker, Y. (2012). Dumb movies for dumb people: Masculinity, the body, and the voice in contemporary action cinema. In *Screening the Male* (pp. 230–244). Routledge.

5 Alberti, J. (2013). "I Love You, Man": Bromances, the construction of masculinity, and the continuing evolution of the romantic comedy. *Quarterly Review of Film and Video, 30*(2), 159–172.

6 Pascoe, G. J. (2015). A qualitative textual and comparative analysis of the representation of masculinity in the action and romantic comedy genres. *Online Journal of Communication and Media Technologies, 5*(3), 1–26.

7 Grant, B. K. (2010). *Shadows of doubt: Negotiations of masculinity in american genre films*. Wayne State University Press.

8 Scharrer, E., & Blackburn, G. (2018). Cultivating conceptions of masculinity: Television and perceptions of masculine gender role norms. *Mass Communication and Society, 21*(2), 149–177.

9 Gilbert, M. A., Giaccardi, S., & Ward, L. M. (2018). Contributions of game genre and masculinity ideologies to associations between video game play and men's risk-taking behavior. *Media Psychology, 21*(3), 437–456.

10 Hine, B., Ivanovic, K., & England, D. (2018). From the sleeping princess to the world-saving daughter of the chief: Examining young children's perceptions of 'old' versus 'new' Disney princess characters. *Social Sciences, 7*(9), 161.

11 Hine, B., England, D., Lopreore, K., Skora Horgan, E., & Hartwell, L. (2018). The rise of the androgynous princess: Examining representations of gender in prince and princess characters of Disney movies released 2009–2016. *Social Sciences, 7*(12), 245.

12 Clarke, L. L., Hine, B., England, D., Flew, P. P., Alzahri, R., Juriansz, S. N., & Garcia, M. J. (2024). The gendered behaviors displayed by Disney protagonists. *Frontiers in Sociology, 9*, 1338900.

13 Agliata, D., & Tantleff-Dunn, S. (2004). The impact of media exposure on males' body image. *Journal of Social and Clinical Psychology, 23*(1), 7–22.

14 Barlett, C. P., Vowels, C. L., & Saucier, D. A. (2008). Meta-analyses of the effects of media images on men's body-image concerns. *Journal of Social and Clinical Psychology, 27*(3), 279–310.

15 Trekels, J., Vangeel, L., & Eggermont, S. (2017). Media ideals and other-sex peer norms among Belgian early adolescents: Equating self-worth with attractiveness. *Journal of Children and Media, 11*(4), 466–484.

16 Giaccardi et al., Media and modern manhood, 151–163.

17 Boyle, K., & Berridge, S. (2014). I love you, man: Gendered narratives of friendship in contemporary Hollywood comedies. *Feminist Media Studies, 14*(3), 353–368.

18 Schlichthorst, M., King, K., Reifels, L., Phelps, A., & Pirkis, J. (2019). Using social media networks to engage men in conversations on masculinity and suicide: Content analysis of Man Up Facebook campaign data. *Social Media+ Society, 5*(4), 2056305119880019.

19 Jones, C., Scholes, L., Johnson, D., Katsikitis, M., & Carras, M. C. (2014). Gaming well: Links between videogames and flourishing mental health. *Frontiers in psychology, 5*, 76833.

20 Parkins, M., & Parkins, J. (2021). Gender representations in social media and formations of masculinity. *Journal of Student Research, 10*(1).

21 Gültzow, T., Guidry, J. P., Schneider, F., & Hoving, C. (2020). Male body image portrayals on instagram. *Cyberpsychology, Behavior, and Social Networking, 23*(5), 281–289.

22 Saiphoo, A. N., & Vahedi, Z. (2019). A meta-analytic review of the relationship between social media use and body image disturbance. *Computers in Human Behavior, 101*, 259–275.

6

SCREEN TIME AND GAMING ADDICTION

6.1 INTRODUCTION

As mentioned in the previous chapter, in recent years, the issue of ever-increasing screen time and gaming addiction has emerged as a significant concern, particularly among men and boys.[1,2] With the advent of increasingly immersive and accessible digital technologies, the prevalence of excessive screen engagement has escalated, leading to concerns about its impact on mental health, social skills, and daily functioning.

This phenomenon is especially pronounced in the male demographic, where gaming is often a popular pastime, where boys and men engage more frequently in gaming than girls and women, and where gaming is still heavily identified as a "male" activity.[3] The addictive nature of many games, combined with the social and competitive aspects of online gaming, has contributed to a growing number of men and boys spending excessive amounts of time in front of screens. This trend is also not limited to leisure activities but extends to the increasing use of digital devices for communication, entertainment, and information. The implications of this trend are profound, affecting not only individual users but also their families, communities, and broader social networks.

As we delve deeper into this chapter, we will explore the factors contributing to this addiction, its wide-ranging effects on different aspects of life, and discuss potential interventions and strategies to foster healthier digital

DOI: 10.4324/9781032709369-8

habits. Addressing this growing concern is crucial, not only for the well-being of men and boys, but also for the health of our digital society at large.

6.2 HISTORICAL CONTEXT AND TECHNOLOGICAL ADVANCEMENTS IN GAMING AND SCREEN TIME

The landscape of gaming and screen time has undergone significant transformations over the past several decades, shaped by technological advancements and changing societal norms.[4] Understanding this evolution is crucial for contextualizing current trends and the impact of gaming addiction.

6.2.1   1970s to 1980s: The Birth of Home Gaming

The late 1970s and early 1980s marked the advent of home gaming consoles with the introduction of systems like the Atari 2600. These early games were simple, with limited graphics and gameplay mechanics. The focus was on short, casual play sessions, often shared with family and friends.

- Notable Games: "Pong," "Space Invaders," "Pac-Man"
- Characteristics: Simple mechanics, local multiplayer, limited graphics

6.2.2   1990s: The Rise of Complex Gaming Systems

The 1990s saw significant advancements in gaming technology with the introduction of 16-bit and 32-bit consoles like the Sega Genesis and Sony PlayStation. Games became more complex, with better graphics, more intricate storylines, and longer gameplay.

- Notable Games: "Sonic the Hedgehog," "Final Fantasy VII," "The Legend of Zelda: Ocarina of Time"
- Characteristics: Improved graphics, deeper narratives, longer playtime, single-player focus

6.2.3   2000s: Online Gaming and Social Interaction

The early 2000s introduced the era of online gaming, fundamentally changing how people interacted with games. Consoles like the Xbox and PlayStation 2, along with PC gaming, facilitated online multiplayer experiences. This period also saw the rise of massively multiplayer online games (MMOs) such as "World of Warcraft."

- Notable Games: "World of Warcraft," "Halo," "Call of Duty"
- Characteristics: Online multiplayer, persistent worlds, social interaction, competitive gameplay

6.2.4 2010s: Mobile Gaming and Accessibility

The 2010s brought the proliferation of smartphones and mobile gaming. Games like "Angry Birds" and "Candy Crush Saga" made gaming more accessible to a broader audience, leading to a significant increase in screen time across all demographics.

- Notable Games: "Angry Birds," "Candy Crush Saga"
- Characteristics: Mobile accessibility, casual gaming, microtransactions

6.2.5 Current Technological Advancements and Their Impact

The current decade is marked by the growing adoption of virtual reality (VR) and augmented reality (AR) technologies. These advancements offer immersive gaming experiences that blur the line between the virtual and physical worlds. VR headsets like the Oculus Rift and AR games like "Pokémon Go" have introduced new dimensions to gaming, enhancing both engagement and the potential for addiction.

6.2.5.1 Virtual Reality (VR)

Virtual reality has revolutionized gaming by creating highly immersive environments that engage multiple senses. Players can experience a heightened sense of presence, making games more compelling and, potentially, more addictive.

- Immersive Experiences: VR games offer 360-degree views and interactive environments that feel real, enhancing engagement.
- Physical Involvement: VR often requires physical movement, which can make the gaming experience more intense and prolonged.
- Examples: "Beat Saber," "Half-Life: Alyx."

6.2.5.2 Augmented Reality (AR)

Augmented reality blends digital content with the physical world, creating interactive experiences that extend beyond traditional screen boundaries. AR games encourage players to explore their real-world environment, adding a layer of physical activity to gaming.

- Real-World Integration: AR games overlay digital elements onto the physical world, making everyday environments part of the game.
- Social Interaction: AR games often have a social component, encouraging players to collaborate or compete in real-world settings.
- Examples: "Pokémon Go," "Ingress."

6.2.5.3   Mobile and Cloud Gaming

The advancements in mobile and cloud gaming have made high-quality games accessible on the go, further increasing screen time. These technologies allow for seamless gameplay across devices, enabling players to continue their gaming sessions anytime, anywhere.

- Accessibility: Mobile and cloud gaming make it possible to play complex games on smartphones and tablets, removing barriers to entry.
- Continuous Engagement: Features like cross-platform play and cloud saves allow for uninterrupted gaming experiences across different devices.
- Examples: "Fortnite," "Genshin Impact," "Google Stadia."

6.2.6   Artificial Intelligence (AI) and Machine Learning

AI and machine learning have enhanced game design by creating more adaptive and personalized gaming experiences. These technologies can tailor gameplay to individual preferences, making games more engaging and difficult to put down.

- Adaptive Gameplay: AI-driven games can adjust difficulty levels and gameplay mechanics based on player behavior.
- Personalization: Machine learning algorithms analyze player data to offer personalized content and recommendations.
- Examples: AI-driven NPCs in games like "The Elder Scrolls V: Skyrim," personalized game recommendations on platforms like Steam.

6.2.7   Implications for Addiction

These technological advancements have increased the potential for gaming addiction by making games more immersive, accessible, and engaging. The integration of social features, reward systems, and real-time updates keeps players engaged for longer periods, making it harder to disconnect.

- *Increased screen time.* The accessibility of gaming on multiple devices encourages continuous play, leading to longer screen time.
- *Enhanced engagement.* Immersive technologies like VR and AR create compelling experiences that are difficult to leave, increasing the risk of addiction.
- *Social pressures.* Online and multiplayer games foster social connections and competitive environments, which can drive excessive gaming to maintain social status.

By understanding the historical context and technological advancements in gaming, we can better address the challenges posed by gaming addiction and develop strategies to promote healthier digital habits. This comprehensive approach is essential for mitigating the negative impacts of excessive screen time and ensuring a balanced relationship with technology.

6.3   CURRENT STATISTICS ON SCREEN TIME AND USAGE

As mentioned in the previous section, the prevalence of screen time and digital media usage has surged dramatically in recent years, particularly among young people. Understanding these statistics is crucial to grasp the extent of the issue and its potential impact on mental health, social skills, and daily functioning. For example, recent studies indicate that the average daily screen time for young people has reached significant levels, with Backlinko[5] reporting that teenagers aged between 13 and 18 years old spend an average of 7 hours and 22 minutes per day on screens for entertainment purposes, excluding schoolwork. This figure highlights the significant integration of digital devices in their daily lives. It is also a notable increase from 2015, when the average was 6 hours and 40 minutes per day.

In younger children (ages 8–12), the average screen time is around 5 hours and 33 minutes per day, which includes activities such as watching videos, playing games, and using social media. This is an increase from 4 hours and 36 minutes per day in 2015. Children under 8 years old also spend a substantial amount of time on screens, averaging about 2.5 hours daily.

6.3.1   Screen Time by Activity

Screen time has increased across all areas of usage too, including:

- *Video watching.* Teenagers spend approximately 3 hours per day watching videos on platforms like YouTube and TikTok, making it the most significant contributor to their screen time.
- *Gaming.* Teenagers spend about 1 hour and 46 minutes daily playing video games. This activity is particularly more common among boys, who generally engage more in gaming compared to girls.
- *Social media.* On average, teenagers spend around 1 hour and 27 minutes per day on social media platforms, such as Instagram, Snapchat, and TikTok.

6.4   FACTORS CONTRIBUTING TO INCREASED SCREEN TIME AND ADDICTION

Like most subjects covered in this book, screen time and screen/gaming addiction is influenced by several factors.

6.4.1   Psychological Factors

Psychological factors play a significant role in screen time and gaming addiction. For many, digital devices and video games provide an escape from reality, offering a sense of achievement, control, and belonging that might be lacking in their real lives.[6] This can be particularly appealing to men and boys who might be facing challenges in their personal or academic lives. The immediate rewards and feedback loops present in many games can also lead to habit formation and, over time, addiction.

6.4.2   Social Factors

Social factors are equally influential. Online communities and multiplayer games create virtual social spaces where men and boys can feel a sense of belonging and acceptance.[7,8] For some, these online interactions might replace real-life social interactions, especially if they feel marginalized or misunderstood in their physical environments. The competitive nature of many games can also create a compelling social dynamic, encouraging continuous play to maintain status within these communities.[9]

6.4.3   Environmental Factors

Environmental factors, including accessibility to digital devices and the increasing push toward online interactions for education, work, and socialization, contribute to the problem.[10] As discussed earlier, the global shift toward a more digitally oriented lifestyle means that men and boys are spending more time than ever in front of screens, with the boundaries between use and overuse becoming increasingly blurred.

6.4.4   Game Design and Online Communities

The design of many games, particularly those that are online and multiplayer, is inherently conducive to addictive behaviors.[11,12,13] These games often employ mechanisms that encourage continuous engagement, such as rewards for regular play, social ranking systems, and ongoing content updates. Additionally, the community aspect of these games can exert a strong social pressure to participate, further entrenching addictive behaviors.

6.5   IMPACT ON MENTAL HEALTH AND COGNITION

The impact, as you can imagine, is widespread. Let's first take a look at mental health and cognitive abilities.

6.5.1   Mental Health

Excessive screen time and addictive gaming have been increasingly linked to various mental health issues among men and boys.[14] Prolonged periods of engagement with digital screens and immersive gaming environments can lead to a range of psychological effects, including increased anxiety, depression, and stress.[15,16,17] Though, importantly, this is related to both the motivation for playing and the level of engagement.[18] These effects are often compounded by the neglect of physical health, lack of sleep, and reduced exposure to outdoor activities, all of which are essential for mental well-being.

6.5.2   Mood

One of the most immediate effects of gaming addiction is on mood. Individuals who spend excessive time gaming or on screens may experience mood swings, irritability, and a general decrease in emotional stability. This can be attributed to the intense emotional experiences and high arousal states associated with gaming, which can lead to a subsequent emotional crash. Additionally, the isolation that often accompanies heavy screen use can exacerbate feelings of loneliness and depression.

6.5.3   Cognition

Cognitive functions can also be affected by excessive gaming and screen time. Attention spans may be reduced, and individuals might find it increasingly difficult to concentrate on tasks that are not as immediately rewarding or stimulating as video games. This may be underpinned by neurological changes that can result from excessive gaming practices.[19] This can affect academic performance in students and productivity in adults. Furthermore, the constant multitasking required in many games can lead to fragmented attention in other areas of life, making it hard to focus on single tasks for extended periods.

It is important to note however that, while there are concerns about the effects of excessive gaming and screen time on cognitive functions, low and moderate gaming can have positive impacts on cognitive performance.[20] For example, research indicates that engaging with video games can enhance various cognitive skills, including problem-solving abilities, spatial navigation, multitasking efficiency, and reaction times.[21] These benefits arise from the complex, strategic thinking and quick decision-making often required in games. Moreover, the neurological adaptations from gaming can enhance focus and cognitive flexibility, which can be beneficial in both academic settings for students and professional environments for adults, but this does depend on the type of game,[22] and even the same type of games can have mixed effects.[23]

6.6   EFFECT ON SOCIAL SKILLS AND RELATIONSHIPS

The impact of excessive screen time and gaming extends to other areas too, such as social skills and interaction with others.

6.6.1   Social Skills Development

Whilst low to moderate gaming does little to harm boys' social skills,[24] excessive screen time and gaming addiction can significantly impact the development of social skills, especially in men and boys.[25] Engaging predominantly in virtual interactions can limit the development of essential interpersonal skills, such as empathy, verbal and nonverbal communication, and conflict resolution. These skills are typically honed through face-to-face interactions, where individuals learn to read and respond to social cues, emotions, and body language. The lack of such real-world social experiences can thus lead to difficulties in understanding and navigating social situations effectively.

6.6.2 Personal Relationships

For individuals struggling with screen time and gaming addiction, personal relationships often suffer. The extensive amount of time spent on screens can lead to neglect of family obligations, friendships, and romantic relationships. This neglect can manifest as a lack of engagement in conversations, failure to attend social gatherings, or ignoring the needs of partners or family members. Over time, this can erode trust and communication in relationships, leading to feelings of resentment and isolation. However, as social spaces in and of themselves, boys and men may still maintain social relationships, just in a digital space. This may be rich in interaction, just in a way very different to real-life interactions.

6.6.3 Isolation

The addictive nature of excessive gaming and screen use can also lead to social isolation. Individuals may find themselves increasingly withdrawing from social activities and interactions to spend more time in the digital world. This isolation can further exacerbate any existing mental health issues, such as anxiety or depression, creating a vicious cycle that makes re-engaging with the social world even more challenging. Though again, it should be noted that some studies indicate that engaging in gaming can compensate for loneliness experienced in real life,[26] and the community offered online may actually prompt increased engagement.

6.7   INFLUENCE ON DAILY LIFE AND RESPONSIBILITIES

The final area of impact is on more day to day elements of life, such as school, work, and physical health.

6.7.1 Impact on Academic and Occupational Performance

Again, whilst some engagement with screens and games, and in the right way, can be beneficial to students, excessive screen time and gaming addiction can have a detrimental impact on academic and occupational performance.[27] In academic settings, students may find it difficult to concentrate on studies or complete assignments on time due to the excessive amount of time spent on screens. This distraction can lead to lower grades, decreased participation in class, and a reduced ability to retain information. In the workplace, similar issues arise. Employees struggling with gaming addiction may exhibit decreased productivity, a lack of focus, and an inability to meet deadlines, potentially jeopardizing their professional development and career progression.

6.7.2   Disruption of Daily Routines

The disruption caused by excessive screen time extends to daily routines and habits. Individuals may experience altered sleep patterns, often staying up late to game or browse the internet, leading to sleep deprivation and its associated consequences, like fatigue and decreased alertness.[28] Regular meals and exercise may also be neglected, as gaming and screen activities consume the time and attention typically allocated to these essential daily activities. This neglect can lead to a sedentary lifestyle, compounding the risk of physical health issues, such as obesity, cardiovascular problems, and musculoskeletal disorders.

6.7.3   Impact on Physical Health

The physical health implications of prolonged screen time and gaming are also significant.[29] Extended periods of inactivity can lead to weight gain and associated health risks. Poor posture and continuous strain on the eyes, neck, and hands can lead to chronic pain and repetitive strain injuries. Moreover, the lack of exposure to natural light and outdoor activities can affect overall physical well-being, contributing to vitamin D deficiency and a weakened immune system.

6.8   CYBERBULLYING AND HOSTILITY IN ONLINE SPACES

Cyberbullying has also emerged as a significant and harmful phenomenon in online spaces, affecting individuals of all ages and backgrounds. For male gamers, bullying on online platform does not always relate to decreased motivation and participation, suggesting that men may simply expect these behaviors as part of their experience.[30,31] However, its impact on women is particularly severe, often manifesting in targeted harassment, threats, and abuse that can have lasting psychological effects. Online platforms, while offering opportunities for communication and engagement, also present environments where anonymity or pseudonymity can embolden harmful behaviors from users, often men. Indeed, even though women make up an increasing proportion of gamers, sexist attitudes toward female gamers are still rife.

6.8.1   Forms of Online Hostility Toward Women

Women in online spaces frequently encounter various forms of hostility, including gender-based harassment, sexual harassment, and doxxing (publishing private information).[32] These interactions can range from unsolicited comments on physical appearance to more aggressive threats. Social media, forums, and gaming communities are notable hot spots where such behavior can proliferate, often exacerbated by the platforms' competitive or contentious nature and their continued identification as "male spaces."[33,34,35,36] This is therefore an important issue for us to acknowledge for men, as the main perpetrators of these behaviors.

6.9   INTERVENTIONS AND TREATMENT APPROACHES

Several sections in this chapter have highlighted that there are positive benefits of online interactions, including in gaming, for boys and men. These include a sense of belonging, healthy competitiveness, and even increased cognitive skills. However, it should be noted that most of these benefits are linked to *low or moderate* use of these platforms, and that excessive use is where many of the negative outcomes arise. As such, it is important to consider what intervention might look like.

6.9.1   Current Intervention Strategies

Intervention strategies for screen time and gaming addiction have evolved as the understanding of these issues deepens. Currently, interventions range from clinical treatment methods to lifestyle and behavioral changes.[37,38,39] Clinical interventions may include cognitive-behavioral therapy (CBT), which helps individuals understand and change the thoughts and behaviors contributing to their addiction. Family therapy is also often recommended, especially for younger individuals, as it addresses the dynamics that may be enabling or exacerbating the addiction. Website: https://americanaddiction-centers.org/video-gaming-addiction.

6.9.2   Treatment Options

Treatment options can vary based on the severity of the addiction. For more severe cases, inpatient treatment programs that offer structured care and withdrawal from gaming and screen environments may be necessary. Outpatient programs, which allow individuals to maintain their daily routines while receiving treatment, can be effective for less severe cases. These programs typically include therapy sessions, support groups, and educational workshops on managing screen time. Additionally, there are now specialized rehabilitation centers that focus specifically on digital and gaming addiction, providing comprehensive, tailored treatment plans. Website: www.netaddictionrecovery.com/.

6.9.3   Digital Detox and Lifestyle Changes

Apart from clinical treatments, digital detox programs, which involve taking a break from all digital devices for a set period, can be beneficial.[40] These programs are often combined with activities that promote physical health, social interaction, and mindfulness. Encouraging regular exercise, outdoor activities, and hobbies that do not involve screens is also crucial in breaking the cycle of addiction. Website: www.itstimetologoff.com/digital-detox-retreats/.

6.9.4   Effectiveness and Accessibility of These Methods

The effectiveness of these interventions varies based on individual circumstances, including the severity of the addiction, personal motivation, and the presence of other mental health conditions. Early intervention tends to be more effective, highlighting the importance of recognizing the signs of addiction promptly. However, one of the challenges in treating screen time and gaming addiction is accessibility. There is still a lack of widespread recognition of this issue as a serious mental health condition, which can make it difficult for individuals to find specialized treatment. Additionally, the cost of treatment can be a barrier for many.

6.10   PROMOTING HEALTHIER DIGITAL HABITS

Beyond specific clinical intervention, softer approaches for more general "screen health" are likely beneficial for boys, men, and all users.

6.10.1   Strategies for Individuals and Families

Developing healthier digital habits is essential in managing and reducing excessive screen time and gaming addiction. For individuals, self-regulation strategies such as setting time limits for gaming and online activities and using apps that monitor and restrict usage can be effective. Creating a balanced daily routine that includes physical activity, social interaction, and hobbies away from screens is also crucial.

To enhance individual self-regulation of gaming habits, practical tips and digital tools can be highly effective. Setting strict time limits for gaming sessions using apps like "Forest" or "Stay Focused" can help individuals stay mindful of their screen time, by blocking access to games after a set period. Establishing a "no-gaming" schedule, such as during meals or just before bed, can also prevent excessive gaming from encroaching on essential daily activities and sleep. For more personalized management, apps that track gaming patterns and provide summaries of daily and weekly usage can offer insightful feedback, helping individuals recognize and modify excessive gaming behaviors. Additionally, engaging in scheduled offline activities such as sports, reading, or spending time with friends and family can provide rewarding alternatives to gaming, ensuring a healthier balance between digital and real-world interactions. These tools and strategies not only aid in reducing screen time but also empower users to take control of their digital life, fostering better overall mental and physical well-being.

Families play a vital role in promoting healthy digital habits. This can include setting clear rules about screen time, especially for younger children, and encouraging alternative activities that do not involve screens. It is also beneficial for families to engage in activities together that do not involve digital devices, like outdoor sports, board games, and reading, to strengthen relationships and provide healthy alternatives to screen time.

6.10.2   The Role of Educational Systems

Educational systems also have a significant part to play in promoting digital well-being. For example, schools can incorporate media literacy into the curriculum to teach students about the impacts of excessive screen time and responsible digital behavior. Moreover, programs that encourage students to engage in extracurricular activities, particularly those that promote physical health and social skills, can provide a healthy balance to screen-based activities. The more innovative these can be, even using the technologies themselves to increase awareness of the issues, the better.[41]

Preventive education in schools and communities also plays a crucial role in raising awareness and combating the risks of screen time and gaming addiction from an early age. Through dedicated educational programs, children and adolescents can be informed about the potential dangers of excessive screen use and be taught strategies to balance their digital activities with physical and social engagements. This approach aims not only to educate but also to embed a sense of responsibility and awareness about digital consumption among young people.

Additionally, schools and community groups can actively implement programs focused on digital literacy, fostering healthy screen habits, and promoting activities that enhance physical health and social interaction. Workshops for parents and caregivers could also feature as part of these initiatives, providing them with the necessary tools to understand and manage their children's digital habits effectively. Meanwhile, educators and community leaders are vital in weaving these themes into the fabric of educational and community life, facilitating student-led projects, expert discussions, and peer mentoring programs that support an integrated approach to digital well-being. Website: www.commonsense.org/education/digital-citizenship.

6.10.3   Policy and Public Health Initiatives

On a broader scale, policy and public health initiatives are crucial in promoting digital well-being. This can include creating guidelines for screen time use, particularly for children and adolescents. Public health campaigns can also raise awareness about the risks of excessive screen time and gaming addiction and provide resources and support for those affected.

Moreover, legislation that requires game developers to include warnings about the potential for addiction, and policies that fund research and treatment for digital addiction, can also be impactful. Additionally, workplaces can implement policies that encourage regular breaks from screens and promote a work culture that values digital disconnection outside of work hours. Website: www.who.int/news/item/24-04-2019-to-grow-up-healthy-children-need-to-sit-less-and-play-more.

6.10.4   Technological Solutions and Tools

A variety of technological solutions and tools has been developed to help combat screen time and gaming addiction.[42] These include software and apps that allow users to monitor and limit their screen time. Parental control apps can also help parents set boundaries for their children's device usage, including setting time limits, blocking certain apps or websites, and scheduling downtime. For adults, apps that track screen time and provide reminders to take breaks can also be effective in managing and reducing excessive use.

Innovations in digital technology are also emerging to address the addictive properties of devices and games. These include features like screen dimming and alerts that remind users to engage in physical activity after prolonged periods of inactivity. Some devices and games are now designed with built-in limits to discourage prolonged use and encourage healthier habits. Websites: www.forestapp.cc/, https://stayfocused.io/.

6.10.5   The Role of the Tech Industry

The tech and gaming industry plays a pivotal role in shaping the landscape of digital consumption, and its efforts to address gaming addiction are increasingly critical.[43,44] Beyond simply recognizing the problem, companies are already actively innovating and implementing measures designed to mitigate addictive behaviors associated with their products.

One significant area of focus is the development of gaming technologies that prioritize user health. For instance, some developers are integrating features that prompt players to take breaks after extended periods of gameplay, a practice known as "forced downtime." Additionally, game designs are increasingly incorporating balanced reward mechanisms that aim to reduce the compulsive engagement driven by reward loops and in-app purchases. These features include setting caps on daily rewards or diminishing returns on continuous play, which discourages prolonged gaming sessions.

Furthermore, the industry is adopting more transparent practices by providing clearer warnings about the potential risks of addiction directly within their games and on their platforms. This includes detailed information about the likelihood of addictive behaviors and guidance on how to recognize signs of addiction.

On the accountability front, regulatory bodies are also stepping in to ensure that these commitments have teeth. For example, some countries have introduced legislation requiring game developers to report on the measures they are taking to prevent addiction and, in some cases, limiting the amount of time minors can spend playing games each day.

Moreover, many companies are now supporting independent research into the long-term effects of gaming. This research is crucial for developing a deeper understanding of the impact of gaming on mental health and can inform future design and regulation. By investing in these areas, the tech industry not only demonstrates a commitment to user well-being but also helps foster a more sustainable and responsible gaming culture. Websites: https://gamespublisher.com/responsible-gaming-and-video-game-addiction-prevention/, https://kindbridge.com/gaming/how-gaming-companies-can-take-a-more-responsible-role-in-fighting-video-game-addiction/.

6.10.6   Tackling Cyberbullying and Gaming Sexism

Efforts to combat cyberbullying and ensure safer online environments for everyone, especially women, might include:

- *Enhanced moderation and reporting mechanisms.* Platforms need robust systems to quickly address reports of harassment. This includes employing advanced moderation tools and training moderators to recognize and act against gender-based attacks.
- *Legal and policy measures.* Updating and enforcing laws that protect against online harassment are crucial. This also involves working with policymakers to ensure these laws reflect the evolving nature of online interactions.
- *Community and support networks.* Building supportive community networks can empower women by providing solidarity and resources to handle and combat cyberbullying. These networks can also promote positive engagement across various platforms.
- *Education and awareness.* Raising awareness about the impact of cyberbullying on women and educating users about digital citizenship can foster more respectful interactions online.

6.11   CONCLUSION

This chapter has highlighted the escalating issue of screen time and gaming addiction among men and boys, a concern that has significant implications for mental health, social skills, academic and occupational performance, and overall well-being. The factors contributing to this addiction are multifaceted, involving psychological, social, and environmental elements, and the impacts are far-reaching, affecting not only the individuals directly involved but also their families, communities, and broader societal structures.

The urgency of addressing screen time and gaming addiction cannot be overstated. As digital technology becomes increasingly ingrained in our daily lives, the potential for addiction and its associated consequences grows. This issue calls for immediate attention and action from all stakeholders, including health-care providers, educators, policymakers, families, and individuals themselves.

There is also a pressing need for broader awareness of the risks associated with excessive screen time and gaming. Public health campaigns, educational programs, and policy initiatives must be developed and implemented to address this growing concern. Moreover, health-care systems need to recognize and treat screen time and gaming addiction as legitimate mental health issues, providing accessible and effective treatment options. Families and educational systems play a crucial role in promoting healthy digital habits from a young age. Encouraging balanced lifestyles, setting boundaries for screen time, and educating children and adolescents about the responsible use of technology are essential steps in preventing addiction.

For individuals, it is vital to be mindful of one's digital consumption and actively seek to maintain a healthy balance between the virtual and the real worlds. Developing hobbies and interests outside of the digital realm, engaging in physical activities, and nurturing face-to-face relationships are key practices that can safeguard against the risks of excessive screen use.

NOTES

1 Su, W., Han, X., Yu, H., Wu, Y., & Potenza, M. N. (2020). Do men become addicted to internet gaming and women to social media? A meta-analysis examining gender-related differences in specific internet addiction. *Computers in Human Behavior, 113*, 106480.
2 André, F., Broman, N., Håkansson, A., & Claesdotter-Knutsson, E. (2020). Gaming addiction, problematic gaming and engaged gaming – Prevalence and associated characteristics. *Addictive Behaviors Reports, 12*, 100324.
3 Leonhardt, M., & Overå, S. (2021). Are there differences in video gaming and use of social media among boys and girls? – A mixed methods approach. *International Journal of Environmental Research and Public Health, 18*(11), 6085.
4 Zhouxiang, L. (2022). *A history of competitive gaming*. Routledge.
5 https://backlinko.com/screen-time-statistics
6 Burén, J., Nutley, S. B., Sandberg, D., Ström Wiman, J., & Thorell, L. B. (2021). Gaming and social media addiction in university students: Sex differences, suitability of symptoms, and association with psychosocial difficulties. *Frontiers in Psychiatry, 12*, 740867.

7   Toombs, A. L., Lee, A., Guo, Z., Buls, J., Westbrook, A., Carr, I., . . . & LaPeter, M. (2022). "We're so much more than the in-game clan": Gaming experiences and group management in multi-space online communities. *Proceedings of the ACM on Human-Computer Interaction, 6*(CSCW2), 1–29.

8   Scholes, L., Mills, K. A., & Wallace, E. (2022). Boys' gaming identities and opportunities for learning. *Learning, Media and Technology, 47*(2), 163–178.

9   Mao, E. (2021). The structural characteristics of esports gaming and their behavioral implications for high engagement: A competition perspective and a cross-cultural examination. *Addictive Behaviors, 123,* 107056.

10 Timotheou, S., Miliou, O., Dimitriadis, Y., Sobrino, S. V., Giannoutsou, N., Cachia, R., . . . & Ioannou, A. (2023). Impacts of digital technologies on education and factors influencing schools' digital capacity and transformation: A literature review. *Education and Information Technologies, 28*(6), 6695–6726.

11 Sirola, A., Savela, N., Savolainen, I., Kaakinen, M., & Oksanen, A. (2021). The role of virtual communities in gambling and gaming behaviors: A systematic review. *Journal of Gambling Studies, 37*(1), 165–187.

12 Gibson, E., Griffiths, M. D., Calado, F., & Harris, A. (2022). The relationship between videogame micro-transactions and problem gaming and gambling: A systematic review. *Computers in Human Behavior, 131,* 107219.

13 Zendle, D., Cairns, P., Barnett, H., & McCall, C. (2020). Paying for loot boxes is linked to problem gambling, regardless of specific features like cash-out and pay-to-win. *Computers in Human Behavior, 102,* 181–191.

14 Purwaningsih, E., & Nurmala, I. (2021). The impact of online game addiction on adolescent mental health: A systematic review and meta-analysis. *Open Access Macedonian Journal of Medical Sciences (OAMJMS), 9*(F), 260–274.

15 Stevens, C., Zhang, E., Cherkerzian, S., Chen, J. A., & Liu, C. H. (2020). Problematic internet use/computer gaming among US college students: Prevalence and correlates with mental health symptoms. *Depression and Anxiety, 37*(11), 1127–1136.

16 Cudo, A., Wojtasiński, M., Tużnik, P., Fudali-Czyż, A., & Griffiths, M. D. (2022). The Relationship between depressive symptoms, loneliness, self-control, and gaming disorder among Polish male and female gamers: The indirect effects of gaming motives. *International Journal of Environmental Research and Public Health, 19*(16), 10438.

17 Li, L., Abbey, C., Wang, H., Zhu, A., Shao, T., Dai, D., . . . & Rozelle, S. (2022). The association between video game time and adolescent mental health: Evidence from Rural China. *International Journal of Environmental Research and Public Health, 19*(22), 14815.

18 Wang, L., Li, J., Chen, Y., Chai, X., Zhang, Y., Wang, Z., . . . & Gao, X. (2021). Gaming motivation and negative psychosocial outcomes in male adolescents: An individual-centered 1-year longitudinal study. *Frontiers in Psychology, 12,* 743273.

19 Mohammadi, B., Szycik, G. R., Te Wildt, B., Heldmann, M., Samii, A., & Münte, T. F. (2020). Structural brain changes in young males addicted to video-gaming. *Brain and Cognition, 139,* 105518.

20 Choi, E., Shin, S. H., Ryu, J. K., Jung, K. I., Kim, S. Y., & Park, M. H. (2020). Commercial video games and cognitive functions: Video game genres and modulating factors of cognitive enhancement. *Behavioral and Brain Functions, 16,* 1–14.

21 Chaarani, B., Ortigara, J., Yuan, D., Loso, H., Potter, A., & Garavan, H. P. (2022). Association of video gaming with cognitive performance among children. *JAMA Network Open, 5*(10), e2235721–e2235721.

22 Aliyari, H., Sahraei, H., Erfani, M., Mohammadi, M., Kazemi, M., Daliri, M. R., . . . & Farajdokht, F. (2020). Changes in cognitive functions following violent and football video games in young male volunteers by studying brain waves. *Basic and Clinical Neuroscience, 11*(3), 279.

23 He, Q., Turel, O., Wei, L., & Bechara, A. (2021). Structural brain differences associated with extensive massively-multiplayer video gaming. *Brain Imaging and Behavior, 15*(1), 364–374.

24 Hygen, B. W., Belsky, J., Stenseng, F., Skalicka, V., Kvande, M. N., Zahl-Thanem, T., & Wichstrøm, L. (2020). Time spent gaming and social competence in children: Reciprocal effects across childhood. *Child Development, 91*(3), 861–875.

25 Salahuddin, S., & Muazzam, A. (2019). Gaming addiction in adolescent boys. *Clinical and Counselling Psychology Review, 1*(2), 01–19.

26 Koban, K., Biehl, J., Bornemeier, J., & Ohler, P. (2022). Compensatory video gaming. Gaming behaviours and adverse outcomes and the moderating role of stress, social interaction anxiety, and loneliness. *Behaviour & Information Technology, 41*(13), 2727–2744.

27 Islam, M. I., Biswas, R. K., & Khanam, R. (2020). Effect of internet use and electronic game-play on academic performance of Australian children. *Scientific Reports, 10*(1), 21727.

28 Kristensen, J. H., Pallesen, S., King, D. L., Hysing, M., & Erevik, E. K. (2021). Problematic gaming and sleep: A systematic review and meta-analysis. *Frontiers in Psychiatry, 12*, 675237.

29 Aziz, N., Nordin, M. J., Abdulkadir, S. J., & Salih, M. M. M. (2021). Digital addiction: Systematic review of computer game addiction impact on adolescent physical health. *Electronics, 10*(9), 996.

30 Prasetyaningtyas, S. W., & Prayogo, A. (2021, October). The effect of cyberbullying in multi-player online gaming environments: Gamer perceptions. In *2021 International Conference on Informatics, Multimedia, Cyber and Information System (ICIMCIS)* (pp. 244–249). IEEE.

31 Kaye, L. S., Hellsten, L. A. M., McIntyre, L. J., & Hendry, B. P. (2022). 'There'sa fine line between trash-talking and cyberbullying': A qualitative exploration of youth perspectives of online gaming culture. *International Review of Sociology, 32*(3), 426–442.

32 Nadim, M., & Fladmoe, A. (2021). Silencing women? Gender and online harassment. *Social Science Computer Review, 39*(2), 245–258.

33 Cote, A. C. (2020). Gaming sexism: Gender and identity in the era of casual video games. In *Gaming sexism*. New York University Press.

34 Ekiciler, A., Ahioğlu, İ., Yıldırım, N., Ajas, İ. İ., & Kaya, T. (2022). The bullying game: Sexism based toxic language analysis on online games chat logs by text mining. *Journal of International Women's Studies, 24*(3), 1–16.

35 Jagayat, A., & Choma, B. L. (2021). Cyber-aggression towards women: Measurement and psychological predictors in gaming communities. *Computers in Human Behavior, 120*, 106753.

36 Vergel, P., La parra-Casado, D., & Vives-Cases, C. (2024). Examining cybersexism in online gaming communities: A scoping review. *Trauma, Violence, & Abuse, 25*(2), 1201–1218.

37 Chen, Y., Lu, J., Wang, L., & Gao, X. (2023). Effective interventions for gaming disorder: A systematic review of randomized control trials. *Frontiers in Psychiatry, 14*, 1098922.

38 Xu, L. X., Wu, L. L., Geng, X. M., Wang, Z. L., Guo, X. Y., Song, K. R., . . . & Potenza, M. N. (2021). A review of psychological interventions for internet addiction. *Psychiatry Research, 302*, 114016.

39 Kumari, S., & Dhiksha, J. (2022). Effect of intervention for gaming addiction among adolescents: A systematic review. *International Journal of Health Sciences, 3*, 431219.

40 Radtke, T., Apel, T., Schenkel, K., Keller, J., & von Lindern, E. (2022). Digital detox: An effective solution in the smartphone era? A systematic literature review. *Mobile Media & Communication, 10*(2), 190–215.

41 Najmi, A. H., Alhalafawy, W. S., & Zaki, M. Z. T. (2023). Developing a sustainable environment based on augmented reality to educate adolescents about the dangers of electronic gaming addiction. *Sustainability, 15*(4), 3185.

42 Gorowska, M., Tokarska, K., Zhou, X., Gola, M. K., & Li, Y. (2022). Novel approaches for treating internet gaming disorder: A review of technology-based interventions. *Comprehensive Psychiatry, 115*, 152312.

43 Griffiths, M. D., & Pontes, H. M. (2020). The future of gaming disorder research and player protection: What role should the video gaming industry and researchers play? *International Journal of Mental Health and Addiction, 18*, 784–790.

44 Shi, J., Potenza, M. N., & Turner, N. E. (2020). Commentary on: "The future of gaming disorder research and player protection: What role should the video gaming industry and researchers play?" *International Journal of Mental Health and Addiction, 18*, 791–799.

Section 3

THE BODY AND SEXUAL BEHAVIOR

7

BODY IMAGE

7.1 INTRODUCTION

As discussed briefly in Chapter 5, body image issues among men and boys are a growing concern,[1] driven largely by societal pressures and media portrayals of masculinity. Traditionally, discussions around body image have predominantly focused on women, but it is becoming increasingly clear that men and boys are also significantly affected. These issues manifest as dissatisfaction with one's physical appearance, driven by a perceived gap between an individual's body and the societal ideals of male physique.

These societal ideals, heavily influenced by media portrayals, often emphasize a narrow range of body types, typically those that are muscular, lean, and tall. This portrayal is pervasive across various media platforms, including movies, television shows, advertisements, and increasingly on social media. The images of "ideal" male bodies are constantly displayed and glorified, creating unrealistic standards that many men and boys find difficult to achieve or maintain.

The impact of these societal pressures and media portrayals is profound. They contribute to a range of mental health issues, including low self-esteem, anxiety, and depression. Moreover, the pursuit of these unattainable body ideals can lead to unhealthy behaviors, such as disordered eating, overexercising, and misuse of substances like steroids.

DOI: 10.4324/9781032709369-10

In this chapter, we will explore the complexities of body image issues among men and boys, examining the influence of societal pressures and media, and the resulting mental and physical health impacts, and discussing strategies to promote healthier body image perceptions and tackle harmful media representations. Addressing these issues is not only crucial for the well-being of men and boys but is also a step toward challenging and changing the narrow definitions of masculinity that pervade our culture.

7.2   HISTORICAL CONTEXT OF MALE BODY IMAGE

Understanding the immediate historical context of male body image provides insight into how societal standards have evolved and the impact these changes have on contemporary issues. Let's just look at the last century alone:

Early 20th Century

Lean and Athletic: In the early 1900s, the ideal male body was characterized by a lean, athletic build, influenced by the physical culture movement which emphasized physical fitness and health.

Cultural Icons: Figures like Charles Atlas promoted the idea that strength and fitness were accessible to all men, regardless of their starting point.

Mid-20th Century

Muscular and Robust: The mid-20th century saw a shift toward a more muscular and robust ideal. This was influenced by the rise of bodybuilding culture and figures like Arnold Schwarzenegger.

Media Influence: Movies and magazines began to feature more muscular actors and models, reinforcing this ideal.

Late 20th Century to Early 21st Century

Diverse Representations: There has been a growing recognition of diverse body types, although the muscular and lean ideal remains prevalent. The late 20th and early 21st centuries also saw an increase in the portrayal of different racial and ethnic backgrounds in media.

Social Media and Technology: The rise of social media platforms has amplified the pressure to conform to these ideals, with influencers and celebrities showcasing their physiques to millions of followers.

We can already see significant change, but where do these changes come from? And what is the relationship between the media and society in creating or perpetuating these ideals?

7.3   SOCIETAL PRESSURES AND MEDIA INFLUENCE

In Chapter 5 we briefly explored just how society and the media play a pivotal role in shaping male body image ideals.[2,3,4] These influences often project an image of masculinity that is tied closely to physical strength, muscularity, and a lean physique. The perpetuation of these ideals across various media platforms creates a powerful societal narrative about what it means to be physically attractive or desirable as a man. The media therefore holds a complex relationship with society, as something that both represents norms as they evolve but also helps to shape these.

In advertising, the portrayal of men with idealized body types is rampant. These images are often used to sell everything from fitness equipment to fashion, implicitly suggesting that success and desirability are linked to achieving a certain physical appearance. This not only sets unrealistic standards but also subtly implies that one's worth is tied to their physicality.

Film and television further reinforce these ideals by frequently casting actors with "ideal" body types in leading roles, especially in roles that are meant to epitomize strength, heroism, or attractiveness. Rarely do mainstream films and TV shows celebrate diverse male body types, particularly in roles that are central or glamorous.

Social media amplifies these issues, given its pervasive nature and the personal interaction it facilitates. Platforms like Instagram and TikTok are flooded with images and videos of "perfect" male bodies, often accompanied by narratives of transformation and discipline.[5] The comparison trap that social media engenders can then lead to feelings of inadequacy and low self-esteem among its users.

The cumulative effect of these societal and media pressures is the creation of unrealistic and homogenous standards of male beauty, and the constant exposure to these ideals can lead to a distorted perception of one's own body, fostering dissatisfaction and negative self-image.

7.4   IMPACT ON MENTAL AND PHYSICAL HEALTH

The body image dissatisfaction that this process creates in men and boys can have profound psychological effects. When individuals perceive a significant gap between their actual body and the ideal body standard set by society and media, it can lead to persistent feelings of inadequacy, low self-esteem, and negative self-perception. This dissatisfaction often goes beyond mere concern with physical appearance, seeping into how individuals value themselves and their worth in society.

The relentless pursuit of an idealized physique can then result in a constant state of self-criticism and monitoring, which can severely impact self-esteem.[6] This negative self-image can pervade many aspects of life, influencing behavior, social interactions, and even decision-making processes.

There is also a clear connection between body image issues and the development of specific mental health disorders like depression and anxiety. Men and boys who are dissatisfied with their bodies are at a higher risk of experiencing symptoms of depression, such as feelings of hopelessness, loss of interest in activities, and persistent sadness.[7] Anxiety, too, can manifest in those who are overly preoccupied with their appearance, leading to social anxiety, excessive worrying about body image, and avoidance of situations where their bodies might be exposed or judged.

Body image issues can also be a contributing factor to the development of eating disorders, such as anorexia nervosa and bulimia, though these are often less recognized in men than in women.[8,9] Furthermore, body dysmorphic disorder (BDD) – a mental health condition where a person spends a lot of time worrying about flaws in their appearance – can be exacerbated by negative body image. BDD often leads to obsessive thoughts and behaviors, significantly impairing daily functioning, including obsession with building muscle.[10]

Body image dissatisfaction can also lead to engagement in risky behaviors.[11] This includes extreme dieting, use of unregulated supplements, and behaviors that border on obsessive, all aimed at achieving a certain body type. These behaviors can have long-term health consequences, including nutritional deficiencies, metabolic imbalances, and physical harm. Interestingly, there are some opposite effects found, with men reporting higher body image satisfaction engaging in risky behaviors, perhaps linked to increased confidence.[12]

The use of anabolic steroids is a particularly concerning behavior linked to body image issues.[13] Steroids are often used to accelerate muscle growth and improve physical appearance. However, their use can lead to severe side effects, including hormonal imbalances, liver damage, increased risk of heart disease, and behavioral changes, such as increased aggression. More on this in the next chapter.

Excessive exercising, while seemingly healthy, can also become problematic when it stems from body dissatisfaction. It can lead to overtraining syndrome, characterized by fatigue, decreased performance, persistent muscle soreness, and increased susceptibility to injuries.[14] This compulsive exercise behavior is often a neglected aspect of body image issues, yet it can have serious physical and mental health implications. Again, more on this in Chapter 8.

7.5 VULNERABLE GROUPS

There are several groups that may be particularly vulnerable to this process and their associated effects.

7.5.1 Adolescents

Adolescents are particularly susceptible to body image issues. This vulnerability is largely due to the physical, emotional, and social changes that occur during puberty, which can heighten self-consciousness about body image. The desire to fit in with peers, combined with exposure to idealized body images in media and online social media, can intensify concerns about physical appearance.[15,16] For adolescent boys, the pressure to quickly gain muscle and achieve an athletic physique can be overwhelming, leading to negative body image and unhealthy behaviors.

7.5.2   LGBTQ+ Individuals

LGBTQ+ individuals face unique challenges regarding body image.[17,18,19] Cultural and societal norms often impose rigid standards of beauty and masculinity, which can be especially difficult for those who may not conform to traditional gender expressions or roles. Within the LGBTQ+ community, there can be additional pressures to conform to certain body ideals, which vary across different groups within the community. For example, gay men often face intense pressure to attain a lean, muscular physique, which is frequently glorified in gay culture and media.[20] These pressures can lead to a higher prevalence of body dissatisfaction and related disorders in LGBTQ+ individuals compared to their heterosexual counterparts.[21,22,23]

7.5.3   Body Image and Gender Identity

Transgender and nonbinary individuals often grapple with body image issues related to gender dysphoria. The distress that arises from a discrepancy between their gender identity and physical appearance can be profound.[24,25] This group may engage in various behaviors to align their physical appearance with their gender identity, which can include dietary restrictions, excessive exercising, or unsupervised medical interventions.[26] These practices can pose significant health risks, especially when not medically supervised.

7.5.4   Additional Sociocultural Factors

Other sociocultural factors, such as race and ethnicity, can further influence body image perceptions among these vulnerable groups.[27,28] Stereotypes and cultural expectations can intersect with mainstream ideals of masculinity, complicating body image issues. For example, men and boys of color may experience a conflict between cultural body norms and those portrayed in Western media.

7.6   STRATEGIES FOR PROMOTING HEALTHIER BODY IMAGE

There are strategies for combatting these issues, but who they are delivered by and in what way are crucial for effectively engaging with men and boys.

7.6.1   Approaches for Individuals

Developing a positive body image is crucial for overall well-being. This can be achieved through various individual strategies:

1. *Cultivating self-awareness.* Individuals can start by recognizing and challenging their negative thoughts and beliefs about their bodies. Understanding the sources of these thoughts and how they are influenced by societal and media standards can help in reframing perceptions.

2. *Practicing self-compassion.* Learning to treat oneself with kindness and understanding, rather than judgment and criticism, can significantly improve body image. This includes accepting one's body as it is and recognizing that self-worth is not solely based on physical appearance.

3. *Mindfulness and body positivity.* Engaging in mindfulness practices can help individuals stay grounded in the present moment and cultivate a more positive relationship with their bodies. Embracing body positivity, which advocates for the acceptance of all body types, can also foster a healthier body image.

Underpinning all this is self-acceptance, a fundamental aspect of developing a positive body image. It involves embracing one's body with all its perceived imperfections and understanding that physical appearance does not define one's value or capabilities. Building self-acceptance can help mitigate the impact of negative societal and media portrayals of ideal bodies.

Building resilience is key to combating negative body image. This can include:

1. *Developing a support system.* Having a supportive network of friends and family who reinforce positive body image can provide a buffer against negative societal influences.

2. *Engaging in positive activities.* Participating in activities that focus on skills, hobbies, or talents rather than appearance can reinforce a sense of accomplishment and self-worth.

3. *Seeking professional help.* In cases where body image issues are significantly impacting mental health, seeking help from a mental health professional can be beneficial. Therapies like cognitive behavioral therapy (CBT) can be effective in addressing negative body image.

Websites: www.nationaleatingdisorders.org/body-image/, https://centerformsc.org/, https://thebodypositive.org/.

7.7 TACKLING MEDIA REPRESENTATIONS

As the origin of many of the issues, tackling unhealthy and unrealistic media representations is critical.

7.7.1 Challenging Media Portrayals of Masculinity

Tackling media representations of masculinity requires a multipronged approach. Media, being a powerful influencer, shapes societal perceptions of what is considered the ideal male body. Challenging these portrayals involves:

1. *Promoting media literacy.* Educating individuals, especially young men and boys, about how media content is produced and the motives behind it can help them critically analyze and question the realism of these portrayals.

2. *Supporting diverse media content.* Actively seeking out and supporting media that portrays a diverse range of male bodies and experiences can help shift industry standards. This includes supporting films, shows, and advertising campaigns that showcase a variety of male body types and reject traditional stereotypes.

Advocacy also plays a critical role in promoting diverse and realistic body types in media. This can be achieved through:

1. *Campaigns and movements.* Participating in or supporting campaigns that advocate for body positivity and diversity in media representation. These movements can influence media creators and advertisers to reconsider their portrayal of male bodies.

2. *Engaging with media creators and advertisers.* Directly engaging with those in the media and advertising industries through discussions, petitions, and collaborations can lead to a more conscious approach in their representation of men and boys.

3. *Role models and influencers.* Promoting and supporting public figures, models, and influencers who represent a broader range of body types and who speak out against unrealistic standards can also be effective in changing the narrative around the male body image.

7.7.2 The Role of Education and Community Support

Education plays an equally crucial role in addressing body image issues among men and boys. Integrating body image education into school curriculums can help young men and boys develop a healthier relationship with their bodies from an early age.[29] This education should focus on:

1. *Understanding body image.* Teaching about what body image is, how it is influenced by societal and media portrayals, and its impact on mental health.

2. *Promoting body positivity.* Encouraging acceptance of all body types and challenging the stereotypes associated with the "ideal" male physique.

3. *Media literacy.* Equipping students with the skills to critically analyze media representations of masculinity and understand the impact of these portrayals on body image.

In communities, workshops and seminars can be organized to educate parents, guardians, and community members about body image issues. These programs can provide tools and resources to support young men and boys struggling with these issues, and can involve:

1. *Peer support groups.* Facilitating peer-led support groups where individuals can share experiences and coping strategies in a safe and non-judgmental environment.

2. *Counseling services.* Providing access to counseling services where men and boys can seek professional help for body image issues.

3. *Mentorship programs.* Establishing mentorship programs where young men and boys can receive guidance and support from positive role models.

Encouraging open discussions about body image is also key to breaking the stigma and silence surrounding this issue. This involves:

1. *Creating safe spaces.* Developing forums, both in-person and online, where individuals can openly discuss body image concerns.

2. *Inclusive community events.* Organizing community events that promote body positivity and inclusivity, showcasing diverse body types and stories.

3. *Engaging men and boys in conversations.* Actively involving men and boys in conversations about body image to validate their experiences and encourage them to seek support.

Websites: www.learningforjustice.org/classroom-resources/lessons/i-see-you-you-see-me-body-image-and-social-justice, https://mhanational.org/blog/how-teach-your-child-body-positivity.

7.7.3   The Role of Sports and Fitness Industry

The sports and fitness industry also plays a significant role in shaping body image ideals. This industry often promotes a specific physical aesthetic, typically one that is muscular, lean, and fit. Through fitness programs, dietary supplements, and targeted advertising, there is a constant emphasis on achieving and maintaining these body standards, but these can be changed:

1. *Fitness Regimes and Body Standards:* Fitness programs can emphasize sustainable, long-term health goals, promoting diverse body types and individual progress. By showcasing a variety of fitness journeys, they can encourage realistic and personalized approaches to health and wellness, celebrating achievements that go beyond physical appearance.

2. *Dietary Supplements:* The marketing of dietary supplements can focus on promoting a balanced and holistic approach to health, highlighting the importance of proper nutrition, safe exercise practices, and the role of supplements as part of a well-rounded lifestyle. This approach can educate consumers on making informed choices that support overall well-being rather than just aesthetic goals.

3. *Advertising Practices:* Advertising in the fitness industry can celebrate a broader range of body types, fitness levels, and health goals. By showcasing diverse models and authentic stories, advertisers can contribute to a more inclusive and realistic portrayal of fitness and health, helping to empower individuals to embrace their unique fitness journeys.

7.7.4   The Impact of Celebrity Culture

Celebrity culture, including film stars, athletes, and social media influencers, significantly impacts body image standards. These public figures often become benchmarks for physical attractiveness and fitness, influencing fans' perceptions of their bodies. Therefore, understanding the influence of celebrity culture is crucial in addressing body image issues. It involves recognizing the curated nature of these images and the reality behind celebrity lifestyles, by looking at the following:

1. *Role of social media influencers.* With the rise of social media, influencers who regularly post about their bodies, workouts, and diets can have

a profound impact on body image, particularly among younger audiences. This can be used for good, with influencers posting less restrictive and unrealistic content.

2. *Celebrity endorsements.* Celebrities endorsing fitness products or cosmetic procedures can reinforce certain body ideals, sometimes leading to unrealistic expectations among their followers. If influencers are careful about who and/or what they endorse, this could have a big impact.

7.7.5   Technological Tools for Positive Body Image

Technology offers tools that can promote a positive body image and mental health. Apps that focus on mindfulness, self-compassion, and body positivity can provide daily affirmations, meditation techniques, and educational content to combat negative body image. Online platforms and forums can offer community support and a space for sharing experiences and coping strategies.

1. *Mental health apps.* Apps designed to improve mental health can offer resources and exercises to help individuals develop a healthier relationship with their bodies.

2. *Body positivity platforms.* Platforms dedicated to body positivity often feature a range of body types and stories, challenging mainstream media's narrow beauty standards.

These technological tools can be a part of a broader strategy to promote positive body image. By providing accessible resources and supportive communities, technology can play a constructive role in helping individuals navigate body image issues.

7.8   CONCLUSION

The issue of body image among men and boys is a significant concern that extends beyond mere physical appearance, deeply impacting mental health, self-esteem, and overall well-being. As we have explored in this chapter, societal pressures and media portrayals contribute to unrealistic and often unattainable standards of male beauty, leading to a wide range of negative effects. These include mental health disorders like depression and anxiety, unhealthy behaviors, and physical health risks. The vulnerability of certain groups, such as adolescents and LGBTQ+ individuals, underscores the urgent need for targeted interventions and support.

Addressing body image issues requires a concerted effort at both societal and individual levels. Societally, there needs to be a shift in how masculinity and male bodies are portrayed in media and popular culture.

This involves advocating for diverse and realistic representations, promoting media literacy, and challenging existing stereotypes that narrow the perception of male beauty. Schools and communities also play a vital role in educating and supporting young men and boys, and mental health professionals and health-care providers need to be cognizant of the unique challenges related to male body image and offer appropriate support and interventions.

At an individual level, empowering men and boys to develop a healthy relationship with their bodies is crucial. This can be achieved through education, fostering self-acceptance, resilience-building, and creating supportive environments where open discussions about body image are encouraged.

NOTES

1 Grogan, S. (2021). *Body image: Understanding body dissatisfaction in men, women and children*. Routledge.
2 Agliata, D., & Tantleff-Dunn, S. (2004). The impact of media exposure on males' body image. *Journal of Social and Clinical Psychology, 23*(1), 7–22.
3 Barlett, C. P., Vowels, C. L., & Saucier, D. A. (2008). Meta-analyses of the effects of media images on men's body-image concerns. *Journal of Social and Clinical Psychology, 27*(3), 279–310.
4 Huang, Q., Peng, W., & Ahn, S. (2021). When media become the mirror: A meta-analysis on media and body image. *Media Psychology, 24*(4), 437–489.
5 Tiggemann, M., & Anderberg, I. (2020). Muscles and bare chests on Instagram: The effect of Influencers' fashion and fitspiration images on men's body image. *Body Image, 35*, 237–244.
6 Mellor, D., Fuller-Tyszkiewicz, M., McCabe, M. P., & Ricciardelli, L. A. (2010). Body image and self-esteem across age and gender: A short-term longitudinal study. *Sex Roles, 63*, 672–681.
7 Barnes, M., Abhyankar, P., Dimova, E., & Best, C. (2020). Associations between body dissatisfaction and self-reported anxiety and depression in otherwise healthy men: A systematic review and meta-analysis. *PLoS One, 15*(2), e0229268.
8 Nagata, J. M., Ganson, K. T., & Murray, S. B. (2020). Eating disorders in adolescent boys and young men: An update. *Current Opinion in Pediatrics, 32*(4), 476–481.
9 Griffiths, S., Murray, S. B., & Castle, D. (2021). Body image disorders in men. *Comprehensive Men's Mental Health, 86*.
10 Rica, R., & Sepúlveda, A. R. (2024). Going deeper into eating and body image pathology in males: Prevalence of muscle dysmorphia and eating disorders in a university representative sample. *European Eating Disorders Review, 32*(2), 363–377.
11 Bornioli, A., Lewis-Smith, H., Smith, A., Slater, A., & Bray, I. (2019). Adolescent body dissatisfaction and disordered eating: Predictors of later risky health behaviours. *Social Science & Medicine, 238*, 112458.
12 Gillen, M. M., Lefkowitz, E. S., & Shearer, C. L. (2006). Does body image play a role in risky sexual behavior and attitudes? *Journal of Youth and Adolescence, 35*, 230–242.

13 Kanayama, G., Hudson, J. I., & Pope Jr, H. G. (2020). Anabolic-androgenic steroid use and body image in men: A growing concern for clinicians. *Psychotherapy and Psychosomatics, 89*(2), 65–73.

14 Carrard, J., Rigort, A. C., Appenzeller-Herzog, C., Colledge, F., Königstein, K., Hinrichs, T., & Schmidt-Trucksäss, A. (2022). Diagnosing overtraining syndrome: A scoping review. *Sports Health, 14*(5), 665–673.

15 Verrastro, V., Liga, F., Cuzzocrea, F., & Gugliandolo, M. C. (2020). Fear the Instagram: Beauty stereotypes, body image and Instagram use in a sample of male and female adolescents. *QWERTY-Interdisciplinary Journal of Technology, Culture and Education, 15*(1), 31–49.

16 Chatzopoulou, E., Filieri, R., & Dogruyol, S. A. (2020). Instagram and body image: Motivation to conform to the "Instabod" and consequences on young male wellbeing. *Journal of Consumer Affairs, 54*(4), 1270–1297.

17 Dahlenburg, S. C., Gleaves, D. H., Hutchinson, A. D., & Coro, D. G. (2020). Body image disturbance and sexual orientation: An updated systematic review and meta-analysis. *Body Image, 35*, 126–141.

18 Filice, E., Raffoul, A., Meyer, S. B., & Neiterman, E. (2020). The impact of social media on body image perceptions and bodily practices among gay, bisexual, and other men who have sex with men: A critical review of the literature and extension of theory. *Sex Roles, 82*, 387–410.

19 Nowicki, G. P., Marchwinski, B. R., O'Flynn, J. L., Griffths, S., & Rodgers, R. F. (2022). Body image and associated factors among sexual minority men: A systematic review. *Body Image, 43*, 154–169.

20 Tran, A., Kaplan, J. A., Austin, S. B., Davison, K., Lopez, G., & Agénor, M. (2020). "It's all outward appearance-based attractions": A qualitative study of body image among a sample of young gay and bisexual men. *Journal of Gay & Lesbian Mental Health, 24*(3), 281–307.

21 Schmidt, M., Taube, C. O., Heinrich, T., Vocks, S., & Hartmann, A. S. (2022). Body image disturbance and associated eating disorder and body dysmorphic disorder pathology in gay and heterosexual men: A systematic analyses of cognitive, affective, behavioral und perceptual aspects. *PLoS One, 17*(12), e0278558.

22 Oshana, A., Klimek, P., & Blashill, A. J. (2020). Minority stress and body dysmorphic disorder symptoms among sexual minority adolescents and adult men. *Body Image, 34*, 167–174.

23 Fabris, M. A., Longobardi, C., Badenes-Ribera, L., & Settanni, M. (2022). Prevalence and co-occurrence of different types of body dysmorphic disorder among men having sex with men. *Journal of Homosexuality, 69*(1), 132–144.

24 Grannis, C., Leibowitz, S. F., Gahn, S., Nahata, L., Morningstar, M., Mattson, W. I., . . . & Nelson, E. E. (2021). Testosterone treatment, internalizing symptoms, and body image dissatisfaction in transgender boys. *Psychoneuroendocrinology, 132*, 105358.

25 Romito, M., Salk, R. H., Roberts, S. R., Thoma, B. C., Levine, M. D., & Choukas-Bradley, S. (2021). Exploring transgender adolescents' body image concerns and disordered eating: Semi-structured interviews with nine gender minority youth. *Body Image, 37*, 50–62.

26 Brewer, G., Hanson, L., & Caswell, N. (2022). Body image and eating behavior in transgender men and women: The importance of stage of gender affirmation. *Bulletin of Applied Transgender Studies, 1*(1–2), 71–95.

27 Gonzales IV, M., & Blashill, A. J. (2021). Ethnic/racial and gender differences in body image disorders among a diverse sample of sexual minority US adults. *Body Image, 36*, 64–73.

28 Thornborrow, T., Onwuegbusi, T., Mohamed, S., Boothroyd, L. G., & Tovée, M. J. (2020). Muscles and the media: A natural experiment across cultures in men's body image. *Frontiers in Psychology, 11*, 501704.

29 Zuair, A. A., & Sopory, P. (2022). Effects of media health literacy school-based interventions on adolescents' body image concerns, eating concerns, and thin-internalization attitudes: A systematic review and meta-analysis. *Health Communication, 37*(1), 20–28.

8

GYM AND STEROID ADDICTION

8.1 INTRODUCTION

Similarly to gaming addiction explored in Chapter 6, in recent years, the prevalence of gym and steroid addiction among men and boys has emerged as a significant concern. This growing trend is largely fueled by societal pressures and the pervasive media portrayals of masculinity that glorify muscular and lean physiques as ideals of male attractiveness and success (as discussed in the previous chapter). The drive to attain these often-unrealistic body standards has led many to frequent gyms obsessively and, in some cases, turn to the use of anabolic steroids.[1]

The allure of rapid physical transformation and the desire to conform to societal standards of masculinity can be powerful motivators. Gyms, as centers of physical improvement, have become focal points for those striving to achieve these ideals. However, for some, what starts as a healthy pursuit of fitness can escalate into an obsession, characterized by excessive and compulsive exercise routines. This gym addiction is often intertwined with steroid use, as men seek faster and more pronounced muscle development than what can be achieved through exercise alone.

The use of steroids, while offering the allure of quick muscle gains, comes with significant risks. These include not only physical health dangers but also psychological impacts, such as dependency and altered mental states. The linkage between societal pressures, media portrayals of masculinity, and

DOI: 10.4324/9781032709369-11

the development of gym and steroid addiction is a complex one. It raises critical questions about the messages we send to men and boys about their bodies and the societal definition of *masculinity*.

In this chapter, we will delve deeper into the phenomenon of gym and steroid addiction, exploring its causes, the risks involved, and how deeply ingrained perceptions of masculinity contribute to this issue. Understanding the roots and ramifications of this problem is crucial in addressing it effectively and promoting healthier, more realistic approaches to body image and physical fitness.

8.2 THE LURE OF THE GYM CULTURE

Gym culture has become increasingly influential in shaping the fitness and body image goals of men and boys. The appeal lies in more than just the pursuit of physical fitness; it encompasses a sense of community, a perception of control over one's body, and the pursuit of an idealized image of masculinity.[2] Gyms are often seen as temples of transformation, where one can sculpt their body to match the ideals promoted by society and media. For many, the gym becomes a space of empowerment and self-improvement, but also of community and fraternity.[3]

There are several aspects that drive this appeal, including:

1. *Community and belonging.* Gyms often provide a sense of community, offering a space where individuals with similar goals can connect and motivate each other.

2. *Perceived control.* Achieving physical goals at the gym can give a sense of control and accomplishment, contributing to self-esteem and body satisfaction.[4]

3. *Media influence.* The influence of media in glorifying muscular physiques fuels the desire to attain similar results, making gyms the go-to place for achieving these goals.

However, while gym culture has many positive aspects, it can sometimes contribute to unhealthy behaviors, including:[5]

1. *Obsession with physical perfection.* Constant exposure to idealized body types can lead to an unhealthy obsession with physical perfection. This may result in overtraining and an excessive focus on appearance over health.

2. *Comparative and competitive nature.* Gyms can foster a competitive environment where individuals compare their progress with others', leading to feelings of inadequacy and low self-esteem.

3.   *Pressure to use enhancements.* The desire to keep up with perceived standards or achieve rapid results can pressure some into using performance-enhancing substances like steroids.[6]

4.   *Pursuit of societal ideals.* The pressure to conform to these media-driven body ideals can drive individuals toward gyms and, in some cases, steroid use as a means to achieve and maintain these standards quickly.

5.   *Unrealistic expectations.* Continuous exposure to idealized body images creates unrealistic expectations, making it difficult for men and boys to feel satisfied with their natural body shape and size, thus fueling the desire to exercise.

The darker side of gym culture includes the risk of developing body dysmorphic disorders, where individuals have a distorted perception of their body, and the normalization of steroid use. The fixation on achieving a muscular and lean physique can thus overshadow the importance of holistic health, including mental well-being.

8.3   UNDERSTANDING STEROID USE

The use of anabolic steroids among men and boys is often rooted in a desire to achieve rapid muscle growth and an enhanced physique, which are seen as markers of masculinity and attractiveness.[7] The motivations for turning to steroids can be complex and multifaceted, including:

1.   *Achieving quick results.* In a society that prizes immediate gratification, steroids offer a quick solution to achieving the muscular build that might take months or years to accomplish through traditional exercise routines.

2.   *Peer pressure and social influence.* Peer influence, especially in environments like gyms, where steroid use might be more common, can play a significant role. Seeing others achieve rapid results can create pressure to use steroids to keep up.

3.   *Competitive edge in sports.* For some athletes, the lure of steroids is in their potential to enhance performance, providing an edge in competitive sports.

The psychology behind steroid use is closely linked to body image and self-perception:

1.   *Body dysmorphia and insecurity.* Many steroid users suffer from body dysmorphic disorders, where despite having muscular physiques, they perceive themselves as smaller or weaker. This distorted self-image drives the continued use of steroids.[8]

2. *Self-esteem and identity.* Steroids are sometimes used as a means to boost self-esteem and self-worth. Achieving the "ideal" body is equated with success, popularity, and masculinity.

3. *Coping mechanism.* For some, steroid use is a way to cope with deeper psychological issues, like depression or anxiety. The temporary boost in confidence and physical appearance can be a way to mask underlying problems.

Indeed, the connection between steroid use and body image issues is undeniable. The societal portrayal of the muscular male body as the pinnacle of masculinity heavily influences this connection, with men and boys who internalize these ideals potentially viewing steroids as a necessary means to achieve these standards, and often overlooking the health risks involved.

8.4   THE DANGERS OF STEROID USE

There are significant risks associated with steroid use, explored here.

8.4.1   Medical Risks of Steroid Use

The use of anabolic steroids, while providing short-term gains in muscle mass and athletic performance, comes with a host of medical risks.[9] These include:

1. *Hormonal imbalances.* Steroids can disrupt the natural balance of hormones in the body, leading to conditions such as gynecomastia (development of breast tissue in men) and testicular atrophy.

2. *Liver damage.* Oral anabolic steroids can have a toxic effect on the liver, potentially leading to liver disease and liver cancer.

3. *Cardiovascular issues.* Steroid use is associated with increased risk of heart disease, including hypertension, increased LDL (bad cholesterol), and decreased HDL (good cholesterol), all of which are risk factors for heart attack and stroke.

4. *Skin problems.* Users may experience acne, oily skin, and other skin conditions due to the hormonal effects of steroids.

8.4.2   Psychological Risks

Psychological effects of steroid use can be equally damaging, including:

1. *Aggression and mood swings.* Commonly referred to as "roid rage,"[10] users may experience significant mood swings and increased aggression.[11,12]

2. *Dependence and withdrawal.* Long-term steroid use can lead to psychological dependence, and withdrawal can result in depression, fatigue, and irritability.

3. *Altered mental health.* There are links between steroid use and mental health disorders like depression and anxiety, particularly upon withdrawal.

8.4.3 Long-Term Health Consequences

The long-term health consequences of steroid use can also be severe and sometimes irreversible, including:[13]

1. *Musculoskeletal damage.* In adolescents, steroid use can cause premature bone aging and stunted growth.

2. *Reproductive system effects.* Long-term use can lead to infertility and reduced sexual function.

3. *Increased risk of infection.* Using nonsterile injection techniques can increase the risk of infections such as HIV/AIDS and hepatitis.

4. *Psychological dependency.* The reliance on steroids for self-esteem and body image can lead to long-term psychological issues, impacting quality of life.

8.5 VULNERABLE POPULATIONS

Certain groups are more susceptible to gym and steroid addiction, often due to specific social and psychological factors.

8.5.1 Adolescents and Young Adults

This group is particularly vulnerable due to the pressures of physical appearance during the formative years.[14] The desire to fit in or stand out among peers can drive them toward gym culture and, in some cases, steroid use.[15] The extra challenges this group may face are:

- *Peer influence.* Strong desire to conform to peer standards of attractiveness and fitness.
- *Media impact.* Heightened susceptibility to media portrayals of ideal bodies.
- *Lack of awareness.* Limited understanding of the long-term consequences of steroid use.

8.5.2   Athletes and Bodybuilders

Competitive environments in sports and bodybuilding can create immense pressure to perform and look a certain way, making steroids an appealing option.[16] Such athletes may be influenced by:

- *Performance pressure.* Intense pressure to enhance performance and physical appearance.
- *Cultural acceptance.* In some athletic cultures, there is an unspoken acceptance or even encouragement of steroid use.

8.5.3   Individuals With Pre-Existing Body Image Issues

Those already struggling with body dissatisfaction or body dysmorphic disorder are at higher risk, as they may view the gym and steroids as solutions to their perceived body flaws.[17] These issues can be particularly acute due to:

- *Distorted self-perception.* Challenges in seeing their bodies realistically, leading to excessive gym attendance and steroid use.
- *Vulnerability to quick fixes.* A tendency to gravitate toward quick solutions like steroids to achieve their ideal body image.

8.5.4   GBT+ Individuals

Members of the gay, bisexual, transgender, and wider queer community may face unique pressures related to body image, exacerbated by cultural and social dynamics within some GBT+ subcultures. These pressures can make gym and steroid use particularly appealing as a means to achieve societal ideals of attractiveness and masculinity, often highlighted within certain segments of the community.[18,19,20] Vulnerabilities in the GBT+ population include:

- *Social and cultural expectations.* Strong cultural emphasis on physical aesthetics within certain GBT+ circles can escalate pressure to attain an idealized body type.
- *Minority stress.* Experiences of discrimination, stigma, and exclusion can contribute to negative self-image and mental health issues, making physical appearance a focal point for personal validation.
- *Internalized homophobia.* Among some GBT+ individuals, internal conflicts about their sexual or gender identity may lead to a greater focus on physical fitness as a means to conform to traditional gender roles or to mitigate perceived deficiencies in other areas of life.
- *Further risks.* There is a potential relationship between steroid use and risky sexual behavior in this population.[21]

8.6   STRATEGIES FOR INTERVENTION AND PREVENTION

Preventing gym and steroid addiction involves early intervention and education, focusing on promoting healthy habits and realistic body expectations,[22] specifically:

1.   *Awareness programs.* Implementing educational programs in schools, gyms, and community centers that inform about the risks associated with steroid use and the importance of balanced fitness routines.

2.   *Promoting healthy body image.* Encouraging a culture that values diverse body types and physical health over appearance. This includes challenging unrealistic media portrayals of masculinity and body standards.

3.   *Support for mental health.* Recognizing and addressing underlying mental health issues like body dysmorphia and low self-esteem that may lead to gym and steroid addiction.

Intervening in cases of gym and steroid addiction requires a multidisciplinary approach, including:

1.   *Medical intervention.* Health-care providers can play a key role in identifying signs of steroid abuse and providing appropriate medical intervention, including referral to specialists.

2.   *Counseling and therapy.* Psychological counseling can help individuals understand the root causes of their addiction and develop healthier coping mechanisms.

3.   *Support groups.* Facilitating or referring to support groups can provide peer support and help individuals understand they are not alone in their struggles.

8.6.1   Role of Health-Care Providers

Health-care providers are critical in both prevention and intervention, as they will be involved in:

1.   *Screening and early detection.* Regular screening for signs of steroid use, especially in high-risk groups.

2.   *Educating patients.* Providing patients with information on the dangers of steroid use and healthier alternatives to achieve fitness goals.

3. *Referral to specialists.* Referring patients to nutritionists, mental health professionals, or addiction specialists when necessary.

8.6.2   Role of Educators and Community Leaders

Educators and community leaders can foster a supportive environment through:

1. *Creating inclusive environments.* Promoting an inclusive culture in schools and communities that values all body types and encourages healthy lifestyle choices.

2. *Educational initiatives.* Implementing educational initiatives that focus on body positivity, the dangers of steroids, and the benefits of healthy exercise and nutrition.

3. *Community engagement.* Organizing community events and workshops that address body image, gym culture, and steroid use, providing platforms for discussion and support.

8.6.3   Preventive Measures in Gyms

Implementing preventive measures in gym settings is also crucial to create an environment that discourages unhealthy practices by providing:

1. *Educational posters and materials.* Displaying posters and materials that educate gym-goers about the risks of steroid use and the importance of balanced fitness practices. This could include information on the signs of addiction and where to seek help.

2. *Workshops and seminars.* Organizing regular workshops or seminars on topics like healthy body image, the dangers of steroid use, and safe training techniques. These could be led by health professionals, experienced trainers, or even former addicts who can share their experiences.

3. *Training for gym staff.* Ensuring that gym staff, including personal trainers and coaches, are trained to recognize signs of gym and steroid addiction. They should be equipped to provide initial guidance and refer individuals to professional help if necessary.

Fostering a gym culture that values health and well-being over appearance is key. Encouraging gym-goers to focus on personal fitness goals rather than compare themselves to others can create a more supportive and less-competitive environment.[23]

8.6.4   Role of Health and Fitness Professionals

Health and fitness professionals are often on the front lines and can play a key role in identifying and addressing gym and steroid addiction by:

1.   *Getting training on recognition.*[24] Educating trainers and coaches on how to recognize the signs of steroid use and addiction.

2.   *Creating open dialogues.* Fostering an environment where athletes feel comfortable discussing body image concerns and pressures.

Health and fitness professionals can also advocate for and model healthy practices, including:

1.   *Promoting balanced training.* Encouraging balanced and sustainable training routines that focus on overall health rather than just appearance or performance.

2.   *Nutritional guidance.* Providing or referring athletes to proper nutritional advice that supports their training without resorting to harmful substances.

8.6.5   Technological Interventions

In the digital age, technology can also play a significant role in both preventing and treating gym and steroid addiction, for example:

1.   *Fitness apps for balanced workouts.* There are numerous fitness apps that focus on promoting balanced and healthy workout routines. These apps can help users track their progress, set realistic goals, and provide guidance on safe exercise practices, reducing the reliance on extreme measures for fitness gains.

2.   *Online support groups and forums.* Digital platforms offer a space for individuals struggling with gym and steroid addiction to find community and support. These forums can provide a sense of solidarity, share success stories, and offer advice on overcoming addiction.

3.   *Virtual counseling services.* Telehealth services can offer counseling and psychological support to those dealing with addiction, making it easier for individuals to seek help, especially if they are hesitant to do so in person.

Wearable devices that monitor physical activity and health metrics can also be useful. They provide real-time feedback on one's physical state, helping to prevent overtraining and promote overall well-being.

8.6.6   Legal and Regulatory Aspects

Understanding the legal framework surrounding anabolic steroids is also crucial, including:

1.   *Controlled substance status.* Explaining how steroids are classified as controlled substances in many jurisdictions, making their unregulated use and distribution illegal.

2.   *Regulatory bodies in sports.* Discussing the role of sports regulatory bodies in monitoring and testing athletes for steroid use.

Outlining the legal consequences of illicit steroid use can also act as a deterrent, including:

1.   *Criminal charges.* Detailing potential criminal charges for possession or distribution of steroids without prescription.

2.   *Bans and suspensions in sports.* Explaining the consequences in the sporting world, including bans and suspensions.

8.7   CONCLUSION

Gym and steroid addictions represent significant concerns in our society, with far-reaching implications for mental and physical health. Driven by unrealistic societal and media portrayals of masculinity, these addictions not only harm individual health but also perpetuate harmful stereotypes about male bodies. Addressing these issues is not just about individual behavior change; it involves challenging and reshaping deep-seated societal norms.

This chapter serves as a call to action for everyone – media professionals, health-care providers, educators, policymakers, and individuals to:

1.   *For media and advertisers.* Reassess and modify the portrayal of male bodies, moving toward more inclusive and realistic representations.

2.   *For health-care providers and educators.* Recognize the signs of gym and steroid addiction and provide appropriate support and interventions.

3.   *For policymakers.* Develop and enforce policies that regulate the portrayal of bodies in media and advertising, and to fund initiatives that promote healthy body image.

4.   *For individuals.* Critically evaluate the media they consume, to advocate for positive change, and to support those struggling with body image issues.

NOTES

1 Mullen, C., Whalley, B. J., Schifano, F., & Baker, J. S. (2020). Anabolic androgenic steroid abuse in the United Kingdom: An update. *British Journal of Pharmacology*, *177*(10), 2180–2198.

2 Andreasson, J., & Henning, A. (2022). "Falling down the Rabbit Fuck Hole": Spectacular masculinities, hypersexuality, and the real in an online doping community. *Journal of Bodies, Sexualities, and Masculinities*, *3*(2), 76–97.

3 Gibbs, N., Salinas, M., & Turnock, L. (2022). Post-industrial masculinities and gym culture: Graft, craft, and fraternity. *The British Journal of Sociology*, *73*(1), 220–236.

4 Lamarche, L., Gammage, K. L., & Ozimok, B. (2018). The gym as a culture of body achievement: Exploring negative and positive body image experiences in men attending university. *SAGE Open*, *8*(2), 2158244018778103.

5 Turnock, L. A. (2021). Rural gym spaces and masculine physical cultures in an 'age of change': Rurality, masculinity, inequalities and harm in 'the gym'. *Journal of Rural Studies*, *86*, 106–116.

6 Christiansen, A. V. (2020). *Gym culture, identity and performance-enhancing drugs: Tracing a typology of steroid use*. Routledge.

7 Kanayama, G., Hudson, J. I., & Pope Jr, H. G. (2020). Anabolic-androgenic steroid use and body image in men: A growing concern for clinicians. *Psychotherapy and Psychosomatics*, *89*(2), 65–73.

8 Bonnecaze, A. K., O'Connor, T., & Aloi, J. A. (2020). Characteristics and attitudes of men using anabolic androgenic steroids (AAS): A survey of 2385 men. *American Journal of Men's Health*, *14*(6), 1557988320966536.

9 de Ronde, W., & Smit, D. L. (2020). Anabolic androgenic steroid abuse in young males. *Endocrine Connections*, *9*(4), R102–R111.

10 Pope Jr, H. G., Kanayama, G., Hudson, J. I., & Kaufman, M. J. (2021). Anabolic-androgenic steroids, violence, and crime: Two cases and literature review. *The American Journal on Addictions*, *30*(5), 423–432.

11 Chegeni, R., Pallesen, S., McVeigh, J., & Sagoe, D. (2021). Anabolic-androgenic steroid administration increases self-reported aggression in healthy males: A systematic review and meta-analysis of experimental studies. *Psychopharmacology*, *238*, 1911–1922.

12 Nelson, B. S., Hildebrandt, T., & Wallisch, P. (2022). Anabolic – androgenic steroid use is associated with psychopathy, risk-taking, anger, and physical problems. *Scientific Reports*, *12*(1), 9133.

13 de Ronde & Smit, Anabolic androgenic steroid abuse in young males, R102–R111.

14 Bonnecaze et al., Characteristics and attitudes of men using anabolic androgenic steroids (AAS), 1557988320966536.

15 Yager, Z., & McLean, S. (2020). Muscle building supplement use in Australian adolescent boys: Relationships with body image, weight lifting, and sports engagement. *BMC Pediatrics*, *20*, 1–9.

16 Karagun, B., & Altug, S. (2024). Anabolic-androgenic steroids are linked to depression and anxiety in male bodybuilders: The hidden psychogenic side of anabolic androgenic steroids. *Annals of Medicine, 56*(1), 2337717.

17 Gawash, A., Zia, H., & Lo, D. F. (2023). Body dysmorphic-induced Androgenic Anabolic Steroids usage and its association with mental health outcomes. *medRxiv*, 2023–01.

18 Star, J. (2021). *Power, discourse, and subjectivity: Contextualizing steroid use among two-spirit gay, bi and queer men in Manitoba* (Master's thesis).

19 Bolding, G., Sherr, L., & Elford, J. (2002). Use of anabolic steroids and associated health risks among gay men attending London gyms. *Addiction, 97*(2), 195–203.

20 Halkitis, P. N., Moeller, R. W., & DeRaleau, L. B. (2008). Steroid use in gay, bisexual, and nonidentified men-who-have-sex-with-men: Relations to masculinity, physical, and mental health. *Psychology of Men & Masculinity, 9*(2), 106.

21 Ip, E. J., Doroudgar, S., Shah-Manek, B., Barnett, M. J., Tenerowicz, M. J., Ortanez, M., & Pope Jr, H. G. (2019). The CASTRO study: Unsafe sexual behaviors and illicit drug use among gay and bisexual men who use anabolic steroids. *The American Journal on Addictions, 28*(2), 101–110.

22 Vinther, A. S. (2023). "The challenge is that steroids are so effective": A qualitative study of experts' views on strategies to prevent men's use of anabolic steroids. *Contemporary Drug Problems, 50*(1), 85–104.

23 Rothmann, J. (2022). Homosociality, homohysteria and the gym. In *Macho men in South African gyms: The idealization of spornosexuality* (pp. 117–153). Springer International Publishing.

24 Izzat, N., Abu-Farha, R., Al-Mestarihi, E., & Alzoubi, K. H. (2023). The awareness and experience of healthcare providers with the use of anabolic androgenic steroids by gym users. *International Journal of Legal Medicine, 137*(6), 1705–1711.

9

CIRCUMCISION

9.1 INTRODUCTION

Circumcision, the surgical removal of the foreskin of the penis, is a practice that dates back thousands of years. Historically, it has been performed for a variety of reasons, including religious rites, cultural traditions, and perceived health benefits. In some cultures, circumcision is viewed as a rite of passage into manhood, while in others, it is more commonly associated with hygienic or preventive health-care practices.

In contemporary society, circumcision remains a widely practiced procedure, with around 37–39% of men circumcised,[1] but it has become a subject of intense debate and scrutiny. The practice intersects various complex issues, including individual rights, religious freedom, cultural tradition, medical ethics, and gender politics.

For many, circumcision continues to hold significant religious and cultural importance, being a key ritual in religions such as Judaism and Islam and practiced in various ethnic and cultural groups around the world. The medical community presents divergent views on circumcision. Some advocate for its health benefits, including reduced risks of certain infections, while others question its necessity and point to the risks and ethical considerations of performing a surgical procedure on nonconsenting infants. The procedure has raised ethical concerns, especially regarding the rights of children to bodily autonomy and the ability to make informed decisions about their bodies.

DOI: 10.4324/9781032709369-12

Given its multifaceted nature, circumcision in contemporary society demands a balanced and informed discourse. It raises fundamental questions about bodily integrity, consent, and the role of tradition in modern medical practice. This chapter seeks to explore these various aspects, offering an in-depth look at why circumcision is conceptualized and practiced in the way it is today, and how it differs significantly in societal and cultural perception from female genital mutilation (FGM).

9.2 HISTORICAL AND CULTURAL BACKGROUND

Let us first progress through a brief background on the historical and cultural significance of the practice.

9.2.1 The Origins of Circumcision

Circumcision is one of the oldest known surgical practices, with its origins steeped in antiquity.[2] Historical evidence suggests that circumcision was practiced in ancient civilizations, including Egyptian, Semitic, and tribal African cultures. Its beginnings are often associated with religious rites, cultural traditions, or symbolic gestures of purity and belonging.

In ancient Egypt, circumcision was a rite of passage for young men, signifying their transition to adulthood. Similarly, in various African cultures, it has long been a crucial part of initiation ceremonies. In Judaism, circumcision, known as *brit milah*, is a covenantal ritual performed on 8-day-old male infants, as commanded in the Torah. In Islam, while not explicitly mentioned in the Quran, it is widely practiced as a Sunnah, influenced by the teachings of the Prophet Muhammad.

9.2.3 Cultural Significance Across Societies

Circumcision holds varying degrees of cultural significance in different societies. Among some tribal and ethnic groups, circumcision continues to be a central cultural practice, signifying bravery, purity, or social status. In modern times, particularly in Western societies, circumcision is often performed for reasons not tied to any religious or cultural traditions but seen as a normative health practice. Over time, the practice of circumcision has evolved, influenced by changes in societal norms, medical practices, and ethical considerations. This evolution reflects a broader dialogue about the role of tradition, health, and individual rights in modern society.

9.3 MEDICAL PERSPECTIVES ON CIRCUMCISION

As noted in the introduction, the medical community is divided on circumcision, as shown in the two sections here.

9.3.1   Medical Benefits of Circumcision

The medical community has identified several potential benefits associated with circumcision,[3] particularly in terms of hygiene and disease prevention, including:

1. *Reduced risk of urinary tract infections (UTIs).* Studies have shown that circumcision can reduce the risk of UTIs in infancy and early childhood.

2. *Prevention of sexually transmitted infections (STIs).* Circumcision has been linked to a lower risk of certain STIs, including HIV. The removal of the foreskin is thought to reduce the likelihood of infections taking hold.

3. *Prevention of penile problems.* Conditions like phimosis and paraphimosis, where the foreskin cannot be retracted or returned to its original position, can be prevented through circumcision.

4. *Reduced risk of penile cancer.* Although rare, circumcision may reduce the risk of penile cancer by preventing the buildup of smegma, which can harbor bacteria and lead to infections.

9.3.2   Medical Risks and Concerns

However, circumcision is not without its risks and complications,[4,5,6] which can include:

1. *Surgical risks.* As with any surgical procedure, there are risks of complications, such as bleeding, infection, and adverse reactions to anesthesia.[7]

2. *Pain and recovery.* The procedure can be painful, and the recovery period may involve discomfort and the risk of irritation or infection.

3. *Long-term sensitivity issues.* There are concerns that circumcision may affect sexual pleasure or sensitivity, although studies on this matter have been inconclusive.[8,9]

9.3.3   The Medical Community's Stance

The stance of the medical community on circumcision varies globally. In some regions, particularly in parts of Africa, medical authorities endorse circumcision for its potential to reduce the spread of HIV. Many medical organizations in other parts of the world, including the American Academy of Pediatrics and the Royal Australasian College of Physicians, adopt a more neutral stance. They recognize the potential benefits but also acknowledge the risks and ethical considerations, advocating for parental choice. It is not surprising, then, that the ethics of performing circumcision on nonconsenting infants for nonmedical reasons is a subject of ongoing debate. Questions routinely arise about bodily autonomy and the right to an intact body.

9.4   PSYCHOLOGICAL IMPACTS

Beyond medical issues, the psychological impact of circumcision on men and boys is a subject of significant importance and complexity.[10,11,12] Unlike physical effects, psychological impacts can be more subtle and vary widely among individuals. Key areas of focus include:

1. *Early childhood experiences.* For infant circumcision, questions arise about the long-term psychological effects of undergoing a surgical procedure at a very young age. Some studies suggest potential links to increased pain sensitivity or anxiety, though findings are not conclusive.

2. *Body image and self-perception.* Men who were circumcised as infants or children may experience mixed feelings about their body image and genital integrity as they grow older, particularly if they feel that the decision was made without their consent.

3. *Cultural and social identity.* In societies where circumcision is the norm, uncircumcised men might feel out of place, and vice versa. This can affect social interactions and feelings of belonging.

9.4.1   Issues of Consent and Bodily Autonomy

The question of consent is central to both the medical and psychological debate on circumcision, and centers around the following:

1. *Infant circumcision.* Performing circumcision on infants raises ethical questions about consent and the right to bodily autonomy. Infants are unable to consent to the procedure, leading to debates about whether parental choice should override the child's right to an intact body.

2. *Informed decision-making.* For older children and adults, the emphasis is on informed consent. This involves understanding the risks, benefits, and implications of the procedure before making a decision.

3. *Cultural and familial pressure.* In many cases, the decision to circumcise is heavily influenced by cultural, religious, or familial expectations, which can complicate the issue of voluntary consent.

9.5 DEBATES DIFFER BY AGE: CHILDHOOD VS. ADULT CIRCUMCISION

Debates also differ by age. Circumcision, when performed in childhood, particularly in infancy, often sparks intense debates centered on consent and the long-term psychological and physical implications. Infants, unable to provide informed consent, are at the heart of ethical controversies, where parental rights, cultural norms, and the child's autonomy clash. Critics argue that circumcising nonconsenting infants could lead to potential psychological distress and a sense of violation of bodily autonomy as they mature. The practice, thus, raises profound ethical questions about consent and the extent to which cultural and religious practices should influence medical decisions made on behalf of a child.

On the other hand, adult circumcision typically involves individuals who can give informed consent, understanding both the risks and benefits associated with the procedure.[13] This capacity for informed decision-making shifts the ethical landscape significantly. Adults opting for circumcision might do so for various reasons, including personal or partner health considerations, cultural identity, or even cosmetic preferences. Here, the debates are less about consent and more about the medical necessity, potential health benefits, and personal autonomy in making health-related decisions.

The differing nature of the debates by age underscores the complex interplay between medical ethics, cultural values, and individual rights. Childhood circumcision remains contentious due to the irreversible nature of the procedure performed on someone who cannot voice their choice. In contrast, adult circumcision, backed by personal consent, often escapes such profound ethical scrutiny despite similar risks and benefits.

9.6 ETHICAL AND LEGAL CONSIDERATIONS

Focusing then on infant circumcision, the practice thus raises several ethical questions, particularly concerning consent and bodily autonomy. The primary ethical concern revolves around performing a permanent surgical procedure on nonconsenting infants. Critics argue that circumcision without immediate medical necessity infringes upon a child's right to bodily integrity and self-determination. On the other hand, proponents often cite cultural and religious rights, arguing that banning circumcision infringes on these freedoms. For many, it is a deeply ingrained ritual with significant spiritual and cultural meaning. The ethical debate often focuses on finding a balance between respecting cultural and religious practices and protecting individual rights, particularly of children.

9.6.1 Legal Status of Circumcision

So, how is ethics translated in law in this case? The legal status of circumcision varies significantly around the world. In many countries, circumcision is legal but subject to regulations, particularly regarding who can perform the procedure and under what conditions. These regulations aim to ensure safety and reduce the risk of complications. Conversely, in some parts of the world, there have been movements to restrict or ban nonmedical circumcision. These are often based on concerns about child welfare, consent, and the necessity of the procedure. The development of legal policies around circumcision often requires sensitivity to cultural and religious practices, leading to diverse legal approaches in different countries, and clear difficulties in balancing ethical considerations in legislation.

9.6.2   The Role of International Law

International law, particularly in the context of children's rights and human rights, plays a crucial role in shaping the legal discourse around circumcision. International conventions, such as the UN Convention on the Rights of the Child, emphasize the right of children to bodily integrity, which is central to the circumcision debate. From a human rights perspective, the practice is often evaluated in terms of its impact on physical and psychological well-being.

9.7   SOCIETAL PRESSURES AND MASCULINITY

And, as is becoming increasingly familiar in this book, there are other influences at play in this debate – specifically the influence of societal perceptions and norms.

9.7.1   The Influence of Societal Pressures on Perceptions of Circumcision

Societal pressures and prevailing cultural norms play a significant role in shaping perceptions of circumcision and its association with masculinity. In many societies, circumcision is viewed as a normative, even necessary, practice for males. It is often linked to societal expectations of what constitutes "normal" or "acceptable" male bodies. In certain cultures, circumcision is seen as a rite of passage into manhood, imbuing it with deep symbolic significance. The procedure is often celebrated as a transition to a new, more mature phase of life.

9.7.2   Media Portrayals of Masculinity

As discussed in previous chapters, media representations contribute to shaping societal perceptions of male identity, which can extend to attitudes toward circumcision.[14] The media often presents idealized images of male bodies, subtly influencing public perceptions of what is considered "normal" or desirable. This includes pornography, which features a high proportion of circumcised actors. The narratives around masculinity in media can also sometimes reinforce the notion that certain physical attributes or procedures, including circumcision, are integral to being a "real man."

9.7.3   The Role of Circumcision in Male Identity Construction

Circumcision can thus play a complex role in the construction of male identity. For some, being circumcised is an integral part of their physical identity, often linked to feelings of belonging to a particular cultural or religious group. However, the decision, or the lack thereof, in the case of infant circumcision, can also have long-lasting psychological impacts on one's sense of autonomy and self-image. In societies where circumcision is the norm, being uncircumcised can lead to feelings of exclusion or difference, impacting social interactions and personal relationships.

9.8   CIRCUMCISION VS. FEMALE GENITAL MUTILATION (FGM)

Circumcision and female genital mutilation (FGM) are both forms of genital alteration, yet they are perceived and treated very differently across societies and cultures.[15] This disparity in perception is often rooted in deep-seated cultural, religious, and historical contexts, compared here:

1. *Circumcision.* Often viewed as a traditional, religious, or even medically beneficial practice, male circumcision is widely accepted in many societies. In some cultures, it is celebrated as a rite of passage or seen as a normative health procedure.

2. *FGM.* Conversely, FGM is internationally condemned as a violation of human rights. It is seen as a practice that undermines the health, rights, and overall well-being of women and girls. Unlike circumcision, FGM has no known health benefits and is known to cause severe physical and psychological harm.

9.8.1   Conceptual Differences in Practices

The fundamental conceptualization of these practices also differs significantly:

1. *Cultural and religious justifications.* Circumcision is often justified through cultural and religious traditions, whereas FGM is typically viewed as a practice that subjugates and controls female sexuality, with no basis in most religious doctrines.

2. *Perceived medical benefits.* Circumcision is sometimes advocated for potential medical benefits, while FGM is not associated with any health advantages and is, in fact, known to be harmful.

3.   *Degree of physical alteration.* The extent of physical alteration and its impact on bodily functions differ between circumcision and FGM, with FGM generally involving more severe alteration and greater risk of long-term health complications.

9.8.2   Understanding the Disparity

The reasons behind the different societal and cultural conceptualizations of these practices are complex and include an appreciation of:

1.   *Gender norms and inequalities.* The contrasting perceptions are often reflective of broader gender norms and inequalities. Male circumcision is sometimes seen as empowering or protective, while FGM is linked to control and subjugation.

2.   *Historical context.* The historical context and evolution of these practices contribute to their current perception. Circumcision has a long history in many cultures as a celebrated tradition, whereas FGM is often seen as a relic of patriarchal control.

3.   *International human rights discourse.* FGM has been a focus of international human rights activism, highlighting its detrimental impact on women's health and rights, which has influenced global perceptions and policies.

9.9   ADVOCACY AND MOVEMENTS

There are several advocacy groups and movements that support the practice of circumcision, often citing cultural, religious, or health-related reasons:

1.   *Religious and cultural advocacy.* Groups within religious communities such as Judaism and Islam actively advocate for circumcision as an essential part of religious practice and cultural identity. Websites: www.circumcision.org/.

2.   *Health advocacy.* Some health advocacy groups support circumcision for its potential medical benefits, including decreased risks of certain infections and diseases. Websites: www.circumcisionaustralia.org/, www.aap.org/.

3.   *Public health campaigns.* In regions with high rates of HIV, public health campaigns may promote circumcision as a preventive measure, backed

by research suggesting its efficacy in reducing transmission rates. Websites: www.who.int/, www.cdc.gov/hiv/risk/male-circumcision. html, www.malecircumcision.org/.

9.9.1 Movements Opposing Circumcision

Conversely, there are movements and organizations strongly opposed to circumcision, advocating for bodily autonomy and informed consent:

1.   *Anticircumcision or intactivist groups.* These groups argue against non-consensual infant circumcision, emphasizing the right to bodily integrity and autonomy. They often advocate for the procedure to be delayed until the individual can make an informed decision. Websites: www. gaamerica.org/, https://intactamerica.org/.

2.   *Human rights organizations.* Some human rights organizations view nonconsensual circumcision as a violation of children's rights, campaigning for its restriction or outright ban. Websites: www.hrw.org/, www.amnesty.org/.

3.   *Medical ethics advocates.* Within the medical community, there are voices that challenge the ethical implications of performing elective surgical procedures on nonconsenting minors. Website: www.doctor-sopposingcircumcision.org/.

9.9.2 Impact on Public Opinion and Policy

The advocacy efforts from both sides have a significant impact on public opinion and policy:

1.   *Shaping public opinion.* Media campaigns, public demonstrations, and educational efforts by advocacy groups play a crucial role in shaping public perceptions and discourse around circumcision.

2.   *Influencing policy.* These movements can influence health policies and legal frameworks. For instance, some countries have seen debates in legislative bodies about the legality and ethics of infant circumcision, leading to policy changes or proposals for new legislation.

3.   *Global perspective.* The issue of circumcision and its advocacy is not limited to any single country or culture, making it a global conversation with varying impacts and policy responses, depending on regional cultural, religious, and legal contexts.

9.10   CONCLUSION

Circumcision is a practice enshrouded in a tapestry of complexity, influenced by a confluence of cultural, religious, medical, ethical, and psychological factors. It stands at a crossroads of tradition and modernity, individual rights and collective beliefs, health benefits and potential risks. The historical roots of circumcision are deep and varied, reflecting its significance across different societies and epochs. Medically, while there are noted benefits, the risks and ethical considerations of performing the procedure, especially on nonconsenting infants, present a contentious debate.

Looking to the future, the discussion on circumcision is likely to continue evolving. Medical advancements, shifting cultural norms, and growing emphasis on individual rights and informed consent are all factors that will shape how this practice is viewed and performed. The balance between respecting cultural and religious practices while safeguarding individual rights, especially of children, will remain a pivotal area of discussion.

The way forward necessitates informed and empathetic discussions on the subject. It involves:

1. *Respectful dialogue.* Engaging in conversations that respect diverse viewpoints and cultural sensitivities, while also considering the rights and well-being of individuals.

2. *Informed decision-making.* Ensuring that decisions about circumcision are made based on accurate information, considering both potential benefits and risks.

3. *Policy and legal considerations.* Crafting policies and laws that reflect ethical considerations, medical perspectives, and cultural practices, aiming to protect the welfare of minors while respecting cultural traditions.

4. *Continued research and education.* Encouraging ongoing research into the medical, psychological, and social aspects of circumcision and disseminating this knowledge to the public, health-care professionals, and policymakers.

NOTES

1 Morris, B. J., Wamai, R. G., Henebeng, E. B., Tobian, A. A., Klausner, J. D., Banerjee, J., & Hankins, C. A. (2016). Estimation of country-specific and global prevalence of male circumcision. *Population Health Metrics, 14*, 1–13.
2 Osserman, J. (2021). *Circumcision on the couch: The cultural, psychological, and gendered dimensions of the world's oldest surgery*. Bloomsbury Publishing USA.

3 Morris, B. J., & Krieger, J. N. (2020). Non-therapeutic male circumcision. *Paediatrics and Child Health, 30*(3), 102–107.

4 Deacon, M., & Muir, G. (2023). What is the medical evidence on non-therapeutic child circumcision? *International Journal of Impotence Research, 35*(3), 256–263.

5 Iacob, S. I., Feinn, R. S., & Sardi, L. (2022). Systematic review of complications arising from male circumcision. *BJUI Compass, 3*(2), 99–123.

6 Shabanzadeh, D. M., Clausen, S., Maigaard, K., & Fode, M. (2021). Male circumcision complications – a systematic review, meta-analysis and meta-regression. *Urology, 152*, 25–34.

7 Shabanzadeh et al., Male circumcision complications – a systematic review, meta-analysis and meta-regression, 25–34.

8 Morris, B. J., & Krieger, J. N. (2020). The contrasting evidence concerning the effect of male circumcision on sexual function, sensation, and pleasure: A systematic review. *Sexual Medicine, 8*(4), 577–598.

9 Bañuelos Marco, B., & García Heil, J. L. (2021). Circumcision in childhood and male sexual function: A blessing or a curse? *International Journal of Impotence Research, 33*(2), 139–148.

10 Tye, M. C., & Sardi, L. M. (2023). Psychological, psychosocial, and psychosexual aspects of penile circumcision. *International Journal of Impotence Research, 35*(3), 242–248.

11 Aydoğdu, B., Azizoğlu, M., & Okur, M. H. (2022). Social and psychological effects of circumcision: A narrative review. *Journal of Applied Nursing and Health, 4*(2), 264–271.

12 Morris, B. J., Moreton, S., Bailis, S. A., Cox, G., & Krieger, J. N. (2022). Critical evaluation of contrasting evidence on whether male circumcision has adverse psychological effects: A systematic review. *Journal of Evidence-Based Medicine, 15*(2), 123–135.

13 Aydogmus, Y., Semiz, M., Er, O., Bas, O., Atay, I., & Kilinc, M. F. (2016). Psychological and sexual effects of circumcision in adult males. *Canadian Urological Association Journal, 10*(5–6), E156.

14 Darby, R. (2005). *A surgical temptation: The demonization of the foreskin and the rise of circumcision in Britain*. University of Chicago Press.

15 Abbott, A. (2020). An analysis of female vs. male circumcision. *Kwantlen Psychology Student Journal*, 8–8.

10

SEXUAL BEHAVIOR AND CONSENT

10.1 INTRODUCTION

Understanding sexual behavior and the concept of consent is crucial, not only for the well-being and safety of individuals, but also for the health of our communities. The ability to understand and respect consent is fundamental to developing healthy sexual relationships and ensuring personal and mutual respect. However, sadly for men and boys, navigating the complexities of sexual behavior and consent is often influenced by a myriad of factors – societal expectations, cultural norms, and media portrayals, to name a few.

Societal attitudes toward masculinity play a particularly significant role in shaping male sexual behavior. Often, there is a cultural narrative that promotes certain stereotypes about male sexuality, such as the emphasis on sexual conquest and aggression. These stereotypes can distort young men's understanding of healthy relationships and consensual sexual encounters. Indeed, stereotypical notions about masculinity can pressure men and boys to conform to certain behaviors, often at the expense of emotional depth and understanding of consent.

On top of this, cultural misconceptions about male sexuality – such as the belief that men are always ready and willing for sex – further complicate the understanding of consent, making it challenging for men and boys to

DOI: 10.4324/9781032709369-13

navigate sexual encounters responsibly. And the media often portrays sexual relationships in a way that glamorizes dominance and aggression, potentially skewing perceptions of what constitutes healthy sexual interactions and the importance of mutual consent.

In this chapter (and later in Chapter 19), we take a deeper exploration into how societal attitudes, cultural norms, and media impact men's and boys' understanding of sexual behavior and consent. The subsequent sections will delve into these aspects, highlighting the need for education and dialogue to promote healthier attitudes and behaviors. This is not just a personal or individual challenge but a societal one, requiring collective effort and change.

10.2   SOCIETAL ATTITUDES TOWARD MALE SEXUALITY

Societal perceptions have a profound impact on shaping male sexual behavior. These perceptions are often ingrained from a young age and reinforced through various social and cultural channels. These include:

1.   *Dominant masculinity norms.* Societal attitudes frequently equate masculinity with sexual prowess and assertiveness.[1] This can pressure men and boys to adopt aggressive and dominant behaviors in sexual contexts, often valuing conquest and performance over emotional connection and mutual satisfaction.

2.   *Expectations of male libido.* There is a widespread belief that men should always desire sex and be ready for it. This expectation can create immense pressure, leading to anxiety and unhealthy sexual behaviors when men feel they do not meet these perceived standards.[2]

3.   *Linking masculinity to sexual conquest.* Often, cultural narratives link masculinity to the ability to attract and engage in sexual activity with multiple partners.[3] This can create unrealistic expectations and pressure to prove one's masculinity through sexual conquests.

4.   *Stigmatization of male vulnerability.* Cultural norms frequently stigmatize male vulnerability, including in sexual contexts. Admitting to insecurities, lack of experience, or even disinterest in sex can be seen as unmasculine.

5.   *The male gender role.* Men and boys often feel pressured to conform to traditional masculine roles, which can include being sexually dominant and experienced. This pressure can deter them from expressing doubts, fears, or a lack of desire. Traditional gender roles also often discourage emotional openness in men, impacting their ability to form emotionally connected and consensual sexual relationships.

Stereotypes about male sexuality contribute significantly to the development of male sexual identity, including:

- *Hypersexualization.* The stereotype of men as inherently hypersexual can lead to a distorted view of what constitutes normal sexual desire and behavior.[4]
- *Inflexibility.* Traditional gender roles often leave little room for men to express vulnerability or uncertainty in sexual situations, potentially leading to a disregard for the concept of consent.

10.2.1   Cultural Influences

Cultural variations also play a significant role in shaping norms and perceptions around male sexuality and sexual behavior. Globally, different societies interpret the concept of masculinity and male sexuality in diverse ways, which can influence male behavior significantly. For example, in many Western cultures, there is a significant emphasis on masculinity being linked with sexual conquest and readiness. Conversely, in some Eastern societies, the expression of male sexuality may be more subdued due to cultural and religious norms emphasizing modesty and restraint.

The influence of these cultural norms on sexual behavior is profound. In societies where masculinity is closely tied to sexual performance and conquest, men may experience pressure to adhere to these expectations, which can lead to unhealthy sexual practices and a misunderstanding of consent. In contrast, in cultures where sexual restraint is valued, men might face different kinds of pressures, such as the stigma associated with expressing sexual desire openly, which can also complicate the understanding and practice of healthy sexual behaviors and consent.

Furthermore, the stigmatization of male vulnerability and the inability to express doubts or disinterest in sex without fear of being perceived as less masculine are common in many cultures. This cultural script contributes to a lack of open communication about sexual preferences and boundaries, which is essential for consensual and healthy sexual relationships.

10.3   MEDIA INFLUENCE ON SEXUAL BEHAVIOR

The media, with its wide-reaching influence, plays a significant role in shaping male perceptions of sexuality and consent. From movies and television shows to advertisements and social media, the portrayal of male sexuality is often narrow and stereotyped. Some notable trends are:

1. *Glamorization of male sexual conquest.* Media often glamorizes and normalizes the notion of male sexual conquest. This portrayal can lead men and boys to believe that aggressive pursuit and dominance are desirable and expected behaviors in sexual encounters.

2.   *Lack of consent representation.* The media frequently fails to depict clear, affirmative consent in sexual scenarios, creating misconceptions about what constitutes consensual sexual interactions.

3.   *Unrealistic sexual standards.* Media portrayals often set unrealistic standards for male sexual performance and physical appearance, or the frequency of sexual practices, contributing to insecurities and distorted expectations about sexual relationships.[5]

The cultural emphasis on male sexual dominance can thus lead to the development of unhealthy attitudes toward sex and relationships, including a disregard for the importance of consent and mutual respect. Moreover, the pressure to conform to these cultural norms can create significant stress and anxiety, potentially leading to issues such as sexual performance anxiety or unhealthy coping mechanisms.

10.4   SELF-IMAGE AND SEXUAL BEHAVIOR

The way men and boys perceive themselves – their self-image – also has a profound impact on their sexual behavior and attitudes. Self-image encompasses not only physical appearance but also self-esteem and the perception of one's own masculinity. There are several specific relationships:

1.   *Body image and sexual confidence.* A positive or negative body image can significantly affect sexual confidence.[6] Men who are dissatisfied with their bodies may feel self-conscious in intimate situations, potentially impacting their sexual performance and desire.

2.   *Self-esteem and sexual relationships.* High or low self-esteem influences how men engage in sexual relationships. Men with low self-esteem might struggle with vulnerability in relationships or feel pressured to behave in certain ways to compensate for perceived shortcomings.

3.   *Masculinity and sexual expectations.* Societal expectations of masculinity can dictate how men perceive their roles in sexual situations. Pressure to conform to traditional masculine norms can lead to aggression or dominance, impacting consent and mutual respect in sexual encounters.

10.5   CONSENT

A crucial part of sexual understanding is consent. Consent is a fundamental concept in sexual relationships, yet it is often misunderstood by those involved and within society.[7,8] At its core, consent is the explicit permission for something to happen or agreement to do something. In sexual contexts, it means all parties involved agree to participate willingly and without coercion, and is guided by three core principles:

1. *Clear and affirmative.* Consent must be clear, affirmative, and ongoing. It is not merely the absence of a "no" but the presence of a voluntary and enthusiastic "yes."

2. *Informed and conscious.* Consent requires that all parties have full knowledge and understanding of what they are consenting to. It cannot be given if someone is incapacitated, under the influence of drugs or alcohol, or under pressure.

3. *Reversible.* Consent is dynamic and reversible. Anyone has the right to change their mind at any point during a sexual encounter.

10.5.1 Challenges in Understanding and Practicing Consent

Despite its importance, many men and boys face challenges in understanding and practicing consent due to various factors:[9,10]

1. *Societal misconceptions.* Prevailing misconceptions about male sexuality – such as the belief that men always want sex – can lead to confusion about the necessity and nature of consent.

2. *Lack of education.* There is often a lack of comprehensive sexual education that emphasizes the importance of consent, leaving many men and boys ill-prepared to navigate consensual sexual encounters.

3. *Cultural and media influences.* Cultural norms and media portrayals that glorify aggression and dominance in male sexuality can obscure the understanding of respectful and consensual relationships.

4. *Peer pressure.* Especially among younger males, peer pressure and expectations can influence attitudes toward consent, often valuing sexual conquest over mutual respect and understanding.

5. *Other attitudes.* Other negative attitudes about sexual behavior, for example, those relating to an acceptance of sexual violence, can also influence perceptions of consent and its necessity.[11]

10.6 HEALTHY SEXUAL RELATIONSHIPS

So, where do we need to get to? Healthy sexual relationships are based on mutual respect, trust, and consent. These relationships are characterized by several key attributes:

1. *Mutual consent.* All parties freely and enthusiastically agree to engage in sexual activities without coercion or pressure.

2. *Open communication.* Partners communicate openly about their desires, boundaries, and any concerns, fostering a safe and understanding environment.

3. *Respect for boundaries.* Each person's boundaries are respected. Consent is ongoing and can be revoked at any time, and this decision is always respected.

4. *Emotional connection.* A healthy sexual relationship often involves an emotional connection, where partners feel valued, cared for, and connected beyond just physical interaction.

5. *Safety and responsibility.* Partners take steps to ensure physical safety, including using protection to prevent STIs and unwanted pregnancies and ensuring that both are physically and mentally comfortable with the activities.

10.6.1   Characteristics of Unhealthy Sexual Relationships

Conversely, unhealthy sexual relationships can be identified by a lack of consent, communication, and respect. They may include:

1. *Coercion or pressure.* One partner feels pressured or forced into sexual activities.

2. *Lack of communication.* There is little to no open discussion about preferences, consent, or boundaries.

3. *Disregard for safety.* Neglecting physical safety, such as not using protection or ignoring one's own or the partner's discomfort.

4. *Emotional neglect or abuse.* The relationship may be marked by emotional neglect, manipulation, or abuse.

10.7   PROMOTING HEALTHIER ATTITUDES AND BEHAVIOURS

Promoting healthy sexual relationships involves several strategies:

1. *Comprehensive sex education.* Education that goes beyond the biological aspects and covers consent, communication, and respectful relationships is crucial.[12]

2. *Role modeling and media representation.* Positive role models and media representations that showcase respectful, consensual relationships can influence societal attitudes.

3. *Open conversations.* Encouraging open discussions about sex, consent, and relationships in various settings, including homes, schools, and communities, can break down taboos and foster understanding.[13]

4. *Support services.* Providing access to support services for advice, counseling, and education about healthy relationships is important, especially for young people navigating their sexual identities.

5. *Empowering individuals.* Empowering both men and women to understand and assert their rights in a relationship, particularly regarding consent and respect.

Confronting body image issues is also crucial for fostering healthy sexual behaviors, with the following identified as key strategies:

1. *Promoting body positivity.* Encouraging body positivity among men and boys, emphasizing that physical attractiveness and worth are not solely based on societal standards, can improve self-image and sexual confidence.

2. *Challenging stereotypes.* Challenging stereotypes around male bodies and sexual prowess can help alleviate the pressure men feel to conform to unrealistic standards.

Building self-esteem is also key to healthy sexual behavior, with the following as absolutely necessities:

1. *Building self-acceptance and awareness.* Fostering self-acceptance and awareness about one's strengths and values can build self-esteem, leading to healthier sexual relationships.

2. *Promoting education and counseling.* Providing education and counseling about body image, self-esteem, and sexuality can help men and boys develop a more positive self-view and healthier sexual behaviors.

Finally, addressing the pressure related to sexual performance is essential, including:

1. *Promoting open communication.* Encouraging open communication about sexual health, performance anxieties, and realistic expectations can alleviate pressure and improve sexual relationships.

2. *Providing professional support.* Professional support, such as therapy or sexual health counseling, can help men dealing with performance anxiety and other related issues.

10.7.1   Strategies for Educating Men and Boys

The key to fostering healthy sexual behavior and understanding consent lies in comprehensive and inclusive education. This education should focus not just on the physical aspects of sex but on emotional intelligence, respect, and communication as well. Such programs should include:

- *Inclusive sex education.* Schools should offer comprehensive sex education that goes beyond the basics of reproduction and contraception to include topics like consent, respectful communication, emotional aspects of sexual relationships, and the debunking of harmful stereotypes.
- *Role models and mentorship.* Positive role models, whether they are family members, teachers, or community leaders, can provide guidance and exemplify respectful attitudes and behaviors. Mentorship programs can help young men navigate their sexual development healthily and responsibly.
- *Workshops and seminars.* Organizing workshops and seminars focused on topics like consent, healthy relationships, and communication skills can provide practical advice and foster understanding.

10.7.2   The Role of Schools

Schools play a crucial role in the early education of men and boys about sexual behavior and consent, and should look closely at:

- *Curriculum development.* Developing a curriculum that includes comprehensive sexual education, focusing on consent and healthy relationships.[14]
- *Creating safe spaces for discussion.* Schools should provide safe spaces where students can discuss these topics openly and without judgment, facilitating healthy dialogues.

10.7.3   The Role of Families

Families also have a significant role in shaping attitudes and behaviors, and should promote the following at home:

- *Open family dialogues.* Encouraging open and honest discussions about sex, relationships, and consent in the family setting can lay a strong foundation for healthy attitudes.[15]

- *Parental guidance and support.* Parents and caregivers can provide guidance and support, helping young men navigate their feelings, relationships, and questions about sexuality.

10.7.4   The Role of Communities

Communities can reinforce these teachings and provide additional support by providing:

- *Community-based programs.* Implementing community-based education and support programs can reach a wider audience and address the diverse needs of young men and boys.
- *Public awareness campaigns.* Campaigns aimed at raising awareness about healthy sexual behaviors and consent can help shift public perception and foster a community ethos of respect and responsibility.

10.7.5   The Role of Technology and Social Media

In an era where technology and social media are integral to daily life, their impact on shaping sexual attitudes and behaviors, particularly among men and boys, is profound and multifaceted, and could influence:

- *Access to information.* Technology has increased access to sexual health information, but not all of it is reliable or accurate. Young men and boys often turn to online sources for information about sex, which can lead to misconceptions if these sources are not credible.
- *Social media and sexual norms.* Social media platforms can perpetuate unrealistic standards of sexual attractiveness and behaviors. The portrayal of relationships and sexual encounters on these platforms often lacks the complexity and nuances of real-life interactions.

Moreover, online communities can both positively and negatively influence sexual attitudes, for example:

Supportive communities. There are online spaces that offer support and education about healthy relationships and sexuality. These communities can be crucial for young men and boys who lack other sources of reliable information.

Toxic communities. Conversely, some online communities may promote harmful attitudes toward sex, reinforcing aggressive or nonconsensual behaviors, and perpetuating myths about male sexuality.

The NO MORE initiative is a great example of an organization dedicated to ending domestic violence and sexual assault by increasing awareness, inspiring action, and fueling cultural change. They provide resources on understanding and practicing consent and support campaigns and initiatives to educate the public on these issues. Website: https://nomore.org/.

10.8   FUTURE DIRECTIONS AND CHALLENGES

Improving understanding and practices around sexual behavior and consent thus involves navigating a series of evolving challenges:

1. *Cultural and social evolution.* As societal norms and cultural perceptions continue to evolve, staying abreast of these changes and reflecting them in educational and policy frameworks are vital.

2. *Technological influence.* The growing influence of technology, particularly social media and online platforms, in shaping attitudes toward sexuality presents both opportunities and challenges in promoting healthy behaviors and consent.

3. *Global diversity.* Recognizing and accommodating the diversity of cultural, religious, and social perspectives on sexuality and consent remain a complex challenge, requiring sensitive and inclusive approaches.

Ongoing research is essential to inform effective strategies and policies, including:

1. *Understanding behavioral trends.* Research into current trends and behaviors in sexual activity and attitudes among different demographics can provide insights for targeted education and intervention.

2. *Evaluating educational programs.* Continued evaluation of sex education programs is necessary to understand their effectiveness and to adapt them to changing societal needs.

3. *Studying the impact of media.* Researching the impact of media and technology on sexual behavior and consent can guide interventions in these areas.

Policy changes are also crucial in institutionalizing healthy attitudes and practices, including:

1. *Comprehensive sex education policies.* Advocating for policies that mandate comprehensive and inclusive sex education in schools is critical.

2. *Legal frameworks around consent.* Strengthening legal frameworks to better define and enforce laws around sexual consent and behavior.

3. *Support for victims and survivors.* Enhancing policies to provide better support and resources for victims and survivors of sexual misconduct.

Put simply, a collective societal effort is key to driving change, where all stakeholders must work together to promote:

1. *Community engagement.* Engaging communities in dialogue and education about healthy sexual behavior and consent.

2. *Media responsibility.* Encouraging media outlets and content creators to portray sexual relationships responsibly and respectfully.

3. *Positive masculinities.* Encouraging a broader, more inclusive understanding of masculinity that embraces respect, empathy, and equality in sexual relationships.

10.9 CONCLUSION

The exploration of sexual behavior and consent among men and boys is more than just an academic exercise; it is a crucial step toward building a society grounded in respect, empathy, and mutual understanding. This chapter has underscored the profound impact of societal attitudes, cultural norms, and media portrayals on shaping perceptions and practices around sexuality and consent.

And it is clear that sexual behavior and understandings of consent are deeply intertwined with broader issues of gender roles, power dynamics, and personal identity. But by addressing these issues, we open pathways to healthier, more respectful relationships and a safer society for all.

Education and open dialogue are paramount in effecting this change. Comprehensive and inclusive sexual education in schools, discussions within families, and broader community dialogues can dismantle harmful stereotypes and foster a deeper understanding of consent and respectful sexual behavior. This chapter thus serves as a call to action for all members of society:

1. *For educators and policymakers.* To implement and support comprehensive sexual education that goes beyond the biological aspects and encompasses consent, respect, and healthy relationships.

2. *For parents and guardians.* To engage in open, honest, and age-appropriate discussions with their children about these topics.

3. *For media and content creators.* To responsibly represent sexual relationships, challenging harmful stereotypes and promoting narratives of consent and respect.

4.   *For individuals.* To reflect on their own attitudes and behaviors, to seek education and understanding, and to be active participants in fostering a culture of respect and consent.

In conclusion, addressing sexual behavior and consent among men and boys is an imperative step toward fostering a society where healthy relationships are the norm and consent is understood and respected by all. Through education, dialogue, and societal effort, we can empower individuals to engage in relationships marked by respect, empathy, and mutual understanding. The path forward requires the commitment of each individual to contribute to this vital change.

NOTES

1 Bareket, O., & Shnabel, N. (2020). Domination and objectification: Men's motivation for dominance over women affects their tendency to sexually objectify women. *Psychology of Women Quarterly, 44*(1), 28–49.

2 Nimbi, F. M., Tripodi, F., Rossi, R., Navarro-Cremades, F., & Simonelli, C. (2020). Male sexual desire: An overview of biological, psychological, sexual, relational, and cultural factors influencing desire. *Sexual Medicine Reviews, 8*(1), 59–91.

3 Prohaska, A., & Gailey, J. A. (2010). Achieving masculinity through sexual predation: The case of hogging. *Journal of Gender Studies, 19*(1), 13–25.

4 Andreasson, J., & Henning, A. (2022). "Falling down the Rabbit Fuck Hole": Spectacular masculinities, hypersexuality, and the real in an online doping community. *Journal of Bodies, Sexualities, and Masculinities, 3*(2), 76–97.

5 Ward, L. M., Epstein, M., Caruthers, A., & Merriwether, A. (2011). Men's media use, sexual cognitions, and sexual risk behavior: Testing a mediational model. *Developmental Psychology, 47*(2), 592.

6 Daniel, S., & Bridges, S. K. (2013). The relationships among body image, masculinity, and sexual satisfaction in men. *Psychology of Men & Masculinity, 14*(4), 345.

7 Javidi, H., Maheux, A. J., Widman, L., Kamke, K., Choukas-Bradley, S., & Peterson, Z. D. (2020). Understanding adolescents' attitudes toward affirmative consent. *The Journal of Sex Research, 57*(9), 1100–1107.

8 Muehlenhard, C. L., Humphreys, T. P., Jozkowski, K. N., & Peterson, Z. D. (2016). The complexities of sexual consent among college students: A conceptual and empirical review. *The Journal of Sex Research, 53*(4–5), 457–487.

9 Orenstein, P. (2020). *Boys & sex: Young men on hook-ups, love, porn, consent and navigating the new masculinity.* Souvenir Press.

10 Ólafsdottir, K., & Kjaran, J. I. (2019). "Boys in power": Consent and gendered power dynamics in sex. *Boyhood Studies, 12*(1), 38–56.

11 Moyano, N., Sánchez-Fuentes, M. D. M., Parra, S. M., Gómez-Berrocal, C., Quílez-Robres, A., & Granados, R. (2023). Shall we establish sexual consent or would you feel weird? Sexual objectification and rape-supportive attitudes as predictors of how sex is negotiated in men and women. *Sexuality & Culture, 27*(5), 1679–1696.

12 Setty, E. (2022). Educating teenage boys about consent: The law and affirmative consent in boys' socio-sexual cultures and subjectivities. *Sex Roles*, *87*(9), 515–535.

13 Hayes, H. M. R., Burns, K., & Egan, S. (2024). Becoming 'good men': Teaching consent and masculinity in a single-sex boys' school. *Sex Education*, *24*(1), 31–44.

14 Waling, A., James, A., & Fairchild, J. (2023). 'I'm not going anywhere near that': Expert stakeholder challenges in working with boys and young men regarding sex and sexual consent. *Critical Social Policy*, *43*(2), 234–256.

15 Wegner, B. (2021). *Raising feminist boys: How to talk with your child about gender, consent, and empathy*. New Harbinger Publications.

11

PORNOGRAPHY

11.1 INTRODUCTION

In the digital age, pornography has become more prevalent and accessible than ever before. The advent of the internet and advanced technology has facilitated easy and often anonymous access to pornographic content. This widespread availability has led to an increase in consumption, making pornography a ubiquitous element in the modern digital landscape.

But the consumption of pornography does not exist in a vacuum; it is deeply intertwined with societal and cultural contexts. For example, while pornography has become more normalized due to its accessibility, it remains a taboo subject in many societies. This dichotomy can create conflicting attitudes and beliefs about its consumption and impact. Moreover, the widespread availability of pornography is influencing sexual norms and expectations, particularly among younger individuals, who may turn to it as a primary source of sexual information.

Significantly, the consumption of pornography often carries different implications for boys and men. Societal expectations and traditional views on masculinity can lead to more permissive attitudes toward male consumption of pornography. These cultural norms may then inadvertently encourage boys and men to view pornography as a rite of passage or a reflection of sexual prowess, which can shape their sexual attitudes and behaviors in profound ways. Understanding these gender-specific

DOI: 10.4324/9781032709369-14

dynamics is crucial for addressing how pornography impacts not only individual consumers but also wider societal sexual ethics and health. Finally, and crucially for this chapter, the consumption of pornography is often seen differently based on gender, with societal attitudes tending to be more accepting of male consumption while stigmatizing female viewership.

And so, as pornography becomes more entrenched in the digital fabric of society, the conversation around it is evolving, and this chapter seeks to understand what that conversation looks like for men and boys.

11.2 THE MODERN HISTORY OF PORNOGRAPHY

Integrating a historical perspective on the evolution of pornography provides essential context for understanding its current impacts and societal perceptions. Historically, pornography has undergone significant transformations, moving from clandestine and often illegal beginnings to a mainstream and highly accessible digital presence. Initially distributed in printed forms, such as pamphlets, books, and magazines, pornography was heavily regulated, with many societies imposing strict laws against its production and distribution. Over time, the advent of film, video, and eventually, digital media, like DVDs, further expanded its reach, gradually loosening the tight grip of censorship. The digital revolution marked a pivotal turn, as the internet facilitated unprecedented access to pornographic content, making it readily available and largely anonymous. This transition from physical to digital media has changed not only the way pornography is consumed but also how it is regulated, with legal frameworks struggling to keep pace with technological advancements and the resulting shifts in social norms.

The rapid advancements in technology are now further significantly reshaping the landscape of pornography, especially with the advent of virtual reality (VR), augmented reality (AR), and artificial intelligence (AI). These technologies are not only enhancing the immersive experience of pornography but also raising complex ethical questions regarding their use.[1,2] VR and AR allow for deeply immersive experiences that can blur the lines between reality and digital fantasy, potentially reinforcing unrealistic expectations about sexual interaction and consent. Moreover, AI's role in generating synthetic pornography, which can include the creation of non-consensual images of individuals, presents profound concerns about privacy, consent, and the unauthorized use of one's image. These technological capabilities could lead to new forms of exploitation and abuse, highlighting the urgent need for updated legal and ethical frameworks to address these evolving challenges. As these technologies continue to advance and become more integrated into everyday life, the potential for harm increases, necessitating a careful consideration of their impacts on society and individual psychology.

11.3   WHO IS USING PORNOGRAPHY: GENDER AND AGE

The consumption of pornography exhibits significant gender differences, influenced by societal attitudes and cultural norms.

Men and boys have a much higher exposure rate to pornography,[3] fueled by several factors:

1   *Normalization and acceptance.* Society tends to view pornography consumption by men and boys as more acceptable. It is often seen as a natural part of male sexuality and even a rite of passage.

2   *Sexual expectations and behavior.* Exposure to pornography can shape men's sexual expectations, emphasizing aggressive or dominant behaviors. This can create unrealistic standards for sexual performance and body image.

3   *Pressure and masculinity.* Traditional views on masculinity encourage men to view pornography as a reflection of sexual prowess, which can influence their sexual attitudes and behaviors profoundly.

4   *Stigmatization and shame.* Women and girls who consume pornography often face greater stigma and shame due to cultural taboos that view female sexuality as more private or less active. This can lead to feelings of guilt and secrecy surrounding their consumption.

5   *Representation and influence.* The portrayal of women in pornography often reinforces submissive and objectified roles, impacting how female viewers perceive their own sexuality and desirability.[4]

6   *Different motivations.* Women may seek out pornography for various reasons, including sexual exploration, understanding their own desires, or fulfilling emotional needs, which can differ from the often visual and performance-focused motivations of men.

11.3.1   Increasingly Younger Users

The accessibility of pornography has also led to its consumption by increasingly younger users, raising significant concerns about its impact on development and sexual education.[5] Issues mainly focus on early exposure often under a lack of guidance:

Early Exposure

• *Curiosity and exploration.* Younger individuals, particularly adolescents, often turn to pornography out of curiosity and a lack of comprehensive sexual education. This early exposure can significantly shape their understanding of sex and relationships.

- *Impact on sexual development.* Exposure to pornography at a young age can impact sexual development, leading to skewed perceptions of normal sexual behavior and body image. This can contribute to unrealistic expectations and confusion about consent and healthy relationships.

Lack of Guidance

- *Inadequate sexual education.* Many young users turn to pornography in the absence of adequate sexual education at home or in school. Without proper guidance, they may internalize the often unrealistic and problematic portrayals of sex found in pornographic content.[6]
- *Misconceptions and risks.* Younger users may develop misconceptions about sex, such as the normalization of risky behaviors or the underrepresentation of consent and communication in sexual encounters, including the use of violence.[7]

11.4   THE IMPACT OF PORNOGRAPHY ON SEXUAL SCRIPTS

Accessed by increasing numbers, pornography has a profound influence on how all viewers including men perceive and internalize sexual norms and behaviors.[8] This impact is especially pronounced in societies where open discussions about sex are limited or taboo. These influences include:

1. *Shaping expectations.* Pornography often becomes a primary source of sexual education, especially for younger men. This can lead to misconceptions about sexual practices, as pornographic content typically prioritizes fantasy over realistic portrayals of sex.

2. *Normalizing certain behaviors.* Frequent exposure to certain types of sexual behaviors in pornography can normalize them in the viewer's mind. This includes aggressive or dominant behaviors that may not align with healthy, consensual sexual interactions in real life.[9]

11.4.1   The Gap Between Pornography and Real-Life Sexual Experiences

The disconnect between the sexual scenarios depicted in pornography and real-life sexual experiences can lead to various issues including:[10]

1. *Unrealistic expectations.* Pornography often portrays an unrealistic standard of body types and sexual performance. Men may feel

pressured to emulate what they see, leading to performance anxiety and dissatisfaction.

2. *Misunderstanding of consent and communication.* Pornography rarely depicts the nuances of consent and verbal communication, potentially leading to misunderstandings about what constitutes a consensual and respectful sexual encounter.

3. *Influence on relationship dynamics.* Expectations formed by pornography can strain intimate relationships, as real-life partners may not conform to the ideals or behaviors portrayed in pornographic material.

11.5   PORNOGRAPHY AND BODY IMAGE ISSUES

Building on discussions in Chapter 7, the consumption of pornography also has a significant impact on men's perceptions of their own bodies and those of their partners. This impact is largely due to the unrealistic portrayals of body types and sexual performance in most pornographic content, resulting in:

1. *Unrealistic standards.* Pornography often features individuals with idealized, and sometimes digitally enhanced, body types. Regular exposure to such portrayals can lead men to develop unrealistic expectations for their own bodies and those of their sexual partners.[11]

2. *Insecurity and comparison.* Men may compare their bodies to the often-unattainable physiques seen in pornography, leading to feelings of inadequacy, low self-esteem, and body dissatisfaction.[12]

3. *Distorted view of normalcy.* The prevalence of certain body types and sexual performances in pornography can distort men's perceptions of what is normal or desirable, potentially impacting their sexual self-esteem and confidence.

11.5.1   The Correlation Between Pornography Consumption and Body Standards

But the relationship between pornography consumption and the development of unrealistic body standards is complex and multifaceted, and includes:

*   *Influence on self-perception.* Regular consumers of pornography may start to perceive the bodies and sexual performance seen in these videos as standards to achieve, contributing to a distorted self-image.

- *Impact on sexual satisfaction.* These unrealistic standards can affect sexual satisfaction, both in terms of personal body image and in expectations of partners' bodies and sexual responses.[13]

- *Consequences for mental health.* The pressure to meet these standards can lead to various mental health issues, including anxiety, depression, and sexual dysfunction.[14,15]

11.6   SEXUAL RISK-TAKING AND PORNOGRAPHY

The consumption of pornography can also have a significant influence on attitudes and behaviors related to sexual risk-taking. This impact is often a by-product of the types of sexual activities and practices commonly depicted in pornographic material, including:

1. *Normalization of risky behaviors.* Pornography often portrays sexual activities without the context of safe sex practices, such as the use of condoms or discussions about sexual health. This can normalize risky behaviors and diminish the perceived importance of safe sex among viewers.

2. *Exploration of high-risk activities.* Exposure to certain types of pornography might encourage individuals to experiment with high-risk sexual activities without fully understanding or acknowledging the potential consequences, including STIs or unintended pregnancies.

3. *Impulsive behavior.* Regular consumption of pornography, especially material that emphasizes spontaneous or high-risk sexual encounters, can contribute to impulsive sexual behaviors in real-life situations.

11.6.1   The Disconnect Between Pornography and Safe Sex Practices

There is a notable disconnect between the portrayal of sex in pornography and the realities of safe and consensual sexual practices, for example:

1. *Lack of condom use.* Condom use is infrequently depicted in mainstream pornography, which can lead to misconceptions, particularly among younger viewers, about the normalcy and necessity of using protection during sex.[16,17]

2. *Misrepresentation of consent and communication.* Pornography often omits the essential aspects of sexual consent and communication, failing to model how partners should discuss and agree upon safe sex practices.[18]

3.   *Unrealistic expectations.* The unrealistic portrayal of sex in pornography, devoid of any real-world consequences, can set false expectations, influencing individuals to engage in risky behaviors without proper precautions.

11.7   PORNOGRAPHY AND SEXUAL RELATIONSHIPS

As the influence of pornography across these various domains takes effect, there is a notable impact on men's attitudes and expectations in their sexual relationships. This influence can manifest in various ways, shaping how men perceive and engage in intimate encounters. It can influence:

1.   *Shaping sexual expectations.* Pornography often portrays an unrealistic picture of sexual activity, leading men to develop skewed expectations about sex. These expectations can include beliefs about partners' appearance, behavior, and willingness to engage in certain sexual acts.

2.   *Sexual performance.* The portrayal of sex in pornography can create unrealistic standards for sexual performance, often leading to anxiety and dissatisfaction in men regarding their sexual abilities and endurance.

3.   *Perceptions of normalcy in sex.* Regular consumption of pornography can lead men to believe that the behaviors and scenarios depicted are commonplace and expected in real-life sexual relationships.

11.7.1   Influence on Consent and Mutual Respect

The portrayal of sex in pornography can also have profound implications for understanding and practicing consent and mutual respect in intimate encounters. Some of the issues are:

1.   *Consent in pornography.* Pornographic content often lacks clear depictions of consent, potentially leading to misunderstandings about the importance of ongoing and enthusiastic consent in real-life sexual interactions.[19]

2.   *Respect for boundaries.* Exposure to pornography that features aggressive or nonconsensual scenarios can blur the lines of respect for partners' boundaries, leading to problematic behaviors in intimate relationships.[20]

3.   *Communication and expectations.* Pornography rarely depicts communication between partners, which is crucial in establishing consent and mutual respect. This lack of portrayal can lead to miscommunications and unmet expectations in actual sexual encounters.

11.7.2   Pornography and Sexual Violence

Beyond the issues within consensual interactions, the complex relationship between pornography and sexual violence has also been a subject of intense academic and societal debate.[21,22] Studies and observations suggest several mechanisms through which pornography could potentially influence attitudes and behaviors associated with sexual violence:

1. *Normalization of aggression.* Pornography, particularly genres that depict aggression or violence as sexually arousing, may normalize such behaviors among frequent consumers. This exposure can blur the lines between consensual sexual activity and coercion, making aggression seem like a permissible or even expected part of sexual encounters.[23]

2. *Desensitization to violence.* Regular consumption of violent pornography may lead to desensitization to sexual violence. This desensitization can reduce empathy for victims of sexual violence and increase the likelihood of dismissing the seriousness of such acts, potentially escalating the acceptance of violence as part of sexual relations.[24]

3. *Influence on sexual scripts.* Pornography often provides a script that some individuals might adopt in real-life sexual encounters. If these scripts include domination, coercion, or violence, they may contribute to similar behaviors in real sexual interactions. The concern is particularly significant in settings where pornography acts as a primary source of sexual education, lacking the context of respect, consent, and communication.[25,26]

4. *Reinforcement of harmful stereotypes.* Pornography can reinforce gender stereotypes that depict men as dominant and women as submissive sexual objects. Such portrayals can contribute to sexist attitudes and can potentially justify or rationalize sexual aggression and violence.[27]

11.8   PROBLEMATIC PORNOGRAPHY CONSUMPTION AND ADDICTION

Even when not resulting in sexual violence, as pornography becomes increasingly accessible the potential for more generally problematic consumption grows, presenting significant challenges to mental and sexual health.[28,29,30] Problematic pornography consumption can escalate into an addiction, characterized by a compulsion to view pornography despite adverse consequences.[31]

Excessive consumption of pornography can strain romantic and sexual relationships. Partners may feel neglected or inadequate compared to the unrealistic standards and scenarios depicted in pornography. This can lead to decreased intimacy, trust issues, and conflicts within relationships. Problematic pornography consumption is also often associated with various mental health issues, including anxiety, depression, and low self-esteem. The guilt and shame tied to perceived overconsumption or the content viewed can exacerbate these feelings.

Overreliance on pornography for sexual satisfaction can also lead to sexual dysfunction in real-life encounters. This includes difficulties with arousal or desire that are not mediated by pornography, as well as issues related to performance anxiety and unrealistic expectations about sex.[32] Indeed, research suggests that heavy pornography consumption can affect the brain similarly to other addictive substances. Changes in neural pathways related to reward and arousal thus make it difficult for individuals to find satisfaction in less-stimulating or nonpornographic sexual activities.[33,34] There is also a potential for escalation, where users seek out more extreme or varied forms of pornography to achieve the same level of arousal, leading to desensitization. This can impact real-life sexual interests and behaviors, potentially encouraging risky or nonconsensual activities.

11.9   ADDRESSING MISLEADING PERCEPTIONS

The misconceptions propagated by pornography can be addressed through targeted strategies aimed at re-educating and informing men and boys about the realities of sexual interactions. This requires:

1. *Comprehensive sex education.* Integrating comprehensive sex education programs in schools and communities that not only cover the basics of reproduction and safe sex but also address the realities versus portrayals of sex in pornography. This education should emphasize the diversity of sexual experiences and the importance of consent and communication in sexual relationships.

2. *Media literacy programs.* Implementing media literacy programs to help men and boys critically analyze and understand the content they consume. This includes discussions on how pornography is produced, its purpose, and the difference between on-screen portrayals and real-life sexual encounters.

3. *Open and honest dialogue.* Encouraging open and honest dialogue in various settings, including schools, homes, and peer groups, about the impact of pornography on sexual expectations and behaviors. Creating safe spaces for these discussions can help dispel myths and encourage healthier attitudes. This can and should include exploring motivations for pornography usage, including life meaning.[35]

11.9.1   Educating on the Difference Between Pornography and Real Life

One of the key areas of focus is in educating men and boys on the differences between pornographic content and real-life sexual interactions, specifically by promoting:

1. *Realistic expectations.* Stressing that real-life sexual experiences vary greatly from person to person and that what is depicted in pornography often does not represent typical sexual encounters.

2. *An understanding consent.* Highlighting the importance of consent in real-life sexual interactions and how pornography often fails to adequately depict this crucial aspect.

3. *An emphasis on healthy relationships.* Focusing on the emotional aspects of sexual relationships, which are often absent in pornography. This includes fostering respect, mutual understanding, and emotional connection with sexual partners.

11.9.2   Addressing Sexual Risk-Taking and Pornography

In addition, mitigating the influence of pornography on sexual risk-taking requires a multipronged approach, including:

1. *Comprehensive sex education.* Educating young people about the realities of safe sex practices, including the importance of using protection and the necessity of informed consent.

2. *Critical media literacy.* Encouraging critical thinking about the content viewed in pornography and its divergence from real-life sexual experiences and responsibilities.

3. *Open conversations.* Promoting open discussions about pornography and its impact on sexual behavior can help individuals differentiate between fantasy and the realities of safe and consensual sex.

11.10   THE ROLE OF EDUCATION AND COUNSELING

Educational initiatives play a crucial role in addressing the impacts of pornography, particularly in forming healthy attitudes toward sex and relationships. Sexual education in schools should, for example, extend beyond the mechanics of sex and contraception to address the psychological and emotional aspects of sexual relationships. This includes discussions about the impact of pornography, understanding consent, and fostering respectful interactions. Education programs should also focus on developing critical thinking skills, enabling young people to discern and critically evaluate the information and images they encounter in pornography and other media. Finally, encouraging parental involvement in sexual education is key. Parents can provide guidance aligned with the family's values and beliefs, creating an open environment for discussing topics like pornography and its effects.

11.10.1   Utilizing Counseling and Therapy

Counseling and therapy can be instrumental in mitigating the negative effects of pornography consumption when necessary,[36,37] including:

1. *Individual counseling.* Professional counseling can help individuals struggling with issues related to pornography consumption, such as addiction, unrealistic sexual expectations, or relationship difficulties.

2. *Cognitive behavioral approaches.* Therapies such as cognitive behavioral therapy (CBT) and acceptance commitment therapy (ACT) can assist in changing harmful patterns of thought and behavior related to pornography use.[38,39]

3. *Group therapy and support groups.* Group therapy or support groups can provide a space for sharing experiences and strategies for coping with the effects of pornography, offering a sense of community and mutual support.

11.11   SOCIETAL AND CULTURAL CHANGE

Addressing the complex issues surrounding pornography also requires significant broader societal and cultural shifts. These changes are essential to alter the current perceptions and practices associated with pornography consumption. This includes:

1. *Redefining norms.* Society needs to move toward a more balanced and realistic understanding of sexuality, where pornography is not the primary educator about sexual norms and behaviors. This shift involves challenging and changing long-held misconceptions and taboos surrounding sex and pornography.

2. *Promoting open discussions.* Encouraging open and healthy discussions about pornography can demystify and destigmatize the topic, leading to a more informed and responsible approach to its consumption.

3. *Raising awareness of impact.* Increasing public awareness about the potential negative effects of pornography on individuals and relationships

is crucial. This awareness can foster a more critical approach to consumption and a better understanding of the difference between pornographic fantasy and real-life intimacy.

11.11.1   Advocacy for Responsible Portrayal

Advocating for the responsible portrayal of sexual content in pornography is vital in promoting healthier sexual attitudes and behaviors. For example, by encouraging the adoption of ethical standards in the production of pornographic content, including the realistic portrayal of bodies, sexual activities, and consent; promoting and supporting pornographic content that depicts a diverse range of bodies, relationships, and sexual practices and which emphasizes consent and mutual respect; and advocating for regulatory measures that ensure the ethical production and distribution of pornography, protecting both performers and consumers.

11.11.2   Responsible Consumption

Educating about and encouraging responsible consumption of pornography are also key, and could be achieved by promoting:

1. *Critical consumption skills.* Teaching skills for critically evaluating and consuming pornography can help individuals distinguish between fantasy and reality and mitigate negative influences.

2. *Resources for parents and guardians.* Providing resources and guidance to parents and guardians on how to discuss pornography with their children, including its potential impacts and the importance of consent and healthy relationships.

11.12   ETHICAL PORNOGRAPHY PRODUCTION AND CONSUMPTION

Indeed, the concept of ethical pornography has gained traction in recent years as a response to the numerous issues associated with mainstream pornographic content. Ethical pornography prioritizes the well-being of performers, emphasizes informed consent, and seeks to present sex in a more realistic and respectful manner. This movement aims to mitigate the negative impacts of traditional pornography on both performers and viewers by promoting healthier and more responsible production and consumption practices.[40]

11.12.1   Principles of Ethical Pornography

Here are the key principles of ethical pornography:

1. Informed Consent

   - *Voluntary participation.* Ethical pornography ensures that all performers participate willingly and fully understand the nature of the work they are engaging in. This involves clear communication and mutual agreement on the boundaries and activities involved.
   - *Transparency.* Contracts and agreements are explicit and transparent, outlining the rights and responsibilities of all parties involved.

2. Fair Treatment of Performers

   - *Safe working conditions.* Producers of ethical pornography provide a safe and respectful working environment. This includes proper hygiene, access to medical care, and support for performers' mental health.
   - *Fair compensation.* Performers are paid fairly and promptly for their work. There is a commitment to equitable pay that reflects the labor and risks involved.
   - *Respect for boundaries.* Performers' boundaries are respected at all times. They have the right to stop a scene if they feel uncomfortable or unsafe.

3. Realistic Portrayals of Sex

   - *Authentic interactions.* Ethical pornography aims to depict sex in a more authentic and relatable manner. This includes showcasing a variety of body types, sexual orientations, and relational dynamics.
   - *Emphasis on consent.* Scenes often include clear depictions of consent, demonstrating how partners communicate and agree on sexual activities.
   - *Varied narratives.* Ethical porn explores diverse sexual experiences and narratives, moving away from stereotypical and formulaic depictions often seen in mainstream pornography.

11.12.2 Benefits of Ethical Pornography

As you might imagine, following these principles comes with several benefits, **including:**

1. Positive Impact on Viewers

   - *Healthy sexual education.* Ethical pornography can serve as a more accurate source of sexual education, showing realistic sexual interactions that emphasize consent and mutual pleasure.
   - *Reduced misconceptions.* By presenting sex more realistically, ethical porn helps reduce the unrealistic expectations and body image issues often perpetuated by mainstream pornography.

2.   Empowerment of Performers

- *Agency and autonomy.* Performers in ethical pornography have greater control over their work, leading to a sense of empowerment and respect.
- *Improved mental health.* A supportive and respectful working environment can significantly improve the mental well-being of performers, reducing the stigma and exploitation often associated with the industry.

11.12.3   How to Support Ethical Pornography

And here are some steps on how to support ethical consumption:

1.   *Seek out ethical producers.* Consumers can support the ethical porn industry by subscribing to platforms and purchasing content from producers who adhere to ethical standards.

- *Research and recommendations.* Utilize resources and recommendations from organizations and websites dedicated to promoting ethical porn.

2.   *Advocate for change.* Engage in discussions about the importance of ethical pornography, and advocate for industry-wide changes.

- *Public awareness campaigns.* Participate in or support campaigns that raise awareness about the benefits of ethical pornography and the issues with mainstream content.

3.   *Educate yourself and others.* Increase your understanding of the ethical issues in pornography, and share this knowledge with others.

- *Workshops and seminars.* Attend or organize educational events that focus on ethical porn and its impact on sexual health and relationships.

11.14   CONCLUSION

The myriad issues presented by pornography are complex and multifaceted, significantly impacting men and, by extension, society. From distorting perceptions of sexual norms and behaviors to fostering unrealistic body image standards, the influence of pornography is pervasive and profound. It often perpetuates misleading sexual scripts, encourages risky sexual behaviors, and can negatively affect the dynamics of sexual relationships.

Pornography, in its current mainstream form, also often fails to depict real-life sexual experiences authentically, overlooking the critical aspects of consent and mutual respect. The gap between the fantasy world of pornography and the reality of sexual relationships can thus lead to confusion, disappointment, and unhealthy attitudes toward sex. The prevalence of pornography also raises concerns about its potential addictive nature and the impact on mental health, particularly when consumed excessively. Addressing these issues necessitates ongoing dialogue and comprehensive education, alongside the promotion of ethical consumption.

Pornography therefore clearly presents significant challenges that require a coordinated and multifaceted response. But by engaging in ongoing dialogue, providing comprehensive education, advocating for responsible consumption, and offering support to those affected, we can work toward mitigating the negative impacts of pornography. Such efforts are crucial in promoting healthier, more realistic attitudes toward sexuality and fostering respectful and consensual sexual relationships.

NOTES

1 Evans, L. (2023). Virtual reality pornography: A review of health-related opportunities and challenges. *Current Sexual Health Reports, 15*(1), 26–35.
2 Dekker, A., Wenzlaff, F., Biedermann, S. V., Briken, P., & Fuss, J. (2021). VR porn as "empathy machine"? Perception of self and others in virtual reality pornography. *The Journal of Sex Research, 58*(3), 273–278.
3 Hen, M., Karsh, N., Langer, E., & Shechter, R. (2020). Gender differences in implicit exposure to cyber-pornography. *The Journal of Social Psychology, 160*(5), 613–623.
4 Scarcelli, C. M. (2015). 'It is disgusting, but . . .': Adolescent girls' relationship to internet pornography as gender performance. *Porn Studies, 2*(2–3), 237–249.
5 www.barnardos.org.uk/blog/how-does-pornography-harm-children
6 Litsou, K., Byron, P., McKee, A., & Ingham, R. (2021). Learning from pornography: Results of a mixed methods systematic review. *Sex Education, 21*(2), 236–252.
7 https://assets.childrenscommissioner.gov.uk/wpuploads/2023/02/cc-a-lot-of-it-is-actually-just-abuse-young-people-and-pornography-updated.pdf
8 Bridges, A. J., Sun, C. F., Ezzell, M. B., & Johnson, J. (2016). Sexual scripts and the sexual behavior of men and women who use pornography. *Sexualization, Media, & Society, 2*(4), 2374623816668275.
9 Fritz, N., & Paul, B. (2017). From orgasms to spanking: A content analysis of the agentic and objectifying sexual scripts in feminist, for women, and mainstream pornography. *Sex Roles, 77*(9), 639–652.
10 Sun, C., Bridges, A., Johnson, J. A., & Ezzell, M. B. (2016). Pornography and the male sexual script: An analysis of consumption and sexual relations. *Archives of Sexual Behavior, 45*(4), 983–994.
11 Tylka, T. L. (2015). No harm in looking, right? Men's pornography consumption, body image, and well-being. *Psychology of Men & Masculinity, 16*(1), 97.
12 Maheux, A. J., Roberts, S. R., Evans, R., Widman, L., & Choukas-Bradley, S. (2021). Associations between adolescents' pornography consumption and self-objectification, body comparison, and body shame. *Body Image, 37*, 89–93.

13 Wright, P. J., & Tokunaga, R. S. (2018). Women's perceptions of their male part-
    ners' pornography consumption and relational, sexual, self, and body satisfac-
    tion: Toward a theoretical model. *Annals of the International Communication
    Association, 42*(1), 55–73.
14 Goldsmith, K., Dunkley, C. R., Dang, S. S., & Gorzalka, B. B. (2017). Pornography
    consumption and its association with sexual concerns and expectations among
    young men and women. *The Canadian Journal of Human Sexuality, 26*(2),
    151–162.
15 Landripet, I., & Štulhofer, A. (2015). Is pornography use associated with sexual
    difficulties and dysfunctions among younger heterosexual men? *The Journal of
    Sexual Medicine, 12*(5), 1136–1139.
16 Tokunaga, R. S., Wright, P. J., & Vangeel, L. (2020). Is pornography consumption
    a risk factor for condomless sex? *Human Communication Research, 46*(2–3),
    273–299.
17 Wright, P. J. (2022). Pornography consumption and condomless sex among
    emerging US adults: Results from six nationally representative surveys. *Health
    Communication, 37*(14), 1740–1747.
18 Marques, A. S., Braga, A. F., Brito, Â., & Arantes, J. (2024). "Do I really need to
    ask?": Relationship between pornography and sexual consent. *Sexuality &
    Culture*, 1–22.
19 Willis, M., Canan, S. N., Jozkowski, K. N., & Bridges, A. J. (2020). Sexual consent
    communication in best-selling pornography films: A content analysis. *The Journal
    of Sex Research, 57*(1), 52–63.
20 Vera-Gray, F., McGlynn, C., Kureshi, I., & Butterby, K. (2021). Sexual violence as
    a sexual script in mainstream online pornography. *The British Journal of
    Criminology, 61*(5), 1243–1260.
21 Mestre-Bach, G., Villena-Moya, A., & Chiclana-Actis, C. (2024). Pornography use
    and violence: A systematic review of the last 20 years. *Trauma, Violence, &
    Abuse, 25*(2), 1088–1112.
22 Brem, M. J., Garner, A. R., Grigorian, H., Florimbio, A. R., Wolford-Clevenger,
    C., Shorey, R. C., & Stuart, G. L. (2021). Problematic pornography use and
    physical and sexual intimate partner violence perpetration among men in bat-
    terer intervention programs. *Journal of Interpersonal Violence, 36*(11–12),
    NP6085–NP6105.
23 Krahé, B., Tomaszewska, P., & Schuster, I. (2021). Links of perceived pornography
    realism with sexual aggression via sexual scripts, sexual behavior, and accep-
    tance of sexual coercion: A study with German university students. *International
    Journal of Environmental Research and Public Health, 19*(1), 63.
24 Carrotte, E. R., Davis, A. C., & Lim, M. S. (2020). Sexual behaviors and violence
    in pornography: Systematic review and narrative synthesis of video content anal-
    yses. *Journal of Medical Internet Research, 22*(5), e16702.
25 Krahé et al., Links of perceived pornography realism with sexual aggression via
    sexual scripts, sexual behavior, and acceptance of sexual coercion, 63.
26 Vera-Gray et al., Sexual violence as a sexual script in mainstream online pornog-
    raphy, 1243–1260.
27 de Heer, B. A., Prior, S., & Hoegh, G. (2021). Pornography, masculinity, and
    sexual aggression on college campuses. *Journal of Interpersonal Violence,
    36*(23–24), NP13582–NP13605.

28 Setyawati, R., Hartini, N., & Suryanto, S. (2020). The psychological impacts of internet pornography addiction on adolescents. *Humaniora, 11*(3), 235–244.

29 Duffy, A., Dawson, D. L., & Das Nair, R. (2016). Pornography addiction in adults: A systematic review of definitions and reported impact. *The Journal of Sexual Medicine, 13*(5), 760–777.

30 De Alarcón, R., de la Iglesia, J. I., Casado, N. M., & Montejo, A. L. (2019). Online porn addiction: What we know and what we don't – A systematic review. *Journal of Clinical Medicine, 8*(1), 91.

31 Taylor, K., & Gavey, N. (2020). Pornography addiction and the perimeters of acceptable pornography viewing. *Sexualities, 23*(5–6), 876–897.

32 Whelan, G., & Brown, J. (2021). Pornography addiction: An exploration of the association between use, perceived addiction, erectile dysfunction, premature (early) ejaculation, and sexual satisfaction in males aged 18–44 years. *The Journal of Sexual Medicine, 18*(9), 1582–1591.

33 Kang, X., Handayani, D. O. D., Chong, P. P., & Acharya, U. R. (2020). Profiling of pornography addiction among children using EEG signals: A systematic literature review. *Computers in Biology and Medicine, 125*, 103970.

34 Gola, M., Wordecha, M., Sescousse, G., Lew-Starowicz, M., Kossowski, B., Wypych, M., . . . & Marchewka, A. (2017). Can pornography be addictive? An fMRI study of men seeking treatment for problematic pornography use. *Neuropsychopharmacology, 42*(10), 2021–2031.

35 Todorovic, L., Huisman, M., & Ostafin, B. D. (2024). Targeting mechanisms for problematic pornography use interventions. *Sexual Health & Compulsivity, 31*(1), 1–28.

36 Roza, T. H., Noronha, L. T., Shintani, A. O., Massuda, R., Lobato, M. I. R., Kessler, F. H. P., & Passos, I. C. (2024). Treatment approaches for problematic pornography use: A systematic review. *Archives of Sexual Behavior, 53*(2), 645–672.

37 Antons, S., Engel, J., Briken, P., Krüger, T. H., Brand, M., & Stark, R. (2022). Treatments and interventions for compulsive sexual behavior disorder with a focus on problematic pornography use: A preregistered systematic review. *Journal of Behavioral Addictions, 11*(3), 643–666.

38 Lotfi, A., Babakhanin, M., & Ghazanfarpour, M. (2021). The effectiveness of intervention with cognitive behavioral therapy on pornography: A systematic review protocol of randomized clinical trial studies. *Health Science Reports, 4*(3), e341.

39 Fraumeni-McBride, J. (2019). Addiction and mindfulness; pornography addiction and mindfulness-based therapy ACT. *Sexual Addiction & Compulsivity, 26*(1–2), 42–53.

40 McKee, A., Dawson, A., & Kang, M. (2023). The criteria to identify pornography that can support healthy sexual development for young adults: Results of an international Delphi panel. *International Journal of Sexual Health, 35*(1), 1–12.

Section 4

EDUCATION AND WORK

12

EDUCATION

12.1 INTRODUCTION

The educational landscape for boys and young men up to the age of 18 presents a unique set of challenges that have significant implications for their academic and personal development. These challenges are multifaceted, impacting various aspects of their educational journey from early childhood through to the end of secondary education. These include but are not limited to:

1. *Learning disparities.* Research indicates that boys often lag behind girls in key educational areas, particularly in reading and writing. This gap can emerge early and may widen as they progress through school.

2. *Engagement in education.* Boys are often less engaged in the educational process, leading to higher dropout rates and lower levels of academic achievement. Factors contributing to this disengagement are complex and varied.

3. *Behavioral issues.* Boys are more likely to face disciplinary actions in school settings, which can further alienate them from the educational environment and impede their academic progress.

DOI: 10.4324/9781032709369-16

The challenges faced by boys and young men in education have far-reaching consequences, extending beyond individual academic outcomes to impact societal development. For example, educational achievements significantly influence future employment opportunities and socioeconomic status. The educational struggles of boys can therefore have long-term implications for their economic stability and career prospects.

Disparities in education also contribute to broader societal issues, including gender-based economic gaps and social inequalities. Moreover, the educational experiences of boys and young men also have profound psychological and social implications. Success or struggle in the educational system can shape self-esteem, social relationships, and overall well-being. Addressing the educational needs of boys is therefore crucial for fostering a more equitable and prosperous society.

Understanding and addressing the unique educational challenges faced by boys and young men are essential. This chapter will explore the issues, their causes, and the potential solutions in more detail.

12.2   THE EDUCATIONAL ACHIEVEMENT GAP

The educational achievement gap between males and females is a well-documented phenomenon, presenting significant disparities in various academic areas.[1,2] This gap, which becomes evident at various stages of schooling, highlights key differences in the educational outcomes of boys and girls. We can track this developmentally across the schooling system:

- *Early indicators.* The gap often starts in early childhood education, with boys typically developing literacy skills like reading and writing at a slower pace compared to girls.[3,4] This disparity can set the tone for future academic challenges.
- *Widening gap in later years.* As children progress through school, this gap can widen.[5,6] Boys are more likely to underperform in standardized tests, particularly in language arts, which includes reading and writing. In contrast, the gap is less pronounced in subjects like mathematics and science but still presents challenges for many boys.
- *Secondary/high school and beyond.* By secondary/high school, the achievement gap often results in higher dropout rates among boys. This trend is concerning because it limits their opportunities for higher education and vocational training, impacting their career prospects and socioeconomic status.

Among the various academic areas, certain subjects emerge as significant points of concern:

- *Reading and literacy.* Reading is a critical area where boys consistently lag behind.[7,8] The reasons are multifaceted, ranging from early developmental differences to variations in interests and engagement strategies. The lower proficiency in reading not only affects performance in language arts but also impacts learning across other subjects, as reading is fundamental to most educational activities.

- *Writing skills.* Similar to reading, writing is another area where boys often underperform.[9] This gap in writing skills can be attributed to differences in language development, as well as to differing interests and attitudes toward writing tasks.

12.3   CONTRIBUTING FACTORS TO THE ACHIEVEMENT GAP

There are several factors with influence and help to create this gap.

12.3.1   Societal Attitudes and Stereotypes

Societal attitudes and stereotypes play a significant role in shaping boys' educational experiences and outcomes. Prevailing notions of masculinity often discourage boys from engaging in academic pursuits perceived as less masculine, like reading or the arts.[10] These societal expectations can limit boys' willingness to explore a wide range of academic interests. Boys are also often expected to be more active and less focused than girls, which can influence how teachers, parents, and peers interact with them in educational settings.[11] These expectations can lead to a self-fulfilling prophecy where boys are less engaged and underperform academically.

12.3.2   Individual Motivations and Gendered Learning Stereotypes

Understanding individual motivations and how they are shaped by gender stereotypes provides a nuanced perspective on engagement and achievement differences between boys and girls.[12,13,14,15] These motivations, informed by societal norms and personal interests, directly influence academic engagement and outcomes.

Stereotypes about gender roles and abilities can significantly influence the motivational dynamics of students. For example, girls may feel discouraged from pursuing subjects like mathematics and science due to persistent stereotypes that suggest these fields are more suitable for boys. Conversely, boys might avoid subjects like language arts or fine arts, seeing them as feminine and thus misaligned with their gender identity.

Self-efficacy, or the belief in one's capabilities to achieve a goal, is often shaped by early experiences and reinforced by societal feedback. Boys who receive positive reinforcement for problem-solving or physical tasks may develop higher self-efficacy in technical or scientific fields, while girls often receive encouragement in areas requiring empathy and communication, bolstering their confidence in humanities or social sciences. These developed efficacies can limit the range of subjects students feel competent in, affecting their academic choices and performances.

The development of interests is crucial in motivating learning and is significantly influenced by gender norms. Boys and girls might choose to engage in activities that conform to their gender identities, impacting their academic pursuits. Boys might be more inclined to engage in competitive environments or choose sports over academic clubs, while girls might opt for activities that emphasize collaboration and social interaction. These preferences shape not only how they engage in learning but also which academic fields they are likely to excel in.

Stereotype threat, the risk of confirming negative stereotypes about one's group, can also adversely affect performance by increasing anxiety and reducing working memory capacity. For instance, girls aware of stereotypes about female performance in math might perform worse on math tests, not due to a lack of ability, but because of the psychological pressure imposed by these stereotypes. Similarly, boys might underperform in reading or writing tasks, where they feel their abilities may be judged as inferior compared to girls'.

12.3.3   Teachers, Teaching Methods, and Classroom Environment

The approach to teaching and the classroom environment are crucial factors in boys' educational achievement, including:

1. *Teaching styles.* Traditional teaching methods, which often emphasize passive learning and prolonged focus, may not align well with the learning styles of many boys, who might benefit more from interactive and hands-on learning experiences.

2. *Teacher expectations.* Teachers themselves may reflect their stereotype knowledge onto children and either explicitly and/or implicitly discourage boys from reading.[16,17]

3. *Classroom dynamics.* Classrooms that lack sufficient physical activity or hands-on learning opportunities can be less engaging for boys, leading to lower levels of participation and interest.

12.3.4   Curriculum Content/Relevance and Education Policy

The content and relevance of the curriculum also contribute to the educational challenges faced by boys, as does broader overarching policy. Issues are found in:

1. *Lack of engaging material.* Boys often struggle with finding the curriculum content relatable or engaging, particularly in subjects like reading

and writing.[18] This disconnection can diminish their interest and motivation to learn.

2. *Limited representation.* The lack of male role models in educational materials, especially in literature and language arts, can affect boys' ability to connect with the content, thereby impacting their interest and engagement.

3. *Policy ignorance.* Whilst there are policies and frameworks in place to address gaps that disadvantage girls (i.e., girls in STEM subjects), there is currently policy blindness to issues affecting boys in many countries.[19]

12.3.5   The Impact of Parents

Different styles of parental involvement, such as supportive guidance versus pressure-driven oversight, can also lead to different outcomes in boys' education. For example, supportive parental engagement, which encourages exploration and learning from mistakes, is linked to higher academic motivation and better emotional health in boys.[20] This contrasts with pressure-driven involvement, which may exacerbate stress and reduce self-confidence, particularly in academic areas where boys may already feel vulnerable or less competent. Some studies also show that parents are generally less involved in boys' education overall, which will have a negative relationship with outcomes.[21]

The expectations parents hold for their sons then significantly affect boys' academic engagement and aspirations. High but realistic expectations can motivate boys to strive for success; however, unrealistic expectations may lead to anxiety and disengagement. It is important for parents to balance their aspirations for their children, with an understanding of their unique capabilities and interests. It is also important for parents, and particularly fathers as male role models, to place value on education for boys and to show interest in their educational pursuits.

12.3.6   The Impact of Technology and Media

As discussed in Chapter 6, the rise of technology and media has brought new challenges and distractions that can impact boys' educational performance. The prevalence of digital devices and media can be particularly distracting for boys, pulling their attention away from academic pursuits. Moreover, media often portrays academic disengagement as a norm for boys, which can reinforce negative stereotypes and influence boys' attitudes toward their education.

12.3.7   The Community's Role

The values and expectations prevalent in a community can also greatly influence boys' attitudes toward education. Communities that value academic achievement can positively impact boys' educational aspirations. Furthermore, community programs and support systems that provide academic assistance, mentorship, and positive role models can be instrumental in encouraging boys to pursue and value education.

12.4   INTERSECTIONALITY AND BOYS' EDUCATION

We also have to look at the type of boys we are speaking about, and how their demographic makeup might influence their achievement and engagement. This includes accounting for:

- *Diverse backgrounds and experiences.* Boys do not experience educational settings and societal expectations uniformly; their experiences vary significantly based on race, socioeconomic status, disability, and more. For example, boys from low-income families may face compounded challenges due to economic disparities that influence their educational outcomes differently from their peers'.
- *Cultural expectations and stereotypes.* Different cultures have varying expectations of masculinity and academic achievement. Exploring how these cultural norms influence boys from different backgrounds can provide a clearer picture of the diverse challenges they face.
- *Impact on engagement and performance.* The intersection of various identity factors can influence how boys engage with the educational system and how they perform academically. For instance, boys with disabilities might experience both ableism and gender-based stereotypes, affecting their educational journey differently than that of boys without disabilities.
- *Tailored strategies for inclusion.* Addressing intersectionality can lead to more effective educational strategies that are tailored to the nuanced needs of boys from diverse backgrounds. This involves creating inclusive educational practices that recognize and address the specific challenges faced by boys with intersecting identities.

12.4.1   Working-Class Boys

One specific and important example of intersectionality and the impact of factors on education outcomes is in the underachievement of working-class boys as, whilst they have some characteristics of groups that are typically thought of as "privileged" or "successful," other elements clearly contribute to lower achievement.

Specifically, working-class boys face a unique set of challenges that contribute to their lower educational outcomes compared to their peers from different racial or socioeconomic backgrounds. Factors such as economic instability, limited access to quality education, and lack of educational support at home can impede their academic progress. Economic hardships then significantly affect the educational experiences of working-class boys, as these barriers often translate into fewer educational resources, less parental involvement due to work constraints, and lower access to extracurricular activities that enhance learning experiences.

Cultural perceptions of masculinity within working-class communities can also play a role in shaping educational outcomes. Often, there is a stronger emphasis on traditional masculinity that undervalues academic achievement in favor of work or trade skills, which can discourage academic engagement and aspiration. Indeed, research shows that working-class boys are more likely to feel alienated or disengaged in school settings that do not cater to their cultural and socioeconomic context. This disengagement is often reflected in higher dropout rates and lower academic achievement.

It is also important to note that the impact of these intersectional characteristics, and indeed just of gender itself, will differ across different countries.

12.5   INTERNATIONAL PERSPECTIVES ON GENDER DYNAMICS IN EDUCATION

To provide a nuanced view of how different educational systems across the globe address or exacerbate challenges related to gender dynamics in education, we must turn to international studies and data.

12.5.1   Educational Attainment and Gender Disparities

Across the globe, educational outcomes and participation levels vary significantly by gender, often influenced by socioeconomic status and cultural factors. In some regions, boys lag behind girls in terms of educational attainment at various levels of education, which is particularly evident in certain sub-Saharan African countries, where primary completion rates for boys are lower than for girls.[22]

In OECD countries, disparities are also evident, with boys more likely to repeat grades during lower secondary education. For instance, in Mexico, a higher percentage of boys repeat a grade compared to the OECD average, indicating a significant challenge in the educational progression for boys at this stage.[23]

12.5.2   Impact of Socioeconomic Factors

As already stated, socioeconomic status plays a crucial role in educational outcomes, often more so than gender alone, and this impact is starkly observed in OECD countries, where children from lower socioeconomic backgrounds exhibit significantly lower educational achievement compared to their wealthier peers.[24]

12.5.3   Global Educational Expenditure and Participation

Investment in education also varies widely. For example, the United States spends significantly on postsecondary education compared to other OECD countries, which could influence the quality and accessibility of education across different demographics.

Participation in early childhood education programs is also a critical factor, with the United States showing lower participation rates for younger children compared to the OECD average, which can impact long-term educational outcomes.[25]

12.5.4   Learning Outcomes and Gender Parity

Internationally, learning outcomes at the end of primary education reveal that girls generally outperform boys in reading across the majority of countries, although the disparities in mathematics tend to be more balanced at the lower secondary level.[26]

These insights underline the complexity of educational challenges faced by boys and the influence of a multitude of factors, including national policies, cultural norms, and economic conditions. Addressing these issues requires a multifaceted approach tailored to the specific contexts of different countries and regions.

12.6   LONG-TERM IMPACTS

The challenges outlined for boys in subjects like reading and literacy can have significant long-term impacts, including on:

1. *Academic performance.* Proficiency in reading is foundational for success in most academic subjects. Boys who struggle with reading may experience broader academic challenges.

2. *Career opportunities.* Literacy skills are critical for most career paths. A lack of proficiency in reading can limit future employment opportunities and career advancement.

3. *Self-esteem and confidence.* Struggles with literacy can affect boys' self-esteem and confidence, influencing their overall attitude toward education and learning.

4. *Subject choice:* These gender dynamics extend to the choices boys make regarding the subjects they study. Boys may steer clear of subjects that are stereotypically seen as feminine, such as literature or arts, due to fear of social stigma or because they do not see these subjects as

aligning with their gender identity. Boys may instead gravitate more toward subjects perceived as more masculine, like sciences or physical education, even if their true interests lie elsewhere.

12.7 SOLUTIONS AND STRATEGIES FOR IMPROVEMENT

To mitigate the challenges faced by boys in education, it is crucial to implement targeted strategies and solutions that address the root causes of these issues.[27,28] A multifaceted approach involving educators, parents, policy-makers, and the community is necessary to make a meaningful impact, including:

1. *Tailored educational approaches.* Developing and implementing teaching methods that cater specifically to the learning styles of boys can significantly improve engagement and performance. This includes more hands-on, experiential learning opportunities, integrating technology, and offering a variety of subject choices that appeal to a range of interests.

2. *Early intervention programs.* Implementing early intervention programs that focus on literacy and language skills can help address the learning gap from a young age. These programs can provide additional support for boys who show early signs of struggle, particularly in reading and writing.

3. *Mentorship and role modeling.* Establishing mentorship programs where boys can connect with positive male role models can have a profound impact.[29,30] These mentors can provide guidance, support, and inspiration, showing boys the value and importance of education.

4. *Acknowledgment of mental health needs.* Schools need to recognize that boys have specific mental health needs that relate to their very experience as boys and the associated masculine attitudes and stereo-types that shape these.[31] Providing safe spaces for boys to explore and resolve these is also essential.

12.7.1 Strategies for Engaging Male Students

Adopting strategies that cater to the learning styles of boys can also make classrooms more engaging and effective, including:

1. *Interactive and hands-on learning.* Incorporating more interactive and hands-on activities can enhance engagement for boys. This includes project-based learning, experiments, and real-world problem-solving tasks.

2. *Incorporating movement and physical activity.* Allowing for movement and physical activity during lessons can help boys channel their energy positively and maintain focus.

3. *Utilizing technology and multimedia.* Leveraging technology and multimedia tools in teaching can be *particularly* effective in capturing boys' interest. Interactive educational software, videos, and online resources can make lessons more dynamic and appealing. Emerging technologies such as artificial intelligence (AI), virtual reality (VR), and adaptive learning systems offer exciting prospects. These tools can be customized to individual learning styles, making them especially advantageous for engaging boys who might not respond as well to conventional educational methods. By incorporating such technologies, educators can create a more inclusive and stimulating learning environment that caters to diverse needs.

4. *Diverse teaching approaches.* Employing a variety of teaching methods to cater to different learning styles is essential. This diversity ensures that all students, not just boys, have the opportunity to learn in ways that best suit them.

5. *Curating inclusive and diverse literature.* Offering a range of engaging literature that appeals to boys is crucial, but it is equally important to ensure that this literature does not simply perpetuate traditional gender stereotypes. Selecting books that feature diverse male protagonists displaying a range of emotions and roles can help challenge existing norms. Additionally, incorporating books written by male authors who explore unconventional themes can also provide relatable content that encourages boys to embrace a broader perspective on masculinity and personal development.

12.7.2   Impact of Extracurricular Activities

Extracurricular activities also play a significant role in the holistic development of boys, offering opportunities to develop skills, build relationships, and enhance academic performance. Participation in sports, arts, clubs, and community service can foster a sense of belonging, improve self-esteem, and provide a productive outlet for energy and creativity, with specific benefits including:

Skill development. Activities like sports, music, and debate help boys develop critical skills, such as teamwork, leadership, time management, and public speaking.

Academic improvement. Research shows that boys who participate in extracurricular activities often perform better academically, as these activities can increase engagement and motivation.

Social connections. Extracurriculars provide a platform for boys to form positive peer relationships and mentorships, reducing feelings of isolation and improving social skills.

Schools and communities should offer a diverse range of extracurricular options to cater to different interests and talents, ensuring all boys can find an activity they enjoy. Moreover, providing access to resources and removing barriers, such as financial constraints or transportation issues, can help more boys participate in these beneficial activities.

12.7.3   Successful Programs and Initiatives

Several programs and initiatives have demonstrated success in addressing the educational challenges faced by boys.

12.7.3.1   Reading and Literacy Programs

1.   *Read to a Child.* This program partners thousands of volunteers who read one-on-one to elementary students in underresourced schools across various metropolitan areas. It aims to build literacy skills and a love for reading through the influence of positive adult role models. Website: https://readtoachild.org/.

2.   *Literacy for Boys.* An online program specifically targeted at boys, using content that appeals to them to improve literacy skills. The program reports significant improvements in reading comprehension, spelling, grammar, and punctuation among its participants. Website: www.literacyforboys.com.au/.

12.7.3.2   STEM Initiatives

FIRST Robotics. This is a well-known international youth organization that operates the FIRST Robotics Competition among other STEM-oriented programs. It combines the excitement of sport with the rigors of science and technology, providing hands-on experience in engineering and technology to students. Website: www.firstinspires.org/.

Code.org. This nonprofit is dedicated to expanding access to computer science in schools and increasing participation by young women and students from other underrepresented groups. Their programs have successfully engaged a large number of boys in computer science education through online courses and local school programs. Website: https://code.org/.

12.7.3.3   *General Attainment Initiatives*

Boys Impact. A UK-wide network of educators who are committed to taking evidence-based approaches in closing the gap in attainment for young men who are eligible for free school meals. Basing their practice in findings from longitudinal research with marginalized young men conducted by the Taking Boys Seriously team at Ulster University, they pilot innovative new projects in regions across England, Scotland, and Northern Ireland. Website: www.boysimpact. com/.

12.7.3.4   *Behavioral and Social Emotional Learning Programs*

The RULER approach. Developed by the Yale Center for Emotional Intelligence, RULER is an evidence-based approach to social and emotional learning that has been adopted by schools to help students, including boys, develop emotional intelligence skills that support better academic and social outcomes. Website: www. rulerapproach.org/.

12.7.4   Encouraging Parental and Community Involvement

The involvement of parents and the community is vital in reinforcing the value of education. By first educating parents about the unique educational needs of boys and involving them in school activities that can enhance parental support for boys' education, we can then encourage the reflection of those attitudes in their interactions with their boys. In addition, community-based programs that offer tutoring, mentorship, and after-school activities can provide additional support and learning opportunities for boys.

12.8   THE WAY FORWARD

To effectively address the educational challenges faced by boys, it is essential to recognize the need for systemic changes in the educational landscape. These changes should aim to create an environment that not only acknowledges the unique needs of boys but also actively works toward supporting their educational journey. We should:

1. *Re-evaluate educational policies.* There is a need for a thorough re-evaluation of existing educational policies to ensure they cater to the diverse learning styles and needs of all students, including boys.[32] This includes revisiting curriculum design, teaching methodologies, and assessment strategies to make them more inclusive and effective for boys.

2. *Focus on teacher training and development.* Teacher training programs should include modules that equip educators with the skills and knowledge to address the specific learning styles of boys.[33] Ongoing professional development should also be provided to help teachers stay updated with the latest research and effective practices in male education.

3. *Incorporate gender sensitivity in education.* Implementing a gender-sensitive approach in education can help in addressing the specific challenges faced by boys. This approach involves understanding and addressing the impact of gender stereotypes and biases on students' learning experiences.

4. *Expand literary choices to challenge stereotypes.* It is crucial to offer boys a selection of literature that not only engages them but also challenges traditional gender stereotypes.[34] By providing access to books that feature male characters in unconventional roles – such as nurturing caregivers, emotional thinkers, or collaborative leaders – educational systems can help reshape perceptions of masculinity.[35]

A collaborative approach involving various stakeholders is critical in driving the necessary changes in education to better support boys. We need:

1. *Collaboration among educators, parents, and policymakers.* Building a strong partnership among educators, parents, and policymakers is vital for the successful implementation of changes in the education system. This collaboration can ensure that policies and practices are aligned with the needs of boys and are effectively communicated and supported across the educational ecosystem.

2. *Community involvement.* Engaging the broader community, including local businesses, nonprofit organizations, and educational experts, can provide additional resources and perspectives in developing and implementing strategies to support boys in education.

3. *Parental involvement.* To optimize parental involvement in education, it is crucial to provide parents with actionable guidelines that emphasize fostering intrinsic motivation in their sons, rather than focusing solely on academic outcomes like grades or test scores. Strategies should include promoting activities that cultivate a love of learning, such as reading for pleasure and engaging in educational activities beyond homework. Encouraging a growth mindset that values effort and perseverance over innate ability can also play a significant role. Additionally, parents should be encouraged to act as advocates for their sons' unique educational needs. This involves proactive communication with teachers

about the child's learning style and any challenges they face, ensuring that educational strategies are adapted to suit their needs, such as incorporating more hands-on learning opportunities and accommodating higher activity levels. These approaches not only support the academic development of boys but also enhance their overall educational experience.

4.   *Advocacy and awareness.* Raising awareness about the educational challenges faced by boys and advocating for their needs are crucial. This can be achieved through campaigns, seminars, and policy discussions that bring attention to the issue and drive public support for necessary changes.

12.9   CONCLUSION

This chapter has delved into the multifaceted educational challenges faced by boys and young men, highlighting crucial areas where they often lag behind and exploring the complex web of factors contributing to these challenges. There is a clear and persistent achievement gap in education between boys and girls, especially evident in areas like reading and literacy. Various factors contribute to this gap, including societal attitudes and stereotypes about masculinity, teaching methods, curriculum content, and the role of parents and the broader community.

Addressing these challenges requires a multifaceted approach, including tailored educational methods, early intervention, mentorship, and the involvement of parents and the community. With these targeted strategies, systemic changes, and collaborative efforts, it is possible to bridge the achievement gap and create an educational environment where boys can thrive and reach their full potential. This endeavor is not just beneficial for boys but is essential for the progress and health of society as a whole as well.

NOTES

1   Evans, D. K., Akmal, M., & Jakiela, P. (2020). Gender gaps in education: The long view. *IZA Journal of Development and Migration, 12*(1).
2   Reeves, R. V., & Smith, E. (2022). Boys left behind: Education gender gaps across the US. Brookings Institution. Retrieved from https://coilink.org/20.500.12592/xnf81v on 31 Aug 2024.
3   Ramirez, G., Fries, L., Gunderson, E., Schaeffer, M. W., Maloney, E. A., Beilock, S. L., & Levine, S. C. (2019). Reading anxiety: An early affective impediment to children's success in reading. *Journal of Cognition and Development, 20*(1), 15–34.
4   McTigue, E. M., Schwippert, K., Uppstad, P. H., Lundetræ, K., & Solheim, O. J. (2021). Gender differences in early literacy: Boys' response to formal instruction. *Journal of Educational Psychology, 113*(4), 690.

5 Yu, J., McLellan, R., & Winter, L. (2021). Which boys and which girls are falling behind? Linking adolescents' gender role profiles to motivation, engagement, and achievement. *Journal of Youth and Adolescence, 50*(2), 336–352.

6 Loh, C. E., Sun, B., & Majid, S. (2020). Do girls read differently from boys? Adolescents and their gendered reading habits and preferences. *English in Education, 54*(2), 174–190.

7 Steinmann, I., Strietholt, R., & Rosén, M. (2023). International reading gaps between boys and girls, 1970–2016. *Comparative Education Review, 67*(2), 298–330.

8 Auxier, B., Stewart, D., Bucaille, A., & Westcott, K. (2019). The gender gap in reading: Boy meets book, boy loses book, boy never gets book back. *2022 Predictions, 94*.

9 Disenhaus, N. (2015). *Boys, writing, and the literacy gender gap: What we know, what we think we know*. The University of Vermont and State Agricultural College.

10 Pansu, P., Régner, I., Max, S., Colé, P., Nezlek, J. B., & Huguet, P. (2016). A burden for the boys: Evidence of stereotype threat in boys' reading performance. *Journal of Experimental Social Psychology, 65*, 26–30.

11 Muntoni, F., Wagner, J., & Retelsdorf, J. (2021). Beware of stereotypes: Are classmates' stereotypes associated with students' reading outcomes? *Child Development, 92*(1), 189–204.

12 Scholes, L. (2019). Differences in attitudes towards reading and other school-related activities among boys and girls. *Journal of Research in Reading, 42*(3–4), 485–503

13 Lundberg, S. (2020). Educational gender gaps. *Southern Economic Journal, 87*(2), 416–439.

14 Schwabe, F., McElvany, N., & Trendtel, M. (2015). The school age gender gap in reading achievement: Examining the influences of item format and intrinsic reading motivation. *Reading Research Quarterly, 50*(2), 219–232.

15 Ashcroft, J. (2017). Do boys' attitudes to reading differ to those of girls? A study into the views of reading within a year three class. *The STeP Journal: Student Teacher Perspectives, 4*(1), 2–14.

16 Boerma, I. E., Mol, S. E., & Jolles, J. (2016). Teacher perceptions affect boys' and girls' reading motivation differently. *Reading Psychology, 37*(4), 547–569.

17 Retelsdorf, J., Schwartz, K., & Asbrock, F. (2015). "Michael can't read!" Teachers' gender stereotypes and boys' reading self-concept. *Journal of Educational Psychology, 107*(1), 186.

18 Van Hek, M., Kraaykamp, G., & Pelzer, B. (2018). Do schools affect girls' and boys' reading performance differently? A multilevel study on the gendered effects of school resources and school practices. *School Effectiveness and School Improvement, 29*(1), 1–21.

19 Hermann, Z., & Kopasz, M. (2021). Educational policies and the gender gap in test scores: A cross-country analysis. *Research Papers in Education, 36*(4), 461–482.

20 de Oliveira Lima, C. L., & Kuusisto, E. (2019). Parental engagement in children's learning: A holistic approach to teacher-parents' partnerships. *Pedagogy in Basic and Higher Education-Current Developments and Challenges*, 973–983.

21 Carter, R. S., & Wojtkiewicz, R. A. (2000). Parental involvement with adolescents' education: Do daughters or sons get more help? *Adolescence, 35*(137).

22 https://uis.unesco.org/en/news/education-data-release
23 www.oecd-ilibrary.org/sites/2a39f90d-en/index.html?itemId=/content/component/2a39f90d-en
24 www.oecd-ilibrary.org/sites/2a39f90d-en/index.html?itemId=/content/component/2a39f90d-en
25 https://nces.ed.gov/blogs/nces/post/education-at-a-glance-2023-putting-u-s-data-in-a-global-context
26 https://uis.unesco.org/en/news/education-data-release
27 Dietrichson, J., Filges, T., Seerup, J. K., Klokker, R. H., Viinholt, B. C., Bøg, M., & Eiberg, M. (2021). Targeted school-based interventions for improving reading and mathematics for students with or at risk of academic difficulties in Grades K-6: A systematic review. *Campbell Systematic Reviews, 17*(2), e1152.
28 Roberts, M. (2021). *The boy question: How to teach boys to succeed in school.* Routledge.
29 Wright, D., & Brownhill, S. (2018). *Men in early years settings: Building a mixed gender workforce* (1st ed.). Jessica Kingsley Publishers.
30 Wood, P., & Brownhill, S. (2018). Absent fathers', and children's social and emotional learning: An exploration of the perceptions of 'positive male role models' in the primary school sector. *Gender and Education, 30*, 172–186. https://doi.org/10.1080/09540253.2016.1187264
31 Pinkett, M. (2023). *Boys do cry: Improving boys' mental health and wellbeing in schools.* Routledge.
32 Nonte, S., Hartwich, L., & Willems, A. S. (2018). Promoting reading attitudes of girls and boys: A new challenge for educational policy? Multi-group analyses across four European countries. *Large-Scale Assessments in Education, 6*, 1–22.
33 Mills, M. (2020). *Teaching boys: Developing classroom practices that work.* Routledge.
34 Scholes, L., Spina, N., & Comber, B. (2021). Disrupting the'boys don't read'discourse: Primary school boys who love reading fiction. *British Educational Research Journal, 47*(1), 163–180.
35 Pinkett, M., & Roberts, M. (2019). *Boys don't try? Rethinking masculinity in schools.* Routledge.

13

HIGHER EDUCATION

13.1   INTRODUCTION

In recent years, a striking gender disparity has emerged in higher education in the UK, characterized by a significant imbalance in the number of female undergraduates compared to their male counterparts.[1] Current statistics reveal that there are around 150,000 more female undergraduates than male in the UK each year.[2] This gap is not just a number; it reflects a deeper issue within the educational landscape (as we began exploring in the previous chapter) and raises critical questions about the factors contributing to this disparity.

Whilst some countries see less of a discrepancy (see Section 13.2), this is a trend that is reflected globally, particularly in the West. It has now reached a point where the implications are profound and far-reaching, impacting not only the individuals involved but also the workforce, societal structures, and future educational policies.

By understanding the magnitude of the issue and its multifaceted causes, the subsequent sections will delve deeper into the societal, cultural, and educational factors contributing to this disparity, setting the groundwork for discussing potential solutions and strategies to address this growing concern.

DOI: 10.4324/9781032709369-17

13.2   HISTORICAL TRENDS IN HIGHER EDUCATION ENROLLMENT

The landscape of higher education enrollment has undergone significant changes over the years, particularly when analyzed through the lens of gender.[3] Historically, higher education in the UK, as in many parts of the world, was predominantly male dominated.[4] However, this trend has shifted dramatically in recent decades.[5]

1. *Early trends.* In the early and mid-20th century, higher education was largely an opportunity afforded to men, with women's participation in universities being relatively rare. Societal norms and legal restrictions often limited women's access to higher education.

2. *Gradual increase in female enrollment.* As societal attitudes began to shift, particularly in the wake of the feminist movements of the 1960s and 1970s, there was a gradual increase in female enrollment in higher education. Legislation and policy changes aimed at promoting gender equality played a significant role in this transformation.

13.2.1   The Emergence and Widening of the Gender Gap

The gender gap in higher education began to emerge and subsequently widen from the late 20th century onward.

*   *Turning point.* The late 20th century marked a turning point when the number of female undergraduates began to surpass that of male undergraduates. This shift was partly due to the changing economic landscape, which placed a higher premium on skills and qualifications that higher education provided.
*   *Factors contributing to the widening gap.* Several factors contributed to the widening of this gap, including changes in the labor market that encouraged more women to pursue higher education, improvements in gender equality, and societal changes in attitudes toward women's education.
*   *Subject choices and cultural shifts.* The gap was further influenced by the subject choices of male and female students, with certain fields of study attracting more women. Cultural shifts also played a role, with changes in perceptions about women's roles in society and the workforce encouraging more women to pursue higher education.

13.2.2   International Comparisons

Analyzing gender disparities in higher education on a global scale provides valuable insights into how different countries address these issues and what strategies have proven successful.[6]

13.2.2.1   Countries With Notable Gender Parity

- *Nordic countries.* Countries like Sweden and Norway have achieved notable gender parity in higher education through policies promoting gender equality, generous parental leave, and robust support systems for students.
- *Germany.* Germany has implemented successful vocational training programs that integrate practical work experience with higher education, appealing to both male and female students.

13.2.2.2   Lessons Learned

- *Policy interventions.* Effective government policies that promote gender equality in education and the workforce can significantly reduce gender disparities.
- *Support systems.* Comprehensive support systems, including financial aid, childcare services, and career counselling, help ensure that all students have equal opportunities to succeed. But more on this in Section 13.6.

13.3   SOCIETAL INFLUENCES ON EDUCATIONAL CHOICES

There are numerous environmental factors which influence educational choices, including the decision to study at all.

13.3.1   Societal Expectations and Norms

Societal expectations and norms play a pivotal role in shaping the educational choices of both men and women. These influences begin early in life and can significantly dictate the trajectory of an individual's educational journey. They include:

1. *Gender-specific expectations.* Traditionally, societal norms have dictated specific roles and expectations for men and women. Men have often been encouraged to pursue careers that emphasize leadership, physical strength, or technical skills, while women have been steered toward roles that are seen as more nurturing or communicative.

2. *Impact on subject choices.* These societal expectations extend to subject choices in higher education. Men may feel societal pressure to choose subjects that align with traditional masculine roles, such as engineering, technology, or business, whereas women may feel more encouraged to pursue fields in the arts, humanities, or social sciences.

13.3.2   The Role of Upbringing

The environment in which children are raised plays a critical role in shaping their future educational choices. These include:

1.   *Family influences.* Family attitudes toward education and specific fields of study can significantly influence children's choices. If a family places a high value on certain professions traditionally associated with one gender, children may be more inclined to follow those paths.

2.   *Early educational experiences.* The encouragement and support children receive in their early learning experiences can also impact their future educational choices. Boys who lack encouragement in reading and writing, for example, may be less likely to pursue courses that heavily involve these skills.

3.   *Economic challenges.* Economic factors play a significant role in men's decisions about higher education.[7] The rising cost of university fees and living expenses can be particularly daunting. Men from lower socio-economic backgrounds may feel the need to enter the workforce immediately after secondary education to support themselves or their families, foregoing higher education.

13.3.3   Other Factors

And there are also several other factors that influence the choice to engage in higher education, including:

1.   *Educational preparedness.* As discussed in the previous chapter, boys' underperformance in secondary education can impact their readiness and eligibility for higher education. Issues with literacy, as well as behavioral and engagement problems in school, can lead to lower academic achievements and reduced opportunities to enter higher education.

2.   *Mental health and well-being.* Mental health issues, which are less frequently discussed and addressed among men, can also act as a barrier. The stress and anxiety associated with the transition to higher education can be daunting, and without adequate support, many men may choose not to pursue further studies.

3.   *Perceptions of higher education.* There is a growing perception among some men that a university degree may not guarantee a better job or career prospects, leading them to question the value of investing in higher education.

4.   *Lack of role models.* The lack of male role models in certain academic fields and in higher education more broadly can deter men from pursuing university degrees. Young men benefit from seeing successful male figures in various fields of study, especially in roles that break traditional stereotypes.

13.4   STEREOTYPES AND SUBJECT CHOICES

Stereotypes associated with different academic fields also play a significant role in contributing to gender disparities in higher education.[8] These stereotypes often dictate which subjects are deemed appropriate or attractive for men and women, influencing their educational and career trajectories, including:

- *Gendered perceptions of subjects.* Certain fields of study are often perceived as inherently "male" or "female." For instance, STEM (science, technology, engineering, and mathematics) fields are traditionally viewed as male-dominated, while subjects like nursing, education, and the arts are seen as more suitable for women. These perceptions can deter students from pursuing interests outside of these gendered norms.[9]
- *Impact on enrollment choices.* The stereotypes surrounding different fields can significantly impact enrollment choices. Men may be less inclined to pursue degrees in fields that are stereotypically seen as feminine, not only due to personal hesitation, but also due to fear of societal judgment or lack of support.

Moreover, the prevalence of gender stereotypes in subjects typically chosen by male students has its own set of implications, including:

- *Reinforcement of masculinity norms.* In male-dominated fields, there is often an implicit reinforcement of traditional masculinity norms, which can create an environment that is less welcoming to women and can perpetuate the gender disparity.
- *Barriers to diversification.* These stereotypes can act as a barrier to diversifying the student population in these fields. Men who do not conform to the traditional masculine archetype might also feel out of place in these subjects, further complicating the issue of gender disparity.

13.5   THE IMPACT OF GENDER DISPARITY IN HIGHER EDUCATION

Gender disparity in higher education, particularly the underrepresentation of men in certain subjects, has significant implications, both in the short and long term. These impacts are felt not only by the individuals directly involved but also by broader society.

13.5.1   Short-Term Impacts

In the immediate context, the gender disparity in higher education can lead to various challenges:

1. *Workforce imbalance.* Certain professions, especially those requiring higher education qualifications, may experience a gender imbalance. Fields traditionally dominated by men may see a shift, which, while beneficial in promoting diversity, can also lead to challenges in workplace dynamics.

2. *Educational experience.* The disparity can affect the educational experience for both genders. A significant imbalance can lead to a lack of diverse perspectives and experiences within the learning environment, potentially impacting academic discussions and collaborations.

3. *Social dynamics on campus.* A skewed gender ratio in universities can alter the social dynamics on campus, potentially impacting student interactions, relationships, and overall campus culture.

13.5.2   Long-Term Impacts

The long-term implications of gender disparity in higher education are then far-reaching:

1. *Workforce and economic consequences.* A persistent gender gap in higher education can lead to broader economic consequences. It could result in a workforce that lacks diversity in certain sectors, impacting innovation, productivity, and economic growth.

2. *Societal roles and perceptions.* This disparity can reinforce or challenge traditional societal roles. As more women enter fields traditionally dominated by men, societal perceptions of gender roles may shift, potentially leading to greater gender equality in various sectors. Conversely, the underrepresentation of men in higher education can perpetuate stereotypes and widen societal divides.

3. *Gender relations and equity.* The education gap can impact gender relations, contributing to disparities in power, earnings, and societal status between men and women. It can also influence personal relationships and family dynamics, especially in cultures where educational attainment is a significant factor in social interactions and partnerships.

13.6   STRATEGIES FOR ADDRESSING THE DISPARITY

The gender gap in higher education requires comprehensive strategies that involve policy changes, educational reforms, and community engagement to create a more balanced and equitable academic environment.

Universities and colleges should implement targeted recruitment programs aimed at attracting more male students, particularly in fields where they are underrepresented. Additionally, support programs that address the specific needs and challenges of male students can help retain and encourage their academic success.

Offering scholarships and financial aid specifically for male students in underrepresented fields could also help alleviate the economic barriers to higher education. Alongside this, establishing mentorship programs where male students can connect with successful male role models in academia can provide guidance and inspiration. This is particularly important in fields that traditionally have fewer male students.

13.6.1   Policy Changes and Educational Reforms

Policy changes and educational reforms are also essential in providing long-term solutions to the gender disparity, including:

1. *Curriculum review and reform.* Reviewing and reforming curricula to ensure they are inclusive and appealing to a diverse student body can help attract a wider range of students. This includes incorporating diverse perspectives and addressing gender stereotypes within academic content.

2. *Flexible learning opportunities.* Implementing flexible learning opportunities, such as part-time courses or online programs, can make higher education more accessible to those who might not be able to commit to traditional full-time programs.

3. *Gender sensitivity training.* Providing gender sensitivity training for educators and administrative staff can help create a more inclusive and supportive environment for all students.

13.6.2   Community-Based Initiatives

Engaging the broader community is also key in changing perceptions and encouraging more men to pursue higher education, such as:

*   *Public awareness campaigns.* Conducting public awareness campaigns to highlight the importance of higher education for men and to

challenge stereotypes that may discourage them from pursuing certain fields of study.
- *Partnerships with schools and organizations.* Building partnerships with schools, nonprofit organizations, and community groups to promote the value of higher education among young men. This could include workshops, talks, and college visits.
- *Support for at-risk youth.* Special attention should be given to at-risk youth, including targeted interventions and mentorship programs, to encourage them to consider higher education as a viable and beneficial path.

13.6.3   Breaking Down Stereotypes

Equally important for achieving gender parity in all fields of study is the addressing and breaking down of stereotypes. This includes:

- *Promoting gender neutrality in subjects.* Efforts must be made to promote the idea that all academic fields are gender-neutral. This involves challenging existing stereotypes and encouraging a more inclusive view of all subjects.
- *Role models and mentorship.* Providing diverse role models and mentors in all fields of study can help break down gender stereotypes. Seeing successful individuals of all genders in various fields can inspire and encourage students to pursue their true interests, regardless of gender norms.

13.7   THE ROLE OF EDUCATIONAL INSTITUTIONS

Universities and colleges themselves play a critical role in addressing gender disparities in higher education. As primary environments where these disparities manifest, these institutions have the responsibility and the capability to implement effective strategies to create a more balanced academic landscape.

For example, higher education institutions should engage in proactive recruitment and outreach efforts aimed at attracting male students, especially in disciplines where they are underrepresented. This could include partnering with schools to provide workshops, career guidance, and scholarships targeted at young men.

Universities and colleges should also develop programs that specifically support the academic and social needs of male students. This can involve tutoring, mentoring, and access to resources that help them navigate the challenges of higher education. It is also crucial for these institutions to cultivate an inclusive culture that values diversity in all its forms. This includes addressing any implicit biases in administrative policies and academic settings that might contribute to the gender gap.

13.7.1   Creating Supportive Environments

Creating supportive environments for male students specifically is key to their academic success and well-being. For example, providing robust mental health and well-being services that cater to the specific needs of male students can help address issues like stress, anxiety, and the pressure to conform to societal expectations.

This could include reviewing and revising curricula and teaching methods to ensure they are inclusive and resonate with a diverse student body, which would have the added benefit of enhancing engagement and academic success for all students. Moreover, encouraging open dialogue about gender disparities and their impacts can help raise awareness and foster understanding among the student and faculty populations.

13.7.2   Societal Change

Higher education institutions also have a role to play in driving broader societal change by conducting research on gender disparities in education and advocating for change at both the policy and societal levels to help address the root causes of these disparities. In addition, engaging with the wider community to challenge stereotypes and norms about gender and education can help shift societal perceptions and encourage more young men to consider higher education.

13.8   CONCLUSION

This chapter has delved into the complex issue of gender disparity in higher education, particularly focusing on the challenges faced by male students in the UK. We have discovered that gender disparity in higher education is a multifaceted issue that requires ongoing attention and collaborative efforts. It is not an issue that can be resolved overnight but requires a sustained and concerted effort from various stakeholders through collaborative strategies, policy and educational reform, and changing societal perceptions.

Through such continued efforts, collaborative strategies, and a commitment to change at both the institutional and societal levels, we can work toward bridging a very clear gap in attainment for men. Indeed, it is imperative that we create a future where higher education is equally accessible and rewarding for all, regardless of gender.

NOTES

1 www.timeshighereducation.com/press-releases/global-universities-address-gender-equality-gaps-remain-be-closed
2 www.hesa.ac.uk/news/19-01-2023/sb265-higher-education-student-statistics

3 O'Connor, P., Carvalho, T., Vabø, A., & Cardoso, S. (2015). Gender in higher education: A critical review. In *The Palgrave international handbook of higher education policy and governance* (pp. 569–584). Palgrave Macmillan London.

4 https://educationalpolicy.org/hello-world/

5 www.universitiesuk.ac.uk/what-we-do/policy-and-research/publications/higher-education-facts-and-figures-2021

6 Stoet, G., & Geary, D. C. (2020). Gender differences in the pathways to higher education. *Proceedings of the National Academy of Sciences, 117*(25), 14073–14076.

7 Reay, D., David, M. E., & Ball, S. J. (2005). *Degrees of choice: Class, race, gender and higher education*. Trentham books.

8 Verniers, C., Bonnot, V., Darnon, C., Dompnier, B., & Martinot, D. (2015). How gender stereotypes of academic abilities contribute to the maintenance of gender hierarchy in higher education. In *Gender and Social Hierarchies* (pp. 26–38). Routledge.

9 Hine, B. (2019). Pick a new# lane: How can we increase boys' participation and interest in literature and language, the arts, nursing, and education and early years? *New Vistas, 5*(1), 24–30.

14

WORK

14.1 INTRODUCTION

The world of work is undergoing a profound transformation, a change that is having a significant impact on men, especially in sectors traditionally dominated by male labor.[1] These include low-paying, manual professions, which have long been the backbone of many economies.

Several distinct changes have occurred, and are occurring, that underpin this shift. First, the rapid advancement of technology and the advent of artificial intelligence (AI) are at the forefront of this transformation, with automation and digitization reshaping industries, and leading to a decline in demand for certain manual jobs traditionally held by men.

Alongside technological progress, economic shifts are altering the nature of employment. There is, and has been for several decades now, a move away from manufacturing and heavy industry to service-oriented and knowledge-based sectors. This transition poses a challenge to those whose skills and experiences are rooted in more traditional industries.

Third, societal needs and priorities are evolving. There is a growing emphasis on sustainable practices, renewable energy, and digital services, sectors that require a different set of skills and expertise than those offered by traditional male-dominated roles.

Understanding the impact of these changes requires a multidimensional view. For example, we must understand that the decline in traditional

DOI: 10.4324/9781032709369-18

male-dominated professions is not just an economic issue; it also has psychological and societal implications. It affects individual self-worth, family dynamics, and broader community structures.

This situation thus necessitates a critical look at how men can adapt to the changing employment landscape. It involves rethinking skills, education, and societal attitudes toward work and gender roles. This will set the stage for discussing the role of policy and education in helping men navigate these changes and highlight the need for strategic planning and support to facilitate this transition.

14.2 HISTORICAL PERSPECTIVES ON MALE-DOMINATED EMPLOYMENT

To understand the current landscape of male-dominated employment, it is essential to look back at its historical context. This mirrors the historical exploration that was taken in Chapter 2, but with this instead focusing much more on men's role as "worker."

Traditionally, certain industries have been predominantly male, both in terms of workforce and cultural perception. This evolution can be traced through various historical periods, each contributing to the current state of male-dominated professions.

14.2.1 Prehistoric and Ancient Times: The Foundations of Male Labor

- *Hunter-gatherer societies.* In early human societies, roles were often divided based on physical capabilities. Men typically took on the roles of hunters, utilizing their physical strength and stamina to procure food, while women gathered plant-based foods and took care of offspring. This division was practical, ensuring the survival of the group.
- *Toolmaking and use.* Men were also involved in creating tools for hunting and defense, which required strength and precision. These early forms of labor laid the groundwork for future specialized roles in societies.

14.2.2 Ancient Civilizations

- *Agriculture and early industries.* With the advent of agriculture, men took on the labor-intensive work of farming, constructing irrigation systems, and building shelters. These tasks required significant physical effort and were thus dominated by men.
- *Crafts and trades.* In ancient civilizations like Mesopotamia, Egypt, Greece, and Rome, men were predominant in skilled trades, such as blacksmithing, masonry, and carpentry. These professions required not only physical strength but also technical knowledge and apprenticeship, which were typically passed from father to son.

- *Military roles.* Men were also the primary warriors and soldiers, defending their communities and expanding territories. Military service was considered a core aspect of masculinity, reinforcing the association of men with strength and protection.

14.2.3   Medieval Times

- *Serfdom and labor.* During the medieval period, the feudal system structured society into rigid classes. Men, particularly those of lower socio-economic status, worked as serfs on the lands of their lords, performing strenuous agricultural labor.
- *Guilds and craftsmen.* The medieval period saw the rise of guilds, which regulated trades and crafts. Guild membership was predominantly male, as most crafts and trades required apprenticeships that were largely inaccessible to women. These guilds controlled the standards of work and often passed down trade secrets through generations of men.
- *Knighthood and chivalry.* The concept of knighthood emerged, where men of noble birth trained from a young age to become knights. This role required rigorous physical training, a deep understanding of martial skills, and a commitment to a code of chivalry, further solidifying the link between masculinity and combat.

14.2.4   The Renaissance

- *Artisans and engineers.* The Renaissance brought about significant advancements in art, science, and engineering. Men like Leonardo da Vinci and Michelangelo were not only artists but also engineers and architects, symbolizing the intellectual and creative heights men could achieve. The period celebrated the "Renaissance man," who was skilled in multiple disciplines.
- *Exploration and trade.* This era was marked by the age of exploration, where men embarked on perilous journeys to discover new lands and trade routes. Figures like Christopher Columbus and Ferdinand Magellan became symbols of bravery and the male spirit of adventure.
- *Scientific endeavors.* Men dominated the emerging scientific fields, conducting experiments and formulating theories that laid the foundation for modern science. This period emphasized rationality and empirical observation, traits culturally ascribed to men.

14.2.5   The Industrial Revolution

- *Mass production and factories.* The Industrial Revolution drastically changed the nature of work. Factories required large numbers of workers to operate machinery, leading to the employment of many men in industrial centers. This period saw a significant shift from agrarian work to industrial labor.

- *Mining and railways.* Industries such as coal mining and railway construction were dangerous and physically demanding, thus attracting predominantly male workforces. These jobs were seen as the backbone of industrial progress and were closely associated with the male identity.
- *Skilled trades and engineering.* The period also saw the rise of skilled trades and engineering professions. Technical knowledge and the ability to innovate were highly valued, and these fields were dominated by men, who had access to education and apprenticeships.

14.2.6   Modern Evolution of Male-Dominated Industries

In modern times, these industries have undergone significant changes, influenced by various factors, including economic shifts and technological advancements.

- *Postwar economic boom and decline.* In the post–World War II era, many Western countries saw a boom in manufacturing and construction, sectors heavily reliant on male labor. However, as economies evolved, many of these industries began to decline, impacted by globalization and the shifting focus to service-oriented sectors.
- *Technological advancements.* The introduction of new technologies in manufacturing, construction, and other traditional industries dramatically changed the nature of work. Automation and computerization began to replace many manual labor jobs, requiring a different skill set that was not always aligned with the traditional workforce.

Several traditional industries are experiencing a decline, influenced by these changing societal trends:

- *Manufacturing industry.* Once the backbone of industrialized economies and a major employer of men, the manufacturing industry has been declining in many developed countries. This is due to factors like automation, globalization, and a shift toward a service-based economy.
- *Mining and heavy industry.* Mining and other heavy industries are also in decline, partly due to environmental concerns and the push toward renewable energy sources. These industries have historically employed large numbers of men and often defined entire communities.
- *Agriculture.* Technological advancements and corporate farming practices have led to fewer jobs in agriculture, a sector that traditionally employed a significant male workforce.

14.2.7   The Impact of Technological Advancements

The rapid advancement of technology in recent decades has been a major catalyst in transforming these traditional industries, including:

- *Automation and job displacement.* Many manual labor jobs that were historically the domain of men have been significantly impacted by automation. Robotics, AI, and machine learning are reshaping the manufacturing and construction industries, leading to job displacement.[2]
- *Changing skill requirements.* The skills required in these evolving industries have shifted. There is a growing need for digital literacy, technical know-how, and adaptability, skills that may not be present in the traditional workforce.

Several industries are at the forefront of this technological disruption:

Manufacturing. Once dominated by manual labor, manufacturing is increasingly automated. Assembly lines that used to require human hands are now operated by robots, leading to a decrease in the demand for traditional manufacturing jobs.

Transportation and logistics. The rise of autonomous vehicles and drone technology is transforming the transportation sector. Jobs like truck driving, a traditionally male-dominated field, are facing significant changes with the advent of self-driving technology.

Construction. Technological advancements in construction, including the use of AI for planning and drones for surveying, are changing the nature of construction work, traditionally a stronghold of male employment.

14.2.8   The Influence of Societal Evolution on Employment

The landscape of employment is also being reshaped not only by technological advancements but also by significant shifts in societal needs and trends. These changes are influencing the nature of employment opportunities, leading to the decline of certain industries and the emergence of new ones. This includes changes in:

- *Shift toward service and knowledge economy.* There is a growing shift from manufacturing and manual labor to service-oriented and knowledge-based sectors. This transition reflects changes in consumer needs, economic priorities, and global market trends. As a result, industries like information technology, health care, and education are expanding, often at the expense of more traditional sectors.
- *Environmental awareness and sustainable practices.* The increasing awareness of environmental issues and the need for sustainable

practices is leading to the growth of industries focused on renewable energy, environmental conservation, and sustainable development. These emerging fields are creating new job opportunities, albeit in areas that may not align with traditional male skill sets or interests.

- *Technology and digital industries.* The technology sector, especially areas related to digital services, software development, and AI, is rapidly expanding. While offering new opportunities, these fields require a different skill set than traditional male-dominated industries.
- *Health-care and social services.* With an aging population and evolving societal needs, health-care and social services are growing sectors. These fields, however, have not traditionally attracted a large male workforce, highlighting a potential area for workforce diversification.
- *Creative and cultural industries.* The creative and cultural industries, including digital media, design, and entertainment, are also on the rise. These industries offer new avenues for employment but may require retraining and upskilling for those transitioning from more traditional roles.

14.3   CHALLENGES FACED BY MEN IN THE EVOLVING JOB MARKET

And so, as the job market evolves rapidly due to technological advancements and societal changes, men face a unique set of challenges. These challenges are not just about acquiring new skills but also involve adapting to a fundamentally altered employment landscape, including:

1. *Skill mismatch and obsolescence.* One of the primary challenges is the mismatch between existing skills and the requirements of new job markets. Men who have spent years or even decades in industries now in decline may find their skills outdated or irrelevant, making it difficult to transition to emerging sectors.

2. *Re-education and reskilling.* The need for re-education and reskilling presents a significant challenge. Many men may need to return to education or training programs to acquire new skills, which can be a daunting and resource-intensive process.

3. *Age-related challenges.* Older men may face age-related challenges when competing in new job markets, where employers often prioritize younger workers, who are perceived as more adaptable or technologically savvy.

14.3.1   Psychological Impact

The psychological impact of these changes on men is profound and multifaceted, including on:

1.   *Identity and self-worth.* For many men, their work is closely tied to their identity and sense of self-worth. Losing a job or being unable to find employment in their field can lead to feelings of inadequacy and a loss of identity.

2.   *Stress and mental health.* The uncertainty and pressure to adapt can lead to increased stress, anxiety, and in some cases, depression. The societal expectation for men to be the breadwinners can exacerbate these mental health issues.[3]

3.   *Family and relationships.* These challenges can also strain family dynamics and personal relationships. The stress of job loss or career change can affect personal interactions and family responsibilities.

14.3.2   Socioeconomic Impact

The socioeconomic implications of these challenges are also significant and affect:

1.   *Economic stability.* The inability to adapt quickly to new job markets can lead to economic instability, affecting not just individual men but also their families and communities.

2.   *Labor market dynamics.* As traditional male-dominated jobs decline, there may be a shift in labor market dynamics, including potential wage gaps and changes in the structure of the workforce.

3.   *Social fabric.* These changes can alter the social fabric of communities, especially those that were heavily reliant on now-declining industries. It can lead to changes in community structures and roles, with far-reaching social implications.

14.3.3   The Skills Gap and Education

The current job market is thus characterized by a significant skills gap, which poses a major challenge for male employment, especially for those transitioning from declining industries. This gap reflects the mismatch between the skills possessed by the workforce and those demanded by employers in emerging sectors. For example, as many industries increasingly integrate technology and automation, there is a growing demand for technological proficiency. Men from traditional, less-tech-focused industries may therefore find their skills outdated or insufficient.

Beyond technical skills, employers are also seeking soft skills, such as adaptability, problem-solving, and communication. The evolving job market requires workers who can navigate complex, dynamic environments, which can be a shift from more traditional, structured work settings. Men seeking to enter new industries may thus face barriers due to a lack of relevant skills, particularly in fast-growing fields like IT, health care, and renewable energy. Moreover, this inability to bridge the skills gap can lead to prolonged periods of unemployment or underemployment, affecting economic stability and growth prospects.

14.4   OPPORTUNITIES IN EMERGING INDUSTRIES

However, as traditional industries face decline due to technological advancements and changing societal needs, new and emerging industries are opening up, offering fresh opportunities for employment. For men looking to transition from traditional roles, these sectors represent a new frontier of possibilities. However, transitioning to these emerging industries requires strategic planning and action, including:

1. *Skills development and education.* For many men, transitioning to new sectors may require going back to school or undertaking vocational training. This might involve earning certifications, degrees, or attending workshops and courses relevant to their desired field.

2. *Leveraging transferable skills.* It is important for men to identify and leverage transferable skills they possess from their previous roles. Skills such as project management, team leadership, and problem-solving are valuable across various industries.

3. *Networking and mentorship.* Building a network in a new industry can be crucial for finding opportunities and understanding industry dynamics. Seeking mentorship from experienced professionals in these emerging sectors can provide guidance and insight during the transition.

14.4.1   Tapping Into Support Resources

Utilizing available resources can facilitate this transition, for example, by utilizing:

1. *Career counseling and job placement services.* Many organizations offer career counseling and job placement services that can help men identify opportunities in new sectors and navigate the job search process.

2. *Government and community programs.* Government-led initiatives and community programs often provide support for workforce retraining and development, especially in rapidly growing sectors.

14.4.2   The Role of Education and Vocational Training

Education and vocational training also play a crucial role in bridging the skills gap, by encouraging and facilitating:

1. *Re-education and lifelong learning.* Higher education institutions and vocational training centers are pivotal in providing re-education and upskilling opportunities. Tailored programs that focus on the needs of men transitioning from traditional industries can facilitate this process.

2. *Access to education and training.* Making education and training programs accessible and affordable is crucial. This includes offering flexible learning options, like part-time courses, online education, and night classes, to accommodate those who may be working or have other commitments.

3. *Industry–academia collaboration.* Collaboration between educational institutions and industries ensures that the training and skills provided are aligned with current market demands. Such partnerships can also provide practical experience and networking opportunities, enhancing employment prospects.

14.4.3   Policy Responses and Support Systems

As the job market evolves rapidly, government and institutional policies play a crucial role in supporting workers affected by these changes. These policies are essential for facilitating smooth transitions for men moving out of declining industries and into emerging sectors. Specifically, we need:

1. *Workforce retraining programs.* Many governments have introduced workforce retraining programs aimed at equipping displaced workers with skills relevant to growing industries. These programs often focus on sectors like technology, health care, and renewable energy.

2. *Educational subsidies and grants.* Policies that provide subsidies or grants for education and training can lower the barriers for men seeking to retrain or upskill. This financial support is crucial for those who might otherwise be unable to afford further education.

3. *Unemployment assistance and career services.* Enhanced unemployment assistance, coupled with career counseling and job placement services, can provide a safety net for those transitioning between jobs. This assistance often includes résumé building, interview preparation, and job search strategies.

14.4.4   Institutional Support Systems

Institutions such as universities, vocational schools, and community colleges also play a key role in supporting workforce transition, by offering:

1. *Flexible learning options.* Offering flexible learning options, including online courses, night classes, and part-time programs, can accommodate those who need to balance education with other commitments.

2. *Partnerships with industries.* Establishing partnerships with industries allows educational institutions to develop programs that align with current job market needs, ensuring that the skills taught are directly relevant to emerging job opportunities.

3. *Apprenticeships and internships.* Apprenticeship and internship programs, often developed in collaboration with industry partners, provide practical, hands-on experience, making them an invaluable part of the transition process.

14.4.5   Community-Based Initiatives

Local community initiatives also contribute significantly to the support system. For example, community centers and local organizations can offer workshops and training sessions in skills that are in demand in the local job market. Networking events and support groups can also provide emotional support, as well as opportunities for professional connections and mentorship.

14.4.6   Addressing Mental Health and Well-Being

Recognizing the psychological impact of career transitions, policies and programs also need to address mental health and well-being, with:

1. *Counseling and mental health services.* Providing access to counseling and mental health services can help men navigate the stresses and challenges associated with changing careers or facing unemployment.

2. *Well-being programs.* Well-being programs that focus on stress management, work–life balance, and resilience can be beneficial for those undergoing significant career changes.

14.4.7   Example Organizations

Here are some example organizations that are already focusing on how to best support men in the workplace:

- Spring Health's Recommendations for Supporting Men's Mental Health
  Description: Spring Health provides strategies for employers to support men's mental health, focusing on working fathers. These include offering one-on-one parent coaching, normalizing mental health conversations in the workplace, providing paid paternity leave, offering flexible work schedules, and increasing access to mental health resources. These measures aim to create a supportive environment that helps men balance work and family responsibilities while maintaining their mental well-being. Website: www.springhealth.com/.
- WorkingDads.co.uk
  Description: WorkingDads.co.uk offers guidance on supporting working fathers, suggesting the creation of parent networks, including dad-specific support groups, and promoting senior role models to normalize parental leave for men. The platform emphasizes the importance of inclusive communication that challenges gender stereotypes and encourages open discussions about work–life balance and childcare responsibilities. Website: www.workingdads.co.uk/.

14.5   THE FUTURE OF MALE EMPLOYMENT

The landscape of male employment is clearly at a pivotal point, with ongoing technological and societal changes shaping its future. Predicting these trends is key to preparing and adapting to the evolving job market. For example, automation and AI are expected to continue growing, impacting a wide range of industries. This trend will likely lead to a further decrease in traditional manual jobs while simultaneously creating new opportunities in tech-driven fields.

The shift toward service and knowledge-based industries is also set to persist, with sectors like health care, education, and digital services expanding. These fields may offer new opportunities for employment, albeit requiring different skill sets. As technology evolves, entirely new job roles that we cannot yet predict are likely to emerge. These roles will require adaptability and a commitment to lifelong learning.

14.5.1   Strategies for Adaptability and Resilience

In the face of these changes, men need to adopt strategies that ensure adaptability and resilience, including these key approaches:

1. *Embracing lifelong learning.* One of the most crucial strategies is a commitment to lifelong learning. This involves continuously updating skills and knowledge to stay relevant in the changing job market.

2. *Flexibility in career paths.* Being open to diverse career paths and being willing to transition between different roles and industries are becoming increasingly important.

3. *Digital literacy and technical skills.* Prioritizing the development of digital literacy and technical skills can position men favorably in the job market, as these skills are becoming essential across various industries.

4. *Soft skills development.* Alongside technical skills, soft skills, such as communication, teamwork, problem-solving, and emotional intelligence, are becoming increasingly valued by employers in the modern workforce.

5. *Entrepreneurship and self-employment.* Exploring entrepreneurship and self-employment as viable career options can also be a way to adapt to the changing job landscape. This path can offer flexibility and the opportunity to capitalize on emerging market trends.

14.5.2 Preparing for the Future

Preparing for the future of employment involves both personal and collective efforts. Governments and educational institutions should continue to evolve policies and curricula to support the development of skills relevant to future job markets. Collaboration between community organizations, industry, and educational institutions can help identify emerging job trends and develop targeted training programs. And as the nature of work changes, prioritizing mental health and well-being will be essential in helping men navigate career transitions and maintain resilience in the face of change.

14.6 CONCLUSION

This chapter has explored the multifaceted and dynamic landscape of male employment in the face of rapid technological and societal changes. The key points discussed provide a comprehensive understanding of the current and future challenges in the job market.

We have highlighted how automation, AI, and shifts in societal needs are fundamentally altering traditional employment sectors, particularly those dominated by men. The challenges men face in adapting to these changes, including skill mismatches and the psychological impact of transitioning from declining industries, have also been underscored.

However, new and emerging industries also present opportunities for employment, underscoring the need for flexibility and adaptability in career paths. And so, the essential roles of policy responses, institutional support, and community initiatives in facilitating smooth transitions for men affected by job market changes have also been discussed.

As the world of work continues to evolve, the ability of men to adapt, learn, and grow is more crucial than ever. This chapter underscores the need for a proactive approach to employment challenges, emphasizing the importance of education, skill development, and comprehensive support systems.

By embracing these strategies, men can navigate the changing employment landscape successfully, ensuring their place in the workforce of the future and contributing positively to the global economy.

NOTES

1 Reeves, R. V. (2022). *Of boys and men: Why the modern male is struggling, why it matters, and what to do about it.* Brookings Institution Press.
2 www.brookings.edu/articles/the-differing-impact-of-automation-on-men-and-womens-work/
3 www.mind.org.uk/news-campaigns/news/mind-survey-finds-men-more-likely-to-experience-work-related-mental-health-problems/

15

WORK–LIFE BALANCE

15.1 INTRODUCTION

Work–life balance refers to the equilibrium that individuals strive to achieve between their professional responsibilities and their personal lives.[1] This balance is essential for maintaining both productivity and overall well-being. When work demands overshadow personal time, it can lead to stress, burnout, and deteriorating mental and physical health. Conversely, neglecting work responsibilities can result in job dissatisfaction and financial instability.

The importance of work–life balance is monumental. It plays a critical role in ensuring that individuals can fulfill their professional duties while also nurturing their personal relationships and interests. Achieving this balance allows for a more holistic and satisfying life experience, fostering mental resilience, emotional stability, and physical health. Moreover, a well-balanced life contributes to higher job satisfaction, improved performance, and greater engagement in both work and personal activities.

In today's fast-paced and ever-connected world, the struggle to maintain a work–life balance is a common challenge for both men and women. Societal expectations and traditional gender roles further complicate this struggle, particularly for men, who are often perceived as primary breadwinners. Understanding the factors that influence work–life balance and finding

DOI: 10.4324/9781032709369-19

effective strategies to manage them are crucial for promoting healthier, more fulfilling lives for everyone.

15.2 SOCIETAL EXPECTATIONS AND TRADITIONAL GENDER ROLES

The history of the working role was covered in the previous chapter, and the progression of work–life balance, or lack of it, largely mirrors this progression. Specifically, as men have traditionally been seen as the working party in households, this has led to a prioritization of work for men above most other elements of life, and most would argue this is out of necessity rather than choice. But let us unpack that a little further and look at the way that those expectations impact work–life balance.

15.2.1 The Breadwinner Role

The concept of the breadwinner role has been a defining element of traditional masculinity for generations. Historically, men have been expected to take on the primary responsibility of providing financial support for their families. This expectation is rooted in patriarchal structures that emphasize male dominance in the public sphere, particularly in economic activities. The breadwinner role not only dictates a man's professional life but also shapes his identity and sense of self-worth. The pressure to meet this expectation can lead to long working hours, high stress levels, and a diminished capacity to engage in family and personal activities, thereby impacting overall well-being.

15.2.2 Societal Pressures and Masculine Norms

Societal pressures and masculine norms play a significant role in shaping men's experiences with work–life balance. From a young age, men are often socialized to value traits such as competitiveness, self-reliance, and stoicism. These cultural norms reinforce the idea that a man's success is measured by his professional achievements and financial contributions.[2] The stigma surrounding vulnerability and emotional expression further complicates men's ability to seek help or openly discuss the challenges they face in balancing work and personal life. These societal pressures create an environment where men feel compelled to prioritize work over personal well-being and familial relationships, often at the expense of their mental and physical health.[3]

15.2.3 Changes in Gender Roles Over Time

While traditional gender roles have long dominated societal expectations, significant changes have occurred over the past several decades. The feminist movement and increasing advocacy for gender equality have challenged the rigid division of labor between men and women. More women have entered the workforce, and there has been a growing recognition of the importance of shared domestic responsibilities. These shifts have begun to redefine what it means to be a man in the modern world, promoting a more balanced approach to work and family life.

Despite these advancements, many men still grapple with the remnants of traditional gender roles. The expectation to be the primary breadwinner persists in many cultures, creating tension between evolving ideals and entrenched norms. However, younger generations are increasingly rejecting these outdated notions, embracing more flexible and equitable approaches to work and family responsibilities. This ongoing evolution in gender roles is crucial for fostering an environment where both men and women can achieve a healthier work–life balance.

Overall, understanding the impact of societal expectations and traditional gender roles on men's work–life balance highlights the need for continued cultural and structural change. By challenging outdated norms and promoting more inclusive and supportive practices, society can help men navigate the complexities of modern life with greater ease and fulfillment.

15.3   THE IMPACT ON MENTAL HEALTH

Work demands can be a significant source of stress and anxiety for men striving to balance their professional and personal lives.[4] The constant pressure to perform, meet deadlines, and achieve career goals can lead to chronic stress. This stress is often exacerbated by the expectation to remain constantly available, thanks to modern technology that blurs the lines between work and personal time. Men may feel overwhelmed by the relentless demands of their job, leading to heightened anxiety and a sense of being perpetually on edge. Over time, this can result in a decreased ability to concentrate, sleep disturbances, and other physical symptoms, such as headaches and high blood pressure.

15.3.1   Depression and Burnout

Chronic stress and anxiety can pave the way for more severe mental health issues, such as depression and burnout. Men experiencing these conditions may struggle with feelings of hopelessness, irritability, and a lack of motivation. The societal pressure to fulfill the breadwinner role can intensify these feelings, as men may perceive themselves as failing if they cannot maintain the expected level of professional success. Burnout, characterized by emotional exhaustion, depersonalization, and reduced personal accomplishment, can further diminish a man's quality of life. It often leads to disengagement from work, strained relationships, and a pervasive sense of fatigue that makes it difficult to manage even daily tasks.

15.4   EFFECTS ON RELATIONSHIPS

Work–life balance also significantly impacts relationship satisfaction. When men struggle to balance their professional and personal lives, it can lead to tension and conflict within their marriages. Long working hours and the stress associated with demanding jobs can reduce the quality time spent with spouses, causing feelings of neglect and dissatisfaction. This can lead to communication breakdowns and a lack of emotional intimacy, which are crucial for maintaining a healthy relationship. Conversely, men who manage to achieve a better work–life balance often report higher levels of marital satisfaction. They are more present and engaged in their marriages, fostering stronger emotional bonds and mutual support.

15.4.1   Parenting and Family Dynamics

Balancing work and family responsibilities is crucial for positive parenting and healthy family dynamics, and this will be explored further in Chapter 17 on fatherhood. When work demands encroach on family time, men may find it challenging to fulfill their roles as active and involved fathers.[5] This can lead to a disconnection from their children's lives, missing out on important milestones and everyday interactions that are vital for building strong parent–child relationships. Moreover, the stress from work can spill over into family life, affecting the overall atmosphere at home.

On the other hand, men who successfully balance work and family life can contribute more meaningfully to parenting. They are able to participate in their children's activities, provide emotional support, and model positive behavior. This active involvement promotes healthier family dynamics, where children feel supported and valued and partners share the responsibilities of raising a family.

15.4.2   Social Connections and Friendships

Work–life balance also affects social connections and friendships. Men who are overwhelmed by work commitments often have limited time and energy to invest in their social lives. This can lead to isolation and a weakened support network, which are important for emotional well-being and stress relief. Friendships offer a crucial outlet for relaxation, shared experiences, and emotional support, which are essential for maintaining mental health.

Maintaining a healthy work–life balance allows men to nurture their social connections and friendships. Regular social interactions contribute to a sense of community and belonging, providing opportunities to unwind and recharge. These relationships can offer different perspectives and support during challenging times, enhancing overall life satisfaction.

15.5   OVERALL WELL-BEING

Maintaining a poor work–life balance can also have significant physical health consequences.[6] Long hours at work and high levels of stress can lead to a sedentary lifestyle, poor diet, and inadequate sleep, all of which contribute to various health issues. Common physical health problems associated with work-related stress include cardiovascular diseases, hypertension, and obesity. Additionally, chronic stress can weaken the immune system, making individuals more susceptible to illnesses and infections. Men who do not prioritize physical health may also experience musculoskeletal problems, such as back pain and repetitive strain injuries, due to prolonged sitting and poor ergonomics.

15.5.1   Emotional and Psychological Well-Being

The struggle to achieve a work–life balance also profoundly affects emotional and psychological well-being. Men facing excessive work demands often experience high levels of stress, anxiety, and depression. The constant pressure to perform and succeed can lead to feelings of inadequacy and low self-esteem. Moreover, the lack of time for relaxation and leisure activities exacerbates these emotional struggles, creating a vicious cycle of stress and mental fatigue.

Emotional well-being is further compromised when men neglect personal relationships and social activities due to work commitments. Isolation and lack of social support can intensify feelings of loneliness and depression. Over time, this can lead to burnout, characterized by emotional exhaustion, detachment from work, and a sense of reduced personal accomplishment. Addressing emotional and psychological well-being is crucial for maintaining a healthy work–life balance and overall quality of life.

15.5.2   Long-Term Life Satisfaction

Achieving a balanced work–life dynamic is essential for long-term life satisfaction, and men who successfully manage their professional and personal responsibilities are more likely to experience a sense of fulfillment and happiness. They can pursue their passions, maintain meaningful relationships, and engage in activities that bring them joy and relaxation. This holistic approach to life enhances overall satisfaction and well-being.

Conversely, an imbalanced work–life dynamic can lead to long-term dissatisfaction and regret. Men who prioritize work over personal life may find themselves missing out on important life experiences and milestones. This can result in a sense of unfulfillment and disappointment in the long run. Additionally, chronic stress and poor health can diminish the quality of life, making it difficult to enjoy achievements and successes.

Prioritizing work–life balance contributes to a sustainable and satisfying life. It allows men to build a life that is rich in experiences, relationships, and personal growth, leading to greater long-term happiness and well-being. By recognizing the importance of balance and taking proactive steps to achieve it, men can enhance their overall life satisfaction and enjoy a healthier, more fulfilling life.

15.6   TECHNOLOGICAL IMPACT

The advent of modern technology, particularly smartphones and remote working tools, has drastically altered the landscape of work–life balance. While technology has facilitated greater flexibility and connectivity, it has also blurred the lines between work and personal life, creating unique challenges and opportunities for achieving balance.

15.6.1   Increased Connectivity and Flexibility

Modern technology allows for increased connectivity and flexibility in the workplace. Employees can work from anywhere at any time, which can lead to greater autonomy and the ability to balance work with personal commitments more effectively. Remote working tools such as videoconferencing platforms, project management software, and cloud-based document sharing have enabled seamless collaboration across geographical boundaries. This flexibility can help employees manage their schedules better, reducing the need for long commutes and allowing for a more adaptable approach to work hours.

15.6.2   Blurred Boundaries and Overwork

However, the same technology that provides flexibility can also lead to the erosion of boundaries between work and personal life.[7] The expectation to be constantly available and responsive can lead to an "always-on" culture, where employees feel compelled to check emails and messages outside of regular working hours. This can result in longer working hours, increased stress, and burnout, as individuals struggle to disconnect from work and enjoy personal time.

Technology can also introduce digital distractions that affect productivity. Social media, instant messaging, and non-work-related online activities can divert attention and time away from work tasks, leading to inefficiencies and the need to work longer hours to compensate. This can further disrupt the balance between work and personal life.

15.6.3   Strategies for Managing Technology Use to Improve Balance

While we are on technology specifically, here are some strategies for managing technology use to improve work–life balance (with more wide ranging strategies discussed shortly):

1. *Establish clear boundaries.* One of the most effective strategies for managing technology use is to establish clear boundaries between work and personal time. Setting specific times for checking and responding to work emails and messages can help create a defined separation. Turning off notifications outside of work hours and using "do not disturb" settings can also reduce the temptation to engage with work-related tasks during personal time.

2. *Utilize technology wisely.* Leveraging technology to enhance productivity and streamline tasks can help manage work more efficiently. Using project management tools to organize tasks, set deadlines, and track progress can improve time management and reduce the need for overtime. Calendar applications can help schedule work tasks and personal activities, ensuring that both are given appropriate attention.

3. *Promote a healthy work culture.* Organizations can promote a healthy work culture by encouraging employees to disconnect after work hours. Leaders should model this behavior by refraining from sending emails or messages during evenings and weekends. Establishing policies that support flexible working arrangements and respect personal time can foster a more balanced work environment.

4. *Practice digital detox.* Regularly practicing digital detox can help reduce the mental strain associated with constant connectivity. Designating specific times or days for unplugging from digital devices can allow individuals to recharge and focus on personal relationships and activities. This can improve overall well-being and prevent burnout.

5. *Encourage open communication.* Encouraging open communication about technology use and work–life balance can help address issues before they become problematic. Employees should feel comfortable discussing their challenges and seeking support from managers and colleagues. Regular check-ins and feedback sessions can provide opportunities to assess and adjust technology use to better support work–life balance.

By adopting these strategies, individuals and organizations can harness the benefits of modern technology while mitigating its potential drawbacks. Achieving a healthy work–life balance in the digital age requires intentional effort and ongoing adjustments to ensure that technology serves as a tool for enhancing, rather than hindering, overall well-being.

15.7   STRATEGIES FOR PROMOTING BETTER BALANCE

Beyond technology specifically, how can men achieve better work–life balance? Most of the upcoming section (as well as many of the issues in this chapter) is applicable to men and women, but I will also draw out where it is relevant specifically to men.

15.7.1   Organizational Policies and Support Systems

Organizations play a crucial role in fostering work–life balance for their employees. Implementing supportive policies and systems can significantly enhance employee well-being and productivity. Flexible work arrangements, such as remote work options, flexible hours, and compressed workweeks, allow employees to manage their time more effectively. Providing access to mental health resources, including counseling services and stress management programs, can help employees cope with work-related pressures.

Creating a culture that values work–life balance is equally important. Organizations can encourage this by promoting regular breaks, discouraging excessive overtime, and recognizing the importance of personal time. Training managers to support their team's work–life balance efforts and implementing family-friendly policies, such as parental leave and childcare support, further contribute to a healthier work environment. Crucially, organizations need to overcome their own prejudices and biases to ensure that all policies are applicable and accessible to male as well as female employees, including fathers.

15.7.2   Time Management and Prioritization Techniques

Effective time management and prioritization are essential for achieving work–life balance. Men can benefit from techniques that help them allocate their time and energy more efficiently. One such technique is the Eisenhower Matrix, which categorizes tasks based on their urgency and importance, helping individuals focus on what truly matters and avoid time-wasting activities.

Setting clear goals and breaking them down into manageable tasks can also improve productivity and reduce overwhelm. Using tools like to-do lists, calendars, and project management software can help organize and track progress. Additionally, learning to delegate tasks and set boundaries around work hours ensures that personal time is protected and respected.

15.7.3   The Role of Communication and Negotiation

Communication and negotiation skills are also vital for maintaining a healthy work–life balance, and men need to communicate their needs and boundaries effectively to their employers, colleagues, and family members. For example, openly discussing workload, deadlines, and personal commitments can lead to better understanding and collaboration in the workplace.

Negotiating flexible work arrangements or reasonable deadlines requires confidence and clarity about one's limits and priorities. Traditionally, it is women that have been seen to struggle with this issue, however men may also struggle to prioritize things that go against the stereotypes of what working men should value, which will affect their confidence. It is therefore important to approach these conversations with a solution-oriented mindset, proposing alternatives that meet both personal and organizational needs. Effective communication and negotiation can reduce work-related stress and create a more supportive environment for balancing professional and personal responsibilities.

15.7.4   Personal Development and Self-Care Practices

Investing in personal development and self-care is crucial for sustaining work–life balance.[8] Workers should prioritize activities that promote physical, emotional, and mental well-being, including regular exercise, a balanced diet, and adequate sleep form the foundation of good health and energy levels. Engaging in hobbies and leisure activities also provides a necessary break from work and fosters creativity and relaxation.

Mindfulness practices, such as meditation and deep breathing exercises, can also help manage stress and improve focus. Building a strong support network of friends, family, and mentors offers emotional support and perspective during challenging times. Setting aside time for self-reflection and personal growth activities, such as reading, learning new skills, or pursuing interests, enhances overall life satisfaction and resilience. For men, there might be a challenge overcoming stereotypes that would normally prohibit engagement with these types of activities.

By integrating these strategies, men can better navigate the demands of work and personal life, achieving a more harmonious and fulfilling balance. Implementing supportive organizational policies, mastering time management, communicating effectively, and prioritizing self-care are all essential steps toward promoting better work–life balance.

15.7.5   Coping Mechanisms and Resilience

There are also various other coping mechanisms and strategies that men can employ to build resilience and improve their mental health. For example, seeking social support is another essential coping mechanism. Talking to friends, family, or a mental health professional can provide much-needed emotional support and perspective. It is important for men specifically to recognize that asking for help is a sign of strength, not weakness.

Building resilience involves developing a positive outlook and focusing on personal growth. Men can benefit from engaging in activities that foster a sense of purpose and fulfillment outside of work, such as hobbies, volunteering, or continuing education. Developing strong time management skills and establishing clear boundaries between work and personal life can also contribute to a healthier balance.

By adopting these coping mechanisms and resilience-building strategies, men can better navigate the challenges of work demands and maintain a healthier mental state. Recognizing the impact of work on mental health and proactively addressing it are essential for achieving a balanced and fulfilling life.

15.7.6   Future Trends

The future of work–life balance will be significantly shaped by emerging trends, such as the gig economy, artificial intelligence (AI), and automation. As more individuals engage in gig work, flexibility in work schedules is expected to become the norm, allowing for a better integration of personal and professional responsibilities. AI and automation will likely reduce the burden of repetitive tasks, freeing up time for more meaningful and creative endeavors. Innovative approaches to future work–life balance challenges will include adaptive work environments, personalized wellness programs powered by AI, and policies promoting continuous learning and skill development to keep pace with technological advancements. These solutions aim to create a more balanced, efficient, and fulfilling work–life experience.

15.8   INTERGENERATIONAL PERSPECTIVES

It is also important to note that work–life balance is perceived and approached differently by various generational cohorts, each shaped by the unique cultural, economic, and technological contexts of their formative years. Understanding these differences is crucial for addressing the specific challenges and needs of each generation, particularly for men, who often face unique pressures related to traditional gender roles and societal expectations. Let's look at each subset in turn:

> *Baby boomers (born 1946–1964).* Baby boomer men were raised during a time when the traditional breadwinner role was heavily emphasized. Many were socialized to prioritize their careers and financial stability above personal well-being and family time. As a result, work–life balance was often seen as secondary to professional success. For many baby boomer men, long working hours and a strong work ethic were viewed as necessary sacrifices for providing for their families.

Generation X (born 1965–1980). Generation X men grew up witnessing their baby boomer parents' work-centric lifestyles and the impact it had on family dynamics. As a result, many have sought a more balanced approach to work and personal life. This generation values independence and flexibility, often striving to achieve a better work–life balance than their predecessors did. They tend to be more skeptical of corporate loyalty and are more likely to seek out work environments that offer flexibility and respect personal time.

Millennials (born 1981–1996). Millennial men entered the workforce during the rise of digital technology and the gig economy. They place a high value on work–life balance and are more likely to prioritize experiences, personal growth, and mental health over traditional career paths. Millennials are comfortable with remote work and flexible schedules, and they often seek employers who offer these benefits. This generation tends to challenge traditional gender roles more openly, advocating for shared domestic responsibilities and equal parenting roles.

Generation Z (born 1997–2012). Generation Z men are the first true digital natives, having grown up with technology as an integral part of their lives. They value flexibility, diversity, and mental health, and they expect work environments to accommodate these priorities. This generation is likely to continue challenging traditional norms around masculinity and work, seeking roles that allow for a more integrated approach to personal and professional life. They are also more vocal about the need for mental health support and work environments that promote overall well-being.

15.8.1   Tailored Strategies for Each Generational Cohort

Now let's see some specific strategies for men in each cohort.

15.8.1.1   *Baby Boomers*

- *Retirement planning and transition support.* Offer programs that help baby boomers transition into retirement, allowing for a gradual reduction in work hours and responsibilities.
- *Health and wellness programs.* Provide resources that focus on physical health and stress management to address the long-term effects of years of hard work.
- *Flexible work arrangements.* Encourage part-time or consulting roles to help baby boomers maintain engagement without the pressures of full-time work.

15.8.1.2   *Generation X*

- *Work flexibility.* Offer flexible work hours and remote work options to help balance professional and personal responsibilities.

- *Career development opportunities.* Provide opportunities for skill development and career growth to keep Gen X engaged and motivated.
- *Family support policies.* Implement family-friendly policies, such as parental leave and childcare support, to reduce the stress of juggling work and family duties.

15.8.1.3 Millennials

- *Flexible work environments.* Emphasize flexibility in work schedules and locations to align with millennials' desire for work–life integration.
- *Mental health resources.* Offer comprehensive mental health support, including counseling and wellness programs, to address the high value this generation places on mental well-being.
- *Purpose-driven work.* Create opportunities for millennials to engage in meaningful work that aligns with their values and allows for personal growth.

15.8.1.4 Generation Z

- *Technological integration.* Leverage technology to provide flexible and remote work options that suit Generation Z's digital fluency.
- *Diversity and inclusion.* Promote a diverse and inclusive work environment that respects and supports various lifestyles and backgrounds.
- *Mental health focus.* Prioritize mental health initiatives, including access to mental health services and creating a supportive work culture that encourages open discussions about well-being.

By understanding and addressing the unique perspectives and needs of each generational cohort, particularly men, organizations can create a more supportive and balanced work environment. This approach not only enhances individual well-being but also fosters greater engagement and productivity across the workforce.

15.9 ECONOMIC IMPLICATIONS

Work–life balance is a critical factor influencing productivity and economic growth. For men, balancing professional and personal responsibilities can lead to improved mental and physical health, increased job satisfaction, and higher overall productivity. When men are able to manage their work–life balance effectively, they are less likely to experience burnout, absenteeism, and turnover, all of which can negatively impact organizational performance and economic growth. Additionally, balanced lives contribute to more innovative and creative thinking, further driving economic progress.

Moreover, work–life balance for men is intrinsically a feminist issue. When men take on a fair share of domestic responsibilities, it supports the advancement of gender equality by alleviating the disproportionate burden often placed on women.[9] This equitable distribution of labor allows women to pursue their careers and contribute to economic growth, leading to a more diverse and inclusive workforce. Encouraging men to engage in family and domestic roles not only benefits their well-being but also fosters a more balanced and productive society.

15.9.1   Cost–Benefit Analysis for Organizations

It is important to highlight that implementing work–life balance initiatives can also yield substantial benefits for organizations. The initial costs of introducing flexible work arrangements, mental health resources, and family-friendly policies are outweighed by the long-term gains in employee productivity and retention. Organizations that support work–life balance for men are also likely to see reduced health-care costs due to lower stress-related illnesses and improved overall employee health.

From a financial perspective, companies with strong work–life balance programs can attract and retain top talent, reducing recruitment and training costs associated with high turnover rates. Moreover, fostering a supportive work environment enhances employee morale and engagement, leading to higher levels of performance and innovation. This, in turn, can drive revenue growth and competitive advantage.

The economic benefits of promoting work–life balance also extend beyond individual organizations. On a macroeconomic level, a workforce that is healthier and more satisfied contributes to greater economic stability and growth. When men are encouraged to balance their work and personal lives, the broader economy benefits from increased productivity, lower health-care costs, and a more equitable distribution of labor between genders, supporting overall societal well-being.

By recognizing the economic implications and prioritizing work–life balance for men, organizations can create a more sustainable and prosperous future for all. This approach not only enhances individual well-being but also drives economic growth and promotes gender equality, underscoring the interconnectedness of work–life balance and broader societal progress.

15.10   CONCLUSION

Achieving work–life balance is an ongoing journey that requires continuous effort and adaptation. As personal and professional demands evolve, so too must the strategies and practices that support balance. Men must remain vigilant in assessing their priorities and making adjustments to ensure that neither work nor personal life is disproportionately impacted. Embracing flexibility and maintaining an open mindset are thus key to navigating this dynamic landscape successfully. Importantly, the journey toward balance is not about perfection but about finding a sustainable and fulfilling equilibrium that enhances overall well-being.

To support men in their quest for better work–life balance, broader cultural and structural changes are essential. Societal norms and expectations around gender roles need to evolve to recognize and value the diverse contributions men make both at work and at home. This includes challenging traditional notions of masculinity that equate success solely with professional achievement and financial provision.

The struggle for work–life balance is clearly a multifaceted challenge that affects men's mental health, relationships, and overall well-being. Looking to the future, it is important to continue advocating for changes that support work–life balance at both individual and systemic levels. Encouraging open dialogue about the challenges and successes of balancing work and personal life can help normalize these experiences and reduce the stigma associated with seeking help. Research and innovation in flexible work practices, mental health support, and organizational development will be crucial in addressing the evolving needs of the workforce.

NOTES

1 Khan, O. F., & Fazili, A. I. (2016). Work life balance: A conceptual review. *Journal of Strategic Human Resource Management, 5*(2).
2 Emslie, C., & Hunt, K. (2009). 'Live to work'or 'work to live'? A qualitative study of gender and work – life balance among men and women in mid-life. *Gender, Work & Organization, 16*(1), 151–172.
3 Rudman, L. A., & Mescher, K. (2013). Penalizing men who request a family leave: Is flexibility stigma a femininity stigma? *Journal of Social Issues, 69*(2), 322–340.
4 Haar, J. M., Russo, M., Suñe, A., & Ollier-Malaterre, A. (2014). Outcomes of work – life balance on job satisfaction, life satisfaction and mental health: A study across seven cultures. *Journal of Vocational Behavior, 85*(3), 361–373.
5 Raiden, A. B., & Räisänen, C. (2013). Striving to achieve it all: Men and work-family-life balance in Sweden and the UK. *Construction Management and Economics, 31*(8), 899–913.
6 Lunau, T., Bambra, C., Eikemo, T. A., van Der Wel, K. A., & Dragano, N. (2014). A balancing act? Work – life balance, health and well-being in European welfare states. *The European Journal of Public Health, 24*(3), 422–427.
7 Adisa, T. A., Gbadamosi, G., & Osabutey, E. L. (2017). What happened to the border? The role of mobile information technology devices on employees' work-life balance. *Personnel Review, 46*(8), 1651–1671.
8 Evans, A. M., Carney, J. S., & Wilkinson, M. (2013). Work – life balance for men: Counseling implications. *Journal of Counseling & Development, 91*(4), 436–441.
9 Chung, H., & Van der Lippe, T. (2020). Flexible working, work – life balance, and gender equality: Introduction. *Social Indicators Research, 151*(2), 365–381.

Section 5

RELATIONSHIPS AND FATHERHOOD

16

FRIENDSHIP AND ROMANCE

16.1 INTRODUCTION

This chapter delves into the nuanced world of male friendships and romantic relationships, exploring how these vital connections are formed, sustained, and sometimes challenged. The focus is on understanding the unique aspects of men's interpersonal relationships across different stages of their lives and in different contexts.

Specifically, the chapter examines the dynamics of male friendships, considering how societal norms, personal growth, and life changes influence these bonds.[1] It investigates how men establish and nurture friendships and the common hurdles they face in maintaining them. It also explores the evolving landscape of dating and romance from a male perspective. It then discusses the challenges posed by modern dating practices, shifts in societal expectations, and the impact of technology. It then considers how changes in traditional institutions like marriage affect men's experiences and expectations in long-term relationships.

Broadly, it aims to provide a comprehensive understanding of these aspects of men's lives, offering insights into the complexities of male friendships and the multifaceted nature of their romantic relationships. It seeks to shed light on the strategies men can employ to navigate these personal connections effectively and the support systems that can aid them in this journey.

DOI: 10.4324/9781032709369-21

16.2   THE FORMATION OF MALE FRIENDSHIPS

The development of male friendships is shaped by numerous factors and changes across the lifespan.

16.2.1   Development Across Life Stages

Male and female friendships evolve through various life stages, influenced by distinct societal and psychological factors:

1. *Childhood and adolescence.* During early and middle childhood, friendships for both boys and girls tend to develop similarly. These friendships are typically formed around shared activities and interests, fulfilling similar psychological needs, such as companionship and mutual support. Schools and neighborhoods play a critical role in facilitating these friendships, which are predominantly about shared experiences and having fun together. As children approach adolescence, however, the importance of gender becomes more pronounced. Interests begin to diverge, and friendships start to take on gendered characteristics, such as differences in group size and conversation dynamics.

2. *Young adulthood.* In young adulthood, the influence of gender on friendships becomes even more pronounced. Friendship groups are increasingly dictated by gendered interests and social roles. Men and women often gravitate toward activities and discussions that align with societal expectations of their gender. For men, friendships often form around shared activities, such as sports, work-related events, or hobbies. Men tend to have a larger number of friends, but these relationships are often characterized by less-intense emotional bonds compared to women's friendships. Women, on the other hand, may have fewer friends but engage in deeper, more emotionally supportive relationships. These differences reflect broader social patterns, where men might prioritize shared activities and practical support while women often seek emotional closeness and detailed personal sharing in their friendships.

3. *Midlife and beyond.* As people age, friendships often revolve around shared life circumstances like family, work, or common hobbies. For men, these friendships tend to focus more on emotional support and shared values, deepening in quality and significance. Additionally, as gendered norms become less salient with age, the nature of men's friendships can change. Older men may start to place more value on emotional intimacy and personal connection, similar to the depth traditionally seen in women's friendships. This shift can be influenced by life experiences, such as retirement, the empty nest syndrome, or personal losses, which encourage men to seek and appreciate deeper, more

emotionally fulfilling relationships. The reduction of societal pressure to conform to traditional gender roles allows for more flexibility in how friendships are formed and maintained in later life.

16.2.2   Societal and Psychological Influences

So, we can see that in childhood and beyond, the nature of male friendships is significantly influenced by societal norms and psychological factors, including:

1. *Societal expectations.* Cultural norms about masculinity can impact how men form and maintain friendships.[2,3] Societal expectations often emphasize independence, emotional stoicism, and competition, which can influence the depth and expression of male friendships.

2. *Emotional expression.* Psychological factors, including how men are socialized to express emotions, play a crucial role. Men may find it challenging to express vulnerability in friendships, impacting the intimacy and supportiveness of these relationships.

3. *Changing social dynamics.* In the modern world, societal changes such as digital communication and urbanization are reshaping how friendships are formed and sustained. Online interactions, for example, can both facilitate and hinder the depth of friendships.

16.2.3   Team Sports and Group Activities

To a greater extent than girls and women, team sports and group activities play a significant role in the formation and maintenance of male friendships.[4] These activities provide structured environments where men can bond over shared goals, experiences, and achievements, including:

1. *Bonding through competition.* Team sports, such as soccer, basketball, and rugby, offer a platform for men to engage in healthy competition and camaraderie. The shared experiences of training, competing, and striving for common goals foster strong bonds among teammates. These friendships often extend beyond the field, creating a sense of brotherhood and mutual support.

2. *Shared accomplishments.* Participating in team sports allows men to celebrate successes and navigate challenges together. The collective joy of winning and the shared disappointment of losing build a sense of unity and trust among team members. These shared experiences can create lasting memories and deepen friendships.

3. *Regular interaction.* Team sports require regular practice sessions, games, and meetings, providing consistent opportunities for interaction and bonding. This regular contact is essential for maintaining friendships, as it allows men to connect and support each other consistently.

4. *Physical and mental well-being.* Engaging in sports promotes physical fitness and mental well-being, which can positively impact friendships. The release of endorphins during physical activity can enhance mood and reduce stress, making men more open to social interactions and emotional connections.

16.2.4   Social Clubs and Community Groups

Social clubs and community groups offer additional avenues for men to form and sustain friendships.[5] These groups often provide opportunities for:

1. *Shared interests.* Social clubs centered on hobbies such as photography, hiking, or cooking attract men with similar interests. These shared passions create common ground for conversation and bonding, making it easier to form friendships.

2. *Community engagement.* Community groups focused on social causes or volunteer work provide opportunities for men to connect while contributing to their communities. Working together toward a common cause fosters a sense of purpose and camaraderie, strengthening the bonds between members.

3. *Support networks.* Social clubs and community groups often serve as support networks, offering emotional and practical support to their members. This sense of community can be especially important during times of personal or professional challenges, providing a safety net of friends who can offer advice, encouragement, and assistance.

4. *Inclusive environments.* Many social clubs and community groups strive to create inclusive environments where members feel welcomed and valued. This inclusivity can help men from diverse backgrounds find common ground and build meaningful friendships.

16.2.5   Virtual Connections

The rise of digital communication technologies has also transformed the way men form and maintain friendships.[6] Virtual connections, facilitated by social media, messaging apps, and video calls, offer new opportunities and challenges for male friendships which help with:

1. *Ease of communication.* Technology enables men to stay connected with friends regardless of geographical distance. Social media platforms and messaging apps allow for instant communication, making it easier to maintain friendships despite busy schedules or physical separation.

2. *Maintaining long-distance friendships.* For men who move away from their hometowns or countries, virtual connections provide a means to maintain existing friendships. Video calls and online chats help bridge the gap, allowing friends to share experiences and support each other in real time.

3. *Online communities.* Virtual spaces such as forums, interest-based groups, and social media communities offer platforms for men to connect with others who share similar interests or experiences. These online communities can provide a sense of belonging and support, especially for men who may feel isolated in their offline lives.

However, while technology facilitates communication, it can also pose challenges. Virtual interactions may lack the depth and emotional richness of face-to-face conversations. Men may find it harder to express vulnerability or build deep emotional connections online compared to in-person interactions.

16.2.6   Gaming Communities

Online gaming communities have become a significant social arena where men can form and maintain friendships. These communities provide unique opportunities for bonding through:

1. *Shared gaming experiences.* Multiplayer games such as Fortnite, World of Warcraft, and Call of Duty create immersive environments where players can collaborate and compete. The shared experiences of strategizing, overcoming challenges, and achieving in-game goals foster strong bonds among gamers.

2. *Social interaction.* Online gaming platforms often include features such as voice chat and messaging, enabling real-time communication during gameplay. These interactions allow players to build camaraderie, share tips, and support each other, enhancing the social aspect of gaming.

3. *Inclusive and diverse communities.* Gaming communities are often diverse, bringing together players from different backgrounds and locations. This diversity can enrich friendships by exposing men to different perspectives and cultures, fostering inclusivity and mutual understanding.

    Support networks. For some men, gaming communities serve as important support networks. The sense of belonging and connection within these communities can provide emotional support, reduce feelings of loneliness, and offer a safe space to discuss personal challenges.

16.4   THE FUNCTION OF MALE FRIENDSHIPS AND HOMOSOCIALITY

Once they are formed, male friendships serve multiple essential functions deeply intertwined with the concept of *homosociality* – the preference for same-sex social relationships.[7] Understanding these functions provides valuable insights into how men navigate their social worlds and maintain emotional well-being.

16.4.1   Emotional Support and Mental Health

Male friendships play a crucial role in providing emotional support, which is vital for mental health.[8] Despite societal norms often discouraging men from expressing vulnerability, close male friendships can offer a safe space for sharing feelings and experiences. This emotional exchange helps in reducing stress, combating loneliness, and fostering a sense of belonging. Friends can act as confidants, offering advice, empathy, and a different perspective on personal issues.

16.4.2   Social Identity and Belonging

Friendships among men also often serve as a foundation for social identity and a sense of belonging. Through shared activities, interests, and experiences, men can form strong bonds that affirm their identity and provide a community. Whether through sports teams, hobby groups, or professional networks, these friendships help men feel connected to a larger group, reinforcing their social roles and personal values.

16.4.3   Homosociality and Social Networks

Homosociality, the tendency for men to seek out and prioritize relationships with other men, significantly shapes male friendships. This phenomenon is not merely about companionship but also about building social networks that can provide various forms of capital, such as career opportunities, social influence, and support systems. These networks often extend into professional and personal realms, creating a web of connections that can be leveraged for mutual benefit.

16.4.4   Shared Activities

Engaging in shared activities is also a common way for men to bond and sustain friendships. Activities like sports, gaming, or DIY projects offer structured environments where men can connect through teamwork and mutual interests. These shared experiences create a sense of camaraderie and collective achievement, reinforcing the friendship through regular interaction and cooperation.

16.4.5   Navigating Social Hierarchies

Male friendships also play a role in navigating social hierarchies. Within homosocial groups, friendships can help men gain status, respect, and influence. By aligning with peers who share similar values or goals, men can reinforce their social standing and create alliances that support their aspirations. These dynamics are evident in various settings, from school playgrounds to corporate boardrooms.

16.4.6   The Rise of Bromance

In recent years, the concept of "bromance" has emerged as a significant cultural phenomenon, reshaping the landscape of male friendships.[9,10] A *bromance*, a close but nonromantic relationship between two men, challenges traditional notions of masculinity by allowing emotional intimacy, affection, and support to flourish. This trend has been influenced by a shift in societal attitudes toward gender roles and emotional expression, where men are increasingly encouraged to break free from the constraints of stoicism and independence. Popular media has played a pivotal role in normalizing bromances, with numerous films, television shows, and public figures celebrating these deep, platonic bonds.[11] Bromances provide a safe space for men to express vulnerability, share personal experiences, and support each other's emotional needs, fostering stronger and more resilient friendships. As such, the rise of bromance marks a progressive step toward more inclusive and emotionally fulfilling male relationships.[12]

16.5   CHALLENGES IN MAINTAINING MALE FRIENDSHIPS

Sadly, some of the masculinity norms we have discussed previously in this book make it hard for men to maintain their friendships.

16.5.1   Navigating the Hurdles of Friendship

Male friendships, while enriching, can encounter various challenges that impact their longevity and depth. Understanding these challenges is key to fostering lasting connections. Some challenges include:

1. *Societal expectations of masculinity.* Societal norms about masculinity often discourage emotional openness and vulnerability, essential aspects of deep, supportive friendships. Men may feel pressure to conform to a stoic, independent ideal, which can hinder the development of close bonds.

2. *Life transitions and priorities.* Major life transitions such as marriage, parenthood, career changes, or relocation can strain friendships. As priorities shift, maintaining old friendships can become challenging, often leading to diminished contact and connection.

3. *Communication barriers.* Men often face barriers in communication, especially when it comes to expressing emotions or discussing personal struggles. This can lead to misunderstandings and a lack of emotional support within friendships.

4. *Lack of initiatives for reconnection.* Unlike romantic relationships, there are fewer societal structures or initiatives that encourage reconnection or strengthening of male friendships, especially when they have been strained or have lapsed.

16.5.2   Changes Postparenthood

The transition to parenthood brings significant changes to a man's life, including shifts in friendships.[13] As new responsibilities and priorities emerge, the dynamics of male friendships often undergo considerable transformation.

1. *Time constraints.* Parenthood introduces a host of new time demands, from childcare duties to family activities. These responsibilities can reduce the amount of time available for socializing with friends. Men may find it challenging to balance their roles as fathers with maintaining pre-existing friendships.

2. *Shifts in priorities.* The arrival of a child often shifts priorities toward family and parenting responsibilities. Activities and interests that once fostered friendships might take a back seat to family needs. This shift can lead to a natural distancing from friends who do not share similar life stages or responsibilities.

3. *Changing social circles.* New fathers may find that their social circles change as they spend more time with other parents. Parenting groups, school activities, and child-centric events become common venues for social interaction, leading to the formation of new friendships based on shared parenting experiences.

4. *Emotional changes.* The emotional impact of becoming a parent can also affect friendships. The joy, stress, and exhaustion associated with parenthood may alter how men relate to their friends. Some men may seek out friends who can empathize with their new experiences, while others may struggle to find common ground with friends who are not parents.

5. *Reduced spontaneity.* Parenthood often requires more planning and less spontaneity in social interactions. The ability to engage in impromptu gatherings or activities may decrease, as family commitments take precedence. This change can affect the frequency and nature of interactions with friends.

Clearly, there is a lot more to do to help men develop and maintain healthy, fruitful friendships.

16.6 THE CHANGING DATING MARKET

Men also face challenges in the formulation of romantic relationships too.

16.6.1 Evolution of the Dating Landscape

The dating landscape has undergone significant changes in recent times, largely influenced by technological advancements and shifting societal norms.[14] This can be attributed to:

1. *Technological impact.* The rise of online dating platforms and apps has transformed the way people meet and interact.[15] This digital revolution offers new opportunities but also presents challenges in terms of navigating online communication and establishing genuine connections.

2. *Shifting societal attitudes.* There is a shift in societal attitudes toward dating, with more emphasis on casual relationships and less on traditional courtship. This change affects how men approach dating and relationships.

3. *Evolutionary models and dating dynamics.* Evolutionary psychology suggests that men and women have evolved different strategies for

selecting mates, influenced by perceived high-value and low-value traits. These models can create confusion and unrealistic expectations in the modern dating scene, as individuals navigate between instinctual preferences and contemporary norms.

4. *Incel behavior and backlash toward feminism.* A growing movement of men identifying as "incels" (involuntary celibates) has emerged, often characterized by frustration and hostility toward perceived societal changes that they believe disadvantage them in the dating market. This group's backlash toward feminism and evolving gender roles can influence broader societal attitudes and behaviors in the dating landscape.

16.6.2   Challenges and Opportunities for Men

Men thus face various challenges and opportunities in this new dating environment, including:

1. *Adapting to online platforms.* Navigating online dating platforms requires adaptability and a different set of skills, such as creating an appealing online profile and effective text communication.

2. *Balancing expectations.* Men must balance traditional expectations with modern dating norms, often navigating ambiguous situations and mixed messages.

3. *Opportunities for broader connections.* The digital age provides opportunities to connect with a more diverse range of people, potentially leading to richer experiences and relationships.

4. *Dealing with rejection.* The fast-paced, often impersonal nature of modern dating can also lead to more frequent experiences of rejection, which men need to manage healthily.

16.7   NAVIGATING MODERN DATING

Navigating the modern dating world requires men to adapt to new technologies and societal changes. The digital era has transformed dating, making skills like digital literacy and effective online communication crucial. They have to keep up with:

1. *Understanding online dating platforms.* Men need to become proficient in using various online dating platforms.[16] This includes creating engaging profiles, understanding the nuances of online communication, and being aware of online dating etiquette.

2. *Effective communication skills.* With the prevalence of texting and mes-saging, effective communication has become key. This means being clear, respectful, and engaging in conversations.

3. *Awareness of social media influence.* Social media plays a significant role in modern dating. Understanding its impact on perceptions and relationships is important for navigating dating successfully.

4. *Balancing online and in-person interactions.* While technology is a use-ful tool, the importance of in-person interactions cannot be understated. Developing the ability to connect in real life remains essential.

5. *Adapting to changing societal norms.* The modern dating scene is marked by changing societal norms around relationships and gender roles. Men must be adaptable and open-minded in their approach to dating.

16.8   LONG-TERM RELATIONSHIPS AND CHANGING INSTITUTIONS

The landscape of long-term relationships, particularly institutions like mar-riage, has undergone significant changes, influencing men's experiences and expectations. This includes:

1. *Shifting views on marriage.* There has been a notable shift in how mar-riage is perceived and experienced. Traditional roles within marriage are evolving, challenging men to adapt to new dynamics in partnership and household responsibilities.

2. *Increased focus on equality and partnership.* Modern relationships often emphasize equality, with a focus on shared responsibilities and emotional support. This shift challenges the traditional view of men as primary providers or decision-makers.

3. *Delayed marriages and changing priorities.* Societal trends show a ten-dency toward delayed marriages and prioritizing personal and career development. Men are navigating how to balance these priorities with the desire for long-term relationships.

4. *Impact of divorce and relationship breakdowns.* Higher rates of divorce and relationship breakdowns have also affected men's approach to long-term relationships, impacting their willingness to commit and their approach to trust and partnership.

16.8.1   Societal Expectations and Norms

These changing societal expectations also play a crucial role in shaping men's experiences in relationships, including:[17]

1. *Balancing independence and commitment.* Navigating the balance between maintaining independence and committing to a shared life is a key challenge in modern relationships.

2. *Communication and emotional intelligence.* The increasing importance of open communication and emotional intelligence in relationships requires men to develop and utilize these skills effectively.

3. *Redefining success in relationships.* Success in long-term relationships is increasingly defined by mutual support, shared growth, and emotional fulfillment, rather than just traditional markers like longevity or societal status.

16.3   CULTURAL AND CONTEXTUAL INFLUENCES ON FRIENDSHIPS AND ROMANTIC RELATIONSHIPS

Truly understanding the dynamics of male friendships and romantic relationships also requires a deep dive into how cultural, sexual orientation, and geographical factors interplay. This section explores the unique practices and expectations in various cultures, the distinctive challenges faced by GBTQ+ men, and the strategies for maintaining long-distance relationships in an increasingly mobile and digitally connected world.

16.3.1   Friendship and Romance in Different Cultural Contexts

Cultural norms and values significantly influence how men form and maintain friendships and romantic relationships.[18], [19] These variations are rooted in societal expectations, traditions, and communal practices that shape interpersonal dynamics.

16.3.1.1   *Cultural Variations*

*   *Collectivist cultures.* In collectivist societies, such as those in many parts of Asia, Africa, and Latin America, friendships and romantic relationships are often deeply embedded in a network of familial and community ties. These relationships emphasize loyalty, group harmony, and long-term commitment. Men in these cultures often form friendships through family connections, educational institutions, or local communities, with regular social gatherings reinforcing these bonds.
*   *Individualist cultures.* In contrast, individualist cultures, like those prevalent in North America and Western Europe, prioritize personal autonomy and self-expression. Friendships and romantic relationships in these contexts may be more fluid, centered on shared interests and activities rather than long-term commitment. While these relationships can be

highly rewarding, they may also be more susceptible to changes in personal circumstances or interests.

16.3.1.2   Expression of Emotions

- *Western cultures.* There is a growing acceptance of emotional openness and vulnerability among men in many Western cultures. However, traditional notions of masculinity that emphasize stoicism and independence can still create barriers to deep emotional connections.
- *Mediterranean and Middle Eastern cultures.* In some Mediterranean and Middle Eastern cultures, expressive forms of emotional bonding among men, such as physical touch and verbal affirmations, are common and enhance the emotional depth of friendships.

16.3.1.3   Immigration and Cultural Adaptation

For men who migrate to new cultural environments, maintaining and forming friendships can present unique challenges and opportunities. The process of adapting to a new culture often requires navigating different social norms and expectations around friendship.

1. *Navigating new social norms.* Immigrant men often face the challenge of understanding and integrating into the social norms of their new environment. This can include adapting to different ways of expressing friendship and emotional support. For instance, men from collectivist cultures may find it challenging to adjust to the more individualistic nature of friendships in Western countries, where friendships might be less interdependent and more centered on shared activities or interests.

2. *Building new friendships.* Forming new friendships in a different cultural context can be daunting. Language barriers, cultural misunderstandings, and social isolation can hinder the process. However, immigrant men often find community and support through cultural associations, religious groups, or local community centers that provide a familiar cultural environment.

3. *Maintaining cultural identity.* While adapting to a new culture, it is also important for immigrant men to maintain connections with their cultural heritage. Friendships with fellow immigrants or individuals from similar cultural backgrounds can provide a sense of continuity and support. These relationships can help men navigate the complexities of cultural adaptation while preserving their cultural identity.

4. *Intercultural friendships.* Developing friendships with individuals from different cultural backgrounds can enrich the immigrant experience. These intercultural friendships provide opportunities for mutual learning and cultural exchange, helping to bridge cultural gaps and foster understanding. For immigrant men, these relationships can also serve as a crucial support system, providing insights into navigating the new cultural landscape.

16.3.2   Friendship and Relationship Dynamics in LGBTQ+ Communities

Men in LGBTQ+ communities navigate a unique set of challenges and experiences in forming and maintaining friendships and romantic relationships. These dynamics are heavily influenced by societal attitudes and the level of acceptance within their communities.

16.3.2.1   *Challenges*

- *Social stigma and discrimination.* GBTQ+ men often face societal stigma and discrimination, which can impact their ability to form and sustain meaningful social connections. This external pressure can lead to feelings of isolation and fear of being open about their identities.
- *Finding community.* GBTQ+ men frequently seek out supportive communities where they can build friendships and romantic relationships free from judgment.[20] These safe spaces are crucial for fostering healthy social networks.

16.3.2.2   *Strategies for Support*

- *Safe spaces.* Creating and promoting safe spaces for GBTQ+ men to meet and connect are vital. These environments provide a sense of security and acceptance, enabling the formation of deep and supportive relationships.[21] There are also other safety benefits associated with friendship for LGBTQ+ individuals when using online apps and in dating.[22, 23]
- *Support groups.* Participating in LGBTQ+ support groups and community organizations can offer a sense of belonging and mutual support, helping men navigate the complexities of their identities.

16.3.3   Long-Distance Friendships and Relationships

In today's globalized world, long-distance friendships and romantic relationships have become increasingly common.[24] These relationships present unique challenges that require specific strategies to sustain.

16.3.3.1   Challenges

- *Communication barriers.* Differences in time zones and limited opportunities for face-to-face interaction can strain long-distance relationships. Maintaining regular and meaningful communication can be difficult.
- *Emotional distance.* The lack of physical presence can make it challenging to maintain emotional intimacy and connection.

16.3.3.2   Strategies for Maintenance

- *Regular communication.* Establishing regular communication routines, such as scheduled video calls and consistent messaging, helps maintain connection and intimacy. Tools like videoconferencing, social media, and messaging apps play a crucial role in bridging the distance.
- *Shared activities.* Engaging in shared activities, even from a distance, can help create a sense of togetherness. This can include watching movies simultaneously, playing online games, or participating in virtual events.
- *Planning visits.* Whenever possible, planning regular visits to spend quality time together can reinforce the bond and provide much-needed physical closeness.

16.9   STRATEGIES FOR BUILDING AND MAINTAINING RELATIONSHIPS

Building and maintaining strong friendships and romantic relationships are crucial for personal well-being. For men, forming these connections can sometimes be challenging due to societal expectations and pressures. Here are specific strategies that can help men navigate these challenges effectively:

1. Practice Open and Honest Communication: Men often face societal pressures to appear strong and stoic, which can make open communication challenging. However, cultivating the ability to express thoughts and feelings clearly and authentically is essential. Start by sharing your thoughts with close friends or partners, and encourage them to do the same. This will create a foundation of trust and mutual understanding.

2. Develop Emotional Intelligence: Emotional intelligence is about recognizing and managing your emotions and understanding the emotions of others. For men, this might mean breaking through the stereotype that emotions are a sign of weakness. Practice empathy by actively listening to others and reflecting on how your actions might affect them. This helps in building deeper, more meaningful connections.

3. Embrace Flexibility and Adaptability: In relationships, rigidity can be a barrier to growth. Being open to change and compromise shows strength and maturity. Whether it's adjusting your expectations or being willing to see things from another's perspective, flexibility can help you navigate the ups and downs of friendships and romantic relationships.

4. Prioritize Regular Engagement and Quality Time: Life can get busy, but making time for the people who matter is crucial. For men, this could mean scheduling regular hangouts with friends or planning meaningful activities with a partner. It's about showing that you value these relationships by investing your time and energy into them.

5. Build Trust and Respect: Trust and respect are foundational elements of any relationship. For men, being consistent, reliable, and supportive are key ways to build these pillars. Show up for your friends and partners when they need you, and always act with integrity. Trust is earned over time, so focus on being a dependable presence in others' lives.

6. Strengthen Conflict Resolution Skills: Disagreements are inevitable, but how you handle them can make or break a relationship. For men, it's important to approach conflicts with a calm and solution-oriented mindset. Practice active listening, avoid escalation, and seek common ground. Effective conflict resolution is about addressing issues directly without letting them fester.

These strategies highlight how men can leverage communication, emotional intelligence, and adaptability to build and maintain fulfilling and enduring relationships. By focusing on these areas, men can form deeper connections that enhance their overall well-being.

16.9.1   Support Systems for Fathers in Particular

While parenthood can strain friendships, it also provides opportunities for building new support systems that are crucial for the well-being of fathers including:

1. *Parenting groups.* Joining parenting groups or dad-specific meetups can offer new fathers a sense of community and shared understanding. These groups provide a space to share experiences, seek advice, and form bonds with other fathers facing similar challenges.

2. *Family-oriented friendships.* Developing friendships with other families can create a support network that benefits both parents and children. Family-oriented activities allow fathers to socialize while their children

play together, fostering relationships that accommodate the needs of the entire family.

3. *Work–life balance.* Employers and communities can support new fathers by promoting work–life balance. Flexible work schedules, paternity leave, and supportive workplace policies can help fathers spend more time with their families without sacrificing their social lives.

4. *Mental health resources.* Access to mental health resources and counseling can help new fathers navigate the emotional challenges of parenthood. Support groups, therapy, and online resources can provide the necessary tools to manage stress and maintain healthy relationships.

5. *Involvement in child's activities.* Actively participating in a child's activities, such as school events, sports, or hobbies, can open new avenues for social interaction. Fathers who engage in these activities often meet other parents, creating opportunities for friendship and mutual support.

6. *Communication with partners.* Open and honest communication with partners about the need for social interaction and personal time is vital. Partners can support each other in maintaining friendships by sharing parenting duties and encouraging each other to pursue social engagements.

16.10 CONCLUSION

This chapter has provided a comprehensive look at the evolving nature of male friendships and romantic relationships. Key points include the development of male friendships across different life stages, the impact of societal expectations and communication barriers, and the evolving dating landscape. Emphasis was placed on the importance of emotional intelligence, adaptability, and communication in maintaining these relationships. The chapter also highlighted the need for policy changes and societal support to aid men in developing healthy relationship skills. In conclusion, understanding and supporting men in building and sustaining meaningful relationships is crucial for their emotional well-being and social fulfillment.

NOTES

1   Greif, G. (2008). *Buddy system: Understanding male friendships*. Oxford University Press.
2   Migliaccio, T. (2010). Men's friendships: Performances of masculinity. *The Journal of Men's Studies*, *17*(3), 226–241.

3 Arxer, S. L. (2011). Hybrid masculine power: Reconceptualizing the relationship between homosociality and hegemonic masculinity. *Humanity & Society, 35*(4), 390–422.

4 Weiss, M. R., & Smith, A. L. (2002). Friendship quality in youth sport: Relationship to age, gender, and motivation variables. *Journal of Sport and Exercise Psychology, 24*(4), 420–437.

5 Swann, C., Telenta, J., Draper, G., Liddle, S., Fogarty, A., Hurley, D., & Vella, S. (2018). Youth sport as a context for supporting mental health: Adolescent male perspectives. *Psychology of Sport and Exercise, 35*, 55–64.

6 Gibbons, E. (2017). *Masculinity, gaming, friendship and intimacy, and sense of community: A comparison of men in virtual and offline domains.* Texas Woman's University.

7 Hammarén, N., & Johansson, T. (2014). Homosociality: In between power and intimacy. *Sage Open, 4*(1), 2158244013518057.

8 McKenzie, S. K., Collings, S., Jenkin, G., & River, J. (2018). Masculinity, social connectedness, and mental health: Men's diverse patterns of practice. *American Journal of Men's Health, 12*(5), 1247–1261.

9 Robinson, S., Anderson, E., & White, A. (2018). The bromance: Undergraduate male friendships and the expansion of contemporary homosocial boundaries. *Sex Roles, 78*(1), 94–106.

10 Robinson, S., & Anderson, E. (2022). *Bromance: Male friendship, love and sport.* Springer Nature.

11 Kulshrestha, S. (2011). I get by with a little help from my bros: An analysis of the male homosocial relationship on 'how I met your mother'. *Inquiries Journal, 3*(1).

12 Scoats, R., & Robinson, S. (2020). From stoicism to bromance: Millennial men's friendships. In *The Palgrave handbook of masculinity and sport* (pp. 379–392). Springer International Publishing.

13 Höfner, C., Schadler, C., & Richter, R. (2011). When men become fathers: Men's identity at the transition to parenthood. *Journal of Comparative Family Studies, 42*(5), 669–686.

14 Eaton, A. A., & Rose, S. (2011). Has dating become more egalitarian? A 35 year review using sex roles. *Sex Roles, 64*, 843–862.

15 Alexopoulos, C., Timmermans, E., & McNallie, J. (2020). Swiping more, committing less: Unraveling the links among dating app use, dating app success, and intention to commit infidelity. *Computers in Human Behavior, 102*, 172–180.

16 Sumter, S. R., Vandenbosch, L., & Ligtenberg, L. (2017). Love me Tinder: Untangling emerging adults' motivations for using the dating application Tinder. *Telematics and Informatics, 34*(1), 67–78.

17 Haywood, C., & Haywood, C. (2018). (Post) Dating masculinities: From courtship to a post-dating world. In *Men, Masculinity and Contemporary Dating* (pp. 25–54). Palgrave Macmillan London.

18 Kaplan, D. (2022). *The men we loved: Male friendship and nationalism in Israeli culture.* Berghahn Books.

19 Wulff, H. (2022). Inter-racial friendship: Consuming youth styles, ethnicity and teenage femininity in South London. In *Youth cultures* (pp. 63–80). Routledge.

20 Roe, S. L. (2015). Examining the role of peer relationships in the lives of gay and bisexual adolescents. *Children & Schools, 37*(2), 117–124.

21 Gillig, T., & Bighash, L. (2019). Gendered spaces, gendered friendship networks? Exploring the organizing patterns of LGBTQ youth. *International Journal of Communication*, *13*, 22.

22 Byron, P., Albury, K., Pym, T., Race, K., & McCosker, A. (2019). Trust in friendship: LGBTQ+ young people and hook-up app safeties. *AoIR Selected Papers of Internet Research*.

23 Byron, P., Albury, K., & Pym, T. (2021). Hooking up with friends: LGBTQ+ young people, dating apps, friendship and safety. *Media, Culture & Society*, *43*(3), 497–514.

24 Belus, J. M., Pentel, K. Z., Cohen, M. J., Fischer, M. S., & Baucom, D. H. (2019). Staying connected: An examination of relationship maintenance behaviors in long-distance relationships. *Marriage & Family Review*, *55*(1), 78–98.

17

FATHERHOOD

17.1 INTRODUCTION

Fatherhood has experienced a remarkable evolution over recent decades, transitioning from traditional roles to more engaged and nurturing forms of parenting.[1] This transformation is not merely a change in behavior but a reflection of broader social dynamics that challenge old stereotypes and create new expectations for what it means to be a father today.

This chapter will explore these themes, examining the historical context of fatherhood, the challenges contemporary fathers face, and the psychological journey of fatherhood. It will also discuss the impact of father involvement on child development, opportunities for change and growth, and strategies for supporting fathers in their parenting roles. Through this comprehensive exploration, I aim to provide a deeper understanding of the evolving nature of fatherhood in today's society.

17.2 THE HISTORICAL CONTEXT OF FATHERHOOD

The role of fathers has undergone significant transformations over time, shaped by various social, economic, and cultural forces.[2] Understanding the historical context of fatherhood provides valuable insights into how and why these changes have occurred.

DOI: 10.4324/9781032709369-22

17.2.1   Evolutionary Perspective on Fatherhood

From an evolutionary standpoint, the role of fathers has been crucial for the survival and success of offspring.[3] In many species, including humans, paternal investment increases the likelihood of offspring survival and success. Anthropologists suggest that early human societies relied on cooperative breeding, where fathers, along with other group members, played significant roles in caring for children. This shared parenting approach ensured that offspring received adequate resources, protection, and socialization, enhancing their chances of survival in a challenging environment.

The evolutionary advantages of paternal investment include not only the provision of resources but also the teaching of essential survival skills and social behaviors. Fathers in early human communities contributed to hunting, protection, and the transmission of cultural knowledge, thereby shaping the development and success of their children.

17.2.2   Anthropological Insights into Fatherhood

Anthropological studies of various indigenous and traditional societies provide further valuable insights into the diverse roles of fathers. In many hunter-gatherer communities, such as the Hadza of Tanzania or the Aka of Central Africa, fathers are deeply involved in the daily lives of their children. They participate in foraging, hunting, and caring for their offspring, demonstrating a high degree of paternal investment. This involvement is not only about providing food and protection but also about bonding, teaching, and playing with their children, which helps strengthen the father–child relationship.

In agricultural and pastoral societies, fathers often hold significant roles as providers and protectors, with their status and responsibilities being closely tied to land and livestock management. For example, in many traditional African and South Asian communities, fathers are central figures in passing down agricultural knowledge and practices, as well as in maintaining social order and family cohesion.

17.2.3   The Impact of Industrialization, Feminism, and Economic Changes

The advent of industrialization in the 19th and early 20th centuries brought about profound changes in family dynamics and fatherhood roles. As economies shifted from agrarian to industrial, many fathers moved from working on family farms to factory and office jobs, which often required long hours away from home. This shift further entrenched the notion of fathers as distant providers, with limited involvement in the emotional and developmental aspects of their children's lives.

17.2.4   Traditional Roles: Providers and Authority Figures

Men were thus then predominantly viewed as providers and authority figures within the family unit. In many cultures, the father's primary responsibility was to ensure the financial stability and security of the household. This role often entailed long working hours and a focus on career advancement, leaving limited time for direct involvement in day-to-day parenting. Fathers were also seen as the primary disciplinarians, tasked with instilling values, discipline, and a sense of responsibility in their children. Emotional nurturing and daily caregiving were largely considered the domain of mothers, reinforcing a clear division of parental roles.

17.2.5   Feminism and the Mid-20th Century

The mid-20th century saw the rise of the feminist movement, which advocated for gender equality and challenged traditional gender roles. Feminism played a crucial role in redefining fatherhood by promoting the idea that parenting responsibilities should be shared more equally between mothers and fathers. This movement also encouraged women to enter the workforce, necessitating a re-evaluation of the father's role in the family. As a result, societal expectations began to shift, recognizing the importance of fathers' active involvement in child-rearing and household duties.

Economic changes in recent decades have further influenced fatherhood roles. The increasing prevalence of dual-income households has necessitated a more balanced division of labor at home. Additionally, the rise of flexible work arrangements and remote work has enabled fathers to spend more time with their families, facilitating greater involvement in parenting.

17.2.6   The Transition to Emotionally Involved and Hands-On Parenting

The transition to a more emotionally involved and hands-on approach to fatherhood is one of the most significant developments in recent decades.[4,5] Modern fathers are increasingly taking on roles that were traditionally seen as maternal, such as providing emotional support, nurturing, and engaging in day-to-day caregiving activities. This shift reflects a broader cultural recognition of the importance of fathers' emotional presence in their children's lives.

Research has shown that children benefit significantly from having involved fathers, leading to better emotional, social, and cognitive outcomes. As a result, contemporary fathers are more likely to prioritize building strong, meaningful relationships with their children. They actively participate in activities such as attending school events, helping with homework, and engaging in recreational activities with their children.

The traditional image of a father as the distant provider has therefore gradually given way to a more involved and nurturing presence.[6] Today's fathers are increasingly participating in activities that were once considered the domain of mothers, such as attending parent–teacher meetings, participating in day-to-day caregiving tasks, and fostering emotional connections with their children. This shift is fueled by a growing recognition of the importance of fatherly involvement in children's overall development, including their emotional, social, and cognitive growth. Fathers now seek to build strong, meaningful relationships with their children, contributing to their well-being in ways that extend beyond financial support.

This evolution toward more egalitarian and involved fatherhood is supported by changing societal norms and policies that recognize the diverse and dynamic nature of modern families. The role of fathers today is thus multifaceted, encompassing not only the traditional aspects of providing and disciplining but also of nurturing, supporting, and being actively present in their children's lives.

As a result, fathers today are navigating a landscape that demands more active participation in their children's lives while also balancing traditional responsibilities. This new paradigm of fatherhood brings both challenges and opportunities as fathers work to integrate their roles as caregivers, providers, and role models in a rapidly changing world.

17.3   THE PSYCHOLOGICAL JOURNEY OF FATHERHOOD

The psychological journey of fatherhood profoundly influences a man's identity, self-perception, and overall mental well-being. This transformative process involves significant shifts in personal values, priorities, and perspectives as fathers adapt to their evolving roles within the family unit.

17.3.1   Identity and Self-Perception as a Father

The transition to fatherhood brings about a substantial shift in identity and self-perception.[7] Men must integrate their new roles as caregivers and role models with their existing personal and professional identities.[8] This often involves reconciling preparental ambitions and lifestyles with the demands and responsibilities of raising children.

For many fathers, this identity shift can be both enriching and challenging. On the one hand, fatherhood provides a sense of purpose and fulfillment, fostering deeper emotional connections and a renewed sense of responsibility. On the other hand, it can also lead to conflicts as fathers strive to balance their new roles with their personal and professional goals. The need to meet societal and self-imposed expectations of being a "good father" can create additional pressure, leading to stress and self-doubt.

Fathers often experience a re-evaluation of their values and priorities as they shift from a focus on individual achievements to a more family-centric perspective. This transition requires a redefinition of masculinity and success, moving away from traditional notions of providing and protecting to include nurturing and emotional availability.

17.3.2   Mental Health Challenges and Support

Fatherhood also brings to light various mental health challenges that are often less discussed compared to those faced by mothers.[9], [10] The pressures of providing, protecting, and being emotionally available can lead to significant stress, anxiety, and even depression.[11] These challenges are compounded by societal norms that may discourage men from expressing vulnerability or seeking help.[12]

The mental health of fathers is crucial not only for their own well-being but also for the health and development of their children. Fathers who experience mental health issues may struggle to engage fully in parenting, affecting their ability to provide emotional support and stability for their children.

It is essential to recognize and address the mental health needs of fathers. Support systems, including counseling, peer support groups, and mental health resources, can provide fathers with the tools they need to navigate the complexities of parenting. Encouraging open discussions about mental health and promoting a culture that supports seeking help are vital steps in ensuring fathers receive the support they need.

17.3.3   The Transition From Individualism to Family-Centric Perspective

The journey of fatherhood also involves a fundamental shift from individualism to a family-centric perspective. This transition can be deeply rewarding as fathers develop a sense of connection and purpose through their roles within the family. However, it also requires significant adjustments in lifestyle, priorities, and time management.

Fathers must learn to balance their personal ambitions and professional responsibilities with the demands of family life. This often involves making sacrifices, such as reducing work hours, giving up personal hobbies, or changing career paths, to be more present for their children. While these changes can be challenging, they also provide opportunities for personal growth and the development of a more holistic and fulfilling identity.

The shift to a family-centric perspective encourages fathers to engage more deeply with their children, fostering strong emotional bonds and providing a stable and supportive environment for their development. It also promotes a more equitable division of parenting responsibilities, benefiting both partners and contributing to a more balanced family dynamic.

17.4   THE ECONOMIC IMPACT OF FATHERHOOD

Fatherhood also carries significant economic implications, influencing both the financial challenges and opportunities that modern fathers face.[13], [14] Understanding these economic dimensions is crucial for appreciating the broader impact of fatherhood on families and society.

17.4.1   Financial Challenges and Considerations for Modern Fathers

Modern fathers often encounter a range of financial challenges as they navigate their roles within the family. These challenges can stem from various factors, including:

1. *Increased financial responsibility.* The arrival of a child brings additional expenses, such as health-care, childcare, education, and general living costs. Fathers may feel heightened pressure to provide financial stability for their families, which can be particularly challenging in economies with high living costs and inadequate social safety nets.

2. *Cost of childcare.* Childcare expenses can constitute a significant portion of a family's budget, especially in households where both parents work. This can strain financial resources and compel fathers to seek additional income or make career adjustments to balance family needs.

3. *Education costs.* Planning for a child's education, from preschool through college and University, involves long-term financial planning and savings. Fathers may need to prioritize education savings accounts, scholarships, and other financial instruments to ensure their children receive quality education without incurring substantial debt.

4. *Health insurance and medical costs.* Ensuring comprehensive health insurance coverage for the entire family is another critical financial consideration. Unforeseen medical expenses can place a considerable burden on family finances, necessitating adequate financial planning and insurance policies.

17.4.2   Economic Benefits of Involved Fatherhood

However, while the financial challenges are considerable, involved fatherhood also offers various economic benefits that can positively impact families and society, including:

a. *Enhanced family stability.* Fathers who actively participate in child-rearing and household responsibilities contribute to a more stable and supportive family environment. This stability can lead to better outcomes for children, reducing long-term social costs associated with education, health care, and social services.

b. *Improved child outcomes.* Research indicates that children with involved fathers tend to perform better academically and exhibit fewer behavioral problems. These positive outcomes can translate into economic benefits, such as higher earning potential and reduced costs related to juvenile delinquency and social welfare programs.

c.   *Increased workforce productivity.* Fathers who achieve a healthy work–life balance are likely to experience reduced stress and improved mental health. This can enhance their productivity and engagement in the workplace, benefiting employers and the broader economy.

d.   *Economic contributions of dual-income families.* In households where both parents work, involved fatherhood supports the economic contributions of dual-income families. This can increase household income, improve financial security, and boost overall economic activity.

17.5   FATHERHOOD ACROSS DIFFERENT CULTURES AND FAMILIES

Fatherhood is a universal experience that varies greatly across different cultures and family dynamics.[15], [16] This diversity in practices, values, and expectations offers a rich tapestry of paternal roles and highlights both the adaptability of fatherhood and the universal aspects of the father–child relationship. By conducting a comparative analysis of fatherhood globally and within different family setups, and by drawing lessons from diverse cultural practices, we can gain valuable insights into the multifaceted nature of being a father.

17.5.1   Comparative Analysis of Fatherhood Globally

Globally, the role of fathers can differ widely based on cultural, social, and economic contexts. In many Western societies, there has been a significant shift toward more egalitarian parenting, with fathers taking on a more active role in childcare and household responsibilities. This trend is driven by changing gender norms, increased participation of women in the workforce, and supportive policies such as paternity leave and flexible work arrangements.

In contrast, in some traditional and collectivist cultures, fathers often retain the role of primary breadwinners and authority figures, with a clear division of labor, where mothers are primarily responsible for day-to-day child-rearing. For example, in many Asian and Middle Eastern cultures, fathers are expected to provide financial stability and discipline, while emotional and nurturing roles are typically fulfilled by mothers.

However, there are also cultures where fathers have long been involved in hands-on parenting. For instance, in some Scandinavian countries, egalitarian parenting has been the norm for decades, supported by comprehensive family policies and social norms that encourage both parents to share childcare responsibilities equally.

17.5.2   Lessons and Insights From Diverse Cultural Practices

Examining fatherhood across different cultures provides valuable lessons and insights that can inform and enhance parenting practices worldwide. One key insight is the importance of community and extended family support in raising children. In many African and Latin American cultures, child-rearing is often a collective effort, involving not just the immediate family but also extended relatives and community members. This collective approach can alleviate the pressures on individual parents and provide children with a broader support network.

Another lesson is the emphasis on work–life balance seen in cultures that prioritize family time over professional achievements. For example, in countries like Sweden and Denmark, societal norms and government policies support parents in taking extended parental leave, ensuring they can spend quality time with their children without sacrificing their careers. This balance promotes better family cohesion and child development.

Additionally, cultural practices that involve fathers in daily rituals and educational activities can strengthen father–child bonds. In some Indigenous cultures, fathers actively participate in teaching their children traditional skills, stories, and values, fostering a deep sense of identity and continuity within the family.

17.5.3   Adaptability of Paternal Roles and Universal Aspects of Father–Child Relationship

Despite the cultural variations in fatherhood, there are universal aspects of the father–child relationship that transcend cultural boundaries. The need for emotional connection, support, and guidance is a fundamental aspect of fatherhood worldwide. Children benefit from the presence of caring and involved fathers, who provide stability, love, and role models for behavior and values.

The adaptability of paternal roles is evident in how fathers navigate and integrate their cultural expectations with the needs of their families. Fathers around the world are increasingly recognizing the importance of being emotionally available and nurturing, regardless of traditional roles. This adaptability allows fathers to provide the best possible support for their children's development, even as cultural norms evolve.

17.5.4   Fathers in Diverse Family Units

Fatherhood within diverse family units, such as same-sex relationships,[17, 18] presents unique dynamics and challenges that enrich our understanding of paternal roles. In these family structures, the roles of fathers are often redefined to ensure a balanced and nurturing environment for the children.

Same-sex couples, particularly those consisting of two fathers, demonstrate the flexibility and adaptability inherent in parenting. They often face societal and legal hurdles that can shape their parenting experience, yet they also exemplify resilience and commitment to their children's well-being. But importantly, studies have shown that children raised by same-sex parents perform equally well, if not better, in various aspects of social, academic, and emotional development compared to their peers in traditional family units.

17.5.5   Challenges and Strengths in Same-Sex Parenthood

One of the significant challenges fathers in same-sex couples encounter is societal acceptance. Despite increasing recognition and rights for LGBTQ+ families in many parts of the world, stigmatization and discrimination persist. These fathers often have to navigate a lack of representation and support systems tailored to their unique needs. However, the challenges faced by these fathers also foster a strong sense of advocacy and community, leading to the establishment of robust support networks and resources.

These fathers also bring a unique set of strengths to parenting. The decision to become parents in a same-sex relationship is often highly intentional, involving thoughtful planning and commitment. This intentionality can translate into high levels of parental involvement and dedication. Moreover, the absence of traditional gender roles allows for a more equitable distribution of parenting responsibilities, promoting a balanced and collaborative approach to childcare and household tasks.

17.5.6   The Role of Extended Families and Communities

Extended families and communities play a crucial role in supporting fathers in same-sex relationships, and acceptance and support from extended family members can significantly impact the well-being of both the parents and the children. Additionally, LGBTQ+ community organizations often provide essential resources, support groups, and social activities that help these fathers navigate their parenting journey. These communities offer a sense of belonging and shared experience, which can be invaluable in overcoming the challenges posed by societal norms and prejudices.

17.5.7   Universal Aspects and Cultural Adaptation

However, it is important to note that despite the unique challenges, the universal aspects of the father–child relationship remain consistent in same-sex fatherhood. The need for emotional connection, stability, and guidance is paramount. These fathers too, like their heterosexual counterparts, strive to provide a nurturing and loving environment for their children. Their adaptability in integrating cultural expectations with the needs of their family exemplifies the universal nature of fatherhood.

17.6   THE IMPACT OF FATHER INVOLVEMENT ON CHILD DEVELOPMENT

The involvement of fathers in their children's lives has a profound and far-reaching impact on child development, effects that are comprehensively covered in a recent report on father involvement in children's educational outcomes.[19] This piece highlights how research consistently demonstrates that active and engaged fatherhood contributes significantly to various aspects of a child's emotional, psychological, educational, and behavioral growth, leading to long-term benefits and success.

17.6.1   Emotional and Psychological Benefits

The emotional presence of a father is crucial for a child's psychological health and well-being. Fathers who are actively involved in their children's lives provide essential emotional support and stability, which helps foster a secure attachment and a strong sense of self-worth in children. Engaged fathers model healthy emotional regulation and coping strategies, which children can learn and emulate.

Children with involved fathers are also less likely to experience mental health issues, such as depression and anxiety. They tend to exhibit higher levels of empathy and social competence, as the emotional engagement from their fathers helps them develop a better understanding of emotions and relationships. The nurturing presence of a father also contributes to a child's overall sense of security and confidence, enabling them to explore the world with a stronger sense of resilience and self-assurance.

17.6.2   Educational and Behavioral Outcomes

Father involvement also has a significant positive impact on a child's educational achievements and behavioral development. Children with active father figures tend to perform better academically, showing higher levels of cognitive development and school readiness. They are also more likely to achieve higher grades, exhibit a greater interest in learning, and pursue higher education.

The presence of an involved father also correlates with better behavioral outcomes. Children with engaged fathers are less likely to engage in delinquent behavior, substance abuse, and other risky activities. They tend to display better self-discipline, higher levels of self-control, and fewer behavioral problems both at home and in school. The consistent involvement of fathers appears to provide children with clear boundaries and expectations, contributing to their overall behavioral development.

17.6.3   Long-Term Development and Success

And the benefits of father involvement extend well into adulthood, influencing long-term development and success. Children who grow up with active and supportive fathers are more likely to develop strong interpersonal relationships, both personal and professional. They exhibit higher levels of social competence, emotional intelligence, and problem-solving skills, which are essential for navigating adult life.

Additionally, the positive influence of an involved father can impact a child's future parenting style and family dynamics. Adults who experienced nurturing and engaged fatherhood are more likely to become involved and supportive parents themselves, perpetuating a cycle of positive parenting practices across generations.

Long-term success is also reflected in the child's career achievements and overall life satisfaction. The confidence, resilience, and work ethic instilled by an involved father contribute to a higher likelihood of professional success and personal fulfillment. The values and skills imparted by fathers play a crucial role in shaping the future trajectories of their children's lives.

17.7   CHALLENGES FACING CONTEMPORARY FATHERS

Contemporary fathers navigate a complex landscape marked by evolving expectations, social norms, and personal aspirations.[20] As they strive to fulfill their roles, they encounter numerous challenges that can impact their ability to engage fully in both their professional and personal lives.

17.7.1   Navigating Work–Life Balance

One of the most pressing challenges for modern fathers is achieving a healthy work–life balance, as discussed in Chapter 15.[21] The economic demands of contemporary society often require fathers to commit substantial time and energy to their careers, which can conflict with their desire to be actively involved in their children's lives. The pressure to provide financially, coupled with the ambition to advance professionally, can lead to long working hours and significant stress.

Fathers who seek to balance their work and family responsibilities often face difficulties in finding flexible work arrangements.[22] While some companies offer paternity leave and flexible working options, these benefits are not universally available, and cultural attitudes toward taking advantage of such policies can vary. Fathers may fear negative career consequences if they prioritize family time over work commitments. This tension can result in feelings of inadequacy and guilt, as fathers struggle to meet the expectations placed on them both at home and in the workplace.

17.7.2   Legal and Social Barriers in Custody and Care

Fathers also encounter significant legal and social barriers, particularly in the context of separation or divorce (and this will be explored in more detail in the next chapter). Despite progress toward gender equality, the legal system in many places still exhibits biases that favor mothers in custody disputes.[23] Fathers may find it challenging to secure equal parenting time or primary custody, even when they are equally capable and willing to care for their children. This can perpetuate the stereotype that mothers are inherently more suitable caregivers.

Social attitudes can also hinder fathers' efforts to be involved in their children's lives postseparation. There can be skepticism and criticism toward fathers seeking custody or significant parenting roles, reinforcing outdated notions about gender roles in parenting. Fathers often have to navigate these biases while advocating for their rights and the well-being of their children. The emotional and financial toll of legal battles can be substantial, further complicating their ability to maintain a strong presence in their children's lives.

17.7.3   Overcoming Stereotypes and Cultural Expectations

Stereotypes and cultural expectations also continue to challenge fathers in their parenting roles. Traditional views often depict men as secondary caregivers, whose primary responsibility is to provide financially rather than participate actively in daily childcare. These cultural norms can create internal and external pressures for fathers, discouraging them from engaging fully in parenting activities.

Fathers who defy these stereotypes by taking on more nurturing and hands-on roles may face judgment or lack of support from their peers, family, and society at large. Overcoming these stereotypes requires a collective shift in perception, recognizing the importance and capability of fathers as primary caregivers. Efforts to change these attitudes involve raising awareness about the positive impact of involved fatherhood on children's development and advocating for a more inclusive understanding of parenting roles.

Additionally, media representation plays a significant role in shaping public perceptions of fatherhood. Positive portrayals of engaged and nurturing fathers can help challenge and eventually change societal norms. Encouraging diverse and realistic representations of fathers in media and popular culture is essential in normalizing the idea that fathers are equally competent and essential in raising their children.

17.8   A SPECIFIC CHALLENGE: LOSS DURING AND AFTER PREGNANCY

The loss of a pregnancy, whether through miscarriage, stillbirth, or neonatal death, is a profoundly painful experience for parents.[24] This type of loss can trigger a wide range of emotions, including grief, anger, guilt, and profound sadness. For fathers, the experience of pregnancy loss can be particularly challenging as societal expectations often place the emotional burden and primary caregiving responsibilities on the mother, leaving fathers to cope with their grief in relative isolation.[25,26,27]

17.8.1   Supporting Fathers Through Pregnancy Loss

In order to support fathers specifically during these events, it is important to do the following:

1. *Acknowledge the grief.* It is crucial to acknowledge that fathers grieve too. Fathers should be encouraged to express their emotions and seek support rather than suppressing their feelings to remain strong for their partners. Acknowledging their grief is the first step toward healing.

2. *Engage in open communication.* Encouraging open and honest communication between partners can help both parents navigate their grief together. Fathers should feel comfortable discussing their feelings and experiences without fear of judgment or minimization.

3. *Provide professional support.* Fathers experiencing pregnancy loss should be provided with access to professional support, such as counseling or therapy. Mental health professionals can offer a safe space for fathers to express their grief and work through their emotions.

4. *Provide peer support groups.* Joining support groups for parents who have experienced pregnancy loss can be beneficial. These groups provide an opportunity for fathers to share their experiences with others who understand their pain, offering mutual support and understanding.

The death of a newborn shortly after birth, known as *neonatal death*, brings a unique set of challenges. Fathers may struggle with feelings of helplessness and confusion as they try to support their partner while coping with their own grief.

17.8.2   Coping Strategies for Fathers

From the perspective of fathers themselves, the following **are likely to** serve them well in coping:

1. *Engage in memorial activities.* Creating memorials or engaging in rituals to honor the lost child can provide a sense of closure and help fathers process their grief. Activities such as planting a tree, creating a memory box, or holding a memorial service can be therapeutic.

2. *Self-care.* Encouraging fathers to take care of their physical and emotional health is essential. This includes maintaining a balanced diet,

engaging in regular exercise, and ensuring they have time to relax and unwind.

3. *Long-term support.* The grief associated with pregnancy and neonatal loss can persist for a long time. Long-term support from family, friends, and mental health professionals can help fathers navigate their ongoing grief and adjust to their new reality.

17.8.3   Impact on Subsequent Pregnancies

Fathers who have experienced pregnancy loss may face heightened anxiety and fear during subsequent pregnancies. These feelings are normal and should be acknowledged and addressed through:

1. *Preparation and support.* Providing fathers with information and support during subsequent pregnancies can help mitigate anxiety. Prenatal counseling and regular communication with health-care providers can offer reassurance and guidance.

2. *Celebrating milestones.* Celebrating each milestone of the new pregnancy can help fathers build confidence and reduce anxiety. Acknowledging and celebrating small achievements can foster a positive outlook.

3. *Involvement in prenatal care.* Encouraging fathers to be actively involved in prenatal care and appointments can help them feel more connected and less anxious. Active involvement can also foster a sense of control and preparedness.

The loss of a pregnancy or newborn is a devastating experience that profoundly affects both parents. It is essential to recognize and support fathers in their grief, providing them with the necessary tools and resources to navigate this difficult time. By acknowledging their pain, promoting open communication, and offering professional and peer support, we can help fathers heal and move forward while honoring the memory of their lost child.

17.9   OPPORTUNITIES FOR CHANGE AND GROWTH

The landscape of fatherhood presents numerous opportunities for change and growth, marked by positive trends in fatherhood engagement and evolving societal norms. By examining successful transitions to nurturing roles through case studies and understanding the shifting perceptions of fatherhood, we can gain valuable insights into the ongoing transformation of paternal roles.

17.9.1   Positive Trends in Fatherhood Engagement

Recent years have witnessed a significant shift toward more engaged and involved fatherhood. Modern fathers are increasingly prioritizing time with their children, taking active roles in caregiving, and participating in day-to-day parenting tasks. This trend reflects a growing recognition of the importance of fatherly involvement in child development and family well-being.

Several factors contribute to this positive trend. Advances in workplace policies, such as the introduction of paternity leave and flexible working arrangements, have enabled fathers to spend more time at home during the critical early stages of their children's lives. Additionally, a broader cultural shift toward gender equality has encouraged men to embrace more nurturing and hands-on parenting roles. As societal norms evolve, the stigma associated with fathers taking on caregiving responsibilities is diminishing, paving the way for more balanced and equitable family dynamics.

17.9.2   Societal Norms and Evolving Perceptions

Societal norms and perceptions of fatherhood are also continually evolving, driven by increased awareness and advocacy for gender equality and inclusive parenting practices. Media representation plays a crucial role in shaping these perceptions, with more positive portrayals of engaged and nurturing fathers in television, movies, and advertising.

As these portrayals become more prevalent, they help normalize the idea that fathers are equally capable and essential in raising their children. This shift challenges the outdated stereotypes that have long confined fathers to the roles of providers and disciplinarians, promoting a more holistic understanding of fatherhood that includes emotional availability and active participation in caregiving.

Educational campaigns and public awareness initiatives further support this evolution by highlighting the benefits of involved fatherhood for both children and families. Workshops, seminars, and community programs aimed at fathers provide valuable resources and support, encouraging men to embrace their parenting roles fully.

17.10   THE ROLE OF TECHNOLOGY IN MODERN FATHERHOOD

Technology has also become an integral part of modern fatherhood, offering various tools and platforms that aid in parenting and shaping perceptions of what it means to be a father today. From practical applications that help manage daily parenting tasks to the influence of social media, technology plays a significant role in supporting and transforming fatherhood.

17.10.1   How Technology Aids in Parenting

Technology provides numerous resources that make parenting more efficient and connected. Mobile apps, online communities, and digital tools offer fathers new ways to engage with and support their children's development. Some key examples include:

1. *Parenting apps.* There are countless apps designed to help fathers with various aspects of parenting, such as tracking their child's developmental milestones, managing schedules, and finding parenting tips. Apps like "Baby Connect" and "Parent Cue" provide real-time information and reminders, making it easier for fathers to stay involved in their children's daily lives.[28]

2. *Health and wellness apps.* Apps like "Wonder Weeks" and "Sprout Baby" help fathers monitor their children's health and development, providing insights into growth patterns, immunization schedules, and common developmental phases. These tools empower fathers with knowledge and support proactive parenting.

3. *Educational apps and games.* Educational apps and interactive games can be used by fathers to support their children's learning. Platforms like "Khan Academy Kids" and "ABCmouse" offer engaging and educational content that fathers can explore with their children, enhancing their learning experiences.

4. *Online communities and forums.* Digital communities provide fathers with a platform to share experiences, seek advice, and find support. Forums like "Reddit's Daddit" and "Fatherly" offer spaces where fathers can discuss challenges, celebrate milestones, and build a sense of community with other fathers.

17.10.2   The Impact of Social Media on Fatherhood Perceptions

Social media has had a profound impact on how fatherhood is perceived and experienced.[29], [30] Platforms like Instagram, Facebook, and Twitter provide fathers with the opportunity to share their parenting journeys, connect with other parents, and engage with a broader audience. This visibility can help normalize diverse expressions of fatherhood and challenge traditional stereotypes. Key impacts include:

1. *Normalization of involved fatherhood.* Social media allows fathers to share their day-to-day parenting activities, from changing diapers to attending school events. By showcasing these moments, social media helps normalize the idea of fathers as active, involved, and nurturing

caregivers, breaking down outdated stereotypes of fathers as distant or uninvolved.

2. *Influence of fatherhood influencers.* The rise of fatherhood influencers and bloggers who share their experiences and insights on parenting has created role models for other fathers. Influencers like "The Dad Lab" and "Father of Daughters" highlight the joys and challenges of fatherhood, providing inspiration and practical advice to their followers.

3. *Community building and support.* Social media facilitates the creation of support networks where fathers can find camaraderie and advice. Hashtags like #DadLife and #Fatherhood connect fathers around the world, fostering a sense of belonging and mutual support.

4. *Public awareness and advocacy.* Social media campaigns and movements can raise awareness about issues related to fatherhood, such as paternity leave, mental health, and gender equality. These platforms provide a voice for advocacy, encouraging societal changes that support and empower fathers.

Clearly by leveraging the benefits of technology, fathers can enhance their parenting experiences, connect with others, and contribute to a more inclusive and diverse understanding of fatherhood.

17.11   FATHERHOOD AND WORKPLACES

Workplace policies and practices play a crucial role in supporting fathers and facilitating a healthy balance between work and family life. Employers can significantly influence the well-being and productivity of fathers through supportive measures and policies.

17.11.1   Workplace Policies Supporting Fatherhood

Several workplace policies are essential in promoting father involvement and supporting the needs of working fathers, including:

1. *Paternity leave.* Offering paid paternity leave allows fathers to spend critical time with their newborns and support their partners during the early stages of parenting. Countries and companies that provide generous paternity leave policies see higher levels of father engagement and satisfaction.

2. *Flexible work arrangements.* Flexible work hours, remote work options, and compressed workweeks enable fathers to balance their professional responsibilities with family commitments. These arrangements

can reduce stress and increase job satisfaction, leading to higher retention rates and employee loyalty.

3.   *Parental leave equality.* Ensuring that both parents have access to equi-
     table parental leave encourages shared parenting responsibilities and
     reduces the gendered division of labor. This promotes a more balanced
     approach to parenting and supports gender equality in the workplace.

4.   *Childcare support.* Employers can offer childcare support through on-site
     day-care facilities, childcare subsidies, or partnerships with local child-
     care providers. This assistance alleviates the burden of childcare costs and
     logistics, making it easier for fathers to remain engaged in their careers.

17.11.2   The Role of Employers in Facilitating Work–Life Balance for Fathers

Employers play a pivotal role in creating a supportive environment for working fathers. By implementing family-friendly policies and fostering a culture
that values work–life balance, employers can facilitate a more inclusive and
productive workplace. Key strategies include:

1.   *Promoting work–life balance.* Employers should actively promote the
     importance of work–life balance through internal communications,
     leadership training, and role modeling by senior management.
     Recognizing and supporting the diverse needs of employees, including
     fathers, contribute to a healthier and more motivated workforce.

2.   *Providing supportive resources.* Offering resources such as employee
     assistance programs (EAPs), counseling services, and parenting work-
     shops can help fathers navigate the challenges of balancing work and
     family life. These resources provide practical support and demonstrate
     the employer's commitment to employee well-being.

3.   *Creating a family-friendly culture.* A family-friendly workplace culture
     encourages employees to prioritize their family responsibilities without
     fear of negative repercussions. Policies that support flexible work,
     parental leave, and childcare should be complemented by a culture
     that respects and values the role of fathers.

4.   *Recognizing and celebrating fatherhood.* Employers can recognize and
     celebrate the contributions of fathers through events, awards, and inter-
     nal communications that highlight the importance of fatherhood.
     Celebrating Father's Day, sharing employee stories, and promoting
     father-friendly initiatives can reinforce the value placed on fathers
     within the organization.

17.12 GENERAL STRATEGIES FOR SUPPORTING FATHERS

Supporting fathers in their parenting roles requires a multifaceted approach involving policy recommendations, community and online resources, and education and awareness campaigns.[31] These strategies aim to create an environment that empowers fathers to engage fully in their children's lives, contributing to healthier families and communities.

17.12.1 Policy Recommendations: Paternity Leave and Legal Rights

Implementing supportive policies is crucial for encouraging father involvement and ensuring that fathers have the necessary legal rights to participate actively in their children's lives, including:

1. *Paternity leave.* Governments and employers should provide paid paternity leave to enable fathers to spend time with their newborns and support their partners during the early stages of parenthood. Paternity leave policies should be flexible, allowing fathers to take leave in a way that suits their family's needs. This support not only benefits the father–child bond but also promotes gender equality by encouraging shared parenting responsibilities.

2. *Legal rights in custody and care.* Legal systems must evolve to ensure that fathers have equal opportunities to gain custody and participate in their children's lives postseparation or postdivorce. Policies should be designed to eliminate biases that favor one parent over the other based on outdated gender norms. Fathers should have access to legal support and advocacy services to navigate custody disputes and secure fair parenting arrangements.

3. *Workplace policies.* Employers should implement family-friendly policies that support fathers, such as flexible work arrangements, on-site childcare, and parental leave equality. Ensuring that fathers have access to the same parental leave benefits as mothers can help normalize involved fatherhood and reduce the stigma associated with men taking time off work for family responsibilities.

17.12.2 Community and Online Resources for Fatherhood Support

Building robust support networks for fathers is also essential for providing them with the resources, advice, and peer support they need to navigate the challenges of parenting, including:

1. *Community programs.* Local communities can establish fatherhood programs that offer workshops, support groups, and parenting classes tailored to the needs of fathers. These programs can provide practical guidance on topics such as child development, coparenting, and work–life balance. Community centers, schools, and religious organizations can play a vital role in hosting and promoting these initiatives.

2. *Online platforms.* Digital resources and online communities offer accessible support for fathers, allowing them to connect with peers, share experiences, and seek advice. Websites, forums, and social media groups dedicated to fatherhood provide a space for fathers to discuss challenges, celebrate milestones, and find camaraderie. Platforms like "Fatherly," "Reddit's Daddit," and "Dad.info" offer valuable information and a sense of community for fathers worldwide.

3. *Helplines and counseling services.* Establishing helplines and counseling services specifically for fathers can provide immediate support for those facing parenting challenges or mental health issues. These services should be easily accessible and staffed by professionals trained to address the unique concerns of fathers.

17.12.3   Education and Awareness Campaigns Targeting Fathers

Raising awareness and educating the public about the importance of father involvement are also crucial for changing societal perceptions and encouraging supportive behaviors.

1. *Public awareness campaigns.* Governments, NGOs, and advocacy groups should launch campaigns that highlight the benefits of involved fatherhood for children, families, and society. These campaigns can use various media channels, including television, radio, social media, and public events, to reach a broad audience. Emphasizing positive stories and role models can help shift public perceptions and normalize active fatherhood.

2. *Parenting education programs.* Educational programs that target fathers should be developed and promoted. These programs can cover a wide range of topics, including child development, effective communication, and healthy coparenting practices. Providing these resources in accessible formats, such as online courses, workshops, and printed materials, ensures that fathers from diverse backgrounds can benefit.

3. *Corporate partnerships.* Partnering with businesses and employers to promote father-friendly policies and practices can amplify the impact of

awareness campaigns. Companies can be encouraged to participate in and support initiatives that promote work–life balance and parental involvement. Highlighting successful case studies of father-friendly workplaces can serve as a model for others to follow.

17.13   EXAMPLES OF FATHERHOOD INITIATIVES

Here are some great examples of organizations already working either with fathers, advocating for fathers, or working with boys affected by father absence.

17.13.1   The Fatherhood Institute

The Fatherhood Institute is a UK charity dedicated to promoting involved fatherhood and supporting men as active caregivers. It focuses on research, policy, and practice to build a society that values and supports fathers. The Institute publishes research reviews, advocates for policy changes, and provides training for professionals in perinatal, early years, education, and social care services. Their mission includes shaping national and local policies to ensure father-inclusive approaches and fostering gender equality in caregiving roles. Website: www.fatherhoodinstitute.org/.

17.13.2   Music.Football.Fatherhood

Music.Football.Fatherhood (MFF) is an online community and platform that provides support and resources for fathers. It serves as a space for dads to share their stories, experiences, and advice on fatherhood. MFF hosts events, publishes articles, and creates content that addresses the diverse challenges and joys of being a dad, all while integrating the passions for music and football. The platform aims to foster a supportive community and promote positive fatherhood. Website: https://musicfootballfatherhood.com/.

17.13.3   Dads Matter

Dads Matter is a UK-based organization dedicated to providing support and resources for fathers experiencing depression, anxiety, or posttraumatic stress disorder (PTSD). Recognizing the unique struggles that fathers face, Dads Matter offers a compassionate, nonjudgmental space for healing and growth. Their services include legal, emotional, and practical assistance to help fathers navigate the complexities of family law and parental alienation.

The organization is committed to advocating for children's well-being, ensuring they retain healthy relationships with both parents. Dads Matter fosters a strong network of support through online forums, peer-to-peer mentoring, and regular events. Their mission is to build stronger, happier communities where dads thrive and families flourish. Website: https://dads-matter.org.uk/.

17.13.4   Dads House

Dads House is a UK-based organization dedicated to supporting fathers, particularly single dads, through practical assistance and community activities. Established in 2008, Dads House offers a variety of services, including regular support meetings, guitar lessons, football sessions, and other social events aimed at reducing isolation and loneliness. The organization is committed to helping dads navigate the challenges of parenting, especially during times of family breakdown or bereavement. Website: www.dadshouse.org.uk/.

17.13.5   Dads Rock

Dads Rock is a Scottish charity dedicated to improving outcomes for children by supporting fathers and families. The organization offers a variety of programs, including weekly playgroups for dads and their children, parenting workshops, music lessons, and one-to-one support for young dads. Their initiatives aim to build confidence, foster strong parent–child relationships, and provide practical parenting skills. Dads Rock is committed to ensuring that dads are supported, valued, and equipped to take an active role in their children's lives. Website: www.dadsrock.org.uk/.

17.13.6   Dad Matters

Dad Matters is a UK-based initiative that supports fathers, especially during the perinatal period. The organization aims to help dads build strong relationships with their babies and partners, by providing practical and emotional support. Their services include peer support groups, one-to-one support, workshops, and outreach sessions at maternity centers and community venues. Dad Matters focuses on helping dads with anxiety, stress, and mental health issues, ensuring they have access to necessary resources and support. Website: https://dadmatters.org.uk/.

17.13.7   North East Young Dads and Lads (NEYDL)

North East Young Dads and Lads (NEYDL) is a dedicated support charity focused on improving the lives of young fathers and expectant dads aged under 26 in the North East of England. Founded in 2015, NEYDL offers a range of services, including peer support, parenting workshops, and social activities designed to help young men play an active and meaningful role in their children's lives. The charity also works to challenge negative societal views of young fathers and advocates for better support and recognition of their needs. Website: www.neydl.uk/.

17.13.8   Lads Need Dads

Lads Need Dads is a UK-based initiative dedicated to supporting boys aged 10–18 who have absent fathers or limited access to positive male role models. Founded in 2015, this community interest company offers a variety of programs, including mentoring, bushcraft, life skill training, and community volunteering. These programs aim to build self-esteem, resilience, and emotional intelligence among boys, helping them avoid potential pitfalls such as poor academic performance, behavioral issues, and mental health struggles. The organization also supports single mothers and carers, providing guidance and training to help them raise their sons effectively. Website: https://ladsneeddads.org/.

17.14   CONCLUSION

The future of fatherhood holds immense potential for positive change, driven by the collective efforts of society, continued research, and an inclusive understanding of parental roles. By addressing the challenges faced by modern fathers and embracing the opportunities for growth and development, we can create a supportive environment that benefits not only fathers but also families and society as a whole.

17.14.1   Role of Society in Facilitating Positive Change

Society plays a crucial role in shaping the future of fatherhood by promoting policies and cultural norms that support and value the contributions of fathers. Key societal actions include:

1.   *Advocating for supportive policies.* Governments and policymakers must prioritize the creation and implementation of policies that support father involvement, such as paid paternity leave, flexible work arrangements, and equitable parental leave. These policies can help alleviate the pressures on fathers and encourage a more balanced approach to parenting.

2.   *Challenging stereotypes.* Media, educational institutions, and community organizations should work together to challenge outdated stereotypes about fatherhood. By portraying diverse and positive images of fathers, society can foster a more inclusive and accurate understanding of what it means to be a father today.

3. *Providing resources and support.* Communities should offer resources and support systems tailored to the needs of fathers. This includes parenting workshops, support groups, counseling services, and online platforms where fathers can share experiences and seek advice.

17.14.2   The Importance of Continued Research and Dialogue

Ongoing research and open dialogue are also essential for understanding the evolving dynamics of fatherhood and identifying effective strategies to support fathers. Key areas of focus include:

1. *Studying fatherhood trends.* Researchers should continue to explore the changing roles and experiences of fathers across different cultures and socioeconomic backgrounds. This research can provide valuable insights into the challenges and opportunities faced by fathers, informing policy and practice.

2. *Evaluating policy impact.* It is important to assess the effectiveness of existing policies and programs designed to support fathers. By evaluating their impact, we can identify best practices and areas for improvement, ensuring that policies are responsive to the needs of fathers and families.

3. *Facilitating dialogue.* Encouraging open conversations about fatherhood within families, communities, and workplaces can help break down barriers and promote understanding. Dialogue can foster empathy, support, and collaboration, enabling fathers to navigate their roles more effectively.

17.14.3   Creating an Inclusive Understanding of Parental Roles for the Benefit of Families and Society

A key aspect of envisioning the future of fatherhood is the creation of an inclusive understanding of parental roles that recognizes the diverse contributions of both mothers and fathers. This inclusive approach can lead to:

1. *Stronger family bonds.* When both parents are equally involved in child-rearing, families can develop stronger emotional connections and a more cohesive family unit. This balanced approach supports the well-being of children and enhances the overall family dynamic.

2. *Gender equality.* Promoting an inclusive understanding of parental roles helps advance gender equality by challenging traditional gender norms and encouraging shared responsibilities. This can lead to more equitable relationships and opportunities for both parents.

3.   *Societal benefits.* Inclusive and supportive parental roles contribute to the overall health and prosperity of society. Children raised in environments where both parents are actively involved are more likely to thrive, leading to better educational, social, and economic outcomes.

In conclusion, envisioning the future of fatherhood requires a concerted effort from society to facilitate positive change, continued research to understand evolving dynamics, and a commitment to creating an inclusive understanding of parental roles. By embracing these principles, we can support fathers in their essential roles, enrich family life, and build a more equitable and thriving society for future generations.

NOTES

1 Lamb, M. E. (2013). The changing faces of fatherhood and father – child relationships: From fatherhood as status to father as dad. In *Handbook of family theories* (pp. 87–102). Routledge.
2 Gray, P. B., & Anderson, K. G. (2010). *Fatherhood: Evolution and human paternal behavior*. Harvard University Press.
3 Machin, A. (2018). *The life of dad: The making of a modern father*. Simon and Schuster.
4 Tan, T. (2016). Literature review on shifting fatherhood. *Masculinities: A Journal of Identity and Culture*, 6, 102–128.
5 Bataille, C. D., & Hyland, E. (2023). Involved fathering: How new dads are redefining fatherhood. *Personnel Review*, *52*(4), 1010–1032.
6 Dermott, E., & Miller, T. (2015). More than the sum of its parts? Contemporary fatherhood policy, practice and discourse. *Families, Relationships and Societies*, *4*(2), 183–195.
7 Johansson, T., & Andreasson, J. (2017). *Fatherhood in transition: Masculinity, identity and everyday life*. Springer.
8 Crespi, I., & Ruspini, E. (2015). Transition to fatherhood: New perspectives in the global context of changing men's identities. *International Review of Sociology*, *25*(3), 353–358.
9 Baldwin, S., Malone, M., Sandall, J., & Bick, D. (2018). Mental health and wellbeing during the transition to fatherhood: A systematic review of first time fathers' experiences. *JBI Evidence Synthesis*, *16*(11), 2118–2191.
10 Baldwin, S., Malone, M., Sandall, J., & Bick, D. (2019). A qualitative exploratory study of UK first-time fathers' experiences, mental health and wellbeing needs during their transition to fatherhood. *BMJ Open*, *9*(9), e030792.
11 Madsen, S. A., & Burgess, A. (2018). Fatherhood and mental health difficulties in the postnatal period. In *Promoting Men's Mental Health* (pp. 74–82). CRC Press.
12 Hayward, R. A., & Honegger, L. N. (2018). Perceived barriers to mental health treatment among men enrolled in a responsible fatherhood program. *Social Work in Mental Health*, *16*(6), 696–712.
13 Hamm, M., Miller, E., Jackson Foster, L., Browne, M., & Borrero, S. (2018). "The financial is the main issue, it's not even the child": Exploring the role of finances

in men's concepts of fatherhood and fertility intention. *American Journal of Men's Health*, *12*(4), 1074–1083.

14 Olsen, L. L., Oliffe, J. L., Brussoni, M., & Creighton, G. (2015). Fathers' views on their financial situations, father – child activities, and preventing child injuries. *American Journal of Men's Health*, *9*(1), 15–25.

15 Strier, R., & Perez-Vaisvidovsky, N. (2021). Intersectionality and fatherhood: Theorizing non-hegemonic fatherhoods. *Journal of Family Theory & Review*, *13*(3), 334–346.

16 Lamb, M. E. (2013). *The father's role: Cross cultural perspectives*. Routledge.

17 Carneiro, F. A., Tasker, F., Salinas-Quiroz, F., Leal, I., & Costa, P. A. (2017). Are the fathers alright? A systematic and critical review of studies on gay and bisexual fatherhood. *Frontiers in Psychology*, *8*, 1636.

18 Feinberg, J. (2020). After marriage equality: Dual fatherhood for married male same-sex couples. *UC Davis Law Review*, *54*, 1507.

19 Hine, B. A. (2022). Teachers' experiences of the impact of fatherlessness on male pupils. Lads Need Dads. https://drbenhine.co.uk/lnd-report-on-fatherless-and-school-achievement-behaviour/

20 Machin, A. J. (2015). Mind the gap: The expectation and reality of involved fatherhood. *Fathering: A Journal of Theory, Research & Practice about Men as Fathers*, *13*(1).

21 Stovell, C., Collinson, D., Gatrell, C., & Radcliffe, L. (2017). Rethinking work-life balance and wellbeing: The perspectives of fathers. In *The Routledge companion to wellbeing at work* (pp. 221–234). Routledge.

22 Kangas, E., Lämsä, A. M., & Jyrkinen, M. (2019). Is fatherhood allowed? Media discourses of fatherhood in organizational life. *Gender, Work & Organization*, *26*(10), 1433–1450.

23 Hine, B. A., & Roy, E. (2023). Lost dads: Findings from the Fathers and Family Breakdown, Separation, and Divorce (FBSD) project. https://drbenhine.co.uk/lost-dads-findings-from-the-fathers-and-family-breakdown-separation-and-divorce-fbsd-project/

24 Faleschini, S., Aubuchon, O., Champeau, L., & Matte-Gagné, C. (2021). History of perinatal loss: A study of psychological outcomes in mothers and fathers after subsequent healthy birth. *Journal of Affective Disorders*, *280*, 338–344.

25 Kothari, A., Bruxner, G., Callaway, L., & Dulhunty, J. M. (2022). "It's a lot of pain you've got to hide": A qualitative study of the journey of fathers facing traumatic pregnancy and childbirth. *BMC Pregnancy and Childbirth*, *22*(1), 434.

26 Kecir, K. A., Rothenburger, S., Morel, O., Albuisson, E., & Ligier, F. (2021). Experiences of fathers having faced with termination of pregnancy for foetal abnormality. *Journal of Gynecology Obstetrics and Human Reproduction*, *50*(1), 101818.

27 Obst, K. L., Oxlad, M., Due, C., & Middleton, P. (2021). Factors contributing to men's grief following pregnancy loss and neonatal death: Further development of an emerging model in an Australian sample. *BMC Pregnancy and Childbirth*, *21*, 1–16.

28 Thomas, G. M., Lupton, D., & Pedersen, S. (2018). 'The appy for a happy pappy': Expectant fatherhood and pregnancy apps. *Journal of Gender Studies*, *27*(7), 759–770.

29 Ammari, T., & Schoenebeck, S. (2015, April). Understanding and supporting fathers and fatherhood on social media sites. In *Proceedings of the 33rd*

Annual ACM Conference on Human Factors in Computing Systems (pp. 1905–1914).

30 Scheibling, C. (2020). Doing fatherhood online: Men's parental identities, experiences, and ideologies on social media. *Symbolic Interaction, 43*(3), 472–492.

31 Henry, J. B., Julion, W. A., Bounds, D. T., & Sumo, J. N. (2020). Fatherhood matters: An integrative review of fatherhood intervention research. *The Journal of School Nursing, 36*(1), 19–32.

18

FAMILY BREAKDOWN, SEPARATION, AND DIVORCE

18.1 INTRODUCTION

Family breakdown, separation, and divorce (FBSD) represent some of the most profoundly disruptive events in a man's life, touching on every aspect of his well-being – emotional, psychological, and often financial. While the societal narrative has made strides in recognizing the broad spectrum of divorce's impact on women and children, the specific vulnerabilities and challenges faced by men in these situations have not been equally illuminated. This chapter seeks to bridge that gap, focusing on the nuanced ways men experience and process the aftermath of family breakdown.

The dissolution of a family unit does not impact all individuals uniformly; men, in particular, encounter unique challenges in the wake of separation. Research indicates that men are extremely vulnerable during and after family separation, with significant implications for their mental health. However, due to long-standing societal norms that equate masculinity with stoicism and emotional resilience, many men struggle in silence, reluctant to seek help or even acknowledge their suffering.

Understanding the experiences of men during these critical junctures is not just an exercise in empathy; it is a crucial step toward providing the support and resources needed to navigate this difficult period. Recognizing the

DOI: 10.4324/9781032709369-23

depth of their vulnerability is key to developing targeted interventions that can address the mental health crisis many separated and divorced men face. Moreover, this understanding can help dismantle the stigma around male vulnerability, encouraging a more supportive and open dialogue about men's emotional and psychological needs during times of personal upheaval.

This chapter aims to delve into the complex tapestry of men's experiences following FBSD, exploring how these events shape their mental health, their relationships, especially with their children, and their overall well-being. It is built upon my "Lost Dads" project, the most extensive examination of this issue to date,[1] as well as my TEDx Talk, "How Can We Separate Better?"[2] By shedding light on these issues, I hope to contribute to a broader conversation about gender, mental health, and societal support, advocating for a world where men's vulnerabilities are acknowledged and addressed with the same urgency and compassion as those of any other member of our society.

18.2   THE IMMEDIATE IMPACT OF SEPARATION

In the immediate aftermath of separation, fathers struggle with their emotions and associated stigma.

18.2.1   Emotional and Psychological Responses

The initial aftermath of separation or divorce ushers in a storm of emotional turmoil and psychological distress for many men. This period is often characterized by a cascade of intense feelings, including sadness, anger, confusion, and in some cases, relief. These emotions are not only natural but are also critical components of the grieving process as men come to terms with the loss of their partnership, shared dreams, and the daily companionship they once knew.

However, the emotional impact of separation is complex and can lead to significant psychological distress. Men may experience depression, anxiety, and a profound sense of loss. The disruption of the familial structure also challenges their identity and roles, not just as partners, but as fathers, providers, and protectors as well. The sense of failure, coupled with worries about the future and the logistics of navigating life postseparation, can be overwhelming. For many men, this period marks one of the most vulnerable times in their lives, laying bare the emotional depth and complexity that societal norms often compel them to hide.

18.2.2   The Stigma of Male Vulnerability

The societal perceptions of male vulnerability play a pivotal role in shaping how men navigate their emotional and psychological responses to separation. Traditionally, masculinity has been equated with stoicism, strength, and an unwavering capacity to withstand emotional distress. This cultural script discourages men from acknowledging their vulnerabilities, much less expressing them or seeking support. The stigma attached to male vulnerability can make men feel isolated in their suffering, exacerbating the psychological toll of their separation.

This reluctance to seek help or express emotions is not without consequence. It can lead to delayed healing, lead to unresolved grief, and in severe cases, contribute to mental health crises. The pressure to "move on" or to quickly rebound into normalcy or new relationships can prevent men from fully processing their loss and can stifle their emotional recovery.

18.3   EXPERIENCES OF ABUSE

Many fathers experience various forms of abusive behavior both during and after the FBSD event, and men's experiences of abuse within relatonships are covered in more detail in Chapter 19. Postseparation abuse specifically can manifest in several ways, significantly impacting the well-being of fathers. The types of abuse often include:

1. *Emotional and psychological abuse.* This is one of the most common forms of abuse that men face postseparation. It involves tactics such as constant belittlement, humiliation, and manipulation designed to undermine the father's confidence and self-worth. Fathers may be subjected to derogatory remarks and continuous criticism, which can lead to severe emotional distress and a decline in mental health.

2. *Verbal abuse.* Verbal abuse includes name-calling, yelling, and threats. This type of abuse often aims to intimidate and control the father, creating an environment of fear and anxiety. Verbal abuse can occur during direct interactions or through indirect means, such as text messages or phone calls.

3. *Physical abuse.* Although less common, some fathers report experiencing physical abuse from their ex-partners. This can include hitting, pushing, or other forms of physical aggression. Such abuse may occur during confrontations or handovers of children.

4. *Financial abuse.* Financial abuse involves controlling or limiting access to financial resources. Fathers may find themselves cut off from joint accounts, burdened with unfair financial obligations, or subjected to excessive demands for child support. This type of abuse can create significant financial strain, making it difficult for fathers to rebuild their lives postseparation.

5. *Legal and administrative abuse.* Fathers often face abuse through legal and administrative channels. This can include false allegations, manipulation of legal processes to delay proceedings, and exploiting legal aid systems to prolong disputes. Such tactics can be emotionally exhausting and financially draining for fathers, who must constantly defend themselves against unfounded accusations.

18.3.2   Parental Alienation and Alienating Behaviors

Parental alienation is a specific and insidious form of postseparation abuse that many fathers encounter.[3,4,5] It involves one parent deliberately attempting to distance the children from the other parent, often through alienating behaviors such as:

1. *Manipulation of the child's perception.* The alienating parent may speak negatively about the other parent in front of the child, portraying them as unloving, irresponsible, or dangerous. This manipulation can create fear, mistrust, and resentment in the child toward the alienated parent.

2. *Control of contact time.* The alienating parent may interfere with scheduled visitations, making it difficult for the other parent to spend time with their children. They may cancel visits at the last minute, refuse to comply with court-ordered custody arrangements, or create logistical barriers to contact.

3. *Denigration and false allegations.* The alienating parent may make false accusations of abuse or neglect, which can have severe legal and emotional consequences for the father. These false allegations can lead to investigations, court hearings, and a further deterioration of the father–child relationship.

4. *Instilling fear in the child.* The alienating parent may instill fear in the child by suggesting that the other parent is harmful or untrustworthy. This fear can prevent the child from wanting to spend time with the alienated parent, further straining their relationship.

18.3.3   The Invisibilization of Abuse

The abuse that men face postseparation is often invisibilized due to societal norms and stereotypes. Several factors contribute to this invisibility:

1. *Societal expectations of masculinity.* Traditional views of masculinity emphasize stoicism, strength, and emotional resilience. Men are often expected to "tough it out" and not show vulnerability. This societal

expectation can prevent men from acknowledging or reporting abuse, leading to underrecognition of their experiences.

2. *Lack of awareness and recognition.* There is a general lack of awareness and recognition of male victims of domestic abuse. Support services and legal systems are often geared toward female victims, leaving male victims without adequate support or resources. This imbalance perpetuates the invisibility of men's experiences of abuse.

3. *Bias in support services.* Many support services, including shelters, counseling, and legal aid, are primarily designed for women. Men seeking help may face skepticism or disbelief, making it difficult for them to access the necessary support. This bias can further marginalize men and discourage them from seeking help.

4. *Stigma and shame.* Men who experience abuse may feel a sense of shame and stigma, believing that admitting to being a victim is a sign of weakness. This internalized stigma can prevent men from reaching out for help and sharing their experiences, contributing to the invisibility of their plight.

18.4   NEGOTIATING CHILD CUSTODY ARRANGEMENTS AND THE FAMILY COURTS

One of the opportunities to enact this abuse comes through the negotiation of child custody arrangements.

18.4.1   Custody Battles and Legal Challenges

One of the most heart-wrenching aspects of family separation for many men is the custody or child contact battle that may ensue. Child contact disputes are not just legal contests; they are deeply emotional processes that can significantly impact a father's mental health and sense of identity. Despite strides toward gender equality in many areas of society, biases in contact cases can still manifest, often leaving men feeling marginalized in the fight for their parental rights. These biases may stem from outdated stereotypes that favor maternal custody or from a presumption that the mother should be the primary caregiver, especially for young children.

The challenges men face in contact procedings are multifaceted. They include navigating complex legal systems, the financial burden of legal fees, and the emotional toll of proving their capability and worthiness as fathers. The stress associated with these challenges can exacerbate existing mental health issues or lead to new ones as men grapple with the fear of losing meaningful contact with their children.

18.4.2   Specific Challenges in Family Courts

There were several challenges highlighted by fathers in my work:

1. *Bias and presumption of maternal custody.* One of the most significant challenges men face in family courts is the enduring bias toward maternal custody. Despite legal frameworks advocating for gender-neutral decisions, many men report feeling that courts are predisposed to favor mothers, especially for young children. This bias often stems from traditional views of mothers as primary caregivers, which can result in fathers being awarded less time with their children or being seen as secondary parents.

2. *Legal and administrative barriers.* Navigating the legal system is often daunting for fathers. The complexity of legal procedures, coupled with a lack of clear guidance, can leave men feeling overwhelmed. Many fathers report that the court processes are slow, inefficient, and biased against them. The need for extensive documentation and proof of their parenting capabilities adds to the burden, making it difficult for fathers to effectively present their case.

3. *Financial strain.* The financial implications of custody battles can be severe. Legal fees can accumulate rapidly, creating significant financial stress. Fathers often have to balance these costs with maintaining their financial responsibilities toward their children and themselves. This financial strain can be exacerbated if the father is also dealing with the loss of a shared household or other financial support systems.

4. *Emotional and psychological toll.* The emotional toll of custody battles cannot be understated. Fathers often experience intense stress, anxiety, and a sense of powerlessness during these proceedings. The fear of losing contact with their children can lead to significant psychological distress, including depression and anxiety. The adversarial nature of court proceedings can also exacerbate these feelings, making the process emotionally draining and demoralizing.

5. *False allegations and parental alienation.* Another challenge fathers face in family courts is dealing with false allegations made by their ex-partners. These allegations can range from accusations of abuse to claims of neglect, which can severely damage a father's case and reputation. Fathers often feel that the courts do not adequately scrutinize these claims, leading to unjust decisions. Additionally, many fathers experience parental alienation, where the other parent actively works to distance the children from them, which can be emotionally devastating and difficult to prove in court.

6. *Lack of support and resources.* Fathers often find themselves with limited support and resources during custody battles. Many report that there are fewer services tailored to their needs compared to those available for mothers. This lack of support can leave fathers feeling isolated and without the necessary guidance to navigate the complex legal landscape effectively.

These specific challenges highlight the need for a more balanced and equitable approach in family court systems, recognizing the essential role that fathers play in their children's lives and ensuring that their rights are protected. Addressing these issues requires comprehensive legal reforms, better support systems, and a cultural shift toward more inclusive and unbiased views of fatherhood.

18.4.3   The Impact of Reduced Contact With Children

When men experience reduced contact with their children postseparation, the impact on their mental health and their identity as fathers can be profound. The father–child relationship is central to many men's understanding of their role and purpose within the family, and a reduction in contact can feel like a loss of part of their identity. This loss can manifest as grief, depression, and a sense of failure, compounding the emotional distress experienced during the separation process.

Reduced interaction with children not only affects the emotional bond but can also lead to feelings of alienation and isolation from the family unit. Men may struggle with the perception that they are no longer "full-time" fathers, which can challenge their views on fatherhood and masculinity. The psychological impact of this can be significant, leading to decreased self-esteem, increased stress, and a sense of disconnection from their children's lives.

Moreover, the impact of decreased contact extends beyond the immediate emotional effects; it can alter the dynamic of the father–child relationship in the long term. The quality and quantity of time spent together are crucial in maintaining strong bonds, and reduced contact can make it challenging to preserve these connections. This situation necessitates a proactive approach to parenting, where fathers seek to maximize the quality of the time they do spend with their children, fostering resilience in themselves and their relationships.

18.5   IMPACT AND SUPPORT

When examining the impact of family breakdown more broadly, men report a variety of issues.

18.5.1   Emotional and Psychological Turmoil

The process of separation and divorce is one of the most emotionally taxing experiences a person can undergo. For men, the emotional and psychological toll of this transition can be profound, often exacerbating pre-existing mental health issues or triggering new ones. The stages of separation – from the initial decision to part ways, through legal proceedings, to the finalization of the divorce – each come with their own set of mental health challenges.

18.5.1.1   Stages and Emotional Responses

There are commonly several stages that men have to progresss through during family breakdown, including:

1. *Initial decision and realization.* The realization that a relationship is ending can lead to a range of intense emotions, including shock, denial, and sadness. Men may struggle with the decision itself, experiencing doubt, guilt, and a profound sense of loss as they contemplate the dissolution of their family unit and the future implications.

2. *Legal proceedings and custody battles.* The legal aspects of separation, including custody battles and financial settlements, are often contentious and stressful. Men may feel overwhelmed by the complexity of legal processes and the adversarial nature of court proceedings. This stage can lead to heightened anxiety, depression, and a sense of powerlessness, particularly if they feel disadvantaged or unjustly treated within the legal system.

3. *Postdivorce adjustment.* Adjusting to life postdivorce involves significant changes in living arrangements, financial status, and social dynamics. Men may struggle with loneliness, identity loss, and the challenge of rebuilding their lives. The uncertainty and disruption of their daily routines can exacerbate feelings of instability and stress.

18.5.1.2   Common Mental Health Issues

During these stages, multiple mental issues can manifest, including:

1. *Depression.* Feelings of sadness and hopelessness are common during and after separation. Depression can be exacerbated by the sense of failure associated with the end of a marriage, the loss of daily interaction with children, and the loneliness of living alone. Symptoms of depression may include persistent sadness, loss of interest in activities,

changes in appetite and sleep patterns, and thoughts of self-harm or suicide.

2. *Anxiety.* The uncertainty and upheaval of separation can lead to significant anxiety. Men may worry about financial stability, future relationships, and their ability to maintain a relationship with their children. Symptoms of anxiety can include excessive worry, restlessness, fatigue, difficulty concentrating, and physical symptoms like heart palpitations and muscle tension.

3. *Posttraumatic stress disorder (PTSD).* In cases where the separation was particularly contentious or involved elements of abuse or trauma, men may experience symptoms of PTSD. These can include flashbacks, nightmares, severe anxiety, and uncontrollable thoughts about the event.

4. *Substance abuse.* Some men may turn to alcohol or drugs as a way to cope with the emotional pain of separation. Substance abuse can provide a temporary escape but often leads to further mental health issues, physical health problems, and strained relationships with friends and family.

18.5.2   Impact on Physical Health

The emotional and psychological stress of separation and divorce can also significantly impact men's physical health. During this tumultuous period, men may experience a range of physical health issues that can exacerbate their overall well-being.

18.5.2.1   Health Issues

These include:

1. *Sleep disturbances.* One of the most immediate physical effects of separation and divorce is on sleep. The anxiety and stress associated with family breakdown can lead to insomnia or disrupted sleep patterns. Men may find it difficult to fall asleep or stay asleep due to racing thoughts and heightened emotional distress. Chronic sleep disturbances can further affect cognitive function, mood, and overall physical health.

2. *Appetite changes.* Stress can significantly alter eating habits. Some men may experience a loss of appetite, leading to unintentional weight loss and malnutrition. Others might turn to food for comfort, resulting in overeating and subsequent weight gain. Both scenarios can lead to

further health complications, including weakened immune systems and nutritional deficiencies.

3.   *Increased risk of chronic illnesses.* Prolonged stress is known to increase the risk of developing chronic illnesses, such as cardiovascular diseases, hypertension, and diabetes. The sustained emotional strain of separation and divorce elevates cortisol levels in the body, which can contribute to high blood pressure, atherosclerosis, and other cardiovascular conditions. Additionally, stress can impair the body's ability to regulate blood sugar levels, increasing the risk of diabetes.

4.   *Weakened immune system.* Chronic stress can weaken the immune system, making men more susceptible to infections and illnesses. This compromised immune response can result in more frequent colds, flu, and other health issues, further impacting overall health.

5.   *Musculoskeletal issues.* The physical manifestations of stress often include muscle tension and pain. Men experiencing significant emotional distress may develop chronic pain conditions, such as back pain, headaches, and joint issues, which can reduce their quality of life and physical functioning.

18.5.3   Impact on Professional Life

Separation and divorce can also profoundly impact men's professional lives, often leading to decreased productivity, reduced job satisfaction, and hindered career advancement. The emotional and psychological stress of navigating a breakup can result in difficulty concentrating, increased absenteeism, and lower overall work performance. Men may also experience a loss of motivation and enthusiasm for their careers as they grapple with personal upheaval. To manage these challenges, it is crucial for men to seek support through counseling, communicate openly with supervisors about their situation, and prioritize self-care practices, such as regular exercise and mindfulness. Additionally, establishing a work–life balance by setting boundaries and seeking flexible work arrangements can help maintain professional stability during this difficult period.

18.5.4   Financial Impact

Family breakdown can have profound financial repercussions for men, influencing their economic stability and future financial well-being. The financial challenges arising from separation and divorce are multifaceted, often leading to both immediate and long-term consequences. Understanding these financial impacts is crucial for men navigating the complexities of family dissolution.

18.5.4.1   Immediate Financial Strain

The immediate aftermath of a separation or divorce typically brings significant financial stress due to several factors:

1. Legal Expenses: Engaging in legal proceedings such as divorce filings, custody battles, and property settlements can incur substantial legal fees. These costs can quickly accumulate, placing a financial burden on men during an already challenging time.

2. Alimony and Child Support Obligations: Men may be required to make regular alimony (spousal support) and child support payments. These financial obligations can significantly reduce disposable income and necessitate adjustments to living standards.

3. Division of Assets: The equitable division of marital assets, including property, savings, investments, and personal belongings, can lead to a reduction in net worth. Men may face the loss of joint assets or the need to purchase out a spouse's share, impacting financial resources.

4. Housing and Living Arrangements: Establishing a new household post-separation often involves upfront costs such as security deposits, moving expenses, and potential increases in rent or mortgage payments. These changes can strain financial resources and necessitate budgeting adjustments.

18.5.4.2   Long-term Financial Consequences

Beyond the immediate financial challenges, family breakdown can lead to enduring financial consequences:

1. Reduced Household Income: The loss of a partner's income can result in a significant decrease in total household earnings. This reduction may affect the ability to maintain previous living standards, save for future goals, or cover ongoing expenses.

2. Increased Debt Levels: Men may incur additional debt to manage the costs associated with separation, including legal fees, moving expenses, and maintaining separate households. This increase in debt can impact credit scores and financial health over time.

3. Impact on Retirement Savings: The division of assets often includes retirement accounts and pensions. Men may find their retirement savings diminished, necessitating adjustments to retirement plans and potentially delaying financial goals related to retirement.

4. Career and Earning Potential: The emotional and psychological stress of family breakdown can affect professional performance, leading to reduced productivity, missed opportunities for advancement, or even job loss. These factors can have long-term implications for earning potential and career progression.

5. Health-Related Expenses: The mental and physical health challenges associated with separation and divorce can lead to increased health-care costs. Addressing issues such as depression, anxiety, or stress-related ailments may require medical treatment, therapy, or medication, adding to financial burdens.

18.5.4   Barriers to Seeking Help

However, significant help-seeking barriers exist for fathers experiencing FBSD, both internal and external. Internal barriers often relate to societal constructions of masculinity that encourage independence and stoicism, as well as negative stereotypes about fatherhood, which limit men's ability to recognize their emotional and mental health needs and forms of victimization. These stereotypes discourage men from seeking support, resulting in many fathers suffering in silence and not accessing the help they desperately need. External barriers include a lack of services, and judgement from others, which are largely informed by those same negative masculinity stereotypes, as well as misleading stereotypes about separation itself.

18.5.5   Healthy vs. Unhealthy Coping

Fathers report coping with FBSD in numerous ways; some healthy, some unhealthy. Healthy coping mechanisms are those that contribute positively to emotional healing and psychological well-being. These can include engaging in physical activity, which not only improves physical health but also offers psychological benefits through the release of endorphins. Seeking therapy or counseling provides a space for men to process their emotions and experiences with a professional helping them understand and work through their feelings rather than suppressing them. Other constructive practices include developing new hobbies, spending time with supportive friends and family, and engaging in mindfulness or meditation to manage stress and anxiety.

Conversely, unhealthy coping mechanisms, while possibly offering a temporary escape from pain, ultimately exacerbate stress and hinder emotional recovery. Substance abuse, whether alcohol, drugs, or misuse of prescription medications, is a common but harmful way some men may try to numb their pain or escape from reality. This not only has dire implications for physical health but can also lead to addiction, deepening depression, and increased anxiety. Similarly, avoidance behaviors, such as withdrawing from social contact or ignoring financial or legal responsibilities, can complicate the situation further and delay the healing process.

18.5.6   The Role of Support Networks

The importance of robust support networks cannot be overstated in navigating the complexities of postseparation life. Friends and family play a crucial role, offering emotional support, practical assistance, and a sense of belonging during a time when men may feel most isolated. These personal connections provide a buffer against the stress of separation, reminding men that they are not alone in their journey.

18.6   STRATEGIES FOR RECOVERY AND RESILIENCE

There are several avenues that fathers can pursue to help cope with FBSD.

18.6.1   Therapeutic Interventions

In the journey toward healing from the aftermath of separation, divorce, or family breakdown, men face a complex web of challenges that require both immediate attention and long-term strategies for emotional recovery and resilience. Effective mental health support and therapeutic approaches tailored to men's needs are fundamental in navigating the recovery process.

Therapy can provide a structured environment for men to explore their feelings, understand their responses to separation, and develop healthy coping mechanisms. Cognitive behavioral therapy (CBT) is particularly effective in addressing depressive symptoms and anxiety by challenging negative thought patterns and promoting more positive thinking and behavior.

In addition to individual therapy, group therapy sessions can offer support through shared experiences. These sessions create a sense of community and reduce feelings of isolation as men realize they are not alone in their struggles. For those facing specific challenges, such as substance abuse or anger management, targeted interventions such as addiction counseling or anger management classes can provide crucial support and strategies for overcoming these issues.

Furthermore, mindfulness-based stress reduction (MBSR) programs and meditation can be beneficial in managing stress, improving emotional regulation, and enhancing overall well-being. These practices encourage presence, awareness, and acceptance, which are vital components of the recovery and healing process.

18.6.2   Building Resilience

Resilience is the capacity to recover from difficulties, adapt to change, and continue moving forward. Building resilience in the face of relationship breakdowns involves several key strategies:

1. *Fostering a growth mindset.* This can help men view challenges as opportunities for learning and personal development rather than insurmountable obstacles. This perspective encourages active engagement with the recovery process and promotes a sense of control over one's path to healing.

2. *Engaging in regular physical activity.* Exercise not only improves physical health but also has a significant positive impact on mental health, reducing symptoms of depression and anxiety and increasing feelings of self-efficacy.

3. *Creating and maintaining a supportive social network.* Strengthening connections with friends, family, and others who provide encouragement and understanding can offer a lifeline during tough times. Additionally, pursuing new interests and hobbies can provide a sense of purpose and joy, contributing to a more fulfilling life postseparation.

4. *Setting realistic goals and celebrating small achievements.* This can motivate continued progress and reinforce a sense of accomplishment. This practice helps men focus on the future with optimism, recognizing their own strength and capacity to overcome adversity.

By investing in their mental health and well-being, embracing growth, and nurturing supportive relationships, men can lay the foundation for a resilient, adaptable, and hopeful future.

18.7   PARENTING STRATEGIES AND LEGAL RIGHTS POSTDIVORCE

Navigating the complexities of parenting and legal rights during and after a divorce can be challenging. Effective coparenting, maintaining strong relationships with children, and understanding legal rights and resources are crucial for ensuring a smooth transition and fostering a stable environment for both parents and children.[6]

18.7.1   Parenting Strategies Postdivorce

Listed are several quickfire bullet pointed sections on different areas of parenting **strategies** post FBSD.

18.7.1.1   Coparenting

- *Effective communication.* Open, respectful, and consistent communication with the ex-partner is essential for successful coparenting. Establish clear boundaries, and keep discussions focused on the well-being of the children. Utilize tools like shared calendars and coparenting apps to coordinate schedules and share important information.
- *Consistency and stability.* Maintain consistent routines and rules across both households to provide stability for the children. Consistency helps children feel secure and understand what to expect, which is crucial during times of change.
- *Conflict resolution.* Develop strategies for resolving conflicts amicably and constructively. This might involve setting aside differences, focusing on the children's needs, and possibly involving a mediator to facilitate discussions when necessary.

18.7.1.2   Maintaining Strong Relationships With Children

- *Quality time.* Prioritize spending quality time with your children. Engage in activities that they enjoy and that strengthen your bond. Regularly scheduled time together reinforces a sense of normalcy and connection.
- *Emotional support.* Be available to listen and provide emotional support to your children. Encourage them to express their feelings, and reassure them that both parents love and support them.
- *Active involvement.* Stay actively involved in your children's lives by attending school events, extracurricular activities, and medical appointments. This involvement shows your commitment and strengthens your relationship.

18.7.2   Legal Rights and Resources

18.7.2.1   Understanding Legal Rights

- *Custody and visitation.* Familiarize yourself with your legal rights regarding custody and visitation. Custody arrangements can vary, including joint custody, sole custody, or shared custody. Understanding these options and your rights can help you advocate for a fair arrangement.
- *Child support.* Learn about your obligations and rights concerning child support. Ensure that the arrangement is fair and that you understand how payments are calculated and enforced.
- *Alimony.* Understand your rights and obligations related to alimony (spousal support). This may involve temporary or long-term payments to support your ex-partner financially.

18.7.2.2   Navigating the Legal System

- *Consulting a lawyer*. Engaging a family law attorney who specializes in divorce and custody issues can provide valuable guidance and representation. A lawyer can help you understand your rights, navigate legal procedures, and advocate for your interests.
- *Legal aid services*. If you cannot afford a private attorney, explore legal aid services that offer support to individuals with limited financial resources. These services can provide legal advice, representation, and assistance with documentation.
- *Online resources*. Utilize online resources and tools to educate yourself about the divorce process, your rights, and available support. Websites, forums, and legal platforms offer valuable information and community support.

18.7.2.3   Strategies for Effective Legal Navigation

- *Documentation*. Keep thorough records of all communications, financial transactions, and legal documents related to the divorce. This documentation can be critical in legal proceedings.
- *Preparation*. Prepare thoroughly for court appearances and meetings with your lawyer. Understanding the process and being organized can significantly improve your ability to navigate the legal system effectively.
- *Support networks*. Lean on support networks, including friends, family, and support groups, for emotional and practical assistance. They can provide guidance, share experiences, and offer encouragement.

18.8   POLICY AND SOCIAL CHANGE RECOMMENDATIONS

The aftermath of separation, divorce, and family breakdown highlights the need for comprehensive policy and social changes to address the challenges faced by men during these transitional times. Addressing these areas through thoughtful policy reform and societal initiatives can significantly impact men's ability to recover and thrive postseparation.

18.8.1   Advocating for Fair Custody Arrangements

Fair custody arrangements are crucial to ensuring that the best interests of children and the rights of both parents are respected and upheld. To achieve this, legal and policy frameworks must evolve to eliminate biases and promote equity in custody decisions. Recommendations include:

1. *Implementing presumption of shared parenting*. Encourage legal systems to start with the presumption of shared parenting, where

appropriate, to affirm the importance of both parents in a child's life, barring situations involving abuse or neglect.

2. *Increasing access to legal resources.* Provide more accessible legal resources and support for fathers navigating the custody process, including legal aid and counseling on their rights and responsibilities.

3. *Enhancing judicial training.* Offer ongoing training for judges and mediators on issues related to gender biases and the dynamics of modern family structures to ensure more balanced decision-making in custody cases.

4. *Promoting mediation and collaborative law.* Encourage mediation and collaborative law as alternatives to contentious court battles, focusing on coparenting arrangements that prioritize the child's well-being while respecting the rights of both parents.

18.8.2 Enhancing Access to Mental Health Services

Improving men's access to mental health resources involves dismantling barriers and expanding services to meet their needs effectively. Recommendations include:

1. *Reducing stigma.* Launch public awareness campaigns to challenge stereotypes about masculinity and mental health, emphasizing that seeking help is a sign of strength. These campaigns can involve sports figures, celebrities, and other influencers men respect and admire.

2. *Expanding services.* Increase funding for mental health services, particularly those targeting men, to expand their availability and reduce wait times. This includes support for group therapy sessions, online counseling options, and crisis intervention services.

3. *Tailoring approaches to men.* Develop and support therapeutic approaches that are specifically designed to engage men, recognizing that traditional therapy settings may not always be the most effective. This could involve more activity-based therapies, online platforms, and outreach in settings where men feel comfortable.

4. *Facilitating access.* Improve the accessibility of mental health services for men by offering flexible hours, online support options, and integrating mental health services into primary care settings where men are more likely to seek help for other issues.

5.   *Training health professionals.* Provide training for health professionals on the unique ways men may express distress and the best strategies for engaging them in mental health care.

18.8.3   Broader Societal Changes

Beyond policy and legal reforms, broader societal changes are necessary to support men and families during and after separation. These changes should focus on valuing both parents and recognizing the impact they have on their children's lives. Recommendations include:

1.   *Valuing both parents equally.* Promote societal recognition of the importance of both parents in a child's life, regardless of marital status. Public campaigns and educational programs can help shift the perception that caregiving is predominantly a maternal role and highlight the essential contributions of fathers to their children's development.

2.   *Encouraging work–life balance.* Advocate for workplace policies that support work–life balance for both parents. This includes promoting flexible work schedules, parental leave for both mothers and fathers, and creating a work culture that values family involvement. Such policies enable both parents to remain actively involved in their children's lives postseparation.

3.   *Supporting father involvement.* Develop and fund community programs that encourage father involvement in all aspects of child-rearing. Parenting classes, father–child activities, and support groups can help fathers develop strong relationships with their children and provide a sense of community and support.

4.   *Challenging gender stereotypes.* Implement educational initiatives aimed at dismantling traditional gender roles and stereotypes that limit the expression of vulnerability in men. Schools, workplaces, and community organizations should promote the idea that seeking help and expressing emotions are healthy behaviors for everyone, regardless of gender.

5.   *Recognizing and addressing parental alienation.* Increase awareness and understanding of parental alienation within the legal and social service systems. Provide training for professionals to recognize signs of parental alienation, and develop intervention strategies to protect the child's relationship with both parents.

By implementing these policy and social change recommendations, society can move toward a more equitable, supportive, and healthy environment for men navigating the challenges of separation, divorce, and family break-down. Fair custody arrangements and enhanced access to mental health services not only benefit men but also promote the well-being of children and the broader community, contributing to a more compassionate and understanding society.

18.9   EXAMPLES OF SUPPORT

Here are some examples of organizations that already work with men fol-lowing family breakdown:

18.9.1   Dads Unlimited

Dads Unlimited is a UK charity dedicated to supporting the emotional safety and mental well-being of men, particularly those facing family separation, domestic abuse, and mental health challenges. They offer a range of ser-vices, including one-to-one mentoring, coparenting workshops, and a spe-cialized domestic abuse victim empowerment service. The organization uses an evidence-based, trauma-informed approach to provide practical and emotional support to help men navigate difficult periods in their lives. Website: www.dadsunltd.org.uk/.

18.9.2   Families Need Fathers

Families Need Fathers is a UK charity that provides information, support, and resources to parents seeking to maintain relationships with their chil-dren following separation or divorce. Their services include a helpline, sup-port meetings, and educational resources on family law. They advocate for shared parenting and work to ensure that children have meaningful relation-ships with both parents. Website: https://fnf.org.uk/.

18.10   CONCLUSION

The journey through FBSD is fraught with emotional, psychological, and practical challenges that can profoundly affect men's lives. This chapter has explored the multifaceted nature of these challenges, from the immediate emotional turmoil and long-term mental health effects to the complexities of navigating child custody and the loss of contact with children. It has high-lighted the significance of distinguishing between healthy and unhealthy coping mechanisms, the indispensable role of support networks, and the critical strategies for recovery and resilience. Moreover, it underscored the necessity for policy and social change, particularly in advocating for fair custody arrangements and enhancing access to mental health services.

The unique challenges faced by men during these difficult times demand our attention and understanding. Recognizing the emotional depth and complexity of men's experiences in the context of family breakdown is the first step toward providing the necessary support. It is not just an individual or family issue but a societal one that calls for a collective response. The stigma around male vulnerability and mental health, which often prevents men from seeking help, needs to be dismantled. Societal norms and perceptions that define masculinity in narrow terms must be challenged and redefined to embrace emotional expression and vulnerability as strengths, not weaknesses.

Supporting men through the challenges of separation, divorce, and beyond is integral to broader societal efforts toward gender equality and mental health awareness. *Gender equality* is not just about addressing the disparities faced by women but also about recognizing and tackling the issues uniquely affecting men. Enhancing men's mental health and well-being enriches the entire fabric of society, contributing to healthier families, communities, and future generations.

As we move forward, it is crucial to continue the dialogue on these issues, advocate for changes in policies and societal attitudes, and provide resources and support tailored to men's needs. The journey toward healing and resilience in the aftermath of family breakdown is challenging, but with collective effort and empathy, we can create a supportive environment that acknowledges and addresses the unique challenges faced by men. In doing so, we not only support individual men in their time of need but also take significant steps toward fostering a more inclusive, equitable, and compassionate society for all.

NOTES

1 Hine, B. A., & Roy, E. (2023). Lost dads: Findings from the Fathers and Family Breakdown, Separation, and Divorce (FBSD) project. https://drbenhine.co.uk/lost-dads-findings-from-the-fathers-and-family-breakdown-separation-and-divorce-fbsd-project/
2 www.youtube.com/watch?v=3aRlfNRs8K0
3 Bates, E. A., & Hine, B. A. (2023). "I was told when I could hold, talk with, or kiss our daughter": Exploring fathers' experiences of parental alienation within the context of intimate partner violence. *Partner Abuse*.
4 Hine, B. A., & Bates, E. A. (2023). "There is no part of my life that hasn't been destroyed": The impact of parental alienation and intimate partner violence on fathers. *Partner Abuse*.
5 Hine, B. A. (2024). Parental alienation – what do we know, and what do we (urgently) need to know? A narrative review. *Partner Abuse*.
6 Hine, B. A. (2023). Parental alienation: A contemporary guide for parents, practitioners and policymakers. *Amazon*.

Section 6

VULNERABLE MEN

19

VIOLENCE

19.1 INTRODUCTION

Violence affects individuals across the spectrum of age, gender, and culture. However, the unique position of men and boys within this context – as both victims and perpetrators – demands a nuanced exploration to unravel the complex dynamics at play.[1,2] This chapter embarks on a critical examination of these dual roles, seeking to shed light on the contributing factors, the impact on individuals and communities, and the pathways toward effective interventions.

The exploration of men and boys in relation to violence is multifaceted, involving an array of factors, including societal norms, cultural expectations, and individual circumstances. The traditional constructs of masculinity, often intertwined with notions of dominance and aggression, play a significant role in shaping behaviors and attitudes toward violence. Moreover, the experiences of men and boys as victims of violence – though significant and profoundly impactful – are frequently overlooked, obscured by prevailing stereotypes and a lack of societal acknowledgment.

Understanding the dynamics of violence requires a careful consideration of the broader societal, psychological, and environmental contexts in which these behaviors manifest. This includes acknowledging the type of violence under examination, the impact of exposure to violence, the influence of media and technology, and the critical role of mental health and substance

DOI: 10.4324/9781032709369-25

abuse. By delving into these areas, this chapter aims to provide a comprehensive overview of the challenges and considerations pertinent to addressing the issues of violence associated with men and boys.

The objective of this exploration is not only to highlight the extent and effects of violence but also to emphasize the urgent need for targeted interventions and support mechanisms. Through a balanced examination of men and boys as both victims and perpetrators of violence, we can begin to formulate strategies that address the root causes, support affected individuals, and ultimately contribute to reducing violence in our communities. This chapter seeks to contribute to the ongoing dialogue on gender, violence, and societal change, advocating for a more inclusive and compassionate approach to understanding and resolving these complex issues.

19.2   UNDERSTANDING THE LANDSCAPE

Violence manifests in myriad forms, each with its distinct characteristics and impacts on the lives of men and boys, and with different roles occupied by men at different rates depending on the type of violence. Understanding these forms is crucial to addressing the root causes and consequences of violence within society. Common forms of violence include:

- *Physical violence.* This form of violence involves physical harm or force against another person. For men and boys, it can occur in various contexts, including domestic settings, schools, workplaces, or public spaces. Physical violence encompasses everything from fighting and assault to more severe forms of harm, such as homicide. Homicide, being one of the most extreme forms of physical violence, has a profound and irreversible impact on families and communities.
- *Emotional and psychological violence.* Often less visible but equally damaging, emotional and psychological violence includes behaviors that harm an individual's mental well-being. For men and boys, this can involve verbal abuse, bullying, intimidation, and manipulation. These actions can leave deep psychological scars, affecting their sense of self-worth and emotional stability.
- *Sexual violence.* This includes acts such as rape, sexual assault, and sexual harassment. Men and boys can be victims of sexual violence, which is often underreported due to stigma, shame, and societal perceptions of masculinity. The impact of sexual violence on male victims can be profound, affecting their mental health, relationships, and overall quality of life.
- *Economic violence.* Economic violence involves controlling a person's access to financial resources, education, or employment, thereby limiting their ability to support themselves and their families. Men and boys can experience economic violence through unfair wages, job discrimination, or financial exploitation.

- *Structural violence.* This form of violence is embedded in social structures and institutions, leading to systematic inequality and discrimination. Though it is typically explored in relation to women and girls – and rightly so – men and boys may also face structural violence in the form of racial discrimination, class inequality, or legal injustices that restrict their opportunities and freedoms.
- *Cultural violence.* Cultural violence refers to aspects of culture that can be used to justify or legitimize direct or structural violence. This includes harmful societal norms and practices, such as those that promote aggressive masculinity or stigmatize mental health issues among men.
- *War and armed conflict.* War and armed conflict represent a large-scale manifestation of violence that significantly impacts men and boys. They may be directly involved as combatants or indirectly affected as civilians. The experiences of war can lead to physical injuries, psychological trauma, displacement, and loss of loved ones. For those who serve in military capacities, the transition back to civilian life can be fraught with challenges, including dealing with posttraumatic stress disorder (PTSD) and reintegrating into society.

19.2.2   Statistical Overview

Globally consistent statistics on violence involving men and boys are challenging to compile, but the available data underscores the significant prevalence of their involvement as both victims and perpetrators, as shown here:

- *Perpetrators of violence.* According to the World Health Organization (WHO), men account for a significant majority of perpetrators in cases of interpersonal violence globally. This is consistent with data from various regions indicating that men are more likely to be involved in acts of violence, including intimate partner violence and sexual violence.[3]
- *Victims of homicide.* Studies indicate that men are more likely to be victims of homicide compared to women. For example, global homicide statistics reveal that men make up approximately 80% of homicide victims worldwide. This statistic highlights the higher risk of lethal violence faced by men.
- *Intimate partner and sexual violence.* The National Intimate Partner and Sexual Violence Survey (NISVS) in the United States reports that nearly 1 in 10 men has experienced severe physical violence by an intimate partner in their lifetime, and 1 in 71 men in the United States has been raped at some point in their lives.[4] In the UK, one in three victims of domestic abuse is male, highlighting that men also face significant risks in domestic settings. Moreover, male victims often face barriers to reporting due to societal stigmas and lack of support services.
- *Bullying and cyberbullying.* The UNESCO Institute for Statistics highlights that, globally, boys report being bullied at similar or slightly higher

rates than girls, depending on the country and the form of bullying. This includes both physical and cyber forms of bullying, which can have long-lasting psychological effects.[5]

- *Conflict and humanitarian settings.* In conflict and postconflict settings, men and boys are often targeted for gender-based violence, including sexual violence. Reports indicate that men and boys have been sexually abused in conflicts across over 25 countries, with significant underreporting due to stigma and cultural norms.[6] The Peace Research Institute Oslo (PRIO) found that men are more likely to be killed during conflicts, underscoring the gender-specific risks in these environments.[7]

And so, men clearly have a complicated relationship with violence, marked by significant risks of both perpetration and victimization. The data underscores the dual nature of men's experiences with violence: while they are frequently the perpetrators of various forms of violence, they are also disproportionately victims, particularly in the contexts of homicide and conflict. This duality highlights the need for comprehensive strategies that address both the causes of male-perpetrated violence, and the support required for male victims, recognizing the unique challenges they face in reporting and recovering from violence.

19.3   CONTRIBUTING FACTORS

The relationship between men, boys, and violence is shaped by a multitude of factors, ranging from deeply ingrained societal norms to individual psychological conditions and environmental influences. Understanding these contributing factors is essential for developing effective strategies to reduce violence and support those affected.

19.3.1   Social and Cultural Influences

Societal norms, cultural expectations, and traditional notions of masculinity play a pivotal role in shaping behaviors and attitudes toward violence.[8,9,10] Culturally embedded ideals of masculinity often associate being a man with strength, dominance, and emotional stoicism. These ideals can pressure men and boys to conform to a specific image of manhood, where aggression is seen as an acceptable, even encouraged, method of expressing dominance or resolving conflicts. The expectation to assert control and avoid showing vulnerability can lead to a higher propensity for violent behaviors as a means of affirming one's masculinity. Furthermore, societal norms that glorify violence as a rite of passage for boys into manhood perpetuate cycles of aggression and dominance. These very same stereotypes also shape men's experiences as victims, and their inability to recognize and seek help following abuse and violence, and in invisibilizing them in societal narratives around violence.

19.3.2 Psychological and Environmental Factors

The interplay of psychological and environmental factors also significantly contributes to the prevalence of violence among men and boys. Mental health issues, such as depression, anxiety, and particularly unaddressed trauma, can increase the risk of both experiencing and perpetrating violence. The lack of accessible mental health resources and stigma around seeking help exacerbates this issue (as discussed in Chapter 3), leaving many men and boys to cope with their psychological distress in unhealthy ways, including through violence.

Substance abuse is another critical factor, with alcohol and drugs often linked to an increased risk of committing acts of violence.[11,12,13] The disinhibiting effects of substances can lower thresholds for aggressive behavior, making violent outbursts more likely. This will be further explored in Chapter 22.

Socioeconomic factors, including poverty, unemployment, and exposure to violence in one's community or household, also significantly impact the likelihood of men and boys being involved in violence.[14] The stress and frustration stemming from economic insecurity and environmental instability can fuel aggression and violence as coping mechanisms.

19.3.3 The Role of Media and Technology

Media portrayals of masculinity and the pervasive influence of the internet and social media platforms also have a profound impact on societal attitudes toward violence.[15] Television, movies, video games, and online content often depict violence as a normative and glorified aspect of masculinity (as was discussed in Chapter 5). These portrayals can normalize aggressive behavior and desensitize individuals to the consequences of violence. Moreover, the anonymity and reach of the internet can amplify violent tendencies through the proliferation of violent content, hate speech, and the radicalization of vulnerable individuals. Social media platforms can also serve as echo chambers that reinforce aggressive behaviors and ideologies, further embedding violence within the cultural fabric of masculinity.

Addressing the complex web of factors contributing to the involvement of men and boys in violence thus invites a multifaceted approach. Interventions must not only target individual behaviors but also challenge societal norms, provide robust mental health and substance abuse support, and foster environments that promote healthy expressions of masculinity. Moreover, media and technology platforms must be held accountable for their role in shaping societal attitudes toward violence and masculinity, advocating for responsible portrayals that reject violence as a component of male identity.

19.3.4   Example Initiatives/Organizations

Here are some examples of initiatives that are seeking to work with men to end their role in violence, specifically in the area of sexual abuse:

1.   Futures Without Violence

     Description: Futures Without Violence is a nonprofit organization dedicated to ending violence against women, children, and families around the world. They provide training for professionals such as doctors, nurses, judges, and coaches on improving responses to violence and abuse. Their initiatives include the "Coaching Boys into Men" program, which trains athletic coaches to teach young men about healthy relationships and respect.

     Website: www.futureswithoutviolence.org/.

2.   MVP Strategies

     Description: MVP Strategies, directed by Jackson Katz, conducts trainings in schools, colleges, communities, and the US Armed Forces to prevent gender-based violence. The program focuses on engaging men as leaders and active bystanders in preventing violence against women and promoting gender equality.

     Website: http://mvpstrategies.net/.

3.   National Organization for Men Against Sexism (NOMAS)

     Description: NOMAS is an activist organization that promotes positive changes for men, advocating for pro-feminist, gay-affirmative, antiracist perspectives. They focus on ending gender-based violence and host an annual national conference to support local and grassroots initiatives.

     Website: https://nomas.org/.

4.   Sonke Gender Justice

     Description: Based in South Africa, Sonke Gender Justice works across the African continent to promote gender equality and prevent gender-based violence. They use a human rights framework to build the capacity of government and civil society to address these issues.

     Website: https://genderjustice.org.za/.

5.   Just Detention International

     Description: This organization focuses on ending sexual abuse in all forms of detention. Just Detention International advocates for the rights and dignity of inmates, promotes public attitudes that support the safety of detainees, and works to hold government officials accountable for preventing prisoner rape.

Website: https://justdetention.org/.

6. RAINN (Rape, Abuse, and Incest National Network)

Description: RAINN operates the National Sexual Assault Hotline and the DoD Safe Helpline for the Department of Defense. They provide support for survivors of sexual violence and carry out programs to prevent sexual violence and ensure perpetrators are brought to justice.

Website: www.rainn.org/.

19.4 MEN AND BOYS AS VICTIMS

The narrative around violence often focuses on men and boys as perpetrators, overshadowing their experiences as victims.[16] This oversight neglects the profound impact that violence has on their lives and the societal barriers they face in seeking recognition and support.[17]

19.4.1 Challenges in Recognition and Response

Societal barriers to acknowledging male victims of violence are multifaceted.[18,19] Stigma plays a significant role; prevailing notions of masculinity equate strength with invulnerability, making it difficult for men and boys to come forward about their experiences with violence. Admitting to being a victim is often seen as a sign of weakness, contradicting societal expectations of male toughness and resilience. This stigma can silence male victims, driving their struggles underground and leaving them to cope in isolation.[20] Moreover, these narratives feed into societal narratives about male violence that normalize these experiences for men and boys and decrease recognition, understanding, awareness, and intervention for those involved.

A direct representation of this lack of awareness is the critical lack of resources specifically tailored to male victims of violence. Many existing support services and shelters are designed with women and children in mind, inadvertently creating a service gap for men and boys in need.[21,22] This gap is not just physical but also psychological, as the support mechanisms that do exist may not adequately address the unique challenges and stigmas that male victims face.

19.4.2 The Impact on Mental and Physical Health

Because the effects of violence on the mental and physical health of men and boys are devastating and enduring.[23] In the short term, victims may experience physical injuries, stress, anxiety, and depression. The immediate aftermath of violence often brings a sense of shock and disbelief, coupled with intense emotional distress.

Long-term effects can be even more profound, affecting every aspect of a victim's life. Chronic health issues, including posttraumatic stress disorder (PTSD), long-standing depression, substance abuse, and increased suicide risk, can all stem from unaddressed violence. These issues are compounded by the societal expectation for men to remain stoic and self-reliant, often discouraging them from seeking the help they need to heal and recover fully.

19.4.3   The Lack of Support Systems and Resources

However, while there are support structures in place for victims of violence, the specific needs of male victims often go unmet due to the gaps in services and the lack of awareness about their experiences.[24] For example, in the domestic violence sector, many existing support services and shelters are designed with women and children in mind, inadvertently creating a service gap for men and boys in need.[25,26] This gap is not just physical but also psychological, as the support mechanisms that do exist may not adequately address the unique challenges and stigmas that male victims face.

Some organizations and initiatives have begun to address this need, offering counseling, support groups, and resources tailored to men and boys. However, these services are not widespread, and their visibility and accessibility remain limited. Identifying and closing these gaps require a concerted effort to raise awareness about the prevalence of male victims of violence and the unique challenges they face. This includes training healthcare providers, educators, and law enforcement on how to recognize and support male victims effectively. Additionally, creating more inclusive and gender-sensitive support services can ensure that men and boys have the resources they need to recover from violence.

The path forward must involve a cultural shift that challenges the stigmas surrounding male vulnerability and victimhood, recognizing that strength lies in seeking help and healing. By acknowledging men and boys as victims of violence and addressing the barriers they face in finding support, society can move toward a more inclusive and compassionate approach to all victims of violence.

19.5   MEN AND BOYS AS PERPETRATORS

As with many chapters and sections in this book, this section could be a whole text in its own right. And so, for brevity, I will focus on two specific areas when examining men as perpetrators – intimate partner violence and gang violence – to capture themes applicable to most other forms.

19.5.1 Intimate Partner Violence

Understanding the pathways that lead men and boys to commit acts of violence is crucial for developing effective strategies to prevent such behavior and intervene when necessary. Often, this is overlooked, with men characterized as inherently or characterologically violence rather than individuals with rich stories and issues that may underpin their violent behavior.

19.5.1.1 Understanding the Pathways

Several key factors can predispose men and boys to engage in violent behavior, and in a much stronger way than simply gender alone, many of which are deeply rooted in societal and environmental conditions:[27,28,29,30,31]

1. *Learned behavior and socialization.* From an early age, boys are often socialized into norms that equate masculinity with toughness and dominance. This socialization process can be reinforced by family, peer groups, and broader cultural messages that valorize aggressive behavior as a means of resolving conflicts or asserting control.

2. *Exposure to violence.* Growing up in environments where violence is prevalent – whether in the home, community, or through media – can normalize aggressive behavior for boys and young men. This exposure can desensitize individuals to the impact of violence and teach them to emulate such behavior in their own lives.

3. *Mental health issues and substance abuse.* Unaddressed mental health challenges and substance abuse can significantly increase the risk of violent behavior. These issues can impair judgment, reduce impulse control, and exacerbate feelings of anger or frustration.

4. *Socioeconomic factors.* Economic insecurity, unemployment, and social marginalization can contribute to feelings of powerlessness and frustration, which some men and boys may attempt to counteract through violence as a misguided form of empowerment or self-assertion.

19.5.1.2 Gender and Gendered Attitudes as Predictors of Violence Perpetration

It would be remiss, however, to not acknowledge that gender and gendered attitudes do also play a critical role in predicting violent behavior among men and boys.[32] These attitudes are deeply ingrained in societal norms and cultural expectations, which can significantly influence the likelihood of violent perpetration. Understanding the impact of these gendered dynamics is essential for addressing the root causes of violence and developing targeted prevention strategies.

1.   *Gender norms and masculinity.* Traditional notions of masculinity often emphasize traits such as dominance, control, and physical strength. Men and boys who strongly identify with these traits may feel pressure to demonstrate their masculinity through aggressive or violent behavior. This connection between masculinity and violence is reinforced by societal expectations and media representations that valorize tough, assertive male figures.

2.   *Power and control dynamics.* Gendered attitudes that endorse male authority and control over others can contribute to the perpetration of violence, particularly in intimate relationships. Men who hold traditional beliefs about gender roles may resort to violence as a means of maintaining power and control over their partners or family members.

3.   *Peer influence and group dynamics.* The influence of peer groups can be a powerful factor in shaping gendered attitudes and behaviors. In many social settings, boys and men may be encouraged or pressured by their peers to conform to aggressive norms and behaviors to gain acceptance or status within the group. This peer reinforcement can perpetuate cycles of violence and aggression.

4.   *Resistance to changing gender roles.* Societal shifts toward more egalitarian gender roles can be perceived as threatening by some men, particularly those who feel their traditional roles are being undermined. This resistance to change can manifest in violent behavior as a way to reassert traditional power structures and resist perceived encroachments on male dominance.

5.   *Attitudes toward violence.* Gendered attitudes that normalize or justify violence as an acceptable means of conflict resolution or self-assertion can also predict violent behavior. Men and boys who internalize these attitudes may be more likely to engage in violent acts, believing them to be a legitimate way to handle disputes or demonstrate strength.

19.5.2   Gang Violence

Gang violence represents a significant area of concern when examining men and boys as perpetrators of violence. Gangs often provide a sense of identity, belonging, and protection for young men and boys who may feel marginalized or disenfranchised by society. However, this affiliation comes at a cost, as involvement in gang activities frequently leads to participation in violent behavior.[33,34] Here are some of the factors that underpin gang involvement and subsequent violence:

1. *Sense of belonging and identity.* For many young men, joining a gang can offer a sense of belonging and identity that they might lack in other areas of their lives. This need for acceptance can drive individuals to conform to the gang's norms, which often include violent behavior as a means of proving loyalty and gaining respect.

2. *Economic incentives.* Gangs can offer economic opportunities through illegal activities, which can be enticing for young men facing poverty and unemployment. The promise of financial gain can be a powerful motivator for participation in gang violence as individuals seek to improve their economic standing.

3. *Peer pressure and social influence.* Similar to other forms of violence, peer pressure within gangs can compel members to engage in violent acts. The desire to be accepted and respected by peers can lead individuals to commit acts of violence that they might not otherwise consider.

4. *Retaliation and territory.* Gang violence is often driven by the need to defend territory or retaliate against rival gangs. This cycle of violence can escalate quickly, as acts of aggression prompt retaliatory attacks, creating a continuous loop of violence that is difficult to break.

5. *Cultural and societal norms.* In some communities, gang involvement and the associated violence can be normalized or even glorified. Cultural narratives that romanticize gang life can influence young men's perceptions of violence, making it seem like a viable or even desirable path. Gang membership and behaviors also represent a glorified and venerated "peak" masculinity that is desirable to boys to pursue.[35]

6. *Trauma and mental health.* Many young men involved in gangs have experienced significant trauma, whether from family violence, community violence, or systemic oppression.[36] This trauma can contribute to mental health issues that make individuals more prone to violent behavior. Additionally, the gang environment itself can perpetuate further trauma, creating a vicious cycle of violence and mental health challenges.

Addressing gang violence requires a multifaceted approach that includes providing economic opportunities, educational support, mental health services, and community-based interventions. By addressing the root causes that lead young men to join gangs and commit acts of violence, it is possible to reduce the prevalence of gang-related violence and help individuals find alternative pathways to belonging and success.

19.6   PREVENTION AND INTERVENTION

Addressing the root causes of violence committed by men and boys requires comprehensive strategies that encompass education, community involvement, and policy reforms:[37]

1. *Education and awareness.* Educational programs that challenge traditional norms of masculinity and promote gender equality can play a critical role in preventing violence. Initiatives that teach emotional intelligence, conflict resolution skills, and healthy relationship practices from an early age can help dismantle harmful stereotypes and equip individuals with the tools to navigate conflicts nonviolently.

2. *Community programs.* Community-based programs that provide positive role models, mentorship, and activities that foster a sense of belonging and self-worth can reduce the allure of violence as a means of gaining respect or status. These programs can also offer safe spaces for men and boys to express vulnerabilities and discuss challenges without judgment.

3. *Policy initiatives.* Policies that address the broader socioeconomic factors contributing to violence are essential. This includes efforts to reduce poverty, improve access to mental health services, and ensure that educational and employment opportunities are accessible to all. Additionally, laws and regulations that promote gun safety, reduce alcohol and substance abuse, and offer support for victims of violence can mitigate risk factors.

4. *Intervention programs.* For individuals who have already exhibited violent behavior, intervention programs that focus on rehabilitation and understanding the underlying causes of their actions are crucial. These programs should aim to provide counseling, support for substance abuse recovery, and education on nonviolent conflict resolution techniques.

5. *Recognizing complex humanity.* It is essential to treat men and boys as human beings with complex stories and lives if we are to truly help them. Understanding the individual narratives, traumas, and socioeconomic conditions that contribute to violent behavior allows for more effective and compassionate intervention strategies. By recognizing their humanity and providing holistic support, society can address the root causes of violence and help men and boys build healthier, nonviolent identities.

Preventing violence among men and boys and intervening effectively when it occurs necessitate a multidimensional approach that addresses the individual, social, and structural contributors to violent behavior. By fostering environments that challenge harmful norms, promote healthy expressions of masculinity, and support individuals in overcoming adversities, society can make significant strides in reducing violence perpetrated by men and boys.

19.6.1   Example Initiatives

Here are some organizations in the UK and worldwide that work in the area of gang violence, to help those involved:

* Gangsline

  Description: Gangsline, founded by former gang member Sheldon Thomas, offers direct support and intervention to individuals involved in gang activity. They provide outreach programs, counseling, and workshops aimed at reducing gang violence and supporting those who wish to leave gang life. Gangsline also offers training to professionals working with gang-affected communities.

  Website: www.gangsline.com/.

* Catch22

  Description: Catch22 provides a variety of services aimed at supporting young people involved in or at risk of gang involvement. Their initiatives include the National County Lines Support and Rescue Service, which helps individuals escape gang life and provides support to victims of gang exploitation. They offer tailored interventions, mentoring, and support to help individuals transition out of gang involvement and lead safer, more fulfilling lives.

  Website: www.catch-22.org.uk/.

* GRASP (Gang Rescue and Support Project)

  Description: GRASP is a peer-run intervention program based in Denver, Colorado. It works with youth who are at risk of gang involvement or are currently active in gangs. The organization also provides support to families of gang victims. Their services include crisis response, community mobilization, parent awareness training, school outreach, hospital intervention, family and youth advocacy, and tattoo removal.

  Website: https://graspyouth.org/.

* Voices Against Violence

  Description: Founded in Pittsburgh, Pennsylvania, Voices Against Violence provides holistic, community-based programs aimed at reducing interpersonal conflict among youth. The organization offers street mediation,

conflict resolution, restorative justice practices, and antiviolence programs. They serve both male and female youth and focus on prevention
and diversion from gang involvement.

Website: www.vavpgh.org/our-story.

- Office of Juvenile Justice and Delinquency Prevention (OJJDP)

  Description: OJJDP supports a variety of programs designed to prevent and
  suppress gang violence. Their initiatives include the Youth Gang Desistance/
  Diversion program and the Comprehensive Gang Model, which provide
  life skills training, mentoring, and support for gang members who wish to
  leave gang life. The South Houston Victims of Gang Violence Support
  Project is an example of their community-based approach.

  Website: https://ojjdp.ojp.gov/.

19.7   STRATEGIES FOR SUPPORT AND CHANGE

Creating a society where the cycle of violence involving men and boys is
broken requires comprehensive strategies that support victims, rehabilitate
perpetrators, and implement policy changes to address the root causes of
violence. This multifaceted approach ensures that all individuals affected by
violence receive the help they need while working toward long-term societal change.

19.7.1   Supporting Male Victims

Enhancing support for male victims of violence involves several key strategies:

1. *Enhancing public awareness.* Raising awareness about the prevalence
   and impact of violence on men and boys is crucial. Public awareness
   campaigns can challenge stereotypes that prevent male victims from
   seeking help and can highlight the importance of recognizing and
   addressing their experiences.

2. *Increasing access to services.* Access to support services tailored to
   the needs of male victims must be expanded. This includes the development of crisis centers, hotlines, and counseling services that cater
   specifically to men and boys. Training for professionals in health care,
   social services, and law enforcement is also essential to ensure they
   can provide appropriate support. An example of an organization that
   provides tailored support to men is the ManKind Initiative in the UK,
   which provides a confidential helpline and support services specifically for male victims of domestic abuse. Website: https://mankind.
   org.uk/.

3.   *Promoting emotional literacy.* Encouraging emotional literacy and resilience among men and boys can empower them to express their feelings and seek help when needed. Educational programs in schools and community settings can play a significant role in promoting healthy emotional expression and challenging harmful norms around masculinity.

19.7.2   Rehabilitation and Reintegration for Perpetrators

Effectively addressing violence committed by men and boys involves not only punishment but also opportunities for rehabilitation and reintegration through:

1.   *Therapeutic interventions.* Offering therapeutic interventions that address the root causes of violent behavior, such as anger management, substance abuse treatment, and trauma-informed therapy, can help perpetrators understand and change their behavior.

2.   *Community-based solutions.* Programs that involve community service, restorative justice practices, and mentorship can facilitate the reintegration of perpetrators into society in a positive and constructive manner. These programs should emphasize accountability, empathy, and the development of healthy relationships.

3.   *Education and training.* Providing education and vocational training to perpetrators, particularly those from disadvantaged backgrounds, can offer pathways to employment and reduce the risk of recidivism by addressing socioeconomic factors linked to violence.

19.7.3   Policy Recommendations

To support male victims and address the causes of violence by men and boys, the following policy changes are recommended:

1.   *Legislation supporting male victims.* Implement legislation that recognizes men and boys as victims of violence and ensures they have equal access to protection and support services, including shelters and legal assistance.

2.   *Funding for support services.* Allocate increased funding to support services for both victims and perpetrators, including specialized programs for men and boys. This funding should also support the training of professionals to work with male victims and perpetrators.

3.   *Preventive education.* Invest in preventive education programs that promote healthy expressions of masculinity, emotional literacy, and nonviolent conflict resolution from an early age.

4. *Research and data collection.* Support research on violence involving men and boys to better understand its prevalence, causes, and effects. This data can inform more effective policies and interventions.

Indeed, despite the significant impact of violence on men and boys, there is a surprising lack of research on their experiences, particularly in specific areas of violence, such as domestic abuse, sexual assault, and community violence. This gap in research hinders the development of targeted interventions and support systems. It is therefore essential to advocate for more comprehensive studies that explore the nuances of male victimization and perpetration.

By implementing these strategies, society can move toward a more compassionate and comprehensive approach to addressing violence, providing support for victims, rehabilitating perpetrators, and ultimately reducing the incidence of violence among men and boys.

19.8   CONCLUSION

This chapter has undertaken a comprehensive examination of the complex relationship between men, boys, and violence, revealing the intricate dynamics of their roles as both victims and perpetrators. Through exploring the contributing factors, including societal norms, psychological and environmental influences, and the impact of media and technology, it becomes clear that violence associated with men and boys is deeply embedded within broader societal structures and cultural expectations.

The discussion underscored the critical challenges faced by male victims of violence, highlighting the societal barriers to recognition and support, and the profound impact on their mental and physical health. It also addressed the pathways leading men and boys to perpetrate violence and outlined strategies for prevention, intervention, and rehabilitation. Central to these strategies is the need for societal change that challenges and dismantles harmful stereotypes surrounding masculinity, promotes gender equality, and fosters a culture of nonviolence and support.

Violence involving men and boys is not an isolated issue; it is a societal problem that demands a societal solution. Breaking down the barriers that prevent male victims from seeking help, addressing the root causes of violence perpetrated by men and boys, and shifting cultural norms toward healthy expressions of masculinity are essential steps in creating a safer, more equitable society for all.

NOTES

1   Archer, J. (Ed.). (2022). *Male violence*. Taylor & Francis.
2   Archer, J. (2022). Introduction: Male violence in perspective. In *Male violence* (pp. 1–20). Routledge.

3 www.who.int/news-room/fact-sheets/detail/injuries-and-violence

4 https://mankind.org.uk/statistics/statistics-on-male-victims-of-domestic-abuse/

5 www.menandboyscoalition.org.uk/statistics/

6 www.icrc.org/en/document/sexual-gender-violence-against-men-boys-lgbtiq

7 https://odi.org/en/insights/male-gender-based-violence-a-silent-crisis/

8 Eibach, J. (2016). Violence and masculinity. *The Oxford handbook of the history of crime and criminal justice* (pp. 229–244). Oxford University Press.

9 Connell, R. W. (2017). On hegemonic masculinity and violence: Response to Jefferson and Hall. In *Crime, criminal justice and masculinities* (pp. 57–68). Routledge.

10 Mshweshwe, L. (2020). Understanding domestic violence: Masculinity, culture, traditions. *Heliyon, 6*(10).

11 Radcliffe, P., Gadd, D., Henderson, J., Love, B., Stephens-Lewis, D., Johnson, A., . . . & Gilchrist, G. (2021). What role does substance use play in intimate partner violence? A narrative analysis of in-depth interviews with men in substance use treatment and their current or former female partner. *Journal of Interpersonal Violence, 36*(21–22), 10285–10313.

12 Rivas-Rivero, E., & Bonilla-Algovia, E. (2022). Adverse childhood events and substance misuse in men who perpetrated intimate partner violence. *International Journal of Offender Therapy and Comparative Criminology, 66*(8), 876–895.

13 Cafferky, B. M., Mendez, M., Anderson, J. R., & Stith, S. M. (2018). Substance use and intimate partner violence: A meta-analytic review. *Psychology of Violence, 8*(1), 110.

14 Reichel, D. (2017). Determinants of intimate partner violence in Europe: The role of socioeconomic status, inequality, and partner behavior. *Journal of Interpersonal Violence, 32*(12), 1853–1873.

15 Wright, P. J., & Tokunaga, R. S. (2016). Men's objectifying media consumption, objectification of women, and attitudes supportive of violence against women. *Archives of Sexual Behavior, 45*, 955–964.

16 Bates, E. A., & Taylor, J. C. (Eds.). (2019). *Intimate partner violence: New perspectives in research and practice* (1st ed.). Routledge. https://doi.org/10.4324/9781315169842

17 Hines, D. (2015). Overlooked victims of domestic violence: Men. *International Journal for Family Research and Policy, 1*(1).

18 Hine, B., Bates, E. A., & Wallace, S. (2022). "I have guys call me and say 'I can't be the victim of domestic abuse'": Exploring the experiences of telephone support providers for male victims of domestic violence and abuse. *Journal of Interpersonal Violence, 37*(7–8), NP5594–NP5625.

19 Widanaralalage, B. K., Hine, B. A., Murphy, A. D., & Murji, K. (2022). "I didn't feel I was a victim": A phenomenological analysis of the experiences of male-on-male survivors of rape and sexual abuse. *Victims & Offenders, 17*(8), 1147–1172.

20 Taylor, J. C., Bates, E. A., Colosi, A., & Creer, A. J. (2022). Barriers to men's help seeking for intimate partner violence. *Journal of Interpersonal Violence, 37*(19–20), NP18417–NP18444.

21 Hine, B., Bates, E. A., Mackay, J., & Graham-Kevan, N. (2022). Comparing the demographic characteristics, and reported abuse type, contexts and outcomes of help-seeking heterosexual male and female victims of domestic violence: Part I – who presents to specialist services? *Partner Abuse, 13*(1), 20–60.

22 Hine, B., Bates, E., Graham-Kevan, N., & Mackay, J. (2022). Comparing abuse profiles, contexts and outcomes of help-seeking heterosexual male and female

victims of domestic violence: Part II – Exit from specialist services. *Partner Abuse*, *13*(2).

23 Hines, D. A., & Douglas, E. M. (2015). Health problems of partner violence victims: Comparing help-seeking men to a population-based sample. *American Journal of Preventive Medicine*, *48*(2), 136–144.

24 Hine et al., "I have guys call me and say 'I can't be the victim of domestic abuse'", NP5594–NP5625.

25 Hine et al., Comparing the demographic characteristics, and reported abuse type, contexts and outcomes of help-seeking heterosexual male and female victims of domestic violence, 20–60.

26 Hine et al., Comparing abuse profiles, contexts and outcomes of help-seeking heterosexual male and female victims of domestic violence.

27 Davis, K. C., Masters, N. T., Casey, E., Kajumulo, K. F., Norris, J., & George, W. H. (2018). How childhood maltreatment profiles of male victims predict adult perpetration and psychosocial functioning. *Journal of Interpersonal Violence*, *33*(6), 915–937.

28 Hine, B. A., Mackay, J., Baguley, T., Graham-Kevan, N., Cunliffe, M., & Galloway, A. (2022). *Understanding perpetrators of Intimate Partner Violence (IPV)*. Home Office.

29 Clare, C. A., Velasquez, G., Martorell, G. M. M., Fernandez, D., Dinh, J., & Montague, A. (2021). Risk factors for male perpetration of intimate partner violence: A review. *Aggression and Violent Behavior*, *56*, 101532.

30 Spencer, C. M., Stith, S. M., & Cafferky, B. (2022). What puts individuals at risk for physical intimate partner violence perpetration? A meta-analysis examining risk markers for men and women. *Trauma, Violence, & Abuse*, *23*(1), 36–51.

31 Li, S., Zhao, F., & Yu, G. (2020). A meta-analysis of childhood maltreatment and intimate partner violence perpetration. *Aggression and Violent Behavior*, *50*, 101362.

32 Miller, E., Culyba, A. J., Paglisotti, T., Massof, M., Gao, Q., Ports, K. A., . . . & Jones, K. A. (2020). Male adolescents' gender attitudes and violence: Implications for youth violence prevention. *American Journal of Preventive Medicine*, *58*(3), 396–406.

33 Wood, J. L., Kallis, C., & Coid, J. W. (2022). Gang members, gang affiliates, and violent men: Perpetration of social harms, violence-related beliefs, victim types, and locations. *Journal of Interpersonal Violence*, *37*(7–8), NP3703–NP3727.

34 Raby, C., & Jones, F. (2016). Identifying risks for male street gang affiliation: A systematic review and narrative synthesis. *The Journal of Forensic Psychiatry & Psychology*, *27*(5), 601–644.

35 Baird, A. (2018). Becoming the 'Baddest': Masculine trajectories of gang violence in Medellín. *Journal of Latin American Studies*, *50*(1), 183–210.

36 Wood, J. L., Kallis, C., & Coid, J. W. (2017). Differentiating gang members, gang affiliates, and violent men on their psychiatric morbidity and traumatic experiences. *Psychiatry*, *80*(3), 221–235.

37 Paymar, M. (2015). *Violent no more: Helping men end domestic abuse*. Turner Publishing Company.

20

HOMELESSNESS

20.1 INTRODUCTION

Homelessness represents one of the most visible and pressing humanitarian crises in modern society, yet the specific plight of homeless men and boys as a gendered issue often goes unnoticed, overshadowed by broader discussions on poverty and housing instability. This chapter seeks to shine a light on this issue, delving into the unique challenges faced by men and boys living without shelter or in unstable housing circumstances. It explores the multifaceted causes behind male homelessness, including mental health issues, substance abuse, economic factors, domestic violence, and the crushing weight of societal expectations.

The perception of homelessness is frequently colored by stereotypes and misconceptions, with homeless men often portrayed as architects of their own misfortune. This narrative overlooks the complex interplay of systemic failures, personal crises, and societal neglect that leads to homelessness. Furthermore, it fails to account for the diversity among the homeless population, where each individual's story is a unique blend of circumstances, choices, and challenges. The reality of male homelessness is far more nuanced, characterized by a spectrum of experiences that defy one-dimensional portrayals.

In this sense, male homelessness is not merely a consequence of individual failings but a societal crisis that reflects our collective failure to

DOI: 10.4324/9781032709369-26

provide for the most vulnerable among us. This chapter aims to bridge the gap between perception and reality, advocating for a compassionate, informed approach to addressing the needs of homeless men and boys. By understanding the root causes and acknowledging the humanity of those affected, we can begin to dismantle the barriers to assistance and advocate for targeted interventions and systemic changes. The journey toward resolving the crisis of male homelessness starts with recognizing its complexity and affirming our commitment to creating a society where no man or boy is left to face the harsh realities of life on the streets alone.

20.2   UNDERSTANDING MALE HOMELESSNESS

Homelessness affects millions worldwide, with men and boys constituting a significant portion of this population. Indeed the data reveals a striking disproportionality: males are hugely overrepresented among the homeless, a trend consistent across various regions and nations. In the UK, around 67.1% of the homeless population is male, compared to 32.9% female, according to the Office for National Statistics[1] and homeless charities.[2] In many urban areas, men make up approximately 70% of the homeless population, a figure that underscores the gendered nature of this crisis.[3,4] The age distribution within this demographic is equally telling, with young men aged 18–24 being particularly vulnerable to homelessness,[5] alongside older men, who face their own unique set of challenges.[6]

These statistics, however, only scratch the surface. Behind the numbers lie complex individual stories of loss, struggle, and survival. The causes of male homelessness are myriad, ranging from economic hardship and unemployment to the breakdown of family relationships and the absence of adequate mental health support. Furthermore, veterans form a significant subset of the homeless male population, facing unique challenges that stem from their service.[7]

20.2.1   Public Perception vs. Reality

Societal perceptions of male homelessness are often fraught with stigma and misunderstanding. Common stereotypes paint homeless men as lazy, unwilling to work, or as perpetrators of their own misfortune. These narratives are not only harmful but also grossly inaccurate, failing to account for the systemic issues and personal tragedies that lead to homelessness.

The reality for homeless men and boys is a daily struggle against hunger, exposure, and danger. Many have experienced significant trauma, both before and after becoming homeless. Far from being unwilling to work, many homeless men actively seek employment but are hindered by barriers such as the lack of a permanent address, limited access to hygiene facilities, and the pervasive stigma of homelessness.

Moreover, the public often overlooks the emotional and psychological toll of homelessness on men, who are socially conditioned to suppress expressions of vulnerability. The societal expectation for men to be self-reliant and stoic compounds their isolation, making it difficult for them to seek help or access support services.

The contrast between public perception and the lived realities of homeless men and boys calls for a shift in discourse. Recognizing the diverse causes of male homelessness and the profound impact it has on individuals is crucial for developing empathetic and effective responses to this issue. By challenging stereotypes and advocating for a nuanced understanding of homelessness, society can begin to address the needs of homeless men and boys with the dignity and support they deserve.

20.3   ROOT CAUSES

There are several factors that influence men's journeys to homelessness.

20.3.1   Mental Health Issues

Untreated mental health conditions stand as a critical and often under-addressed factor leading to homelessness among men and boys.[8] Disorders such as depression, anxiety, schizophrenia, and posttraumatic stress disorder (PTSD) can significantly impair an individual's ability to maintain employment, manage finances, and sustain relationships. The stigma surrounding mental health, particularly among men, who are culturally conditioned to avoid showing weakness, often prevents them from seeking help (as explored in Chapter 3). Without adequate support and treatment, mental health issues can spiral into crisis situations, leaving men and boys vulnerable to losing their homes and finding themselves without shelter.

20.3.2   Substance Abuse

Substance abuse is both a cause and consequence of homelessness, creating a vicious cycle that is difficult to break.[9,10] For many men and boys, turning to alcohol or drugs can be a coping mechanism for underlying issues, such as trauma or mental health disorders. However, substance abuse only exacerbates these problems, undermining an individual's health, social connections, and financial stability. The loss of employment and the depletion of savings to sustain addiction can swiftly lead to homelessness. Moreover, the challenges of overcoming substance abuse are magnified without stable housing, making recovery a far more daunting task for those already on the streets. More on this in Chapter 22.

20.3.3   Economic Factors

Economic instability is a fundamental driver of homelessness, with unemployment, underemployment, and the lack of affordable housing being key contributors. The loss of a job or insufficient income to cover basic living expenses leaves many men and boys unable to afford housing. Moreover, the global housing crisis, characterized by skyrocketing rents and a shortage of affordable housing options, exacerbates the situation. For those living paycheck to paycheck, an unexpected financial setback – a medical emergency, a car repair, or a job loss – can swiftly lead to eviction and homelessness. The economic vulnerability faced by men and boys highlights the need for systemic solutions that address the root causes of financial instability and housing insecurity.

20.3.4   Domestic Violence and Childhood Abuse

Domestic violence and childhood abuse are significant yet often overlooked factors contributing to male homelessness.[11,12,13] Men and boys who are victims of abuse face unique challenges that can lead to housing instability and homelessness. For example, men who are victims of domestic violence may find it difficult to seek help due to societal expectations and stigmas surrounding masculinity. Cultural norms often portray men as strong and self-reliant, leading to a reluctance to admit victimization or to reach out for support. This hesitation can result in prolonged exposure to abusive situations, increasing the likelihood of homelessness as the individual's physical, and mental, health deteriorates.

The pathways from domestic violence victimization to homelessness for men can include:

1. *Isolation from support networks.* Abusers often isolate their victims from friends, family, and other support networks. This isolation can be particularly pronounced for men, who may already be less likely to have strong social support due to societal expectations. Without a support network to turn to, men may find themselves with no safe place to go when they leave an abusive situation.

2. *Economic abuse.* Abusive partners may exert control over finances, making it difficult for the victim to access money, maintain employment, or save for the future. Economic abuse can leave men financially destitute and unable to secure stable housing once they escape the abusive environment.

3. *Legal and custody issues.* Men may face additional challenges in legal battles, particularly in cases involving child custody. Misconceptions and biases in the legal system can disadvantage male victims, leading to unfavorable outcomes that may contribute to their homelessness. Losing custody of children or being unfairly treated in court can further destabilize their lives.

4. *Mental health impacts.* The trauma of domestic violence can lead to severe mental health issues, such as PTSD, depression, and anxiety. These conditions can impair a man's ability to function in daily life, maintain employment, and secure housing. The stigma surrounding men's mental health can exacerbate these issues, as men may be less likely to seek help or acknowledge their struggles.

5. *Lack of services.* There is a notable lack of services and shelters specifically geared toward male victims of domestic violence. Many domestic violence services are tailored primarily to women, leaving men with fewer options for emergency housing and support. This gap in services can force men to remain in abusive situations or face homelessness.

20.3.5   Military Participation

Military service, particularly combat duty, exposes individuals to high levels of stress and trauma, which can lead to significant mental health issues, such as PTSD, depression, and anxiety.[14] These conditions can severely impact a veteran's ability to reintegrate into civilian life, maintain employment, and secure stable housing. The transition from military to civilian life can be fraught with difficulties, including the loss of the structure and support that the military provides. Veterans may struggle with finding adequate employment that matches their skills and experience, leading to economic instability and, ultimately, homelessness. Additionally, the stigma surrounding mental health within the military culture often prevents veterans from seeking help, exacerbating their vulnerabilities.

20.3.6   Incarceration

Incarceration is another significant factor contributing to male homelessness.[15,16,17,18] Men who have been incarcerated face numerous barriers upon release, including limited job opportunities, stigma, and legal restrictions that can impede their ability to secure housing. The experience of incarceration can erode social networks and support systems, leaving individuals without a safety net when they re-enter society. Moreover, the criminal justice system often disproportionately affects men, particularly those from marginalized communities, leading to higher rates of incarceration and subsequent homelessness. The lack of support and resources for reintegration, coupled with the societal stigma attached to having a criminal record, makes it challenging for formerly incarcerated men to achieve stability and avoid homelessness.

20.3.7   Societal Expectations and Masculinity

Societal pressures and norms around masculinity significantly contribute to the risk of homelessness for men and boys. The expectation to be the primary provider, combined with cultural norms that discourage expressions of vulnerability, places enormous pressure on men. When faced with economic hardship, family breakdown, or personal crisis, the perceived failure to live up to these expectations can be devastating.[19,20] Additionally, the stigma against seeking help for financial troubles, mental health issues, or substance abuse reinforces a harmful cycle of silence and suffering. This isolation can lead to the erosion of social support networks, ultimately resulting in homelessness. Moreover, masculinity norms can contribute to becoming trapped in a cycle of homelessness, due to a reluctancy to help seek, and to embody the "tough" lifestyle.[21,22]

Addressing the root causes of male homelessness thus requires a holistic approach that acknowledges the interplay between mental health, substance abuse, societal expectations, and economic factors. By understanding these underlying issues, efforts to combat homelessness can be more targeted, compassionate, and effective, offering hope and support to those caught in the grip of this crisis.

20.4   CHALLENGES FACED BY HOMELESS MEN AND BOYS

Homeless men and boys navigate a landscape marked by numerous challenges that exacerbate their situation and hinder their path to stability. The barriers to accessing essential services, coupled with significant health concerns and profound social isolation, paint a bleak picture of the daily realities faced by this vulnerable population.

20.4.1   Access to Services

Accessing homeless and mental health services presents numerous obstacles for men and boys. One significant barrier is the gender bias inherent in many support systems, which are often designed with the primary aim of assisting women and children. This bias can manifest in a scarcity of shelters that accept single men or have the resources to address their specific needs. Mental health services, too, may not be tailored to the unique challenges faced by men, particularly those related to societal expectations of masculinity. Furthermore, bureaucratic hurdles, lack of awareness about available resources, and the stigma surrounding homelessness and mental health issues can deter men and boys from seeking the help they desperately need.

20.4.2   Health Concerns

The physical and mental health challenges faced by homeless men and boys are both acute and chronic, significantly impacting their well-being and quality of life.[23] Physically, the harsh conditions of living without shelter can lead to a range of health problems, from respiratory infections and untreated injuries to chronic conditions like hypertension and diabetes that go unmanaged. Nutrition deficiencies and inadequate access to clean water and sanitation facilities exacerbate these health issues.

Mentally, the stress and trauma of homelessness can trigger or worsen mental health disorders, such as depression, anxiety, and PTSD. The lack of privacy, constant insecurity, and daily struggles for survival can take a profound toll on psychological well-being. Moreover, the absence of a support network and societal stigmatization can leave individuals feeling hopeless and isolated, further deteriorating their mental health.

20.4.3   Social Isolation

Social isolation represents one of the most crippling aspects of homelessness for men and boys. The stigma associated with being homeless can lead to societal detachment, where individuals feel marginalized and disconnected from the community. This stigma often extends to personal networks, resulting in the breakdown of relationships with family and friends. The loss of these social connections not only deepens the emotional impact of homelessness but also removes potential avenues for support and assistance. Furthermore, the competitive nature of life on the streets can hinder the formation of new, supportive relationships among the homeless community, exacerbating feelings of isolation and loneliness.

20.4.4   Perceptions of Masculinity

Homelessness also profoundly impacts men's perceptions of their masculinity.[24] Traditional societal norms often equate masculinity with the ability to provide and protect, roles that become difficult to fulfill when homeless. This inability can lead to feelings of shame, inadequacy, and a diminished sense of self-worth. Many homeless men struggle with the stigma that their situation contradicts societal expectations of male strength and independence. These pressures can exacerbate mental health issues, as men might be less likely to seek help due to the fear of appearing weak or vulnerable.

20.4.5   Fatherhood Challenges

Homelessness also severely affects men's roles as fathers.[25] The instability and insecurity of homelessness make it challenging for men to maintain consistent relationships with their children. Fathers experiencing homelessness often face legal and systemic barriers that hinder their ability to participate in their children's lives, such as custody battles and the lack of a permanent address. The stress and preoccupation with daily survival needs can further detract from their capacity to engage in active and supportive parenting.

Moreover, societal and legal systems often fail to recognize or support homeless fathers, focusing predominantly on mothers and children. This lack of support can lead to feelings of helplessness and frustration, compounding the emotional toll of homelessness and contributing to a cycle of disengagement from their children.

20.5 INTERSECTIONALITY AND DIVERSE EXPERIENCES

Understanding homelessness among men and boys also requires an intersectional approach that considers how race, ethnicity, sexual orientation, and disability intersect with gender. These intersections create unique experiences and challenges that must be addressed to develop effective and inclusive solutions. Each section next contains a few bullet points on how that particularly demographic characteristic might affect men's experiences of homelessness.

20.5.1   Race and Ethnicity

- *Disproportionate impact.* Men and boys from racial and ethnic minority groups often face higher rates of homelessness due to systemic racism, economic inequality, and discrimination in housing and employment.[26] For instance, in the United States, African American and Native American men are disproportionately represented among the homeless population.[27]
- *Barriers to services.* Language barriers, cultural differences, and mistrust of authorities can hinder access to essential services for minority homeless populations. Tailoring services to be culturally sensitive and inclusive can help bridge these gaps.
- *Police and judicial system.* Minority men and boys often experience higher rates of incarceration and interactions with the police, contributing to their risk of homelessness. Discriminatory practices in the judicial system exacerbate these challenges.

20.5.2   Sexual Orientation

- *LGBTQ+ homelessness.* GBTQ+ men and boys are at a higher risk of homelessness due to family rejection, discrimination, and violence.[28,29] They often face additional stigma and barriers when seeking shelter and services.[30,31]
- *Inclusive shelters.* Many shelters do not provide safe and inclusive environments for LGBTQ+ individuals, forcing them to choose between staying in unsafe conditions or living on the streets. Creating LGBTQ+-inclusive shelters and support services is crucial.
- *Mental health.* The mental health impact of discrimination and violence against LGBTQ+ individuals can lead to higher rates of mental health issues and substance abuse, further complicating their ability to secure stable housing.

20.5.3   Disability

- *Physical and mental disabilities.* Men and boys with disabilities face significant challenges in accessing housing that accommodates their needs. Physical disabilities require accessible housing, while mental disabilities may necessitate specialized support services.[32]
- *Discrimination and stigma.* Individuals with disabilities often encounter discrimination in the housing market and within shelter systems. The stigma associated with disabilities can also affect their ability to secure employment and financial stability.
- *Service gaps.* Many homeless services are not equipped to handle the specific needs of disabled individuals, leaving them with inadequate support. Integrating disability services with homeless support systems is essential for addressing these gaps.

20.5.4   Combined Effects

- *Compounded challenges.* When multiple factors intersect, such as being a disabled LGBTQ+ person of color, the challenges can be compounded, creating even greater barriers to stable housing and support.[33] These compounded challenges require multifaceted and intersectional approaches to support and intervention.
- *Tailored interventions.* Interventions must be tailored to address the unique needs arising from these intersections. This includes providing culturally competent services, ensuring accessibility, and fostering inclusive environments.

20.6   TARGETED INTERVENTION

To effectively address the crisis of male homelessness, targeted interventions that recognize and cater to the specific needs of this population are essential. However, many reviews in this area have not considered how gender may influence the effectiveness of intervention.[34,35] Similarly, whilst in the UK there are effective interventions like Veterans Aid, Crisis Skylight Centres, Forward Trust, Combat Stress, St. Mungo's, and the Prince's Trust, very few explicitly state or acknowledge the specific needs of men. These programs offer comprehensive support, including emergency housing, mental health services, substance abuse treatment, and employment assistance. However, they often do not highlight or tailor their services to address the unique challenges faced by homeless men, such as societal expectations of masculinity and the stigma surrounding mental health and vulnerability. This gap underscores the need for more gender-sensitive approaches in addressing male homelessness.

Such interventions should not only aim to provide immediate relief but also foster long-term stability and reintegration into society. Three critical areas where targeted interventions can make a significant impact include tailored support services, mental health and substance abuse treatment, and employment and education programs.

20.6.1   Tailored Support Services

There is therefore a pressing need for the development and expansion of services specifically designed for homeless men and boys. These services should go beyond the provision of shelter to include access to health care, legal assistance, and social support tailored to the unique challenges faced by this demographic. Recognizing that men may be hesitant to seek help due to societal stigma or feelings of shame, these services should be marketed in a way that emphasizes dignity, respect, and confidentiality. Efforts should be made to create a welcoming environment that encourages men and boys to access the support they need without fear of judgment. Additionally, shelters and support services should be equipped to address the specific physical and psychological health needs of men, providing a holistic approach to care that facilitates recovery and resilience.

20.6.2   Mental Health and Substance Abuse Treatment

Addressing the root causes of homelessness first requires a focus on mental health and substance abuse treatment. Accessible, comprehensive treatment programs are crucial for homeless men and boys, many of whom struggle with these issues. These programs should offer a range of services, from crisis intervention and detoxification to long-term therapy and rehabilitation, all tailored to the individual's needs. Recognizing the interconnectedness of mental health, substance abuse, and homelessness, these treatment programs should be integrated with other support services to provide a coordinated approach to care. This integration ensures that men and boys receive not only treatment but also assistance with housing, employment, and other essential services, facilitating a more effective and sustainable recovery.

20.6.3   Employment and Education Programs

Economic stability is the next critical factor in preventing and overcoming homelessness. As such, programs that offer pathways to employment and self-sufficiency are vital. These programs should provide homeless men and boys with access to education and vocational training, job placement services, and ongoing support to ensure successful integration into the workforce. Special consideration should be given to overcoming the barriers that homeless individuals face in seeking employment, such as lack of identification, gaps in employment history, and limited access to transportation. By equipping men and boys with the skills, resources, and confidence they need to secure and maintain employment, these programs can help break the cycle of homelessness and pave the way for a more stable and independent future.

20.6.4 The Use of Technology

Technology can play a pivotal role in addressing the issue of male homelessness by enhancing access to services and support.[36] Mobile apps and online platforms can provide critical information about available shelters, food resources, and health services.[37] These tools can also facilitate the coordination of care, allowing service providers to share information and track the progress of individuals seeking help. Moreover, virtual support groups and telehealth services can offer mental health support and counseling, making these services more accessible to those who may feel stigmatized seeking help in person.[38] By leveraging technology, we can create more efficient and inclusive support systems that better address the needs of homeless men and boys.

Through the implementation of targeted interventions that address the specific needs of homeless men and boys, it is possible to make significant strides in alleviating this crisis. By providing tailored support services, comprehensive mental health and substance abuse treatment, and pathways to employment and education, society can offer hope and opportunity to those who have been marginalized, helping them rebuild their lives and reintegrate into the community.

20.7 SYSTEMIC CHANGES

Addressing the crisis of male homelessness also requires systemic changes that go beyond immediate interventions, focusing on policy reforms, community engagement, and preventative strategies. By implementing these changes, we can create a more supportive environment for homeless men and boys, ultimately aiming to prevent homelessness before it starts.

20.7.1 Policy Recommendations

To provide better support for homeless men and boys, several policy changes are essential:

1. *Housing-first initiatives.* Policies should prioritize housing-first models, which provide homeless individuals with stable housing as a preliminary step before addressing other issues, such as employment, substance abuse, or mental health. This approach has been shown to improve long-term outcomes by providing a stable foundation from which individuals can rebuild their lives.

2. *Health-care reform.* Access to health care is a critical issue for homeless men, many of whom suffer from untreated physical and mental health conditions. Policies should aim to reform health-care systems to ensure

that homeless individuals have access to comprehensive health services, including preventive care, mental health support, and substance abuse treatment. This could include expanding Medicaid coverage or providing targeted funding for health services within homeless shelters and support programs.

3. *Affordable housing policies.* To prevent homelessness, there must be a significant investment in affordable housing. Policies should encourage the development of low-income housing units and provide rental assistance programs to keep housing affordable for those at risk of homelessness. Additionally, protections against eviction and discrimination in housing can provide further stability for vulnerable populations.

4. *Integrated support services.* Policies should promote the integration of support services to provide a holistic approach to assisting homeless men and boys. This includes coordinating between housing services, health-care providers, employment agencies, and educational institutions to ensure that individuals receive comprehensive support.

20.7.2   Community Engagement

Community awareness and involvement also play a vital role in addressing male homelessness. Raising awareness about the issue can help break down the stigma and misconceptions surrounding homelessness, encouraging a more compassionate and proactive community response. Communities can support homeless men and boys through volunteer work, donations, and advocacy for policy changes. Local businesses and organizations can also contribute by providing employment opportunities, educational programs, and in-kind support. Engaging the community in these efforts not only helps address the immediate needs of homeless individuals but also fosters a more inclusive and supportive environment.

20.7.3   The Involvement of Homeless Individuals in Solutions

Engaging homeless men and boys in the creation and implementation of solutions to homelessness is crucial for developing effective, tailored interventions, for example, through:

1. *Empowerment through participation.* Engaging homeless men and boys in the development and implementation of homelessness solutions ensures that interventions are tailored to their actual needs and circumstances.

2. *Insightful feedback.* Their firsthand experiences provide valuable insights that can lead to more effective and practical strategies.

3. *Fostering ownership.* Involving homeless individuals in decision-making processes fosters a sense of ownership and empowerment, which can enhance the success and sustainability of the programs.

4. *Building trust.* Active participation can help build trust between service providers and the homeless community, encouraging more individuals to seek help and support.

20.7.4   Breaking the Cycle

Preventing homelessness also requires addressing its root causes early on. This involves:

1. *Early intervention programs.* Identifying and supporting at-risk individuals through early intervention programs in schools, health-care settings, and community centers can prevent homelessness before it starts. These programs can offer counseling, family support services, and assistance with housing and employment.

2. *Education and employment opportunities.* Providing access to education and employment opportunities for at-risk populations can help prevent the economic instability that often leads to homelessness. This includes vocational training, apprenticeship programs, and support for continuing education.

3. *Substance abuse and mental health programs.* Investing in comprehensive substance abuse and mental health programs that are accessible to all individuals can prevent the downward spiral that often results in homelessness. This includes expanding access to mental health care, providing preventive services, and supporting rehabilitation and recovery programs.

20.7.5   Example Organizations

There are several UK organizations that assist homeless individuals, including Crisis (www.crisis.org.uk/), Shelter (https://england.shelter.org.uk/), St. Mungo's (www.mungos.org/), and those outlined in the following. However, it should be noted that with this being a hugely gendered issue, a greater gendered focus is likely needed:

•   Single Homeless Project (SHP)

    Description: SHP offers supported accommodation and a range of services to homeless individuals across London. They focus on helping men with multiple and complex needs, including those leaving prison, to reintegrate into society and achieve long-term recovery.

Website: www.shp.org.uk/.

- Alabaré Christian Care and Support

  Description: Alabaré provides support and accommodation to vulnerable and homeless people, including veterans. Their services aim to empower individuals to live independently, by offering tailored support, including mental health services and training programs.

  Website: https://alabare.co.uk/.

- Help the Homeless

  Description: Help the Homeless is a grant-giving trust that funds grassroots charities working to support homeless people across the UK. They prioritize organizations that assist the most vulnerable individuals, helping them transition to healthy, independent lives.

  Website: www.help-the-homeless.org.uk/.

- Glass Door

  Description: Glass Door runs the UK's largest network of open-access shelters, providing emergency accommodation and support services to homeless people in London. They offer vital essentials and connect individuals to services that help them move out of homelessness.

  Website: www.glassdoor.org.uk/.

20.8 CONCLUSION

The crisis of male homelessness, with its complex web of causes and consequences, stands as a pressing yet often overlooked challenge within our society. Throughout this chapter, we have explored the multifaceted nature of homelessness among men and boys, delving into its root causes – ranging from mental health issues and substance abuse to economic instability and the rigid confines of societal expectations. We have also examined the unique challenges faced by homeless men and boys, such as barriers to accessing vital services, health concerns, and the profound isolation that compounds their plight.

Targeted interventions, including the development of tailored support services, comprehensive mental health and substance abuse treatment, and programs that provide pathways to employment and education, are critical for addressing the immediate needs of homeless men and boys. However, to achieve lasting change, we must also advocate for systemic reforms that address the underlying causes of homelessness. This includes policies that prioritize housing-first initiatives, health-care reform, and the creation of affordable housing, as well as community engagement efforts that raise awareness and foster a supportive environment.

The crisis of male homelessness is not insurmountable, but it requires a concerted effort from all sectors of society. Policymakers must champion and implement reforms that ensure homeless men and boys have access to the resources and support they need. Service providers should strive to offer holistic and tailored services that address the specific challenges faced by this population. The community at large has a role to play in breaking down stigma, supporting local initiatives, and advocating for policy changes.

By doing so, we can move closer to a society where no man or boy is left without shelter and support, and where homelessness is no longer a neglected crisis but a priority for collective action and compassion. Together, we can pave the way for a future where homelessness among men and boys is not just alleviated but prevented, ensuring dignity, stability, and hope for all.

NOTES

1 www.ons.gov.uk/peoplepopulationandcommunity/housing/articles/peopleexpe riencinghomelessnessenglandandwales/census2021
2 https://england.shelter.org.uk/professional_resources/policy_and_research/pol icy_library/homelessness_in_england_2021
3 https://policyinstitute.iu.edu/news-media/stories/2021-pit-count-homeless.html
4 www.abs.gov.au/statistics/people/housing/estimating-homelessness-census/ latest-release
5 https://homeless.org.uk/knowledge-hub/young-and-homeless-2021/
6 Pope, N. D., Buchino, S., & Ascienzo, S. (2020). "Just like jail": Trauma experiences of older homeless men. *Journal of Gerontological Social Work, 63*(3), 143–161.
7 www.crisis.org.uk/ending-homelessness/homelessness-knowledge-hub/ homelessness-monitor/england/the-homelessness-monitor-england-2021/
8 Spicer, B., Smith, D. I., Conroy, E., Flatau, P. R., & Burns, L. (2015). Mental illness and housing outcomes among a sample of homeless men in an Australian urban centre. *Australian & New Zealand Journal of Psychiatry, 49*(5), 471–480.
9 Kim, M. M., Ford, J. D., Howard, D. L., & Bradford, D. W. (2010). Assessing trauma, substance abuse, and mental health in a sample of homeless men. *Health & Social Work, 35*(1), 39–48.
10 Rodriguez-Moreno, S., Vázquez, J. J., Roca, P., & Panadero, S. (2021). Differences in stressful life events between men and women experiencing homelessness. *Journal of Community Psychology, 49*(2), 375–389.
11 Deck, S. M., & Platt, P. A. (2015). Homelessness is traumatic: Abuse, victimiza- tion, and trauma histories of homeless men. *Journal of Aggression, Maltreatment & Trauma, 24*(9), 1022–1043.
12 Hine, B. A., Hoppe, I., & Los, G. (2024). Experiences of men made homeless as a result of domestic violence. *Policy Report*.
13 Woodhall-Melnik, J., Dunn, J. R., Svenson, S., Patterson, C., & Matheson, F. I. (2018). Men's experiences of early life trauma and pathways into long-term homelessness. *Child Abuse & Neglect, 80*, 216–225.
14 Fargo, J., Metraux, S., Byrne, T., Munley, E., Montgomery, A. E., Jones, H., . . . & Culhane, D. (2012). Prevalence and risk of homelessness among US veterans. *Preventing Chronic Disease, 9*.

15 Greenberg, G. A., & Rosenheck, R. A. (2008). Jail incarceration, homelessness, and mental health: A national study. *Psychiatric Services, 59*(2), 170–177.

16 Moschion, J., & Johnson, G. (2019). Homelessness and incarceration: A reciprocal relationship?. *Journal of Quantitative Criminology, 35*, 855–887.

17 Rodriguez-Moreno et al., Differences in stressful life events between men and women experiencing homelessness, 375–389.

18 Remster, B. (2021). Homelessness among formerly incarcerated men: Patterns and predictors. *The ANNALS of the American Academy of Political and Social Science, 693*(1), 141–157.

19 Rice, A., Kim, J. Y. C., Nguyen, C., Liu, W. M., Fall, K., & Galligan, P. (2017). Perceptions of masculinity and fatherhood among men experiencing homelessness. *Psychological Services, 14*(2), 257.

20 Dej, E. (2018). When a man's home isn'ta castle: Hegemonic masculinity among men experiencing homelessness and mental illness. *Containing madness: Gender and 'psy' in institutional contexts* (pp. 215–239). Springer International Publishing.

21 Umamaheswar, J. (2022). "On the street, the only person you gotta bow down to is yourself": Masculinity, homelessness, and incarceration. *Justice Quarterly, 39*(2), 379–401.

22 Lorentzen, J. M. (2017). Power and resistance: Homeless men negotiating masculinity. *Qualitative Sociology Review, 13*(2), 100–120.

23 Munoz, M., Crespo, M., & Pérez-Santos, E. (2005). Homelessness effects on men's and women's health. *International Journal of Mental Health, 34*(2), 47–61.

24 Liu, W. M., Stinson, R., Hernandez, J., Shepard, S., & Haag, S. (2009). A qualitative examination of masculinity, homelessness, and social class among men in a transitional shelter. *Psychology of Men & Masculinity, 10*(2), 131.

25 Rice et al., Perceptions of masculinity and fatherhood among men experiencing homelessness, 257.

26 Jones, M. M. (2016). Does race matter in addressing homelessness? A review of the literature. *World Medical & Health Policy, 8*(2), 139–156.

27 May, J. (2015). Racial vibrations, masculine performances: Experiences of homelessness among young men of colour in the Greater Toronto Area. *Gender, Place & Culture, 22*(3), 405–421.

28 Ecker, J., Aubry, T., & Sylvestre, J. (2019). A review of the literature on LGBTQ adults who experience homelessness. *Journal of Homosexuality, 66*(3), 297–323.

29 McCann, E., & Brown, M. (2019). Homelessness among youth who identify as LGBTQ+: A systematic review. *Journal of Clinical Nursing, 28*(11–12), 2061–2072.

30 McCarthy, L., & Parr, S. (2022). Is LGBT homelessness different? Reviewing the relationship between LGBT identity and homelessness. *Housing Studies*, 1–19.

31 Matthews, P., Poyner, C., & Kjellgren, R. (2019). Lesbian, gay, bisexual, transgender and queer experiences of homelessness and identity: Insecurity and home (o) normativity. *International Journal of Housing Policy, 19*(2), 232–253.

32 Zamorano, S., González-Sanguino, C., Sánchez-Iglesias, I., Sáiz, J., Salazar, M., Vaquero, C., . . . & Muñoz, M. (2022). The stigma of mental health, homelessness and intellectual disability, development of a national stigma survey with an intersectional gender perspective. *International Journal of Clinical Trials, 9*(4), 286–292.

33 Markowitz, F. E., & Syverson, J. (2021). Race, gender, and homelessness stigma: Effects of perceived blameworthiness and dangerousness. *Deviant Behavior, 42*(7), 919–931.

34 Munthe-Kaas, H. M., Berg, R. C., & Blaasvær, N. (2018). Effectiveness of interventions to reduce homelessness: A systematic review and meta-analysis.
Campbell Systematic Reviews, 14(1), 1–281.

35 O'Shaughnessy, B. R., & Michelle Greenwood, R. (2020). Empowering features
and outcomes of homeless interventions: A systematic review and narrative synthesis. *American Journal of Community Psychology, 66*(1–2), 144–165.

36 Thurman, W., Semwal, M., Moczygemba, L. R., & Hilbelink, M. (2021).
Smartphone technology to empower people experiencing homelessness:
Secondary analysis. *Journal of Medical Internet Research, 23*(9), e27787.

37 Garvin, L. A., Hu, J., Slightam, C., McInnes, D. K., & Zulman, D. M. (2021). Use
of video telehealth tablets to increase access for veterans experiencing homelessness. *Journal of General Internal Medicine, 36*, 2274–2282.

38 Lal, S., Elias, S., Sieu, V., & Peredo, R. (2023). The use of technology to provide
mental health services to youth experiencing homelessness: Scoping review.
Journal of Medical Internet Research, 25, e41939.

21

THE ARMY, PRISON, THE POLICE, AND THE CARE SYSTEM

21.1 INTRODUCTION

Institutional environments such as the army, prison, the police force, and the care system play a pivotal role in shaping the lives and identities of the men within them (for example, in homelessness – as explored in the previous chapter). These settings, characterized by their structured nature and inherent stressors, impose unique challenges on all within them, but especially men, who make up the majority of participants in these systems. It affects their mental health, relationships, and sense of self. This chapter delves into these complexities, aiming to uncover the nuanced experiences of men navigating life in these demanding contexts.

The army, with its rigorous discipline and the potential for combat exposure, places immense pressure on soldiers, often pushing the boundaries of physical and mental endurance. The prison system, marked by confinement and a culture of violence, impacts inmates in profound ways, affecting their psychological well-being and future prospects. The police force, tasked with maintaining law and order, exposes officers to high-stress situations that can take a toll on their mental health and alter their perception of community and self. Finally, the care system, which often provides a cold and unyielding environment for boys in care, can do lasting damage for years to come.

DOI: 10.4324/9781032709369-27

These institutional settings, while distinct in their purposes and cultures, share commonalities in the way they reinforce traditional notions of masculinity. Strength, stoicism, and dominance are often valorized, sometimes at the expense of emotional well-being and mental health. The expectation to conform to these ideals can further exacerbate the challenges faced by men in these environments, leading to issues such as PTSD, depression, and strained personal relationships.

Understanding the experiences of men in the army, prison, police force, and in care is crucial for identifying the support systems and interventions needed to foster resilience and well-being. This chapter seeks to highlight the significance of these institutional settings in shaping men's lives, advocating for targeted strategies to address the unique challenges they present. Through this exploration, we aim to contribute to a broader conversation about masculinity, mental health, and the societal structures that influence them.

21.2 THE ARMY

In the UK, men make up approximately 91% of the armed forces, with women comprising about 9%. In the United States, women represent about 17% of active-duty military personnel.[1]

21.2.1 Challenges and Pressures

Men in the military face a unique set of rigorous demands that test their physical, mental, and emotional resilience. The challenges of military life extend beyond the battlefield, encompassing the stress of training, the anticipation of deployment, and the realities of combat exposure. These experiences can be compounded by the pressure to adhere to traditional masculine norms that valorize stoicism, toughness, and self-reliance.[2] Such expectations often discourage expressions of vulnerability or seeking help, creating an environment where emotional struggles are internalized. The impact of combat exposure is particularly profound, exposing soldiers to traumatic events that can leave lasting psychological scars. Moreover, the military's hierarchical structure and the necessity for cohesion place additional pressures on individuals to conform, further intensifying the challenges they face.

21.2.2 Impact on Mental Health and Relationships

The mental health of men in the military can be significantly affected by their service. Conditions such as posttraumatic stress disorder (PTSD), depression, and anxiety are prevalent among soldiers, stemming from both combat exposure and the high-stress military environment.[3,4,5] The effects of these mental health challenges are not confined to the individuals alone; they also place a considerable strain on family and personal relationships and can result in suicide ideation.[6] The transition back to civilian life can exacerbate these strains, as soldiers and their loved ones navigate the complexities of reintegration.[7] The altered dynamics can lead to misunderstandings, emotional distance, and conflict, further impacting the well-being of both the veterans and their families.

21.2.3   Strategies for Support

Recognizing the unique mental health needs of soldiers, various programs and interventions have been developed to offer support both during service and post discharge. These include:

1. *Resilience training.* Programs aimed at building psychological resilience among soldiers, preparing them to handle the stresses of military life and combat. These training programs focus on developing coping strategies, emotional intelligence, and stress management techniques.

2. *Mental health services.* Access to mental health professionals who specialize in military-related trauma is crucial. Counseling and therapy services, both individual and group, provide spaces for soldiers to process their experiences and receive treatment for conditions like PTSD. It is also critical to tackle the stigma associated with male active personnel and veterans seeking such help.[8,9]

3. *Peer support.* Peer support programs facilitate connections among soldiers and veterans, offering a network of understanding and empathy. These programs leverage shared experiences to provide mutual support, advice, and camaraderie.

4. *Family support initiatives.* Recognizing the impact of military service on families, these initiatives offer resources and counseling designed to strengthen family relationships and ease the reintegration process. They provide education on the challenges of post deployment life and strategies for effective communication and support.

5. *Breaking down hegemonic representations.* There is some suggestion that there are already changes underway in how the army is presented as a performance of masculinity, both through diversifying representation in campaigns and also in relation to the qualities valued and how these are framed.[10] Newer advertisements frame masculinity more progressively and focus on the teamwork and bonding elements rather than aggression and success.

By highlighting and expanding these support strategies, we can better address the mental health needs of soldiers, aiding their transition from military to civilian life and enhancing their overall well-being. It is imperative that these support systems are widely accessible, removing barriers to help-seeking and fostering an environment where the well-being of soldiers is a priority.

21.2.4   Examples Organizations

Following are some organizations that work to support military personnel, including men.

21.2.4.1   UK Organizations

- Help for Heroes

  Help for Heroes is a UK-based charity that provides lifelong support to service personnel and veterans who have suffered injuries or illnesses as a result of their service. The charity offers a range of services, including physical and mental health support, career advice, and community reintegration programs. Help for Heroes aims to empower veterans and their families to live fulfilling and independent lives.

  Website: www.helpforheroes.org.uk/.

- Walking With the Wounded

  Walking With the Wounded supports veterans who have been physically, mentally, or socially disadvantaged by their service. The charity focuses on helping veterans reintegrate into society through employment support, mental health services, and training programs. Walking with the Wounded works to ensure that veterans can lead independent and productive lives.

  Website: walkingwiththewounded.org.uk/.

- The Royal British Legion

  The Royal British Legion is the UK's largest armed forces charity, providing support to serving and ex-serving personnel and their families. The charity offers a wide range of services, including financial assistance, social support, and remembrance activities. The Royal British Legion also campaigns on behalf of the Armed Forces community to ensure their needs are met.

  Website: www.britishlegion.org.uk/.

- Forward Assist

  Forward Assist provides support, advice, guidance, and advocacy through various projects aimed at helping veterans overcome social isolation and improve their mental and physical health. Their interventions aim to reduce the negative impact of social isolation and loneliness.

  Website: www.forward-assist.com/.

- Combat Stress

  Combat Stress is the UK's leading mental health charity for veterans, offering free treatment and support to ex-servicemen and ex-service-women of the UK Armed Forces. They provide comprehensive mental health services to help veterans rebuild their lives.

  Website: https://combatstress.org.uk/.

- HighGround

  HighGround provides advice and support to service leavers and veterans about jobs and careers in the land-based sector, including Rural Weeks at Bicton College. They aim to improve the well-being and employment prospects of veterans through connections to land-based industries.

  Website: https://highground-uk.org/.

21.2.4.2   Around the World

- American Red Cross – Services for Military and Veteran Families

  The American Red Cross provides support to military members, veterans, and their families, offering emergency communication services, financial assistance, and programs designed to improve morale and well-being during and after service.

  Website: www.redcross.org/.

- United Service Organizations (USO)

  The USO supports American service members by providing programs and services that boost morale and help military personnel stay connected to their families. The organization operates more than 250 centers worldwide and offers a variety of support programs.

  Website: www.uso.org/.

- Boeing's Military and Veterans Engagement

  Boeing supports veterans and military families through philanthropic investments, employment opportunities, and integrated transition services. They work closely with military-focused organizations to address the challenges faced by service members during their transition to civilian life.

  Website: www.boeing.com/.

- National Resource Directory (NRD)

  The NRD is a partnership among the Departments of Defense, Labor, and Veterans Affairs that connects service members, veterans, their families, and caregivers to programs and services that support their recovery, rehabilitation, and reintegration.

  Website: https://nrd.gov/.

21.3   THE PRISON SYSTEM

In the UK, the prison population is overwhelmingly male, with men constituting 96% of those incarcerated. Similarly, in the United States, men account for about 93% of the prison population.[11] And these types of proportions are reflected globally.

21.3.1   The Reality of Incarceration

The experience of incarceration imposes profound psychological impacts on men, characterized by a complex interplay between violence, isolation, and the loss of autonomy. Prisons, often environments of heightened violence and aggression,[12] expose inmates to daily stresses and threats that can exacerbate existing mental health conditions or catalyze new ones. The pervasive sense of isolation, both physical and emotional, from being cut off from the outside world and familial connections, further compounds these psychological burdens. Additionally, the loss of autonomy over daily life, from simple choices like when to eat or sleep to more significant decisions about personal growth and development, strips individuals of their agency, leading to feelings of helplessness and despair. This environment not only hinders personal development but also poses significant barriers to the mental and emotional well-being of incarcerated men.

Masculinities within prison spaces operate under a unique and often brutal hierarchy that enforces traditional and hypermasculine behaviors.[13,14,15] Incarcerated men frequently navigate a culture where dominance, physical strength, and emotional stoicism are necessary for survival and respect. Displays of vulnerability can be perceived as weaknesses, making it dangerous for inmates to express emotions or seek mental health support. This hypermasculine code often exacerbates conflicts and fuels a cycle of violence as men strive to assert their dominance and avoid being perceived as weak. Furthermore, the rigid enforcement of these masculine norms contributes to a toxic environment that can entrench harmful behaviors and hinder rehabilitation efforts.

Queer masculinity in these spaces faces additional layers of complexity and discrimination.[16] Men who identify as queer or display nontraditional masculine behaviors often confront heightened stigma and violence, both from fellow inmates and, at times, from correctional staff. This intersection of homophobia and hypermasculinity can lead to severe marginalization, making it even more challenging for queer men to navigate the prison environment. They may be forced to conceal their identities to avoid targeting, which exacerbates feelings of isolation and impacts their mental health profoundly. Additionally, straight-identifying men may find themselves forced to engage in or occupy queer spaces as a part of prison hierarchies and survival strategies, which can create further internal conflict and stress. These men might adopt queer behaviors as a means of protection or gaining favor, complicating their own sense of identity and contributing to the overall complexity of masculinity in prison.

Understanding the dynamics of both traditional and queer masculinities in prison is crucial for developing interventions that promote healthier expressions of identity and support mental health among all inmates, fostering an environment where diverse forms of masculinity can coexist without fear of retribution.

21.3.2   Rehabilitation vs. Punishment

The prison system stands at a crossroads between two fundamentally different approaches: rehabilitation and punishment. The debate over the effectiveness of these approaches is crucial in determining the outcomes for incarcerated men. Rehabilitation, focusing on treating the underlying causes of criminal behavior through education, therapy, and skill development, aims to prepare inmates for a successful re-entry into society. Conversely, a punitive approach, emphasizing retribution and deterrence, often overlooks the root causes of criminal behavior, potentially reinforcing harmful behaviors and identities. This dichotomy raises critical questions about the goals of incarceration and its impact on individuals. Evidence increasingly suggests that rehabilitation programs significantly reduce recidivism rates and foster positive societal re-entry by addressing the psychological, educational, and vocational needs of inmates, challenging the efficacy of a purely punitive model.

21.3.3   Support and Reintegration

The importance of support and reintegration programs for male prisoners is significant. Rehabilitation initiatives, including mental health counseling, educational courses, vocational training, and substance abuse treatment,[17] are essential in addressing the multifaceted needs of incarcerated men.[18] These programs not only aid in the personal development of inmates but also equip them with the skills and coping mechanisms necessary for life outside prison. Upon release, reintegration support becomes crucial in ensuring a smooth transition back into society. This includes assistance with finding housing and employment, reconnecting with family, and accessing community-based support services. Such comprehensive support systems are vital in reducing recidivism, aiding individuals in rebuilding their lives, and ultimately contributing to safer, healthier communities.

The discussion surrounding the prison system's impact on men underscores the need for a shift toward a more rehabilitative and supportive approach. By focusing on addressing the root causes of criminal behavior and providing meaningful support for reintegration, we can foster environments that not only respect the dignity and potential of incarcerated individuals but also enhance public safety and community well-being.

21.3.4   Example Organizations

Here are some examples of organizations that are supporting prisoners, including men, both within prisons and postsentence.

21.3.4.1 UK Organizations

- A Band of Brothers

  A Band of Brothers (ABOB) is a UK-based charity dedicated to supporting young men involved in the criminal justice system. The organization provides intensive mentorship and rites-of-passage programs designed to help these young men transition into adulthood with a sense of belonging, purpose, and connection. ABOB's programs include one-to-one mentoring, residential weekends, and ongoing support to help young men build positive futures and avoid reoffending.

  Website: https://abandofbrothers.org.uk/.

- St. Giles Trust

  St. Giles Trust offers a range of services to support people facing severe disadvantage, including those who are or have been involved in the criminal justice system. They provide mentoring, employment training, and housing assistance to help individuals reintegrate into society.

  Website: www.stgilestrust.org.uk/.

21.3.4.2 Global Organizations

- Hope for Prisoners

  This organization helps men, women, and young adults re-enter the workforce and their communities. Their programs include leadership training, financial literacy workshops, and technology training to equip participants with skills for successful reintegration.

  Website: https://hopeforprisoners.org/.

- The National Reentry Network for Returning Citizens

  This network supports formerly incarcerated individuals by providing advocacy, support services, and community reintegration programs. Their "one-stop shop" model offers a variety of services aimed at rebuilding lives postincarceration.

  Website: https://thenationalreentrynetwork.org/.

- Vera Institute of Justice

  Vera Institute works to end mass incarceration and improve the justice system. They provide research, advocacy, and policy recommendations to help reduce incarceration rates and support re-entry programs.

  Website: www.vera.org/.

- DOVE (Developing Organizing Visions for Everyone)

  DOVE offers re-entry and crime prevention programs designed for system-impacted individuals. They provide support in connecting to services, social justice advocacy, and gang prevention.

  Website: www.dovebayarea.org/.

- Center for Community Transitions
  This organization helps formerly incarcerated individuals find employment and reintegrate into their communities. They offer various programs focused on employment training, life skills development, and community support.

  Website: https://centerforcommunitytransitions.org/.

21.4   THE POLICE FORCE

In the UK, men account for 65.3% of the workforce. In the United States, men represent about 88% of full-time law enforcement officers,[19] and forces are male dominated worldwide.

21.4.1   Occupational Stressors

Men in law enforcement face a myriad of occupational stressors that can significantly impact their mental health and well-being. The nature of police work often involves high-stress situations, such as dealing with violent crimes, life-threatening scenarios, and the constant pressure to remain vigilant. These stressors are compounded by the internalization of the hypermasculine "tough cop" persona, a cultural construct within the police force that valorizes stoicism and emotional detachment.[20] This expectation to embody an unwavering figure of authority and strength can inhibit officers from expressing vulnerabilities or seeking support, leading to increased risks of burnout, PTSD, and other stress-related conditions. The cumulative effect of these pressures not only affects the officers' mental health but can also impact their decision-making, job performance, and interactions with the public.

21.4.2   Community Relations and Identity

The role of law enforcement in the community and its impact on officers' personal identity and relationships are complex and multifaceted. Police officers often grapple with the dual identity of being a member of the community they serve and an enforcer of the law. This dichotomy can lead to tensions in personal relationships and a sense of isolation from the community. Furthermore, the current climate of scrutiny and criticism toward law enforcement practices can exacerbate these challenges, affecting officers' sense of self and their perception of their role in society. Striking a balance between authority and community member requires navigating societal expectations, personal values, and the inherent responsibilities of policing, all of which can deeply influence officers' identities both on and off duty.

21.4.3   Resilience and Support Mechanisms

Fostering resilience and providing comprehensive support mechanisms for police officers are essential steps toward mitigating the mental health challenges associated with law enforcement work. Strategies for supporting officers' mental health include:

1. *Stress management programs.* Implementing stress management and mindfulness training can help officers develop coping strategies to manage the psychological demands of their work. These programs should focus on emotional regulation, resilience building, and the promotion of mental wellness.

2. *Emotional support and counseling services.* Providing access to counseling services and peer support groups where officers can safely express their feelings and experiences is crucial. These services should be confidential and easily accessible, encouraging officers to seek help without fear of stigma or professional repercussions.

3. *Community engagement initiatives.* Engaging in community outreach and partnership programs can help bridge the gap between law enforcement and the communities they serve. These initiatives can foster mutual understanding, respect, and collaboration, enhancing officers' roles within the community and improving public perceptions of policing.

4. *Leadership training.* Training for police leadership should include components on recognizing the signs of mental health struggles among their ranks and creating an environment that encourages support-seeking and prioritizes officer well-being.

By addressing the unique pressures faced by men in law enforcement and implementing targeted support and resilience strategies, we can better support the mental health and overall well-being of police officers. This approach not only benefits the officers themselves but also enhances the quality of policing, community relations, and public trust in law enforcement.

21.5   CROSS-INSTITUTION ISSUES

21.5.1 Masculinity and Institutional Culture

As outlined earlier, institutional cultures within the army, prison, and police force are all deeply intertwined with traditional norms of masculinity, often emphasizing strength, stoicism, and aggression as ideal traits. These environments can reinforce a narrow view of what it means to be a man, placing immense pressure on individuals to conform to these expectations. In the military, the valorization of physical toughness and emotional resilience can deter soldiers from acknowledging psychological distress or seeking support. Similarly, in prisons, the culture of masculinity promotes a hyper-vigilant demeanor as a means of protection and survival, often at the expense of emotional well-being. Within the police force, the "tough cop" persona fosters a culture where showing vulnerability is equated with weakness, impacting officers' mental health and their interactions with the community.[21]

The effects of these institutional cultures on men's health and behavior are profound. Adherence to rigid masculine norms can lead to unhealthy coping mechanisms, such as substance abuse, and can exacerbate mental health conditions like depression and PTSD. Moreover, the suppression of emotions and avoidance of help-seeking behaviors can hinder personal relationships, creating barriers to social support that is crucial for mental health and resilience.

21.5.2   Mental Health Awareness and Intervention

The critical need for mental health support and intervention across all institutional settings cannot be overstated. Despite the growing recognition of mental health issues among men in the army, prison, and police force, significant barriers to accessing care persist, largely due to the stigma associated with seeking help. Systemic changes are essential to address these challenges, including the implementation of comprehensive mental health programs that are sensitive to the unique contexts of each institution. These programs should offer accessible, confidential, and nonjudgmental support, aiming to destigmatize mental health issues and encourage individuals to seek help without fear of reprisal or judgment.

In addition to programmatic support, institutional cultures themselves must evolve to embrace a broader understanding of masculinity that includes vulnerability and emotional expression as strengths rather than weaknesses. Leadership within these institutions plays a critical role in driving this cultural shift, modeling supportive behaviors, and promoting mental health awareness as a priority.

Creating environments that support mental health and challenge traditional norms of masculinity requires concerted effort and commitment from all levels of institutional leadership, as well as broader societal support. By fostering cultures that prioritize well-being, encourage help-seeking, and respect diverse expressions of masculinity, we can improve the health and behavior of men in these critical sectors, ultimately benefiting the individuals themselves and the communities they serve.

21.6   IMPACT ON MINORITY GROUPS

Men from minority groups often face unique challenges and discrimination within institutional environments such as the army, prison, and police force. These experiences are shaped by intersecting factors of race, ethnicity, and systemic biases that can exacerbate the pressures and mental health challenges already present in these settings.

21.6.1   Challenges Faced by Minority Men

These include:

1. *Systemic discrimination and racism.* Minority men frequently encounter systemic discrimination and racism within these institutions. In the military, for instance, they might face biases in recruitment, promotions, and disciplinary actions. Similarly, in the police force, minority officers can experience racial profiling and discriminatory practices both from within their departments and from the communities they serve.

2. *Cultural isolation.* The lack of representation and support networks can lead to cultural isolation for minority men in these environments. They may struggle to find mentors or colleagues who share similar backgrounds and experiences, which can hinder their professional development and emotional well-being.

3. *Heightened scrutiny.* Minority men often face heightened scrutiny and pressure to prove themselves in ways that their peers may not. This can lead to increased stress and anxiety as they must navigate not only the demands of their roles but also the additional burden of overcoming racial biases and stereotypes.

21.6.2   Example: Police Officers and the Black Lives Matter Movement

The Black Lives Matter (BLM) movement has highlighted the complex and often conflicting identities that minority police officers must navigate. Black officers, in particular, face the challenge of balancing their professional responsibilities with their membership in a racial group that has historically been subjected to police violence and discrimination.

21.6.2.1   Balancing Dual Identities

• *Professional loyalty vs. racial solidarity.* Black police officers often find themselves caught between their duty to uphold the law and their solidarity with the BLM movement, which protests against police brutality and systemic racism. This dual identity can create significant internal conflict and stress.

- *Community relationships.* Black officers may experience strained relationships with both their colleagues and the communities they serve. Within the police force, they might be seen as less loyal or trustworthy, while in their communities, they may be viewed as enforcers of a system that oppresses their racial group.

21.6.2.2 *Specific Challenges*

- *Isolation.* Black officers can feel isolated within their departments, where they might be one of the few minority individuals. This isolation can be compounded by a lack of understanding or support from their peers regarding the racial issues highlighted by the BLM movement.
- *Mental health impact.* The stress of navigating these dual identities can take a significant toll on mental health. Black officers may experience higher levels of anxiety, depression, and burnout, exacerbated by the need to suppress their personal experiences of racism to fit into the institutional culture.

21.7 CULTURAL CHANGES AND POLICY INTERVENTIONS

To address the pervasive issues of masculinity and mental health within the army, prison, and police force, significant cultural changes and policy interventions are needed. These reforms should aim to create environments that support mental health, challenge traditional norms of masculinity, and provide comprehensive support systems for the individuals within these institutions. Here are some quick fire recommendations:

21.7.1 Cultural Changes

1. *Redefining masculinity.* Promote a broader, more inclusive understanding of masculinity that values emotional expression, vulnerability, and mutual support. Institutions should actively work to dismantle the stigmas associated with seeking help and expressing emotions, encouraging a culture where mental health is prioritized.

2. *Leadership training.* Institutional leaders must be equipped with the knowledge and skills to recognize and address mental health issues among their ranks. Leadership training should include components on mental health awareness, supportive communication, and strategies for fostering an inclusive environment.

3. *Peer support networks.* Establish and strengthen peer support networks where individuals can share their experiences and offer mutual support. These networks can play a crucial role in normalizing conversations

about mental health and providing informal but essential emotional support.

4.   *Inclusive policies.* Develop and implement policies that explicitly support diverse expressions of masculinity, including those of queer individuals. These policies should aim to create a safe and inclusive environment where all forms of masculinity are respected and valued.

21.7.2   Policy Interventions

1.   *Comprehensive mental health programs.* Implement comprehensive mental health programs tailored to the unique needs of individuals in the army, prison, and police force. These programs should offer accessible, confidential, and nonjudgmental support, including counseling, therapy, and resilience training.

2.   *Mandatory mental health training.* Make mental health training mandatory for all personnel within these institutions. This training should cover recognizing signs of mental distress, basic mental health first aid, and the importance of seeking help. Regular refresher courses should be included to ensure ongoing awareness.

3.   *Support for families.* Develop support programs for the families of individuals within these institutions. These programs should offer resources and counseling to help families understand the challenges their loved ones face and provide strategies for effective communication and support.

4.   *Monitoring and evaluation.* Establish mechanisms for the regular monitoring and evaluation of mental health programs and policies. Feedback from participants should be actively sought and used to continually improve these initiatives.

5.   *Collaboration with mental health professionals.* Foster collaboration between institutional leaders and mental health professionals to ensure that mental health programs are evidence-based and effective. This collaboration can help in designing programs that are tailored to the specific needs of the institution.

21.7.3   Institutional Reforms

1.   *Rehabilitation-oriented approaches.* Shift toward rehabilitation-oriented approaches in prisons and the military, focusing on addressing the root causes of behavioral issues and preparing individuals for successful reintegration into society. This includes providing education, vocational training, and substance abuse treatment.

2.   *Community engagement.* Enhance community engagement initiatives within the police force to build trust and improve relations between law enforcement and the communities they serve. These initiatives should focus on transparency, accountability, and collaboration with community leaders.

3.   *Stigma reduction campaigns.* Launch campaigns aimed at reducing the stigma associated with mental health issues and seeking help. These campaigns should use various platforms, including social media, to reach a broad audience and normalize conversations around mental health.

4.   *Comprehensive rehabilitation and re-entry programs.* Develop and implement comprehensive rehabilitation and re-entry programs for incarcerated men that focus on mental health and successful reintegration into society. These programs should include individualized mental health assessments and treatments, addressing issues such as PTSD, depression, and substance abuse. Additionally, providing life skills training, such as financial literacy, anger management, and effective communication, is essential for holistic rehabilitation. These programs should also offer robust postrelease support, including job placement services, housing assistance, and ongoing counseling, to ensure that former inmates have the resources and support needed to rebuild their lives and reduce recidivism. Collaboration with community organizations and employers to create pathways for employment and integration into the community is also crucial for the success of these programs.

21.7.4   Societal Support

1.   *Public awareness.* Increase public awareness about the mental health challenges faced by individuals in the army, prison, and police force. Public education campaigns can help in shifting societal perceptions and fostering a more supportive environment for these individuals.

2.   *Advocacy for policy change.* Encourage advocacy for policy changes that support mental health and well-being within these institutions. This can involve working with policymakers, nonprofit organizations, and other stakeholders to push for reforms at local, national, and international levels.

3.   *Research and development.* Support research into the mental health needs of individuals in these institutional settings to inform evidence-based policy and practice. Continued research can provide insights into effective interventions and help in the development of new support strategies.

By implementing these cultural changes and policy interventions, we can create environments that not only support the mental health and well-being of men in the army, prison, and police force but also foster a more inclusive and understanding society. These efforts will ultimately lead to healthier individuals, more effective institutions, and stronger communities.

21.8 BOYS IN THE CARE SYSTEM

Boys in the care system, including foster families and residential care, face unique and multifaceted challenges that can significantly impact their development, well-being, and future prospects. These challenges are often exacerbated by societal expectations and systemic shortcomings, making it imperative to address their specific needs. These include:

1. *Instability and attachment issues.* Boys in the care system often experience frequent placement changes, leading to instability that disrupts the formation of secure attachments. This lack of consistent, nurturing relationships can result in difficulties with trust, emotional security, and healthy relationship-building in the future.

2. *Behavioral problems.* There is a prevalent stereotype that boys are more prone to behavioral issues, which can lead to harsher disciplinary measures and increased placement disruptions. This perception not only stigmatizes boys but can also result in a cycle where their behavior worsens due to negative reinforcement and lack of appropriate support.

3. *Mental health concerns.* Boys (and girls) are at a high risk for mental health issues, such as anxiety, depression, and PTSD.[22] The trauma from abuse, neglect, or family separation, combined with the instability of care placements, exacerbates these issues. Unfortunately, mental health services tailored specifically to boys' needs are often inadequate or inaccessible.

4. *Academic challenges.* Frequent changes in living situations often lead to disruptions in education. Boys may face biases that affect their academic experiences, and without stable support, they are at risk of disengagement and lower educational attainment (and this is on top of the challenges outlined in previous chapters on education). This instability can hinder their future opportunities.

5. *Identity and self-esteem issues.* The lack of consistent, positive male role models can negatively impact boys' self-esteem and identity formation. Additionally, societal pressures to conform to traditional masculine norms can discourage boys from expressing vulnerability or seeking help, further complicating their emotional development.

21.8.1   Strategies for Supporting Boys in the Care System

Addressing the unique challenges faced by boys in the care system requires targeted, thoughtful strategies designed to meet their specific needs and support their overall well-being. These include:

1.   *Ensuring stable placements and continuity of care.* Minimizing placement disruptions is crucial for the emotional and psychological stability of boys in care. Efforts should be made to keep boys in stable, nurturing environments, where they can form lasting, supportive relationships with caregivers.

2.   *Behavioral support and positive reinforcement.* Implementing behavioral support programs that emphasize positive reinforcement over punitive measures can help address and manage behavioral issues effectively. Caregivers should be trained in trauma-informed care to better understand and respond to boys' needs.

3.   *Providing access to comprehensive mental health services.* Boys in care should have access to tailored mental health services, including counseling and therapy that address the specific traumas and challenges they face. Programs should aim to reduce stigma around seeking mental health support and be readily accessible.

4.   *Offering educational support and advocacy.* Ensuring that boys receive consistent academic support through tutoring and advocacy is essential. Collaboration between child welfare agencies and educational institutions can help provide the necessary resources and stability to support boys' academic success.

5.   *Connecting boys with positive male role models and mentors.* Establishing mentoring programs that link boys with positive male role models can significantly impact their development. Mentors can offer guidance, support, and stability, helping boys build self-esteem and aspire to achieve their goals.

6.   *Encouraging emotional expression and building resilience.* Creating environments that promote emotional expression and resilience is crucial. Programs should focus on developing emotional literacy, teaching boys healthy coping mechanisms, and encouraging them to seek help when needed.

7.   *Engaging and supporting families.* Whenever possible, involving biological families in the care process and providing them with support can help maintain important connections for boys. Family therapy and

reunification programs can aid in rebuilding these relationships and providing a sense of stability and belonging.

Boys in the care system face a range of specific challenges that require targeted, multifaceted approaches to support their development and well-being. By prioritizing stability, mental health, educational support, positive role models, and emotional resilience, we can create a more supportive environment for boys in care. These strategies will help them overcome the adversities they face and build a brighter future. It is essential that child welfare policies and practices continuously evolve to meet the unique needs of boys in the care system, ensuring they receive the comprehensive support necessary to thrive.

21.9 CONCLUSION

This chapter has traversed the complex terrain of men's experiences within institutional settings, such as the army, prison, and the police force, shedding light on the unique challenges these environments pose to men's mental health, relationships, and sense of self. Through examining the rigorous demands, mental stress, and the pressures to conform to traditional masculine norms, we have uncovered how these institutional cultures can exacerbate issues of vulnerability and hinder the pursuit of help and emotional support.

The exploration into the realms of the army, prison, and police force reveals a common thread: the need for systemic change to address the pervasive issues of masculinity and mental health within these environments. The pressures to adhere to outdated norms of stoicism and toughness not only compromise the well-being of men but also impact their behavior, their ability to form and maintain healthy relationships, and their overall effectiveness within their roles.

As we conclude, it is imperative to issue a call to action for policymakers, institutional leaders, and society at large. Recognizing the unique challenges faced by men in these settings is just the first step. There is a dire need for targeted support strategies that cater specifically to the mental health and well-being of men in the army, prison, and police force. This includes implementing comprehensive mental health programs, fostering environments that challenge the traditional norms of masculinity, and promoting a culture that values emotional literacy and resilience.

Moreover, institutional leaders must play a pivotal role in driving cultural change, advocating for policies that prioritize mental health support, and dismantling the stigma associated with seeking help. Society, too, has a part to play in shifting perceptions of masculinity to encompass a broader, more inclusive understanding that recognizes emotional vulnerability as a strength rather than a weakness.

The journey toward fostering an environment that supports the mental health, resilience, and positive identity development for men in demanding institutional contexts is long and complex. However, by committing to these targeted support strategies and systemic changes, we can pave the way for a future where men in these settings are not only more effective in their roles but also lead healthier, more fulfilling lives. This not only benefits the individuals themselves but also has a profound impact on the institutions they serve and society at large.

NOTES

1 https://commonslibrary.parliament.uk/research-briefings/cbp-7930/
2 Richard, K., & Molloy, S. (2020). An examination of emerging adult military men: Masculinity and US military climate. *Psychology of Men & Masculinities, 21*(4), 686.
3 Duncan, J. M., Reed-Fitzke, K., Ferraro, A. J., Wojciak, A. S., Smith, K. M., & Sánchez, J. (2020). Identifying risk and resilience factors associated with the likelihood of seeking mental health care among US army soldiers-in-training. *Military Medicine, 185*(7–8), e1247–e1254.
4 Rhead, R., MacManus, D., Jones, M., Greenberg, N., Fear, N. T., & Goodwin, L. (2022). Mental health disorders and alcohol misuse among UK military veterans and the general population: A comparison study. *Psychological Medicine, 52*(2), 292–302.
5 Ganz, A. P. D. Y., Yamaguchi, C., Koritzky, B. P. G., & Berger, S. E. (2021). Military culture and its impact on mental health and stigma. *Journal of Community Engagement & Scholarship, 13*(4).
6 Kieran, D. (2021). 'It changed me as a man': Reframing military masculinity in the army's 'shoulder to shoulder' suicide prevention campaign. *Journal of War & Culture Studies, 14*(3), 306–323.
7 Allen, E. S., Rhoades, G. K., Stanley, S. M., & Markman, H. J. (2010). Hitting home: Relationships between recent deployment, posttraumatic stress symptoms, and marital functioning for Army couples. *Journal of Family Psychology, 24*(3), 280.
8 Clary, K. L., Pena, S., & Smith, D. C. (2023). Masculinity and stigma among emerging adult military members and veterans: Implications for encouraging help-seeking. *Current Psychology, 42*(6), 4422–4438.
9 Spector-Mersel, G., & Gilbar, O. (2021). From military masculinity toward hybrid masculinities: Constructing a new sense of manhood among veterans treated for PTSS. *Men and Masculinities, 24*(5), 862–883.
10 Jester, N. (2021). Army recruitment video advertisements in the US and UK since 2002: Challenging ideals of hegemonic military masculinity? *Media, War & Conflict, 14*(1), 57–74.
11 https://commonslibrary.parliament.uk/research-briefings/sn04334/
12 Maguire, D. (2021). Vulnerable prisoner masculinities in an English prison. *Men and Masculinities, 24*(3), 501–518.
13 Yvonne, J. (2017). Men behind bars: "Doing" masculinity as an adaptation to imprisonment. In *Crime, Criminal Justice and Masculinities* (pp. 381–400). Routledge.
14 Ricciardelli, R., Maier, K., & Hannah-Moffat, K. (2015). Strategic masculinities: Vulnerabilities, risk and the production of prison masculinities. *Theoretical Criminology, 19*(4), 491–513.4

15 Michalski, J. H. (2017). Status hierarchies and hegemonic masculinity: A general theory of prison violence. *British Journal of Criminology, 57*(1), 40–60.
16 Hefner, M. K. (2018). Queering prison masculinity: Exploring the organization of gender and sexuality within men's prison. *Men and Masculinities, 21*(2), 230–253.
17 Doyle, M. F., Shakeshaft, A., Guthrie, J., Snijder, M., & Butler, T. (2019). A systematic review of evaluations of prison-based alcohol and other drug use behavioural treatment for men. *Australian and New Zealand Journal of Public Health, 43*(2), 120–130.
18 Timler, K., Brown, H., & Varcoe, C. (2019). Growing connection beyond prison walls: How a prison garden fosters rehabilitation and healing for incarcerated men. *Journal of Offender Rehabilitation, 58*(5), 444–463.
19 www.gov.uk/government/statistics/police-workforce-england-and-wales-31-march-2023/police-workforce-england-and-wales-31-march-2023
20 Silvestri, M. (2017). Police culture and gender: Revisiting the 'cult of masculinity'. *Policing: A Journal of Policy and Practice, 11*(3), 289–300.
21 Steinþórsdóttir, F. S., & Pétursdóttir, G. M. (2022). To protect and serve while protecting privileges and serving male interests: Hegemonic masculinity and the sense of entitlement within the Icelandic police force. *Policing and Society, 32*(4), 489–503.
22 Jacobsen, H., Bergsund, H. B., Wentzel-Larsen, T., Smith, L., & Moe, V. (2020). Foster children are at risk for developing problems in social-emotional functioning: A follow-up study at 8 years of age. *Children and Youth Services Review, 108,* 104603.

22

SUBSTANCE USE AND MISUSE

22.1 INTRODUCTION

Substance misuse and alcoholism represent some of the most pressing public health challenges facing men and boys today. This complex issue, rooted
in a web of societal, psychological, and environmental factors, not only
devastates the lives of individuals but also has profound implications for
families, communities, and society at large. It has arisen in numerous previous chapters, and so many of the relationships between substance use and
misuse and other outcomes (e.g., homelessness) have already been explored.
This chapter aims to dissect the intricacies of these issues among men and
boys, offering a comprehensive exploration of their causes, consequences,
and the critical need for effective interventions.[1]

It does so because the prevalence of substance misuse and alcoholism is
disproportionately high among men and boys, influenced by a confluence of
factors that encourage or normalize substance use as a coping mechanism,
a rite of passage, or a means to affirm one's masculinity. These behaviors,
often initiated during adolescence or young adulthood, can set the stage for
a lifetime of challenges, including addiction, health deterioration, and social
isolation.

The consequences of substance misuse and alcoholism extend far beyond
the individual, affecting every facet of society. On a personal level, addiction
can lead to significant health problems, mental health disorders, and a
marked decline in quality of life. Relationships with family and friends suffer,
employment opportunities diminish, and the ability to function effectively in

DOI: 10.4324/9781032709369-28

daily life is severely compromised. Societally, the ripple effects are seen in increased health-care costs, lost productivity, and a higher burden on criminal justice and social services systems.

This chapter seeks not only to shed light on the critical issue of substance misuse and alcoholism among men and boys but also to underscore the urgent need for comprehensive strategies that address the root causes of addiction, provide support for those struggling, and foster environments that promote healthy, substance-free lifestyles. Through this exploration, we aim to contribute to a broader understanding and more effective resolution of this pervasive challenge.

22.2   CONTRIBUTING FACTORS

There are several factors that contribute to **substance use and misuse by** men and boys.

22.2.1   Societal Expectations

The influence of societal norms and expectations around masculinity plays a significant role in substance misuse and alcoholism among men and boys.[2,3] Traditional masculine roles often emphasize stoicism, toughness, and self-reliance, discouraging expressions of vulnerability or emotional distress. This pressure to conform to an idealized version of manhood can lead individuals to seek escape or solace in alcohol and drugs as a means to cope with emotional pain or stress in silence.[4] Furthermore, the stigma attached to seeking help for emotional or psychological issues exacerbates this problem, trapping men in a cycle of substance misuse as a socially acceptable method of managing their struggles.

22.2.2   Mental Health Issues

There is also a profound interplay between mental health disorders – such as depression, anxiety, and PTSD – and substance misuse.[5] Men and boys suffering from untreated or inadequately addressed mental health conditions may turn to alcohol or drugs as a form of self-medication, attempting to alleviate symptoms or numb emotional pain. This form of coping not only fails to address the underlying mental health issue but also increases the risk of developing a dependency or addiction. The cycle of mental health issues and substance misuse creates a complex challenge that necessitates integrated treatment approaches to effectively address both concerns.

22.2.3   Peer Pressure and Social Environment

The influence of peer groups and social settings also significantly impacts substance misuse among men and boys.[6] Social norms and behaviors within these groups often play a crucial role in shaping individuals' attitudes toward alcohol and drug use. For many, substance use is initiated or perpetuated in social contexts where it is normalized or even celebrated as a marker of social belonging or masculinity. Peer pressure can intensify these influences, making it challenging for individuals to resist engaging in substance misuse without risking social exclusion or ridicule. It can also act as a route to interact with each other without the stigma around male relationships and male touch.[7]

22.2.4   Trauma and Adversity

Past trauma and adverse experiences are also critical factors in the likelihood of developing substance misuse issues.[8,9,10] Experiences of childhood abuse, neglect, exposure to violence, or other traumatic events can have long-lasting effects on an individual's mental and emotional well-being. For many men and boys, substance misuse becomes a way to cope with the pain and memories of these experiences. The link between trauma and addiction highlights the need for trauma-informed care within substance misuse treatment, recognizing the deep-seated roots of addiction that stem from past adversities.

22.2.5   Externalizing Coping Mechanisms in Men

Men often tend to externalize their coping mechanisms due to societal expectations that discourage the expression of internal emotional struggles. This externalization can manifest as substance misuse, aggression, or other outward behaviors that temporarily mask emotional distress. Men may choose substance use as a coping mechanism because it provides an immediate, albeit temporary, escape from their problems without requiring them to confront their emotions directly. This approach aligns with the societal ideal of male stoicism and self-reliance but ultimately leads to negative outcomes, such as addiction and further emotional isolation.

22.2.6   Other Factors

These include:

> *Genetic and biological factors.* Genetic predispositions and biological factors also play a significant role in substance misuse among men. Certain genetic markers may increase the susceptibility to addiction, and biological differences can influence how substances affect men differently from women.
>
> *Economic and occupational stress.* Economic hardships, job loss, or high-stress occupations contribute significantly to substance misuse among men. The pressure to fulfill the provider role can lead men to

use alcohol or drugs as a means to cope with the stress and anxiety related to economic and occupational challenges.

Cultural and ethnic considerations. Substance misuse varies significantly across different cultural and ethnic groups. Cultural background influences attitudes toward substance use and coping mechanisms, and understanding these differences is crucial for effective prevention and treatment.

Impact of relationship dynamics. The quality of personal relationships and familial support systems can influence substance misuse. Men in troubled relationships or with weak family support systems may be more prone to substance misuse, highlighting the need for strong social support networks.

Access to treatment and health care. The availability and accessibility of mental health and substance misuse treatment services are critical in addressing substance misuse. Barriers such as cost, availability, and stigma can prevent men from seeking the help they need, exacerbating the issue. Improving access to comprehensive care is essential for effective treatment and recovery.

22.3   CONSEQUENCES OF ADDICTION

The consequences of substance use and addiction are wide ranging and explored as follows.

22.3.1   Health Impacts

Prolonged substance misuse and alcoholism have devastating effects on both physical and mental health. Physically, chronic diseases such as liver cirrhosis, cardiovascular problems, and various forms of cancer are significantly more prevalent among those with long-term alcohol and substance use disorders. Furthermore, substance misuse can lead to cognitive impairments, including memory loss, decreased attention span, and impaired decision-making abilities. These health issues are compounded by a general neglect of personal health and well-being, leading to deteriorated conditions that might not be directly related to substance use but are worsened by it. The risk of mortality also increases, not just from health complications, but from accidents or incidents related to impaired judgment under the influence of substances as well.

22.3.2   Social and Relationship Impacts

The ripple effects of substance misuse extend deeply into personal relationships and social functioning. Relationships with family, friends, and romantic partners often suffer, as the trust and communication necessary for healthy relationships are eroded by the behaviors associated with addiction.

Substance misuse can lead to financial instability, further straining relation-ships and contributing to an environment of stress and conflict. Employment is also adversely affected, with increased absenteeism, decreased productiv-ity, and a higher risk of unemployment among those struggling with addic-tion. The loss of employment affects not only the individual's economic status but also their social identity and self-esteem, deepening the cycle of misuse as a form of coping.

22.3.3   Community and Societal Impacts

On a broader scale, widespread substance misuse and alcoholism have sig-nificant implications for public health, safety, and economic productivity. Communities face increased health-care costs due to the treatment of condi-tions related to substance misuse, alongside the costs associated with acci-dents and injuries under the influence. Public safety is compromised by increased rates of crime and violence associated with substance abuse. Economically, the loss of productivity due to absenteeism, workplace acci-dents, and the overall decrease in employability of individuals struggling with addiction costs societies billions annually. Furthermore, the intergen-erational impact of substance misuse, where children in households affected by addiction are at a higher risk of engaging in similar behaviors, perpetu-ates the cycle of substance misuse and its associated costs to society.

22.3.4   Other Outcomes of Addiction

Substance misuse and addiction also contribute to a range of other severe outcomes, including violence (see Chapter 19), homelessness (see Chapter 20), and exacerbated mental health issues (see Chapter 3). Specifically, addiction often leads to violent behavior, either due to the disinhibitory effects of sub-stances or as a means to acquire drugs or alcohol. This violence can occur in domestic settings, contributing to family breakdowns, or in public, affecting community safety.

Homelessness is another tragic consequence, as addiction can erode per-sonal relationships, financial stability, and the ability to maintain housing. Individuals struggling with substance use disorders are disproportionately represented among the homeless population, creating a vicious cycle where homelessness exacerbates addiction, and vice versa.

Moreover, mental health issues such as depression, anxiety, and PTSD are both causes and consequences of substance misuse. The co-occurrence of these disorders with addiction creates a complex clinical picture that requires integrated treatment approaches. The stigma associated with both addiction and mental health issues often prevents individuals from seeking help, further entrenching their struggles.

The consequences of addiction are clearly thus far-reaching, affecting not just the individual struggling with substance misuse but also the wider network of relationships and the community at large. Recognizing these impacts is crucial for developing comprehensive strategies that address not only the treatment and recovery of individuals but also the societal structures that contribute to and are affected by substance misuse and alcoholism.

22.4 PREVENTION, TREATMENT, AND RECOVERY STRATEGIES

There are many avenues to intervention in this area, but few are tailored to the needs of men.

22.4.1 Prevention Programs

The cornerstone of addressing substance misuse and alcoholism lies in effective prevention programs. Early intervention and education play critical roles in preventing the onset of substance misuse, particularly among youth and at-risk populations. Programs that foster awareness about the dangers of substance abuse, while also teaching coping skills for stress and emotional distress, can significantly reduce the likelihood of substance misuse. Schools, community centers, and health-care settings are ideal platforms for implementing these preventive measures, offering accessible information and support. Additionally, engaging families and caregivers in prevention efforts ensures a supportive environment that can deter substance misuse. Tailored programs that recognize the unique pressures faced by young men and boys, including societal expectations of masculinity, can be particularly effective in mitigating the risk of developing substance use disorders.

22.4.2 Tailored Treatment Approaches

For those already experiencing substance misuse and alcoholism, tailored treatment approaches that address the specific needs of men and boys are essential.[11] Gender-sensitive counseling and support groups can provide a safe space for men to explore the underlying issues contributing to their substance use, including challenges related to masculinity and societal expectations.[12,13] Integrated treatment programs that address co-occurring mental health conditions, such as depression or PTSD, alongside substance misuse, offer a more holistic approach to recovery. Recognizing the complex interplay between mental health and substance abuse is key to developing effective treatment plans that address all aspects of an individual's well-being.

22.4.3 Recovery and Reintegration Support

The journey to recovery extends beyond the cessation of substance use; ongoing support is crucial for maintaining long-term sobriety and facilitating successful reintegration into society. Community-based recovery programs that offer continued counseling, peer support groups, and relapse prevention strategies play a significant role in supporting individuals in their recovery journey. Additionally, providing opportunities for employment and education can help reintegrate recovering individuals into society, offering a sense of purpose and direction. The role of social support networks, including family, friends, and community members, is crucial; these networks provide the emotional support and encouragement necessary to sustain recovery efforts. Recognizing and celebrating milestones in the recovery process can further reinforce the individual's commitment to sobriety and personal growth.

22.4.4   The Role of Technology in Prevention and Treatment

Technological advancements have revolutionized the prevention and treatment of substance misuse, providing innovative tools that enhance accessibility, support, and effectiveness. Here is a quickfire list of some of the technological solutions available.

22.4.4.1   Telehealth Services

- *Increased accessibility.* Telehealth services have expanded access to treatment for individuals struggling with substance misuse, particularly those in remote or underserved areas. Through virtual consultations, patients can receive professional counseling, medication management, and continuous monitoring without the need for in-person visits.
- *Confidential support.* Telehealth offers a level of privacy that can encourage more individuals to seek help, reducing the stigma associated with substance misuse treatment.

22.4.4.2   Mobile Apps

- *On-demand support.* Mobile apps designed for substance misuse prevention and recovery provide users with immediate access to resources, including educational materials, coping strategies, and crisis intervention tools. Apps like "Sober Grid" and "Recovery Record" offer real-time support and community connection.
- *Personalized monitoring.* These apps often include features for tracking sobriety, setting recovery goals, and monitoring progress, which can help individuals stay motivated and accountable in their recovery journey.

22.4.4.3   Online Support Groups

- *Community and peer support.* Online support groups and forums offer a platform for individuals to connect with others who are experiencing similar challenges. These groups provide emotional support, shared

experiences, and practical advice, fostering a sense of community and belonging.
- *Flexible engagement.* The online nature of these support groups allows for flexible participation, enabling individuals to seek support at any time, regardless of their location or schedule.

22.4.4.4   Data-Driven Insights

- *Predictive analytics.* Advanced data analytics can help identify patterns and predict relapses, allowing for timely interventions. Health-care providers can use these insights to tailor treatment plans and improve outcomes.
- *Behavioral insights.* Technology can track and analyze behavioral data, providing insights into triggers and habits associated with substance misuse. This information can be crucial for developing personalized prevention and treatment strategies.

22.4.4.5   Comprehensive Care Integration

- *Coordinated care.* Digital platforms can facilitate the integration of various aspects of care, from primary health care to specialized substance misuse treatment, ensuring a holistic approach to recovery. This coordination helps streamline the treatment process and improve continuity of care.

By harnessing the power of technology, we can create more accessible, effective, and personalized approaches to preventing and treating substance misuse, ultimately improving outcomes for individuals struggling with addiction.

Implementing comprehensive strategies encompassing prevention, tailored treatment, and ongoing recovery support is crucial in addressing substance misuse and alcoholism among men and boys. By fostering environments that promote early intervention, provide gender-sensitive treatment, and support long-term recovery, we can significantly mitigate the impact of substance misuse and enable individuals to lead healthier, more fulfilling lives.

22.5   CONCLUSION

Throughout this exploration of substance misuse and alcoholism among men and boys, we have delved into the complexities of this pervasive issue, uncovering the societal expectations, mental health challenges, and environmental factors that contribute to its prevalence. We have seen how traditional notions of masculinity can push men and boys toward substance use as a coping mechanism, and how this choice can spiral into addiction, with wide-ranging consequences for health, relationships, and societal well-being.

The urgent need for societal, policy, and cultural shifts to address this issue is clear. Substance misuse and alcoholism are not merely individual failures but are symptoms of broader systemic issues that require collective action to resolve. This includes dismantling harmful stereotypes around masculinity, increasing access to mental health care, and creating environments that support open discussions about substance use and recovery.

As we conclude, it is clear that a call to action is needed. Policymakers must prioritize funding for prevention programs and ensure that treatment and recovery services are accessible and tailored to the unique needs of men and boys. Health-care providers should be trained to recognize the signs of substance misuse and provide gender-sensitive care. Community leaders can play a crucial role in fostering supportive environments that encourage individuals to seek help without fear of judgment. And society at large must shift its perspective on addiction, viewing it not as a moral failing but as a complex health issue that requires compassion, understanding, and support.

By adopting comprehensive, inclusive approaches to prevention, treatment, and recovery, we can offer men and boys affected by substance misuse and alcoholism the support they need to overcome addiction and move toward healthier, more fulfilling lives. This effort will not only benefit those directly affected but will also contribute to the overall health and well-being of our communities, paving the way for a future where substance misuse is understood, treated, and ultimately, prevented.

NOTES

1 Woodford, M. S. (2012). *Men, addiction, and intimacy: Strengthening recovery by fostering the emotional development of boys and men*. Routledge.
2 Becker, J. B., McClellan, M., & Reed, B. G. (2016). Sociocultural context for sex differences in addiction. *Addiction Biology, 21*(5), 1052–1059.
3 Hunt, G., & Antin, T. (2019). Gender and intoxication: From masculinity to intersectionality. *Drugs: Education, Prevention and Policy, 26*(1), 70–78.
4 Darcy, C. (2020). Men and the drug buzz: Masculinity and Men's motivations for illicit recreational drug use. *Sociological Research Online, 25*(3), 421–437.
5 Link, B. G., Struening, E. L., Rahav, M., Phelan, J. C., & Nuttbrock, L. (1997). On stigma and its consequences: Evidence from a longitudinal study of men with dual diagnoses of mental illness and substance abuse. *Journal of Health and Social Behavior*, 177–190.
6 Studer, J., Baggio, S., Grazioli, V. S., Mohler-Kuo, M., Daeppen, J. B., & Gmel, G. (2016). Risky substance use and peer pressure in Swiss young men: Test of moderation effects. *Drug and Alcohol Dependence, 168*, 89–98.
7 Farrugia, A. (2015). "You can't just give your best mate a massive hug every day" young men, play and MDMA. *Contemporary Drug Problems, 42*(3), 240–256.
8 Clark, C. B., Reiland, S., Thorne, C., & Cropsey, K. L. (2014). Relationship of trauma exposure and substance abuse to self-reported violence among men and women in substance abuse treatment. *Journal of Interpersonal Violence, 29*(8), 1514–1530.

9 Cosden, M., Larsen, J. L., Donahue, M. T., & Nylund-Gibson, K. (2015). Trauma symptoms for men and women in substance abuse treatment: A latent transition analysis. *Journal of Substance Abuse Treatment, 50*, 18–25.

10 Choi, N. G., DiNitto, D. M., Marti, C. N., & Choi, B. Y. (2017). Association of adverse childhood experiences with lifetime mental and substance use disorders among men and women aged 50+ years. *International Psychogeriatrics, 29*(3), 359–372.

11 Polak, K., Haug, N. A., Drachenberg, H. E., & Svikis, D. S. (2015). Gender considerations in addiction: Implications for treatment. *Current Treatment Options in Psychiatry, 2*, 326–338.

12 Gueta, K., Gamliel, S., & Ronel, N. (2021). "Weak is the new strong": Gendered meanings of recovery from substance abuse among male prisoners participating in narcotic anonymous meetings. *Men and Masculinities, 24*(1), 104–126.

13 Bäcklin, E. (2022). Supporting masculinities: Wounded healing and masculinity in peer support organizations for people with experiences of criminality and substance abuse. *Victims & Offenders, 17*(6), 872–892.

Section 7

INTERSECTIONALITY AND INTERVENTION

23

GENDER AND ETHNICITY, RELIGION, CULTURE, CLASS, AND SEXUALITY

23.1 INTRODUCTION

In today's increasingly diverse and complex society, understanding the experiences of men and boys necessitates an approach that goes beyond generalized assumptions and looks at the nuanced ways in which various aspects of identity intersect.[1] Originally coined to describe how race and gender intersect to shape the experiences of Black women, *intersectionality* has evolved into a critical tool for examining the multifaceted experiences of individuals across a spectrum of identities. It acknowledges that gender, ethnicity, religion, culture, class, and sexuality are not isolated factors but interwoven elements that collectively influence one's life and interactions with the world. Indeed, in the first chapter of this book, the importance of intersectionality was highlighted, and throughout the book, the intersectional approach has been interwoven and explored.

As seen so far, for men and boys, intersectionality sheds light on how societal expectations and pressures vary significantly across different backgrounds and contexts. A one-size-fits-all approach to understanding the challenges they face is therefore clearly insufficient. For example, the experience of masculinity can be vastly different for a young Black man living in

DOI: 10.4324/9781032709369-30

an urban environment compared to that of a White man in a rural setting. Factors such as cultural background, socioeconomic status, and sexual orientation further complicate these experiences, each layer adding its own set of challenges and expectations.

Recognizing the importance of these intersecting identities is crucial in addressing the issues faced by men and boys. It allows us to see the unique vulnerabilities and strengths that arise from their specific contexts, informing more effective and empathetic approaches to support and intervention. Whether it is in the realm of mental health, education, employment, or social relationships, an intersectional approach enables us to tailor our strategies to meet the diverse needs of men and boys, ensuring that no one is left behind due to oversimplified assumptions about their experiences.

In this chapter we will explore the various dimensions of identity that shape the lives of men and boys more broadly and discuss how acknowledging these intersections can lead to more inclusive and supportive environments for everyone across a range of issues. By embracing an intersectional lens, we not only enrich our understanding of the complexities of male identities but also contribute to building a society that values and addresses the unique experiences of all its members.

23.2   ETHNICITY AND CULTURAL BACKGROUND

Ethnicity and cultural background play significant roles in shaping the experiences and identities of men and boys, influencing everything from the expression of masculinity to the expectations placed upon them by their communities and wider society.[2,3] These factors contribute to a rich tapestry of experiences which, while enriching, can also complicate the navigation of societal norms and personal identity development. Cultural norms dictate specific roles and behaviors deemed acceptable for men and boys, which can vary widely between different ethnic groups. For instance, certain cultures may place a strong emphasis on familial responsibility and community involvement as core components of masculinity, while others might prioritize individual achievement and independence.

The diversity in cultural backgrounds among men and boys leads to a wide array of understandings of what it means to be a man, which can both challenge and reinforce broader societal norms. This diversity can enrich communities by offering varied perspectives on gender, work, and family life, contributing to a more holistic understanding of masculinity in a multicultural context.

23.2.1   Strengths Derived From Ethnic and Cultural Diversity

Ethnic and cultural diversity also brings significant strengths and resilience. Diverse cultural backgrounds provide men and boys with unique perspectives and skills, enriching the social fabric of communities. The ability to navigate multiple cultural contexts can foster adaptability, empathy, and a deep understanding of cultural nuances, which are valuable in an increasingly globalized world.

Furthermore, strong community and familial ties, often emphasized in various cultural traditions, can provide a robust support network for men and boys. These networks can offer emotional support, guidance, and a sense of belonging, which are crucial for mental health and well-being.

Cultural traditions and practices also serve as a source of strength and pride, offering men and boys a firm grounding in their identities and values. Celebrating one's cultural heritage can foster a positive sense of self and resilience in the face of challenges, providing a counternarrative to the stereotypes and discrimination they may encounter.

23.2.2   Challenges Derived From Ethnic and Cultural Diversity

Despite the strengths derived from ethnic and cultural diversity, men and boys often face unique challenges related to their backgrounds. Racism and discrimination are significant issues that can affect their social experiences, mental health, and opportunities for success. Ethnic minority men and boys may encounter stereotypes that impact how they are perceived by others, including assumptions about their behavior, intelligence, and potential for success. These stereotypes can limit opportunities for education and employment, perpetuating cycles of poverty and inequality.

Additionally, the pressure to assimilate into the dominant culture while also maintaining one's cultural heritage can create internal conflicts and identity struggles. Men and boys navigating multiple cultural identities may feel they must suppress certain aspects of their cultural background to fit in, leading to feelings of alienation and loss of identity.

Thus, acknowledging the role of ethnicity and cultural background is essential in understanding the diverse experiences of men and boys. By recognizing the challenges they face and the strengths they bring, society can move toward more inclusive and supportive practices that honor and celebrate cultural diversity. This approach not only benefits men and boys from various backgrounds but also enriches the entire community by fostering understanding, empathy, and cooperation across cultural divides.

23.3   RELIGIOUS INFLUENCES

Religious beliefs and practices exert a profound influence on the lives, values, and day-to-day experiences of men and boys, shaping their perceptions of themselves and the world around them. Religion can play a central role in defining moral values, ethical behaviors, and life goals, often providing a framework for understanding one's place in the world. For many, religious communities offer guidance, support, and a sense of belonging, which can be particularly influential during the formative years and in moments of personal crisis or transition.

However, the impact of religion on men and boys is not uniform and can vary significantly, depending on the specific beliefs, practices, and cultural

23.4   SOCIOECONOMIC FACTORS

The influence of class and socioeconomic status on the lives of men and boys is profound, permeating every aspect of their existence, from the opportunities available to them to their overall health and well-being.[9,10,11] Socioeconomic status determines access to quality education, nutritious food, safe housing, and health care – all fundamental components that contribute to a healthy and productive life. For men and boys from lower socioeconomic backgrounds, limited access to these essential resources can significantly hinder their ability to achieve their potential, impacting their future employment opportunities, income levels, and social mobility.

Moreover, socioeconomic status can shape the experiences of masculinity, with societal expectations often placing pressure on men and boys to be the primary providers for their families. In contexts where economic opportunities are scarce or unstable, this expectation can contribute to stress, anxiety, and feelings of inadequacy. The chronic stress associated with financial instability and poverty also has direct implications for physical and mental health, increasing the risk of developing a range of health issues, from cardiovascular diseases to depression and substance misuse.

23.4.1   Economic Inequality and Access to Resources

Economic inequality exacerbates the challenges faced by men and boys from disadvantaged backgrounds, creating a wide chasm between those with ample resources and those struggling to meet basic needs. In societies where wealth is highly concentrated, access to resources such as quality education, health care, and employment opportunities can become highly stratified, further entrenching socioeconomic divides. For boys growing up in poverty-stricken areas, the lack of access to educational opportunities and extracurricular activities can stifle their development and limit their future prospects, setting in motion a cycle of poverty that can be difficult to break.

The relationship between economic inequality and social mobility is complex, with socioeconomic status often acting as both a determinant and outcome of an individual's social mobility. Men and boys from lower socioeconomic backgrounds may find it challenging to ascend the economic ladder due to systemic barriers, such as discrimination, inadequate education systems, and limited access to networking opportunities. This lack of social mobility not only affects individual lives but can also have broader implications for society, contributing to social unrest and diminishing the overall quality of life for entire communities.

23.4.3   Addressing Socioeconomic Disparities

To improve the opportunities, health, and well-being of men and boys, it is thus crucial to address the underlying socioeconomic disparities that limit their potential. This requires a multifaceted approach that includes policy interventions aimed at reducing poverty, improving access to quality education and health care, and creating more equitable employment opportunities. Efforts to support men and boys must also consider the specific challenges posed by socioeconomic status, providing targeted support that addresses their unique needs and circumstances.

Investing in programs that provide mentorship, job training, and access to mental health services can help men and boys from disadvantaged backgrounds overcome barriers to success, promoting healthier lives and greater social mobility. By acknowledging and addressing the impact of socioeconomic factors, society can work toward creating a more inclusive and equitable environment that supports the well-being and success of all men and boys, regardless of their background.

The socioeconomic factors that shape the lives of men and boys are thus critical determinants of their opportunities, health, and overall well-being. By understanding and addressing the relationship between economic inequality, access to resources, and social mobility, we can foster a society that supports the growth and development of every individual, paving the way for a more equitable and prosperous future for all.

23.5 SEXUALITY AND GENDER IDENTITY

The experiences of men and boys who identify as GBTQ+ are deeply influenced by their interactions with societal norms, cultural expectations, and the pervasive reality of discrimination.[12] For many, their journey of self-discovery and identity formation is navigated within environments that may not recognize or value their authentic selves.[13] The societal pressures to conform to traditional notions of masculinity can be particularly challenging for GBTQ+ men and boys, who may find these norms at odds with their true identities.[14] This discordance can lead to internal conflicts, affecting their sense of self-worth and belonging.

Discrimination, both overt and subtle, remains a significant challenge for LGBTQ+ individuals. Homophobia, transphobia, and bigotry can manifest in various aspects of their lives, from family rejection to institutional discrimination, impacting access to education, health care, and employment. Such experiences not only inflict emotional pain but also contribute to higher rates of mental health issues within the LGBTQ+ community, including anxiety, depression, and suicidal thoughts.

23.5.1 Navigating Societal Norms and Discrimination

Navigating societal norms and discrimination requires resilience and, often, a conscious effort to seek out supportive communities and spaces. The strength found in LGBTQ+ communities and ally networks can offer crucial emotional support, validation, and advocacy, counteracting the negative impacts of discrimination. However, the burden of constantly defending one's identity and rights can be exhausting and detrimental to one's well-being.

The challenges faced by GBTQ+ men and boys are compounded by inter-sectionality, where aspects of their identity such as race, ethnicity, religion, and socioeconomic status intersect with their sexual orientation and gender identity, creating unique and complex experiences of discrimination and marginalization. Recognizing and addressing these intersecting identities are essential in understanding the full scope of their experiences and the multifaceted nature of the discrimination they face.

23.5.2   The Importance of Supportive Environments and Acceptance

Creating supportive environments and fostering acceptance are critical in promoting the well-being of GBTQ+ men and boys.[15] Acceptance from fam-ily, friends, and society at large plays a significant role in their mental and emotional health, contributing to a positive sense of self and reducing the risk of mental health issues. Educational and workplace policies that explic-itly protect LGBTQ+ rights and promote inclusivity can create safer spaces that acknowledge and value diversity.

Supportive environments also extend to the availability of LGBTQ+-specific resources and services that address the unique challenges faced by this community, including counseling services, support groups, and health care tailored to their needs. Such resources not only provide necessary sup-port but also affirm the identities of GBTQ+ men and boys, contributing to a stronger sense of community and belonging.

The experiences of GBTQ+ men and boys are thus shaped by a complex interplay of societal norms, discrimination, and the search for acceptance. By fostering supportive environments that celebrate diversity and promote inclusivity, society can better support the well-being and happiness of GBTQ+ individuals. Acknowledging the challenges they face and taking active steps toward acceptance and support are essential in ensuring that all men and boys have the opportunity to live authentically and thrive.

23.6   INTERSECTIONAL VULNERABILITIES AND STRENGTHS

The concept of intersectionality reveals that individuals do not experience life through a single lens of identity but, rather, through multiple, overlap-ping identities that interact with each other and with societal structures in complex ways. For men and boys, this means that their experiences are shaped not only by their gender but also by their ethnicity, cultural back-ground, socioeconomic status, religion, sexuality, and more. This intersec-tion of identities can expose them to unique vulnerabilities, where the challenges associated with one aspect of their identity are compounded by those related to another.[16,17]

For instance, a young man of color may face systemic racism that impacts his access to education and employment opportunities, which is further complicated by socioeconomic factors. If this individual is also part of the LGBTQ+ community, he may experience additional layers of discrimination and stigma, heightening his vulnerability to mental health issues, social isolation, and economic instability.[18] Similarly, religious beliefs may offer solace and community to some men and boys but could also be a source of conflict and exclusion for others, depending on how their identities align with or diverge from the norms and expectations of their faith communities.

23.6.1   Highlighting Strengths, Resilience, and Contributions

While recognizing vulnerabilities is crucial, it is equally important to highlight strengths, resilience, and contributions of diverse groups of men and boys. Intersectional identities can provide men and boys with unique perspectives and experiences that contribute to their resilience in the face of adversity. For example, the ability to navigate multiple cultural contexts can foster adaptability and empathy, skills that are invaluable in an increasingly globalized world.

The solidarity found within communities – whether based on shared ethnicity, cultural background, or sexual orientation – can also offer powerful sources of support and affirmation. These communities not only provide a sense of belonging and identity but also serve as platforms for advocacy and change, challenging societal norms and working toward greater inclusivity and equity.

Moreover, the contributions of men and boys from diverse backgrounds enrich society as a whole. Their experiences and perspectives can inspire creativity, drive innovation, and foster a deeper understanding of the complex world we share. Recognizing and valuing these contributions is essential in moving toward a more inclusive and equitable society.

Acknowledging the intersectional vulnerabilities and strengths of men and boys thus allows for a more nuanced understanding of their experiences and needs. By addressing the unique challenges they face while also celebrating their resilience and contributions, we can work toward creating a society that supports the well-being and success of all its members, regardless of their intersecting identities. This approach not only benefits individuals but also strengthens the fabric of communities and society at large, promoting a world where diversity is recognized as a source of strength and innovation.

23.7   STRATEGIES FOR INCLUSIVE SUPPORT

Addressing the needs of men and boys in all their diversity requires strategies that are as multifaceted as their identities. Recognizing the complexity of these identities is the first step toward developing and implementing support systems that are both inclusive and culturally sensitive. Here are some key recommendations for creating such strategies and highlights examples of successful programs and initiatives:

1. *Intersectional training for service providers.* Educators, health-care providers, social workers, and other professionals should receive training that emphasizes an intersectional understanding of masculinity. This training would equip them to recognize and address the unique challenges faced by men and boys from diverse backgrounds, ensuring that support services are responsive to their specific needs.

2. *Community-based approaches.* Developing support strategies that are rooted in the community can ensure that they are culturally relevant and accessible. Engaging community leaders and members in the creation and implementation of these strategies can foster trust and ensure that programs are well-suited to the community's needs.

3. *Safe spaces for open dialogue.* Creating environments where men and boys feel safe to express their vulnerabilities, share their experiences, and seek support is crucial. These spaces can be physical, such as community centers or support groups, or virtual platforms that offer anonymity and flexibility.

4. *Tailored mental health services.* Mental health services should be tailored to address the specific concerns of men and boys, taking into account factors such as cultural background, sexual orientation, and socioeconomic status. This might include offering services in multiple languages or providing counseling that is informed by an understanding of different cultural norms around masculinity and mental health.

5. *Inclusive educational programs.* Educational curricula should be designed to include discussions on gender, sexuality, cultural diversity, and emotional literacy. Such programs can help deconstruct harmful stereotypes and encourage a more inclusive understanding of masculinity from an early age.

23.7.1   Examples of Successful Programs and Initiatives

And here are some examples of initiatives or organizations that are already doing these things:

•   *The Man Box Project.* This initiative focuses on challenging traditional notions of masculinity and promoting a healthier, more inclusive understanding of what it means to be a man. Through workshops and discussions, the project addresses the impact of rigid gender norms on men's mental health and relationships.

- *Brothers in Arms.* Based in Scotland, this mental health service is specifically aimed at men and boys, offering support through digital platforms that provide resources, counseling, and a community forum. The service recognizes the barriers men often face in seeking help and provides a confidential and accessible support system.
- *RAINN's Sexual Assault Support for Men and Boys.* Recognizing that men and boys are also victims of sexual violence, RAINN offers specialized support services that are sensitive to the unique challenges they face. The program provides counseling, resources, and advocacy, emphasizing the importance of acknowledging and addressing sexual violence against all genders.
- *The Trevor Project.* Dedicated to LGBTQ+ youth, the Trevor Project offers crisis intervention and suicide prevention services through phone, text, and online platforms. The project also provides resources for young people exploring their sexual orientation and gender identity in the context of diverse cultural and religious backgrounds.

Implementing inclusive support strategies requires a concerted effort from all sectors of society, including policymakers, educators, health-care providers, and community organizations. By adopting an intersectional approach, we can ensure that support systems are responsive to the diverse needs of men and boys, promoting their well-being and contributing to a more equitable society.

23.8   CONCLUSION

Throughout this exploration of the intersectional approach to understanding men and boys, we have delved into the complex layers that constitute individual identities and experiences. This journey has underscored the profound impact that factors such as gender, ethnicity, religion, culture, class, and sexuality have on shaping the lives of men and boys. By examining how these dimensions intersect, we gain a richer, more nuanced understanding of the unique challenges and strengths that define their experiences in a diverse and changing world.

The key insights garnered from this exploration reveal that no man or boy lives a monolithic experience; instead, their lives are a tapestry woven from multiple strands of identity, each adding color and texture to their existence. It is clear that adopting an intersectional perspective is not merely an academic exercise but a crucial step toward developing more empathetic, effective, and inclusive support systems. Such systems are capable of recognizing and addressing the varied needs of men and boys, ensuring that no one is left behind due to oversimplified or monolithic approaches to gender and identity.

contexts of different faiths, like Islam,[4] Hinduism,[5] Judaism,[6] Buddhism,[7] and Christianity.[8] Religious teachings and community expectations can also influence various aspects of masculinity, from the roles men are expected to play within families and communities to the ways in which they are encouraged to express – or suppress – emotions and vulnerabilities.

23.3.1   Religious Identity and Masculinity

The intersection of religious identity with masculinity and societal expectations can create unique challenges for men and boys. In some religious traditions, masculinity is closely tied to ideas of leadership, strength, and moral integrity, with men often expected to serve as spiritual leaders within their families and communities. These expectations can reinforce traditional gender roles, placing pressure on men and boys to conform to specific models of behavior that may not align with their personal beliefs or experiences.

Conversely, certain religious teachings may emphasize values such as compassion, empathy, and nonviolence, which can challenge prevailing cultural notions of masculinity. Men and boys who embrace these aspects of their faith may find themselves at odds with societal expectations that equate masculinity with aggression and emotional stoicism. Navigating these conflicting pressures can be a source of tension, requiring individuals to reconcile their religious beliefs with their personal identities and the broader cultural norms surrounding masculinity.

23.3.2   The Role of Religion in Shaping Values and Challenges

Religion can also shape the values and challenges faced by men and boys in more subtle ways. For example, religious teachings on sexuality, marriage, and family life can influence men's attitudes toward relationships, gender roles, and personal conduct. Adhering to these teachings can provide a sense of purpose and direction, but it can also lead to internal conflicts, particularly in societies where secular values differ significantly from religious ones.

Furthermore, the experience of religious discrimination or marginalization can impact the well-being and social integration of men and boys from minority faith communities. Encounters with prejudice and exclusion can affect their sense of identity and belonging, potentially leading to feelings of isolation or alienation.

Understanding the influence of religious beliefs and practices is thus crucial for comprehensively addressing the experiences of men and boys. By acknowledging the interplay between religious identity, masculinity, and societal expectations, we can foster a more nuanced and empathetic approach to supporting individuals in their diverse journeys. Recognizing the challenges and values instilled by religion allows for the development of more inclusive and culturally sensitive interventions that respect and honor the complex identities of men and boys across different faiths.

As I conclude this chapter, I issue a call to action for researchers, policy-makers, practitioners, and communities to embrace and integrate intersectional perspectives in their work with men and boys. Researchers are encouraged to further investigate the intersections of identity that impact men's and boys' lives, contributing to a body of knowledge that supports evidence-based interventions. Policymakers must consider the diverse realities of men and boys in crafting legislation and policies that promote equity and access to resources. Practitioners, whether in education, health care, or social services, should apply intersectional frameworks in their practice, ensuring that their support is responsive to the unique contexts of those they serve.

Communities, too, play a vital role in fostering environments of inclusivity, cultural sensitivity, and solidarity across differences. By cultivating spaces where men and boys feel seen, heard, and supported in all aspects of their identities, we can contribute to the dismantling of barriers that divide us. This collective effort toward understanding and support is not just beneficial for men and boys but enriches our entire society as well, promoting a world where empathy, respect, and mutual support prevail.

In embracing intersectionality, we open the door to a more inclusive, equitable, and compassionate approach to addressing the needs of men and boys. It is through this lens that we can truly appreciate the complexity of their experiences and work together to build supportive environments that acknowledge and celebrate the diversity of all individuals.

NOTES

1 Thompson Jr, E. H., & Bennett, K. M. (2015). Measurement of masculinity ideologies: A (critical) review. *Psychology of Men & Masculinity, 16*(2), 115.
2 Wong, Y. J., Liu, T., & Klann, E. M. (2017). The intersection of race, ethnicity, and masculinities: Progress, problems, and prospects. In R. F. Levant & Y. J. Wong (Eds.), *The psychology of men and masculinities* (pp. 261–288). American Psychological Association. https://doi.org/10.1037/0000023-010.
3 Wong, Y. J., Horn, A. J., & Chen, S. (2013). Perceived masculinity: The potential influence of race, racial essentialist beliefs, and stereotypes. *Psychology of Men & Masculinity, 14*(4), 452.
4 Inhorn, M. C. (2012). *The new Arab man: Emergent masculinities, technologies, and Islam in the Middle East*. Princeton University Press.
5 Banerjee, S. (2012). *Make me a man!: Masculinity, Hinduism, and nationalism in India*. State University of New York Press.
6 Imhoff, S. (2017). *Masculinity and the making of American Judaism*. Indiana University Press.
7 Chladek, M. R. (2021). Defining manhood: Monastic masculinity and effeminacy in contemporary Thai Buddhism. *The Journal of Asian Studies, 80*(4), 975–995.
8 Krondorfer, B. (Ed.). (2013). *Men and masculinities in Christianity and Judaism: A critical reader*. SCM Press.
9 Ingram, N., & Waller, R. (2014). Degrees of masculinity: Working and middle-class undergraduate students' constructions of masculine identities. In *Debating modern masculinities: Change, continuity, crisis?* (pp. 35–51). Palgrave Pivot.

10 Roberts, S. (2013). Boys will be boys . . . won't they? Change and continuities in contemporary young working-class masculinities. *Sociology*, *47*(4), 671–686.
11 Thompson & Bennett, Measurement of masculinity ideologies, 115.
12 Philaretou, A. G., & Allen, K. R. (2001). Reconstructing masculinity and sexuality. *The Journal of Men's Studies*, *9*(3), 301–321.
13 Pascoe, C. J. (2012). *Dude, you're a fag: Masculinity and sexuality in high school*. University of California Press.
14 Salvati, M., Passarelli, M., Chiorri, C., Baiocco, R., & Giacomantonio, M. (2021). Masculinity threat and implicit associations with feminine gay men: Sexual orientation, sexual stigma, and traditional masculinity. *Psychology of Men & Masculinities*, *22*(4), 649.
15 Snapp, S. D., Watson, R. J., Russell, S. T., Diaz, R. M., & Ryan, C. (2015). Social support networks for LGBT young adults: Low cost strategies for positive adjustment. *Family Relations*, *64*(3), 420–430.
16 Christensen, A. D., & Jensen, S. Q. (2014). Combining hegemonic masculinity and intersectionality. *NORMA: International Journal for Masculinity Studies*, *9*(1), 60–75.
17 Kimmel, M. S., & Coston, B. M. (2018). Seeing privilege where it isn't: Marginalized masculinities and the intersectionality of privilege. In *Privilege* (pp. 161–179). Routledge.
18 Alexander, B. K. (2006). *Performing Black masculinity: Race, culture, and queer identity*. Rowman Altamira.

24

EFFECTIVE INTERVENTIONS AND STRATEGIES

24.1 INTRODUCTION

As outlined throughout this book, men and boys face a myriad of challenges that significantly impact their mental, physical, and emotional well-being. Addressing these challenges requires more than just isolated efforts; it necessitates a comprehensive and strategic approach that recognizes the complexity and diversity of their experiences. This chapter focuses on identifying and implementing effective interventions and strategies to address these challenges, emphasizing the importance of holistic and intersectional solutions. This more general approach can be taken alongside the many more specific suggestions given throughout this book.

Interventions aimed at supporting men and boys must be designed with careful consideration of their unique circumstances and needs. The guiding principles outlined in this chapter are crucial for the success of any intervention, policy change, service, or educational initiative targeting this demographic. These principles ensure that interventions are not only effective but also inclusive, culturally sensitive, and tailored to the specific contexts of men and boys from diverse backgrounds.

The six principles discussed in this chapter are designed to provide a broad framework for developing and implementing interventions, including:

DOI: 10.4324/9781032709369-31

1. *Universal access and culturally responsive practices.* Ensuring that all men and boys, regardless of their background, have access to the support they need. Recognizing and respecting the diverse cultural backgrounds of men and boys, and tailoring interventions to be relevant and respectful of cultural norms and values.

2. *Intersectional frameworks.* Considering the complex interplay of various identity factors such as gender, ethnicity, religion, culture, class, and sexuality.

3. *Gender inclusivity.* Ensuring that the needs of men and boys are fully catered for and form part of the central structure of any service or intiative designed to assist them.

4. *Evidence-based.* Grounding interventions in the latest research and best practices, with a commitment to continuous evaluation and improvement.

5. *Multisector collaboration.* Encouraging multisector collaboration to address complex issues through coordinated efforts.

6. *Proactive measures: preventive and early.* Emphasizing preventive measures and early intervention to address issues before they become more serious.

These guiding principles provide a foundation for creating effective, compassionate, and sustainable interventions that can significantly improve the lives of men and boys. By adhering to these principles, policymakers, educators, service providers, and community leaders can develop initiatives that not only address immediate challenges but also contribute to long-term positive change. This chapter serves as a blueprint for fostering a more inclusive, equitable, and supportive environment for men and boys, ultimately enhancing their well-being and promoting a healthier society for all.

24.2   PRINCIPLE 1: UNIVERSAL ACCESS AND CULTURALLY RESPONSIVE PRACTICES

To ensure that interventions effectively reach and benefit all men and boys, it is essential that they are inclusive, accessible, and culturally sensitive. This means designing programs and services that cater to individuals from diverse backgrounds, including those from marginalized or underserved communities. It also involves recognizing and respecting the diverse cultural backgrounds of men and boys, tailoring interventions to be relevant and respectful of cultural norms and values.

24.2.1   Implementation Strategies

1. Sliding-Scale Fee Structures and Free Services

    - *Income-based pricing.* Develop sliding-scale fee structures that adjust costs based on an individual's income level. This approach ensures that financial constraints do not prevent access to necessary services.
    - *Scholarships and grants.* Provide scholarships, grants, or subsidies for those who cannot afford to pay, ensuring that financial aid is readily available and easily accessible.
    - *Pro bono services.* Encourage professionals and organizations to offer pro bono services or volunteer time to support men and boys who are in need but cannot afford to pay.

2. Strategic Location of Services

    - *Community-centered locations.* Place services in community centers, schools, and other easily accessible locations to ensure they are within reach for those who need them most. This includes setting up mobile units that can travel to remote or underserved areas.
    - *Public transportation accessibility.* Ensure that service locations are well-connected to public transportation networks, making it easier for men and boys without private transport to attend.
    - *Decentralized service points.* Create multiple service points within a city or region to reduce travel time and costs for individuals, particularly in rural or suburban areas.

3. Multilingual Materials and Services

    - *Language accessibility.* Offer all informational materials, support services, and communication in multiple languages to cater to nonnative speakers. This includes translating documents, websites, and promotional materials.
    - *Bilingual staff.* Employ bilingual or multilingual staff members who can communicate effectively with individuals from different linguistic backgrounds.
    - *Cultural competence training.* Provide cultural competence training for all staff to ensure they are sensitive to and respectful of cultural differences, enhancing their ability to communicate and connect with individuals from diverse backgrounds.

4. Engagement with Cultural Advisors and Community Leaders

    - *Collaborative program design.* Engage cultural advisors or community leaders in the design and implementation of programs to ensure they are culturally relevant and respectful. This collaboration helps build trust and ensures that interventions are well-received by the target population.

- *Ongoing community involvement.* Maintain ongoing relationships with community leaders and cultural advisors to continually adapt and improve programs based on community feedback and changing needs.

5.   Use of Physical Activity and Sports

- Physical activity and sports can serve as powerful interventions for improving the mental health and well-being of men and boys. Regular exercise is linked to reduced anxiety and depression, improved mood, and enhanced self-esteem.

6.   Digital and Online Interventions

- *Telehealth services.* Telehealth services allow individuals to receive professional support from the comfort of their homes, making it easier for those in remote areas or with mobility issues to access care.
- *Online support groups.* Digital support groups offer a sense of community and belonging, providing a platform for men and boys to share experiences, offer mutual support, and receive guidance from peers and professionals.
- *Mobile apps.* Mobile apps designed for mental health and well-being provide users with immediate access to resources, including educational materials, coping strategies, and crisis intervention tools. Apps like "Sober Grid" and "Recovery Record" offer real-time support and community connection. These apps often include features for tracking mental health progress, setting recovery goals, and monitoring daily activities, which can help individuals stay motivated and accountable in their recovery journey.
- *Positive social media use.* Social media and online communities can provide support networks, raise awareness about mental health issues, and offer platforms for sharing experiences and finding encouragement. These communities can help men and boys feel less isolated and more connected to others facing similar challenges.

24.3   PRINCIPLE 2: INTERSECTIONAL FRAMEWORKS

Understanding that men and boys experience challenges differently based on the intersections of gender, ethnicity, religion, culture, class, and sexuality is crucial for effective interventions. A holistic and intersectional approach ensures that these intersecting identities are considered and interventions are designed to address multiple aspects of an individual's life simultaneously.

24.3.1   Implementation Strategies

1. Comprehensive Needs Assessments

   - *Individualized assessments.* Conduct comprehensive needs assessments that consider all aspects of an individual's identity, including socioeconomic status, cultural background, and personal experiences. These assessments help identify the unique challenges faced by each individual.
   - *Community assessments.* Perform broader community assessments to understand the common issues and needs within specific communities, allowing for the design of interventions that are both personalized and community-focused.

2. Multifaceted Program Design

   - *Integrated services.* Design multifaceted programs that address multiple needs simultaneously, such as combining mental health support with employment training, educational support, and substance abuse treatment. This holistic approach ensures that all aspects of an individual's well-being are addressed.
   - *Collaborative partnerships.* Form partnerships with organizations across various sectors (e.g., health care, education, social services) to provide comprehensive support. These collaborations help create a network of services that can address the complex and interconnected challenges faced by men and boys.

3. Flexible and Adaptive Programming

   - *Responsive interventions.* Design interventions that are flexible and can be adapted to meet changing needs and circumstances. Be prepared to modify programs based on feedback and evolving challenges.
   - *Pilot programs and feedback loops.* Develop pilot programs with built-in mechanisms for feedback and adjustment. This iterative process allows for continuous improvement and ensures that interventions remain effective and relevant.

4. Strength-Based Approaches

   - *Empowerment and resilience.* Focus on the strengths and potential of men and boys rather than just their problems. Encourage resilience and empowerment through positive reinforcement and skill-building.
   - *Positive role models.* Highlight diverse and positive male role models who exemplify healthy behaviors and relationships.

5.   Innovative and Creative Therapies

- *Engagement through creativity.* Incorporate innovative and creative therapeutic approaches, such as art therapy, music therapy, and adventure therapy, that can be particularly effective for engaging men and boys. These therapies provide alternative means of expression and healing, which can be especially beneficial for those who may be reluctant to engage in traditional talk therapies.
- *Therapeutic environments.* Create therapeutic environments that foster creativity and engagement, such as outdoor adventure settings, art studios, and music rooms. These environments can help men and boys feel more comfortable and open to participating in therapy.

By implementing these comprehensive strategies, interventions can become truly inclusive, accessible, and culturally sensitive, ensuring that men and boys from all walks of life have the support they need to thrive. This approach not only promotes equity but also enhances the overall effectiveness of programs and services, by reaching a broader and more diverse audience. The combined focus on inclusivity, cultural relevance, and holistic approaches ensures that interventions are well-rounded and capable of addressing the complex needs of men and boys in a comprehensive manner.

24.4   PRINCIPLE 3: GENDER INCLUSIVITY

Interventions aimed at supporting men and boys must be specifically shaped to address their unique needs, recognizing that gender-specific challenges require tailored approaches. It is essential that these efforts focus on the well-being of men without compromising the needs of other genders. A gender-inclusive approach ensures that supporting men and boys is done thoughtfully, contributing positively to the broader landscape of gender equality, rather than detracting from it.

24.4.1   Implementation Strategies

1.   Tailored Support for Men and Boys

- *Targeted intervention design.* Develop and implement interventions that are specifically tailored to address the unique challenges faced by men and boys. This could include mental health support, educational programs, or community initiatives designed to improve their well-being.
- *Communication strategies.* Craft communication materials that highlight the specific benefits of these interventions for men, while also showing how such support can indirectly benefit other genders. For example, improving men's mental health not only benefits them directly but can also create healthier family dynamics.

- *Gender-specific goals.* Set clear, gender-specific goals for interventions, ensuring that the distinct needs of men and boys are at the forefront of the initiative. At the same time, consider how these goals can complement broader gender equality objectives.

2. Collaboration with Gender Equality Organizations

- *Partnerships for comprehensive approaches.* Work with gender equality organizations to ensure that interventions for men and boys are part of a holistic approach to gender issues. Collaboration can help integrate men's issues into the broader conversation without sidelining other genders.
- *Joint programs and resources.* Develop and fund joint programs that, while focused on men, also consider the interconnectedness of gender dynamics. Pooling resources can enhance the reach and effectiveness of these programs, benefiting all genders in the long term.

3. Gender-Sensitive Program Design and Evaluation

- *Inclusive stakeholder engagement.* While the primary focus is on men, involve representatives from various gender groups in program design and evaluation to ensure a balanced and fair approach. This helps identify any potential biases and ensures that the programs are sensitive to all genders.
- *Gender impact assessments.* Conduct gender impact assessments to understand how interventions designed for men might affect other genders. Use these insights to refine the programs, ensuring that they are inclusive without diluting their focus on men's specific needs.

4. Education and Training on Gender Issues

- *Targeted gender awareness training.* Provide education and training that emphasizes the importance of addressing the specific needs of men and boys within the broader context of gender equality. This training should cover how supporting men can contribute to overall gender balance.
- *Workshops and seminars.* Organize events that educate participants on the importance of focused support for men, while also contextualizing this within the larger framework of gender equality.

By prioritizing the unique needs of men and boys in these interventions, while also ensuring that such efforts are inclusive and do not disadvantage other genders, we can create a more equitable and supportive society. This approach not only addresses the specific challenges faced by men but also contributes to the broader goals of gender equality, fostering a more cohesive and thriving community for everyone.

24.5 PRINCIPLE 4: RESEARCH-INFORMED INTERVENTIONS

Effective interventions for men and boys must be grounded in the latest research and best practices. This approach ensures that programs are not only based on sound evidence but are also continuously improved to meet evolving needs and challenges. Implementing evidence-based practices involves regular evaluation and feedback mechanisms to ensure that interventions remain effective and relevant.

24.5.1 Implementation Strategies

1. Establish Partnerships with Academic Institutions

   - *Collaborative research.* Partner with universities and research institutions to stay updated on current research findings and emerging trends relevant to men and boys. These partnerships can facilitate access to cutting-edge studies and innovations in intervention strategies.
   - *Research grants and funding.* Apply for research grants to fund studies that evaluate the effectiveness of interventions. This funding can support longitudinal studies that provide deeper insights into long-term outcomes and impacts.

2. Regular Program Evaluations

   - *Data collection and analysis.* Implement systematic data collection methods to monitor the effectiveness of interventions. Use quantitative and qualitative data to assess program outcomes and identify areas for improvement.
   - *Feedback loops.* Establish feedback mechanisms that allow participants and stakeholders to provide input on program effectiveness. Regularly review this feedback to make data-driven improvements and adjustments to interventions.

24.6 PRINCIPLE 5: MULTISECTOR COLLABORATION

Addressing the complex challenges faced by men and boys requires coordinated efforts across multiple sectors. Collaboration between education, health, social services, and the criminal justice system is essential to provide comprehensive and integrated support. Multisector collaboration ensures that interventions are holistic and address the interconnected aspects of men's and boys' lives.

24.6.1   Implementation Strategies

1.   Create Interdisciplinary Teams

- *Cross-sector expertise.* Assemble teams with professionals from various sectors, including health-care providers, educators, social workers, and criminal justice experts. These interdisciplinary teams can design and deliver interventions that are well-rounded and comprehensive.
- *Shared objectives.* Establish clear goals and objectives that align across sectors to ensure cohesive and unified efforts. Regular meetings and communication channels can help maintain alignment and coordination.

2.   Formal Partnerships with Organizations

- *Memorandums of understanding (MOUs).* Develop formal agreements with partner organizations to outline roles, responsibilities, and shared goals. MOUs can facilitate collaboration and ensure commitment from all parties involved.
- *Resource sharing.* Pool resources and expertise from different organizations to enhance the capacity and reach of interventions. Shared funding, facilities, and personnel can significantly improve program delivery and effectiveness.

24.6.2   Additional Principle: Responsive Programming

Interventions must also be designed with flexibility and adaptability in mind. As needs and circumstances change, programs should be able to adjust accordingly. This responsiveness ensures that interventions remain relevant and effective, even in dynamic and evolving contexts. Being prepared to modify programs based on feedback and emerging challenges is crucial for sustained success.

24.6.2.1   *Implementation Strategies*

1.   Develop Pilot Programs

- *Testing and refinement.* Implement pilot programs with built-in mechanisms for feedback and adjustment. Pilot programs allow for testing new approaches on a smaller scale before wider implementation. Use feedback from participants and stakeholders to refine and improve these programs.
- *Scalability plans.* Design pilot programs with scalability in mind, ensuring that successful elements can be expanded to broader populations.

2.   Training Staff for Adaptability

- *Continuous professional development.* Provide ongoing training for staff to equip them with the skills and knowledge needed to adapt to changing needs. This includes training in new methodologies, cultural competence, and emerging best practices.
- *Responsive support systems.* Create support systems that encourage staff to be proactive and responsive to participants' needs. This may include regular supervision, peer support networks, and opportunities for professional growth.

24.6.3   Integrated Implementation

By integrating evidence-based practices, multisector collaboration, and responsive programming, interventions for men and boys can be both effective and adaptable. Combining these principles ensures that programs are grounded in research, benefit from diverse expertise, and remain flexible to meet changing needs. This integrated approach enhances the capacity to address the complex and multifaceted challenges faced by men and boys, leading to more successful and sustainable outcomes.

In summary, effective interventions must be research-informed, collaborative, and adaptive. Establishing partnerships with academic institutions, conducting regular program evaluations, fostering multisector collaboration, creating interdisciplinary teams, and developing flexible and responsive programs are key strategies to achieve these principles. By adhering to these guidelines, interventions can provide comprehensive, culturally sensitive, and accessible support to men and boys, ultimately improving their well-being and contributing to a more inclusive and equitable society.

24.7   PRINCIPLE 6: PROACTIVE MEASURES

Proactive measures in prevention and early intervention are essential to address issues affecting men and boys before they escalate into more serious problems. Focusing on early support can significantly reduce long-term negative outcomes, promote healthier lifestyles, and improve overall well-being. This principle emphasizes the importance of anticipating potential challenges and providing timely, appropriate resources to mitigate their impact.

24.7.1   Implementation Strategies

1.   Screening and Early Detection Programs

- *Educational settings.* Implement regular screening and early detection programs in schools to identify academic, behavioral, and emotional issues among boys. This includes regular health checkups, psychological assessments, and academic evaluations.

- *Health and wellness screenings.* Conduct periodic health screenings in schools to monitor physical and mental health indicators, providing referrals to health-care providers as needed.
- *Behavioral assessments.* Utilize tools such as surveys, teacher observations, and peer reviews to identify early signs of behavioral or emotional distress. Establish protocols for timely intervention by school counselors or psychologists.
- *Workplaces.* Develop workplace wellness programs that include regular screenings for stress, anxiety, depression, and substance abuse among male employees. These programs should also offer resources for coping and support.
- *Employee assistance programs (EAPs).* Encourage the implementation of EAPs that provide confidential assessments, short-term counseling, and referrals for employees experiencing personal or work-related issues.
- *Wellness initiatives.* Organize health fairs, on-site medical check-ups, and workshops on stress management and mental health awareness to promote early detection and intervention.
- *Community centers.* Establish screening programs in community centers to reach men and boys in various age groups and backgrounds, focusing on both physical and mental health.
- *Community health outreach.* Collaborate with local health organizations to provide free or low-cost health screenings, vaccinations, and wellness checks in community centers.
- *Mobile health units.* Deploy mobile health units to underserved areas to offer screenings and basic health-care services, ensuring broader accessibility.

2. Education and Awareness Campaigns

- *Promoting help-seeking behavior.* Launch public education campaigns to reduce stigma around seeking help and to promote the benefits of early intervention. These campaigns should target both men and boys and their support networks, including families and communities.
- *Mental health literacy.* Develop materials that educate men and boys about common mental health issues, their symptoms, and the importance of early intervention. Use various media channels, such as social media, websites, and community events, to disseminate this information.
- *Role models and testimonials.* Feature testimonials from respected public figures, community leaders, and peers who have successfully sought help. Personal stories can humanize the experience and encourage others to seek assistance.
- *School-based programs.* Integrate mental health and well-being education into school curricula to teach boys about recognizing

and addressing early signs of stress, anxiety, and other mental health issues.

- *Curriculum integration.* Include lessons on emotional intelligence, stress management, and coping strategies as part of health and physical education classes.
- *Peer support programs.* Establish peer mentoring and support programs where older students or trained peer counselors can provide guidance and support to younger students facing difficulties.
- *Workplace awareness.* Conduct workshops and training sessions in workplaces to educate employees and management about the importance of early intervention and the resources available to support mental and physical health.
- *Manager training.* Train managers and supervisors to recognize early signs of distress among employees and to respond appropriately, providing support or referrals as needed.
- *Employee wellness programs.* Offer workshops on stress management, healthy living, and work–life balance to promote a proactive approach to health and well-being.
- *Community outreach.* Engage with local organizations, religious institutions, and social groups to spread awareness about early intervention programs and available resources.
- *Community workshops.* Organize workshops and seminars in community centers and churches to educate the public about the importance of early intervention and available support services.
- *Information campaigns.* Distribute pamphlets, flyers, and other informational materials in public places such as libraries, gyms, and recreational centers to reach a wider audience.

3. Early Intervention Services

- *Counseling and support groups.* Provide access to counseling services and support groups that focus on early intervention. These should be available in schools, workplaces, and community centers and should be tailored to meet the specific needs of men and boys.
- *School counseling services.* Ensure that schools have sufficient counseling staff to provide individual and group counseling sessions for students in need.
- *Workplace support groups.* Create support groups in workplaces where employees can share experiences and coping strategies in a safe and confidential environment.
- *Community-based counseling.* Offer low-cost or free counseling services in community centers, focusing on early intervention for mental health and substance abuse issues.
- *Hotlines and online support.*

- *24/7 hotlines.* Establish and promote hotlines that provide immediate support and crisis intervention for men and boys experiencing distress.
- *Online counseling services.* Develop online platforms where men and boys can access counseling and support anonymously and conveniently, reducing barriers to seeking help.

4. Policy Advocacy

- *Legislative support.* Advocate for policies that support preventive measures and early intervention programs. This includes funding for mental health services in schools, workplaces, and communities.
- *Funding for mental health programs.* Lobby for increased government funding and grants for mental health programs targeting men and boys.
- *Mandatory health screenings.* Support legislation that requires regular health and wellness screenings in schools and workplaces.
- *Insurance coverage.* Work toward ensuring that preventive and early intervention services are covered by health insurance policies, to reduce financial barriers.
- *Insurance advocacy.* Advocate for insurance policies that cover mental health screenings, counseling services, and preventive health care.
- *Employer-sponsored plans.* Encourage employers to include comprehensive mental health and wellness coverage in their employee benefit plans.

By implementing these proactive measures, it is possible to address issues affecting men and boys before they become more serious. Early detection, education, and intervention can significantly reduce long-term negative outcomes, promoting healthier lifestyles and improving overall well-being. This comprehensive approach to prevention and early intervention not only enhances individual lives but also contributes to the well-being of families and communities.

24.8 CONCLUSION

In addressing the myriad challenges faced by men and boys, this chapter has provided a comprehensive framework for developing and implementing effective interventions and strategies. By adhering to the six guiding principles outlined – universal access and culturally responsive practices, intersectional frameworks, gender inclusivity, evidence-based approaches, multisector collaboration, and proactive measures – policymakers, educators, service providers, and community leaders can ensure that their efforts are both impactful and sustainable.

Inclusivity, accessibility, and cultural sensitivity are essential for reaching all men and boys, especially those from marginalized or underserved communities. Ensuring that interventions are culturally relevant and accessible promotes equity and enhances the overall effectiveness of programs.

Holistic and intersectional approaches recognize the complex interplay of various identity factors, such as gender, ethnicity, religion, culture, class, and sexuality. By designing multifaceted programs that address multiple needs simultaneously and forming collaborative partnerships, interventions can provide comprehensive support that addresses the interconnected challenges faced by men and boys.

Gender-inclusive perspectives ensure that efforts to support men and boys are effective, by centering and acknowledging their needs. Moreover, a balanced gender approach emphasizing mutual benefits and collaboration inevitably contributes to a more inclusive and equitable society for everyone.

Evidence-based interventions are grounded in the latest research and best practices. Regular evaluations and feedback mechanisms ensure that programs remain effective and relevant, continuously improving to meet evolving needs and challenges.

Multisector collaboration involves coordinated efforts across various sectors, such as education, health, social services, and the criminal justice system. This collaboration ensures that interventions are holistic and address the diverse aspects of men's and boys' lives.

Proactive measures in prevention and early intervention are crucial for addressing issues before they escalate into more serious problems. Early detection, education, and intervention can significantly reduce long-term negative outcomes and promote healthier lifestyles.

By integrating these principles into their work, stakeholders can develop and implement initiatives that not only address immediate challenges but also contribute to long-term positive change. This chapter therefore serves as a blueprint for fostering a more inclusive, equitable, and supportive environment for men and boys, ultimately enhancing their well-being and promoting a healthier society for all. The successful implementation of these strategies will not only improve the lives of men and boys but also contribute to the overall well-being and resilience of communities and society as a whole.

25

CONCLUSION

This chapter exists simply to reiterate the urgent need for societal transformation to address the unique challenges faced by men and boys. Throughout this book, we have explored a wide range of issues that impact the lives of men and boys, whilst considering the complex interplay of gender, ethnicity, religion, culture, class, and sexuality.

In each section, I have highlighted several critical areas that demand attention and action:

1. *Mental health and the media.* The pervasive mental health issues among men and boys, including depression, anxiety, and suicide, require comprehensive mental health services and destigmatization campaigns to encourage help-seeking behavior. The role of media in shaping male identity and perpetuating narrow definitions of masculinity calls for more diverse and realistic portrayals to foster healthier self-images and relationships.

2. *Body image, physical health, and sexual behavior.* The pressures of maintaining an ideal body image and the resultant issues, such as gym addiction and steroid misuse, highlight the need for promoting positive body image and healthy lifestyle choices. Moreover, understanding and promoting healthy sexual behaviors and consent are fundamental to fostering respectful and fulfilling relationships.

DOI: 10.4324/9781032709369-32

3. *Educational and employment disparities.* Addressing the educational achievement gap and adapting to the changing employment landscape are crucial for ensuring that men and boys can thrive in an evolving world.

4. *Relationships and fatherhood.* Facing the challenges men and boys face in creating and maintaining both platonic and romantic relationships, as well as the challenges and opportunities associated with fatherhood, and when parental relationships break down is also crucial.

5. *Vulnerable men.* Men in institutional settings, those struggling with substance misuse, and the homeless face distinct challenges that require targeted and compassionate interventions.

6. *Intersectionality.* Recognizing the intersecting identities of men and boys and how these intersections influence their experiences is essential for developing effective and inclusive interventions.

7. *Support systems and interventions.* From digital and online platforms to community-based programs, the importance of accessible, tailored, and comprehensive support systems cannot be overstated.

Throughout our exploration, a recurring theme has been the complementary nature of addressing men's issues alongside the ongoing fight for gender equality. Emphasizing the well-being of men and boys does not detract from the progress made in women's rights; instead, it reinforces the need for a balanced and inclusive approach to gender equality.

We have also underscored the importance of public consciousness. Raising awareness about the challenges faced by men and boys, and their broader societal impact, is a critical step toward fostering empathy, understanding, and cooperation among various stakeholders.

25.1   CALL TO ACTION

And so, what can be done?

- *For policymakers.* Implement policies that support mental health services, education, employment opportunities, and inclusive health care for men and boys from diverse backgrounds.
- *For educators and employers.* Create supportive environments that address the unique needs of men and boys, promoting lifelong learning and adaptability in the workforce.
- *For health-care providers.* Develop and offer comprehensive mental and physical health services tailored to the needs of men and boys.

- *For communities and families.* Foster open dialogues about masculinity, mental health, and healthy relationships, creating a supportive network that encourages positive growth and development.
- *For media and influencers.* Promote diverse and realistic portrayals of men and boys, challenging harmful stereotypes and fostering a culture of inclusion and respect.
- *For researchers and academics.* Conduct and disseminate research that deepens our understanding of the unique challenges faced by men and boys, ensuring that interventions are evidence-based and effective.
- *For NGOs and advocacy groups.* Develop campaigns and programs that specifically address the needs of men and boys, ensuring that these efforts are integrated into broader gender equality initiatives.
- *For mentors and role models.* Actively mentor and provide positive examples for young men and boys, guiding them toward healthy, responsible, and fulfilling lives. Show them the importance of seeking help and maintaining strong mental and physical health.
- *For faith and community leaders.* Use your platforms to encourage open discussions about the challenges men and boys face, and provide support networks within your communities that address their specific needs.
- *For social service providers.* Ensure that services are accessible to men and boys, particularly those who may be reluctant to seek help. Tailor outreach and support programs to reduce barriers to access and encourage engagement.
- *For philanthropists and funders.* Invest in initiatives and organizations that focus on the well-being of men and boys, particularly those that address mental health, education, and social support. Your contributions can help scale effective programs and reach more individuals.
- *For law enforcement and judicial systems.* Implement training and policies that address the specific needs of men and boys, particularly in areas such as mental health, domestic violence, and rehabilitation. Ensure that systems are supportive and not punitive where possible.
- *For technology developers and social media platforms.* Create digital tools and platforms that promote positive mental health and well-being among men and boys. Ensure that online spaces are safe and supportive, and actively combat toxic behaviors and stereotypes.
- *For unions and worker organizations.* Advocate for workplace policies that support the mental and physical health of men and boys, including paternity leave, mental health days, and access to counseling services.
- *For sports and recreational organizations.* Promote healthy masculinity through sports programs that emphasize teamwork, respect, and mental well-being. Provide resources and support for athletes' mental health, and challenge harmful stereotypes within sports culture.
- *For individuals (incuding you!).* Engage in self-reflection and conversations with those around you to challenge your own perceptions of

masculinity and support the men and boys in your life. Advocate for their well-being and encourage their participation in mental health and community support services.

25.2 CONCLUSION

Put simply, by addressing the challenges outlined with urgency and sensitivity, we can promote a more inclusive, equitable, and compassionate society for all.

Let us, therefore, all move forward with a commitment to understanding, supporting, and uplifting men and boys, ensuring their well-being and contributions are valued and recognized in our collective journey toward gender equality.

References

Abbott, A. (2020). An analysis of female vs. male circumcision. Kwantlen Psychology Student Journal, 8–8.

Adisa, T. A., Gbadamosi, G., & Osabutey, E. L. (2017). What happened to the border? The role of mobile information technology devices on employees' work-life balance. Personnel Review, 46(8), 1651–1671.

Agliata, D., & Tantleff-Dunn, S. (2004). The impact of media exposure on males' body image. Journal of Social and Clinical Psychology, 23(1), 7–22.

Alberti, J. (2013). "I Love You, Man": Bromances, the construction of masculinity, and the continuing evolution of the romantic comedy. Quarterly Review of Film and Video, 30(2), 159–172.

Alexander, B. K. (2006). Performing Black masculinity: Race, culture, and queer identity. Rowman Altamira.

Alexopoulos, C., Timmermans, E., & McNallie, J. (2020). Swiping more, committing less: Unraveling the links among dating app use, dating app success, and intention to commit infidelity. Computers in Human Behavior, 102, 172–180.

Aliyari, H., Sahraei, H., Erfani, M., Mohammadi, M., Kazemi, M., Daliri, M. R., . . . & Farajdokht, F. (2020). Changes in cognitive functions following violent and football video games in young male volunteers by studying brain waves. Basic and Clinical Neuroscience, 11(3), 279.

Allen, E. S., Rhoades, G. K., Stanley, S. M., & Markman, H. J. (2010). Hitting home: Relationships between recent deployment, posttraumatic stress symptoms, and marital functioning for Army couples. Journal of Family Psychology, 24(3), 280.

Alvermann, D., Wynne, E., & Wright, W. (2021). Tales from TikTok: Gender and cultural intersectionalities. In Genders, cultures, and literacies (pp. 198–211). Routledge.

Ammari, T., & Schoenebeck, S. (2015, April). Understanding and supporting fathers and fatherhood on social media sites. In Proceedings of the 33rd Annual ACM Conference on Human Factors in Computing Systems (pp. 1905–1914).

Anderson, E. (2010). Inclusive masculinity: The changing nature of masculinities. Routledge.

André, F., Broman, N., Håkansson, A., & Claesdotter-Knutsson, E. (2020). Gaming addiction, problematic gaming and engaged gaming – Prevalence and associated characteristics. Addictive Behaviors Reports, 12, 100324.

Andreasson, J., & Henning, A. (2022). "Falling down the Rabbit Fuck Hole": Spectacular masculinities, hypersexuality, and the real in an online doping community. Journal of Bodies, Sexualities, and Masculinities, 3(2), 76–97.

Andriessen, K., Krysinska, K., Kõlves, K., & Reavley, N. (2019). Suicide postvention service models and guidelines 2014–2019: A systematic review. Frontiers in Psychology, 10, 491007.

Antons, S., Engel, J., Briken, P., Krüger, T. H., Brand, M., & Stark, R. (2022). Treatments and interventions for compulsive sexual behavior disorder with a focus on problematic pornography use: A preregistered systematic review. Journal of Behavioral Addictions, 11(3), 643–666.

Archer, J. (2022a). Introduction: Male violence in perspective. In Male violence (pp. 1–20). Routledge.

Archer, J. (Ed.). (2022b). Male violence. Taylor & Francis.

Arxer, S. L. (2011). Hybrid masculine power: Reconceptualizing the relationship between homosociality and hegemonic masculinity. Humanity & Society, 35(4), 390–422.

Ashcroft, J. (2017). Do boys' attitudes to reading differ to those of girls? A study into the views of reading within a year three class. The STeP Journal: Student Teacher Perspectives, 4(1), 2–14.

Auxier, B., Stewart, D., Bucaille, A., & Westcott, K. (2019). The gender gap in reading: Boy meets book, boy loses book, boy never gets book back. 2022 Predictions, 94.

Aydoğdu, B., Azizoğlu, M., & Okur, M. H. (2022). Social and psychological effects of circumcision: A narrative review. Journal of Applied Nursing and Health, 4(2), 264–271.

Aydogmus, Y., Semiz, M., Er, O., Bas, O., Atay, I., & Kilinc, M. F. (2016). Psychological and sexual effects of circumcision in adult males. Canadian Urological Association Journal, 10(5–6), E156.

Aziz, N., Nordin, M. J., Abdulkadir, S. J., & Salih, M. M. M. (2021). Digital addiction: Systematic review of computer game addiction impact on adolescent physical health. Electronics, 10(9), 996.

Bäcklin, E. (2022). Supporting masculinities: Wounded healing and masculinity in peer support organizations for people with experiences of criminality and substance abuse. Victims & Offenders, 17(6), 872–892.

Baird, A. (2018). Becoming the "Baddest": Masculine trajectories of gang violence in Medellín. Journal of Latin American Studies, 50(1), 183–210.

Baldwin, S., Malone, M., Sandall, J., & Bick, D. (2018). Mental health and wellbeing during the transition to fatherhood: A systematic review of first time fathers' experiences. JBI Evidence Synthesis, 16(11), 2118–2191.

Baldwin, S., Malone, M., Sandall, J., & Bick, D. (2019). A qualitative exploratory study of UK first-time fathers' experiences, mental health and wellbeing needs during their transition to fatherhood. BMJ Open, 9(9), e030792.

Banerjee, S. (2012). Make me a man!: Masculinity, Hinduism, and nationalism in India. State University of New York Press.

Bañuelos Marco, B., & García Heil, J. L. (2021). Circumcision in childhood and male sexual function: A blessing or a curse? International Journal of Impotence Research, 33(2), 139–148.

Bareket, O., & Shnabel, N. (2020). Domination and objectification: Men's motivation for dominance over women affects their tendency to sexually objectify women. Psychology of Women Quarterly, 44(1), 28–49.

Barlett, C. P., Vowels, C. L., & Saucier, D. A. (2008). Meta-analyses of the effects of media images on men's body-image concerns. Journal of Social and Clinical Psychology, 27(3), 279–310.

Barnes, M., Abhyankar, P., Dimova, E., & Best, C. (2020). Associations between body dissatisfaction and self-reported anxiety and depression in otherwise healthy men: A systematic review and meta-analysis. PloS One, 15(2), e0229268.

Bataille, C. D., & Hyland, E. (2023). Involved fathering: How new dads are redefining fatherhood. Personnel Review, 52(4), 1010–1032.

Bates, E. A., & Hine, B. A. (2023). "I was told when I could hold, talk with, or kiss our daughter": Exploring fathers' experiences of parental alienation within the context of intimate partner violence. Partner Abuse.

Bates, E. A., & Taylor, J. C. (Eds.). (2019). Intimate partner violence: New perspectives in research and practice (1st ed.). Routledge.

Becker, J. B., McClellan, M., & Reed, B. G. (2016). Sociocultural context for sex differences in addiction. Addiction Biology, 21(5), 1052–1059.

Belus, J. M., Pentel, K. Z., Cohen, M. J., Fischer, M. S., & Baucom, D. H. (2019). Staying connected: An examination of relationship maintenance behaviors in long-distance relationships. Marriage & Family Review, 55(1), 78–98.

Bennett, S., Robb, K. A., Zortea, T. C., Dickson, A., Richardson, C., & O'Connor, R. C. (2023). Male suicide risk and recovery factors: A systematic review and qualitative metasynthesis of two decades of research. Psychological Bulletin, 149(7–8), 371.

Blakemore, J. E. O., Berenbaum, S. A., & Liben, L. S. (2013). Gender development. Psychology Press.

Boerma, I. E., Mol, S. E., & Jolles, J. (2016). Teacher perceptions affect boys' and girls' reading motivation differently. Reading Psychology, 37(4), 547–569.

Bolding, G., Sherr, L., & Elford, J. (2002). Use of anabolic steroids and associated health risks among gay men attending London gyms. Addiction, 97(2), 195–203.

Bonnecaze, A. K., O'Connor, T., & Aloi, J. A. (2020). Characteristics and attitudes of men using anabolic androgenic steroids (AAS): A survey of 2385 men. American Journal of Men's Health, 14(6), 1557988320966536.

Bornioli, A., Lewis-Smith, H., Smith, A., Slater, A., & Bray, I. (2019). Adolescent body dissatisfaction and disordered eating: Predictors of later risky health behaviours. Social Science & Medicine, 238, 112458.

Bowie, J., Brunckhorst, O., Stewart, R., Dasgupta, P., & Ahmed, K. (2022). Body image, self-esteem, and sense of masculinity in patients with prostate cancer: A qualitative meta-synthesis. Journal of Cancer Survivorship, 16(1), 95–110.

Boyle, K., & Berridge, S. (2014). I love you, man: Gendered narratives of friendship in contemporary Hollywood comedies. Feminist Media Studies, 14(3), 353–368.

Brem, M. J., Garner, A. R., Grigorian, H., Florimbio, A. R., Wolford-Clevenger, C., Shorey, R. C., & Stuart, G. L. (2021). Problematic pornography use and physical and sexual intimate partner violence perpetration among men in batterer intervention programs. Journal of Interpersonal Violence, 36(11–12), NP6085–NP6105.

Brewer, G., Hanson, L., & Caswell, N. (2022). Body image and eating behavior in transgender men and women: The importance of stage of gender affirmation. Bulletin of Applied Transgender Studies, 1(1–2), 71–95.

Bridges, A. J., Sun, C. F., Ezzell, M. B., & Johnson, J. (2016). Sexual scripts and the sexual behavior of men and women who use pornography. Sexualization, Media, & Society, 2(4), 2374623816668275.

Burén, J., Nutley, S. B., Sandberg, D., Ström Wiman, J., & Thorell, L. B. (2021). Gaming and social media addiction in university students: Sex differences, suitability of symptoms, and association with psychosocial difficulties. Frontiers in Psychiatry, 12, 740867.

Butler, J. (2004). Undoing gender. Routledge.

Butler, J. (2020). Performative acts and gender constitution: An essay in phenomenology and feminist theory. In Feminist theory reader (pp. 353–361). Routledge.

Byron, P., Albury, K., & Pym, T. (2021). Hooking up with friends: LGBTQ+ young people, dating apps, friendship and safety. Media, Culture & Society, 43(3), 497–514.

Byron, P., Albury, K., Pym, T., Race, K., & McCosker, A. (2019). Trust in friendship: LGBTQ+ young people and hook-up app safeties. AoIR Selected Papers of Internet Research.

Cadaret, M. C., & Speight, S. L. (2018). An exploratory study of attitudes toward psychological help seeking among African American men. Journal of Black Psychology, 44(4), 347–370.

Cafferky, B. M., Mendez, M., Anderson, J. R., & Stith, S. M. (2018). Substance use and intimate partner violence: A meta-analytic review. Psychology of Violence, 8(1), 110.

Carneiro, F. A., Tasker, F., Salinas-Quiroz, F., Leal, I., & Costa, P. A. (2017). Are the fathers alright? A systematic and critical review of studies on gay and bisexual fatherhood. Frontiers in Psychology, 8, 1636.

Carrard, J., Rigort, A. C., Appenzeller-Herzog, C., Colledge, F., Königstein, K., Hinrichs, T., & Schmidt-Trucksäss, A. (2022). Diagnosing overtraining syndrome: A scoping review. Sports Health, 14(5), 665–673.

Carrotte, E. R., Davis, A. C., & Lim, M. S. (2020). Sexual behaviors and violence in pornography: Systematic review and narrative synthesis of video content analyses. Journal of Medical Internet Research, 22(5), e16702.

Carter, R. S., & Wojtkiewicz, R. A. (2000). Parental involvement with adolescents' education: Do daughters or sons get more help? Adolescence, 35(137).

Chaarani, B., Ortigara, J., Yuan, D., Loso, H., Potter, A., & Garavan, H. P. (2022). Association of video gaming with cognitive performance among children. JAMA Network Open, 5(10), e2235721–e2235721.

Chatzopoulou, E., Filieri, R., & Dogruyol, S. A. (2020). Instagram and body image: Motivation to conform to the "Instabod" and consequences on young male wellbeing. Journal of Consumer Affairs, 54(4), 1270–1297.

Chegeni, R., Pallesen, S., McVeigh, J., & Sagoe, D. (2021). Anabolic-androgenic steroid administration increases self-reported aggression in healthy males: A systematic review and meta-analysis of experimental studies. Psychopharmacology, 238, 1911–1922.

Chen, Y., Lu, J., Wang, L., & Gao, X. (2023). Effective interventions for gaming disorder: A systematic review of randomized control trials. Frontiers in Psychiatry, 14, 1098922.

Chladek, M. R. (2021). Defining manhood: Monastic masculinity and effeminacy in contemporary Thai Buddhism. The Journal of Asian Studies, 80(4), 975–995.

Choi, E., Shin, S. H., Ryu, J. K., Jung, K. I., Kim, S. Y., & Park, M. H. (2020). Commercial video games and cognitive functions: Video game genres and modulating factors of cognitive enhancement. Behavioral and Brain Functions, 16, 1–14.

Choi, N. G., DiNitto, D. M., Marti, C. N., & Choi, B. Y. (2017). Association of adverse childhood experiences with lifetime mental and substance use disorders among men and women aged 50+ years. International Psychogeriatrics, 29(3), 359–372.

Christensen, A. D., & Jensen, S. Q. (2014). Combining hegemonic masculinity and intersectionality. NORMA: International Journal for Masculinity Studies, 9(1), 60–75.

Christiansen, A. V. (2020). Gym culture, identity and performance-enhancing drugs: Tracing a typology of steroid use. Routledge.

Chung, H., & Van der Lippe, T. (2020). Flexible working, work – life balance, and gender equality: Introduction. Social Indicators Research, 151(2), 365–381.

Clare, C. A., Velasquez, G., Martorell, G. M. M., Fernandez, D., Dinh, J., & Montague, A. (2021). Risk factors for male perpetration of intimate partner violence: A review. Aggression and Violent Behavior, 56, 101532.

Clark, C. B., Reiland, S., Thorne, C., & Cropsey, K. L. (2014). Relationship of trauma exposure and substance abuse to self-reported violence among men and women in substance abuse treatment. Journal of Interpersonal Violence, 29(8), 1514–1530.

Clarke, L. L., Hine, B., England, D., Flew, P. P., Alzahri, R., Juriansz, S. N., & Garcia, M. J. (2024). The gendered behaviors displayed by Disney protagonists. Frontiers in Sociology, 9, 1338900.

Clary, K. L., Pena, S., & Smith, D. C. (2023). Masculinity and stigma among emerging adult military members and veterans: Implications for encouraging help-seeking. Current Psychology, 42(6), 4422–4438.

Connell, R. W. (2017). On hegemonic masculinity and violence: Response to Jefferson and Hall. In Crime, criminal justice and masculinities (pp. 57–68). Routledge.

Connell, R. W. (2020). Masculinities. Routledge.

Connell, R. W., & Messerschmidt, J. W. (2005). Hegemonic masculinity: Rethinking the concept. Gender & Society, 19(6), 829–859.

Cosden, M., Larsen, J. L., Donahue, M. T., & Nylund-Gibson, K. (2015). Trauma symptoms for men and women in substance abuse treatment: A latent transition analysis. Journal of Substance Abuse Treatment, 50, 18–25.

Cote, A. C. (2020). Gaming sexism: Gender and identity in the era of casual video games. In Gaming sexism. New York University Press.

Crespi, I., & Ruspini, E. (2015). Transition to fatherhood: New perspectives in the global context of changing men's identities. International Review of Sociology, 25(3), 353–358.

Cudo, A., Wojtasiński, M., Tużnik, P., Fudali-Czyż, A., & Griffiths, M. D. (2022). The Relationship between depressive symptoms, loneliness, self-control, and gaming disorder among Polish male and female gamers: The indirect effects of gaming motives. International Journal of Environmental Research and Public Health, 19(16), 10438.

Curtin, S. C., & Hedegaard, H. (2019). Suicide rates for females and males by race and ethnicity: United States, 1999 and 2017.

Dahlenburg, S. C., Gleaves, D. H., Hutchinson, A. D., & Coro, D. G. (2020). Body image disturbance and sexual orientation: An updated systematic review and meta-analysis. Body Image, 35, 126–141.

Daniel, S., & Bridges, S. K. (2013). The relationships among body image, masculinity, and sexual satisfaction in men. Psychology of Men & Masculinity, 14(4), 345.

Darby, R. (2005). A surgical temptation: The demonization of the foreskin and the rise of circumcision in Britain. University of Chicago Press.

Darcy, C. (2020). Men and the drug buzz: Masculinity and Men's motivations for illicit recreational drug use. Sociological Research Online, 25(3), 421–437.

Davis, K. C., Masters, N. T., Casey, E., Kajumulo, K. F., Norris, J., & George, W. H. (2018). How childhood maltreatment profiles of male victims predict adult perpetration and psychosocial functioning. Journal of Interpersonal Violence, 33(6), 915–937.

Deacon, M., & Muir, G. (2023). What is the medical evidence on non-therapeutic child circumcision? International Journal of Impotence Research, 35(3), 256–263.

De Alarcón, R., de la Iglesia, J. I., Casado, N. M., & Montejo, A. L. (2019). Online porn addiction: What we know and what we don't – A systematic review. Journal of Clinical Medicine, 8(1), 91.

Deck, S. M., & Platt, P. A. (2015). Homelessness is traumatic: Abuse, victimization, and trauma histories of homeless men. Journal of Aggression, Maltreatment & Trauma, 24(9), 1022–1043.

Dej, E. (2018). When a man's home isn't a castle: Hegemonic masculinity among men experiencing homelessness and mental illness. In Containing madness: Gender and "psy" in institutional contexts (pp. 215–239). Springer International Publishing.

de Heer, B. A., Prior, S., & Hoegh, G. (2021). Pornography, masculinity, and sexual aggression on college campuses. Journal of Interpersonal Violence, 36(23–24), NP13582–NP13605.

Dekker, A., Wenzlaff, F., Biedermann, S. V., Briken, P., & Fuss, J. (2021). VR porn as "empathy machine"? Perception of self and others in virtual reality pornography. The Journal of Sex Research, 58(3), 273–278.

de Oliveira Lima, C. L., & Kuusisto, E. (2019). Parental engagement in children's learning: A holistic approach to teacher-parents' partnerships. In Pedagogy in basic and higher education-current developments and challenges (pp. 973–983).

Dermott, E., & Miller, T. (2015). More than the sum of its parts? Contemporary fatherhood policy, practice and discourse. Families, Relationships and Societies, 4(2), 183–195.

de Ronde, W., & Smit, D. L. (2020). Anabolic androgenic steroid abuse in young males. Endocrine Connections, 9(4), R102–R111.

Dietrichson, J., Filges, T., Seerup, J. K., Klokker, R. H., Viinholt, B. C., Bøg, M., & Eiberg, M. (2021). Targeted school-based interventions for improving reading and mathematics for students with or at risk of academic difficulties in Grades K-6: A systematic review. Campbell Systematic Reviews, 17(2), e1152.

Disenhaus, N. (2015). Boys, writing, and the literacy gender gap: What we know, what we think we know. The University of Vermont and State Agricultural College.

Donnelly, K., & Twenge, J. M. (2017). Masculine and feminine traits on the Bem Sex-Role Inventory, 1993–2012: A cross-temporal meta-analysis. Sex Roles, 76, 556–565.

Doyle, M. F., Shakeshaft, A., Guthrie, J., Snijder, M., & Butler, T. (2019). A systematic review of evaluations of prison-based alcohol and other drug use behavioural treatment for men. Australian and New Zealand Journal of Public Health, 43(2), 120–130.

Duffy, A., Dawson, D. L., & Das Nair, R. (2016). Pornography addiction in adults: A systematic review of definitions and reported impact. The Journal of Sexual Medicine, 13(5), 760–777.

Duncan, J. M., Reed-Fitzke, K., Ferraro, A. J., Wojciak, A. S., Smith, K. M., & Sánchez, J. (2020). Identifying risk and resilience factors associated with the likelihood of seeking mental health care among US army soldiers-in-training. Military Medicine, 185(7–8), e1247–e1254.

Eaton, A. A., & Rose, S. (2011). Has dating become more egalitarian? A 35 year review using sex roles. Sex Roles, 64, 843–862.

Ecker, J., Aubry, T., & Sylvestre, J. (2019). A review of the literature on LGBTQ adults who experience homelessness. Journal of Homosexuality, 66(3), 297–323.

Edley, N. (2017). Men and masculinity: The basics. Routledge.

Eibach, J. (2016). Violence and masculinity. In The Oxford handbook of the history of crime and criminal justice (pp. 229–244). Oxford University Press.

Ekiciler, A., Ahioğlu, İ., Yıldırım, N., Ajas, İ. İ., & Kaya, T. (2022). The bullying game: Sexism based toxic language analysis on online games chat logs by text mining. Journal of International Women's Studies, 24(3), 1–16.

Emslie, C., & Hunt, K. (2009). "Live to work" or "work to live"? A qualitative study of gender and work – life balance among men and women in mid-life. Gender, Work & Organization, 16(1), 151–172.

Evans, A. M., Carney, J. S., & Wilkinson, M. (2013). Work – life balance for men: Counseling implications. Journal of Counseling & Development, 91(4), 436–441.

Evans, D. K., Akmal, M., & Jakiela, P. (2020). Gender gaps in education: The long view. IZA Journal of Development and Migration, 12(1).

Evans, L. (2023). Virtual reality pornography: A review of health-related opportunities and challenges. Current Sexual Health Reports, 15(1), 26–35.

Fabris, M. A., Longobardi, C., Badenes-Ribera, L., & Settanni, M. (2022). Prevalence and co-occurrence of different types of body dysmorphic disorder among men having sex with men. Journal of Homosexuality, 69(1), 132–144.

Faleschini, S., Aubuchon, O., Champeau, L., & Matte-Gagné, C. (2021). History of perinatal loss: A study of psychological outcomes in mothers and fathers after subsequent healthy birth. Journal of Affective Disorders, 280, 338–344.

Fargo, J., Metraux, S., Byrne, T., Munley, E., Montgomery, A. E., Jones, H., . . . & Culhane, D. (2012). Prevalence and risk of homelessness among US veterans. Preventing Chronic Disease, 9.

Farrugia, A. (2015). "You can't just give your best mate a massive hug every day" young men, play and MDMA. Contemporary Drug Problems, 42(3), 240–256.

Feinberg, J. (2020). After marriage equality: Dual fatherhood for married male same-sex couples. UC Davis Law Review, 54, 1507.

Filice, E., Raffoul, A., Meyer, S. B., & Neiterman, E. (2020). The impact of social media on body image perceptions and bodily practices among gay, bisexual, and other men who have sex with men: A critical review of the literature and extension of theory. Sex Roles, 82, 387–410.

Fisher, K., Seidler, Z. E., King, K., Oliffe, J. L., & Rice, S. M. (2021). Men's anxiety: A systematic review. Journal of Affective Disorders, 295, 688–702.

Franklin II, C. W. (2012). The changing definition of masculinity. Springer Science & Business Media.

Fraumeni-McBride, J. (2019). Addiction and mindfulness; pornography addiction and mindfulness-based therapy ACT. Sexual Addiction & Compulsivity, 26(1–2), 42–53.

Freeman, A., Mergl, R., Kohls, E., Székely, A., Gusmao, R., Arensman, E., . . . & Rummel-Kluge, C. (2017). A cross-national study on gender differences in suicide intent. BMC Psychiatry, 17, 1–11.

Fritz, N., & Paul, B. (2017). From orgasms to spanking: A content analysis of the agentic and objectifying sexual scripts in feminist, for women, and mainstream pornography. Sex Roles, 77(9), 639–652.

Fuentes, A. (2021). Searching for the "roots" of masculinity in primates and the human evolutionary past. Current Anthropology, 62(S23), S13–S25.

Ganz, A. P. D. Y., Yamaguchi, C., Koritzky, B. P. G., & Berger, S. E. (2021). Military culture and its impact on mental health and stigma. Journal of Community Engagement & Scholarship, 13(4).

Garvin, L. A., Hu, J., Slightam, C., McInnes, D. K., & Zulman, D. M. (2021). Use of video telehealth tablets to increase access for veterans experiencing homelessness. Journal of General Internal Medicine, 36, 2274–2282.

Gawash, A., Zia, H., & Lo, D. F. (2023). Body dysmorphic-induced Androgenic Anabolic Steroids usage and its association with mental health outcomes. medRxiv, 2023–01.

George, J., Quamina-Aiyejina, L., Cain, M., & Mohammed, C. (2009). Gender issues in education and intervention strategies to increase participation of boys. Ministry of Education.

Giaccardi, S., Ward, L. M., Seabrook, R. C., Manago, A., & Lippman, J. (2016). Media and modern manhood: Testing associations between media consumption and young men's acceptance of traditional gender ideologies. Sex Roles, 75, 151–163.

Gibbons, E. (2017). Masculinity, gaming, friendship and intimacy, and sense of community: A comparison of men in virtual and offline domains. Texas Woman's University.

Gibbs, N., Salinas, M., & Turnock, L. (2022). Post-industrial masculinities and gym culture: Graft, craft, and fraternity. The British Journal of Sociology, 73(1), 220–236.

Gibson, E., Griffiths, M. D., Calado, F., & Harris, A. (2022). The relationship between videogame micro-transactions and problem gaming and gambling: A systematic review. Computers in Human Behavior, 131, 107219.

Gilbert, M. A., Giaccardi, S., & Ward, L. M. (2018). Contributions of game genre and masculinity ideologies to associations between video game play and men's risk-taking behavior. Media Psychology, 21(3), 437–456.

Gilgoff, J. N., Wagner, F., Frey, J. J., & Osteen, P. J. (2023). Help-seeking and man therapy: The impact of an online suicide intervention. Suicide and Life-Threatening Behavior, 53(1), 154–162.

Gillen, M. M., Lefkowitz, E. S., & Shearer, C. L. (2006). Does body image play a role in risky sexual behavior and attitudes? Journal of Youth and Adolescence, 35, 230–242.

Gillig, T., & Bighash, L. (2019). Gendered spaces, gendered friendship networks? Exploring the organizing patterns of LGBTQ youth. International Journal of Communication, 13, 22.

Gola, M., Wordecha, M., Sescousse, G., Lew-Starowicz, M., Kossowski, B., Wypych, M., . . . & Marchewka, A. (2017). Can pornography be addictive? An fMRI study of men seeking treatment for problematic pornography use. Neuropsychopharmacology, 42(10), 2021–2031.

Goldsmith, K., Dunkley, C. R., Dang, S. S., & Gorzalka, B. B. (2017). Pornography consumption and its association with sexual concerns and expectations among young men and women. The Canadian Journal of Human Sexuality, 26(2), 151–162.

Gonzales IV, M., & Blashill, A. J. (2021). Ethnic/racial and gender differences in body image disorders among a diverse sample of sexual minority US adults. Body Image, 36, 64–73.

Gorowska, M., Tokarska, K., Zhou, X., Gola, M. K., & Li, Y. (2022). Novel approaches for treating Internet Gaming Disorder: A review of technology-based interventions. Comprehensive Psychiatry, 115, 152312.

Grannis, C., Leibowitz, S. F., Gahn, S., Nahata, L., Morningstar, M., Mattson, W. I., . . . & Nelson, E. E. (2021). Testosterone treatment, internalizing symptoms, and body image dissatisfaction in transgender boys. Psychoneuroendocrinology, 132, 105358.

Grant, B. K. (2010). Shadows of doubt: Negotiations of masculinity in American genre films. Wayne State University Press.

Gray, P. B., & Anderson, K. G. (2010). Fatherhood: Evolution and human paternal behavior. Harvard University Press.

Greenberg, G. A., & Rosenheck, R. A. (2008). Jail incarceration, homelessness, and mental health: A national study. Psychiatric Services, 59(2), 170–177.

Greif, G. (2008). Buddy system: Understanding male friendships. Oxford University Press.

Griffiths, M. D., & Pontes, H. M. (2020). The future of gaming disorder research and player protection: What role should the video gaming industry and researchers play? International Journal of Mental Health and Addiction, 18, 784–790.

Griffiths, S., Murray, S. B., & Castle, D. (2021). Body image disorders in men. Comprehensive Men's Mental Health, 86.

Grogan, S. (2021). Body image: Understanding body dissatisfaction in men, women and children. Routledge.

Gueta, K., Gamliel, S., & Ronel, N. (2021). "Weak is the new strong": Gendered meanings of recovery from substance abuse among male prisoners participating in narcotic anonymous meetings. Men and Masculinities, 24(1), 104–126.

Gültzow, T., Guidry, J. P., Schneider, F., & Hoving, C. (2020). Male body image portrayals on insta-gram. Cyberpsychology, Behavior, and Social Networking, 23(5), 281–289.

Haar, J. M., Russo, M., Suñe, A., & Ollier-Malaterre, A. (2014). Outcomes of work – life balance on job satisfaction, life satisfaction and mental health: A study across seven cultures. Journal of Vocational Behavior, 85(3), 361–373.

Hadar-Shoval, D., Alon-Tirosh, M., Asraf, K., Tannous-Haddad, L., & Tzischinsky, O. (2022). The association between men's mental health during COVID-19 and deterioration in economic status. American Journal of Men's Health, 16(2), 15579883221082427.

Hadley, D. (2015). Masculinity in medieval Europe. Routledge.

Halkitis, P. N., Moeller, R. W., & DeRaleau, L. B. (2008). Steroid use in gay, bisexual, and nonidenti-fied men-who-have-sex-with-men: Relations to masculinity, physical, and mental health. Psychology of Men & Masculinity, 9(2), 106.

Hamm, M., Miller, E., Jackson Foster, L., Browne, M., & Borrero, S. (2018). "The financial is the main issue, it's not even the child": Exploring the role of finances in men's concepts of fatherhood and fertility intention. American Journal of Men's Health, 12(4), 1074–1083.

Hammarén, N., & Johansson, T. (2014). Homosociality: In between power and intimacy. Sage Open, 4(1), 2158244013518057.

Harrington, C. (2021). What is "toxic masculinity" and why does it matter? Men and Masculinities, 24(2), 345–352.

Hayes, H. M. R., Burns, K., & Egan, S. (2024). Becoming "good men": Teaching consent and mas-culinity in a single-sex boys' school. Sex Education, 24(1), 31–44.

Hayward, R. A., & Honegger, L. N. (2018). Perceived barriers to mental health treatment among men enrolled in a responsible fatherhood program. Social Work in Mental Health, 16(6), 696–712.

Haywood, C., & Haywood, C. (2018). (Post) dating masculinities: From courtship to a post-dating world. In Men, masculinity and contemporary dating (pp. 25–54). Palgrave Macmillan London.

He, Q., Turel, O., Wei, L., & Bechara, A. (2021). Structural brain differences associated with exten-sive massively-multiplayer video gaming. Brain Imaging and Behavior, 15(1), 364–374.

Hefner, M. K. (2018). Queering prison masculinity: Exploring the organization of gender and sexu-ality within men's prison. Men and Masculinities, 21(2), 230–253.

Hen, M., Karsh, N., Langer, E., & Shechter, R. (2020). Gender differences in implicit exposure to cyber-pornography. The Journal of Social Psychology, 160(5), 613–623.

Henry, J. B., Julion, W. A., Bounds, D. T., & Sumo, J. N. (2020). Fatherhood matters: An integrative review of fatherhood intervention research. The Journal of School Nursing, 36(1), 19–32.

Hermann, Z., & Kopasz, M. (2021). Educational policies and the gender gap in test scores: A cross-country analysis. Research Papers in Education, 36(4), 461–482.

Hine, B. (2019). Pick a new #lane: How can we increase boys' participation and interest in literature and language, the arts, nursing, and education and early years? New Vistas, 5(1), 24–30.

Hine, B. (2022). Teachers' experiences of the impact of fatherlessness on male pupils. Lads Need Dads. https://drbenhine.co.uk/lnd-report-on-fatherless-and-school-achievement-behaviour/

Hine, B. (2024). Parental Alienation – What do we know, and what do we (urgently) need to know? A narrative review. Partner Abuse.

Hine, B., & Bates, E. A. (2023). "There is no part of my life that hasn't been destroyed": The impact of parental alienation and intimate partner violence on fathers. Partner Abuse.

Hine, B., Bates, E. A., Graham-Kevan, N., & Mackay, J. (2022). Comparing abuse profiles, contexts and outcomes of help-seeking heterosexual male and female victims of domestic violence: Part II – Exit from specialist services. Partner Abuse, 13(2).

Hine, B., Bates, E. A., Mackay, J., & Graham-Kevan, N. (2022). Comparing the demographic char-acteristics, and reported abuse type, contexts and outcomes of help-seeking heterosexual male and female victims of domestic violence: Part I – Who presents to specialist services? Partner Abuse, 13(1), 20–60.

Hine, B., Bates, E. A., & Wallace, S. (2022). "I have guys call me and say 'I can't be the victim of domestic abuse'": Exploring the experiences of telephone support providers for male victims of domestic violence and abuse. Journal of Interpersonal Violence, 37(7–8), NP5594–NP5625.

Hine, B., England, D., Lopreore, K., Skora Horgan, E., & Hartwell, L. (2018). The rise of the androgynous princess: Examining representations of gender in prince and princess characters of Disney movies released 2009–2016. Social Sciences, 7(12), 245.

Hine, B., Hoppe, I., & Los, G. (2024). Experiences of men made homeless as a result of domestic violence. Policy Report.

Hine, B., Ivanovic, K., & England, D. (2018). From the sleeping princess to the world-saving daughter of the chief: Examining young children's perceptions of "old" versus "new" Disney princess characters. Social Sciences, 7(9), 161.

Hine, B., Mackay, J., Baguley, T., Graham-Kevan, N., Cunliffe, M., & Galloway, A. (2022). Understanding Perpetrators of Intimate Partner Violence (IPV). Home Office.

Hine, B., & Roy, E. (2023). Lost dads: Findings from the Fathers and Family Breakdown, Separation, and Divorce (FBSD) project. https://drbenhine.co.uk/lost-dads-findings-from-the-fathers-and-family-breakdown-separation-and-divorce-fbsd-project/

Hines, D. (2015). Overlooked victims of domestic violence: Men. International Journal for Family Research and Policy, 1(1).

Hines, D. A., & Douglas, E. M. (2015). Health problems of partner violence victims: Comparing help-seeking men to a population-based sample. American Journal of Preventive Medicine, 48(2), 136–144.

Hoeve, M., Colins, O. F., Mulder, E. A., Loeber, R., Stams, G. J. J., & Vermeiren, R. R. (2015). Trauma and mental health problems in adolescent males: Differences between childhood-onset and adolescent-onset offenders. Criminal Justice and Behavior, 42(7), 685–702.

Höfner, C., Schadler, C., & Richter, R. (2011). When men become fathers: Men's identity at the transition to parenthood. Journal of Comparative Family Studies, 42(5), 669–686.

Howson, R. (2006). Challenging hegemonic masculinity. Routledge.

Huang, Q., Peng, W., & Ahn, S. (2021). When media become the mirror: A meta-analysis on media and body image. Media Psychology, 24(4), 437–489.

Hunt, G., & Antin, T. (2019). Gender and intoxication: From masculinity to intersectionality. Drugs: Education, Prevention and Policy, 26(1), 70–78.

Hygen, B. W., Belsky, J., Stenseng, F., Skalicka, V., Kvande, M. N., Zahl-Thanem, T., & Wichstrøm, L. (2020). Time spent gaming and social competence in children: Reciprocal effects across childhood. Child Development, 91(3), 861–875.

Iacob, S. I., Feinn, R. S., & Sardi, L. (2022). Systematic review of complications arising from male circumcision. BJUI Compass, 3(2), 99–123.

Imhoff, S. (2017). Masculinity and the making of American Judaism. Indiana University Press.

Ingram, N., & Waller, R. (2014). Degrees of masculinity: Working and middle-class undergraduate students' constructions of masculine identities. In Debating modern masculinities: Change, continuity, crisis? (pp. 35–51). Palgrave Pivot.

Inhorn, M. C. (2012). The new Arab man: Emergent masculinities, technologies, and Islam in the Middle East. Princeton University Press.

Ip, E. J., Doroudgar, S., Shah-Manek, B., Barnett, M. J., Tenerowicz, M. J., Ortanez, M., & Pope Jr, H. G. (2019). The CASTRO study: Unsafe sexual behaviors and illicit drug use among gay and bisexual men who use anabolic steroids. The American Journal on Addictions, 28(2), 101–110.

Islam, M. I., Biswas, R. K., & Khanam, R. (2020). Effect of internet use and electronic game-play on academic performance of Australian children. Scientific Reports, 10(1), 21727.

Izzat, N., Abu-Farha, R., Al-Mestarihi, E., & Alzoubi, K. H. (2023). The awareness and experience of healthcare providers with the use of anabolic androgenic steroids by gym users. International Journal of Legal Medicine, 137(6), 1705–1711.

Jablonka, I. (2022). A history of masculinity: From patriarchy to gender justice. Penguin UK.

Jacobsen, H., Bergsund, H. B., Wentzel-Larsen, T., Smith, L., & Moe, V. (2020). Foster children are at risk for developing problems in social-emotional functioning: A follow-up study at 8 years of age. Children and Youth Services Review, 108, 104603.

Jagayat, A., & Choma, B. L. (2021). Cyber-aggression towards women: Measurement and psychological predictors in gaming communities. Computers in Human Behavior, 120, 106753.

Javidi, H., Maheux, A. J., Widman, L., Kamke, K., Choukas-Bradley, S., & Peterson, Z. D. (2020). Understanding adolescents' attitudes toward affirmative consent. The Journal of Sex Research, 57(9), 1100–1107.

Jester, N. (2021). Army recruitment video advertisements in the US and UK since 2002: Challenging ideals of hegemonic military masculinity? Media, War & Conflict, 14(1), 57–74.

Johansson, T., & Andreasson, J. (2017). Fatherhood in transition: Masculinity, identity and everyday life. Springer.

Jones, C., Scholes, L., Johnson, D., Katsikitis, M., & Carras, M. C. (2014). Gaming well: Links between videogames and flourishing mental health. Frontiers in Psychology, 5, 76833.

Jones, M. M. (2016). Does race matter in addressing homelessness? A review of the literature. World Medical & Health Policy, 8(2), 139–156.

Kahn-John, M., Badger, T., McEwen, M. M., Koithan, M., Arnault, D. S., & Chico-Jarillo, T. M. (2021). The Diné (Navajo) Hózhó Lifeway: A focused ethnography on intergenerational understanding of american indian cultural wisdom. Journal of Transcultural Nursing, 32(3), 256–265.

Kanayama, G., Hudson, J. I., & Pope Jr, H. G. (2020). Anabolic-androgenic steroid use and body image in men: A growing concern for clinicians. Psychotherapy and Psychosomatics, 89(2), 65–73.

Kang, X., Handayani, D. O. D., Chong, P. P., & Acharya, U. R. (2020). Profiling of pornography addiction among children using EEG signals: A systematic literature review. Computers in Biology and Medicine, 125, 103970.

Kangas, E., Lämsä, A. M., & Jyrkinen, M. (2019). Is fatherhood allowed? Media discourses of fatherhood in organizational life. Gender, Work & Organization, 26(10), 1433–1450.

Kaplan, D. (2022). The men we loved: Male friendship and nationalism in Israeli culture. Berghahn Books.

Karagun, B., & Altug, S. (2024). Anabolic-androgenic steroids are linked to depression and anxiety in male bodybuilders: The hidden psychogenic side of anabolic androgenic steroids. Annals of Medicine, 56(1), 2337717.

Kareithi, P. J. (2014). Hegemonic masculinity in media. Media and Gender: A Scholarly Agenda for the Global Alliance on Media and Gender, 30, 27–29.

Kaye, L. S., Hellsten, L. A. M., McIntyre, L. J., & Hendry, B. P. (2022). "There's a fine line between trash-talking and cyberbullying": A qualitative exploration of youth perspectives of online gaming culture. International Review of Sociology, 32(3), 426–442.

Kecir, K. A., Rothenburger, S., Morel, O., Albuisson, E., & Ligier, F. (2021). Experiences of fathers having faced with termination of pregnancy for foetal abnormality. Journal of Gynecology Obstetrics and Human Reproduction, 50(1), 101818.

Kennedy, A. J., Brumby, S. A., Versace, V. L., & Brumby-Rendell, T. (2020). The ripple effect: A digital intervention to reduce suicide stigma among farming men. BMC Public Health, 20, 1–12.

Khan, O. F., & Fazili, A. I. (2016). Work life balance: A conceptual review. Journal of Strategic Human Resource Management, 5(2).

Kieran, D. (2021). "It changed me as a man:" Reframing military masculinity in the Army's "shoulder to shoulder" suicide prevention campaign. Journal of War & Culture Studies, 14(3), 306–323.

Kim, M. M., Ford, J. D., Howard, D. L., & Bradford, D. W. (2010). Assessing trauma, substance abuse, and mental health in a sample of homeless men. Health & Social Work, 35(1), 39–48.

Kimmel, M. S. (2016). 6 masculinity as homophobia. In Race, class, and gender in the United States: An integrated study (p. 59).

Kimmel, M. S. (2018). The contemporary "crisis" of masculinity in historical perspective. In The making of masculinities (Routledge Revivals) (pp. 121–153). Routledge.

Kimmel, M. S., & Coston, B. M. (2018). Seeing privilege where it isn't: Marginalized masculinities and the intersectionality of privilege. In Privilege (pp. 161–179). Routledge.

King, K., Schlichthorst, M., Turnure, J., Phelps, A., Spittal, M. J., & Pirkis, J. (2019). Evaluating the effectiveness of a website about masculinity and suicide to prompt help-seeking. Health Promotion Journal of Australia, 30(3), 381–389.

King, T. L., Shields, M., Sojo, V., Daraganova, G., Currier, D., O'Neil, A., . . . & Milner, A. (2020). Expressions of masculinity and associations with suicidal ideation among young males. BMC Psychiatry, 20, 1–10.

Koban, K., Biehl, J., Bornemeier, J., & Ohler, P. (2022). Compensatory video gaming: Gaming behaviours and adverse outcomes and the moderating role of stress, social interaction anxiety, and loneliness. Behaviour & Information Technology, 41(13), 2727–2744.

Kothari, A., Bruxner, G., Callaway, L., & Dulhunty, J. M. (2022). "It's a lot of pain you've got to hide": A qualitative study of the journey of fathers facing traumatic pregnancy and childbirth. BMC Pregnancy and Childbirth, 22(1), 434.

Krahé, B., Tomaszewska, P., & Schuster, I. (2021). Links of perceived pornography realism with sexual aggression via sexual scripts, sexual behavior, and acceptance of sexual coercion: A study with German university students. International Journal of Environmental Research and Public Health, 19(1), 63.

Kristensen, J. H., Pallesen, S., King, D. L., Hysing, M., & Erevik, E. K. (2021). Problematic gaming and sleep: A systematic review and meta-analysis. Frontiers in Psychiatry, 12, 675237.

Krondorfer, B. (Ed.). (2013). Men and masculinities in Christianity and Judaism: A critical reader. SCM Press.

Kubrin, C. E., & Wadsworth, T. (2009). Explaining suicide among blacks and whites: How socioeconomic factors and gun availability affect race-specific suicide rates. Social Science Quarterly, 90(5), 1203–1227.

Kulshrestha, S. (2011). I get by with a little help from my bros: An analysis of the male homosocial relationship on "how I met your mother". Inquiries Journal, 3(1).

Kumari, S., & Dhiksha, J. (2022). Effect of intervention for gaming addiction among adolescents: A systematic review. International Journal of Health Sciences, (III), 431219.

Lal, S., Elias, S., Sieu, V., & Peredo, R. (2023). The use of technology to provide mental health services to youth experiencing homelessness: Scoping review. Journal of Medical Internet Research, 25, e41939.

Lamarche, L., Gammage, K. L., & Ozimok, B. (2018). The gym as a culture of body achievement: Exploring negative and positive body image experiences in men attending university. SAGE Open, 8(2), 2158244018778103.

Lamb, M. E. (2013a). The changing faces of fatherhood and father – child relationships: From fatherhood as status to father as dad. In Handbook of family theories (pp. 87–102). Routledge.

Lamb, M. E. (2013b). The father's role: Cross cultural perspectives. Routledge.

Landripet, I., & Štulhofer, A. (2015). Is pornography use associated with sexual difficulties and dysfunctions among younger heterosexual men? The Journal of Sexual Medicine, 12(5), 1136–1139.

Langelier, D. M., Jackson, C., Bridel, W., Grant, C., & Culos-Reed, S. N. (2021). Coping strategies in active and inactive men with prostate cancer: A qualitative study. Journal of Cancer Survivorship, 1–11.

Leonhardt, M., & Overå, S. (2021). Are there differences in video gaming and use of social media among boys and girls? – A mixed methods approach. International Journal of Environmental Research and Public Health, 18(11), 6085.

Li, L., Abbey, C., Wang, H., Zhu, A., Shao, T., Dai, D., . . . & Rozelle, S. (2022). The association between video game time and adolescent mental health: Evidence from Rural China. International Journal of Environmental Research and Public Health, 19(22), 14815.

Li, S., Zhao, F., & Yu, G. (2020). A meta-analysis of childhood maltreatment and intimate partner violence perpetration. Aggression and Violent Behavior, 50, 101362.

Link, B. G., Struening, E. L., Rahav, M., Phelan, J. C., & Nuttbrock, L. (1997). On stigma and its consequences: Evidence from a longitudinal study of men with dual diagnoses of mental illness and substance abuse. Journal of Health and Social Behavior, 177–190.

Lippa, R. A. (2016). Biological influences on masculinity. In Y. J. Wong & S. R. Wester (Eds.), APA handbook of men and masculinities (pp. 187–209). American Psychological Association. https://doi.org/10.1037/14594-009.

Litsou, K., Byron, P., McKee, A., & Ingham, R. (2021). Learning from pornography: Results of a mixed methods systematic review. Sex Education, 21(2), 236–252.

Liu, W. M., Stinson, R., Hernandez, J., Shepard, S., & Haag, S. (2009). A qualitative examination of masculinity, homelessness, and social class among men in a transitional shelter. Psychology of Men & Masculinity, 10(2), 131.

Loh, C. E., Sun, B., & Majid, S. (2020). Do girls read differently from boys? Adolescents and their gendered reading habits and preferences. English in Education, 54(2), 174–190.

Lorentzen, J. M. (2017). Power and resistance: Homeless men negotiating masculinity. Qualitative Sociology Review, 13(2), 100–120.

Lotfi, A., Babakhanin, M., & Ghazanfarpour, M. (2021). The effectiveness of intervention with cognitive behavioral therapy on pornography: A systematic review protocol of randomized clinical trial studies. Health Science Reports, 4(3), e341.

Lunau, T., Bambra, C., Eikemo, T. A., van Der Wel, K. A., & Dragano, N. (2014). A balancing act? Work – life balance, health and well-being in European welfare states. The European Journal of Public Health, 24(3), 422–427.

Lundberg, S. (2020). Educational gender gaps. Southern Economic Journal, 87(2), 416–439.

Lynch, L., Long, M., & Moorhead, A. (2018). Young men, help-seeking, and mental health services: Exploring barriers and solutions. American Journal of Men's Health, 12(1), 138–149.

Machin, A. J. (2015). Mind the gap: The expectation and reality of involved fatherhood. Fathering: A Journal of Theory, Research & Practice about Men as Fathers, 13(1).

Machin, A. J. (2018). The life of dad: The making of a modern father. Simon and Schuster.

Madsen, S. A., & Burgess, A. (2018). Fatherhood and mental health difficulties in the postnatal period. In Promoting Men's Mental Health (pp. 74–82). CRC Press.

Maguire, D. (2021). Vulnerable prisoner masculinities in an English prison. Men and Masculinities, 24(3), 501–518.

Maheux, A. J., Roberts, S. R., Evans, R., Widman, L., & Choukas-Bradley, S. (2021). Associations between adolescents' pornography consumption and self-objectification, body comparison, and body shame. Body Image, 37, 89–93.

Mao, E. (2021). The structural characteristics of esports gaming and their behavioral implications for high engagement: A competition perspective and a cross-cultural examination. Addictive Behaviors, 123, 107056.

Mardani, A., Farahani, M. A., Khachian, A., & Vaismoradi, M. (2023). Fear of cancer recurrence and coping strategies among prostate cancer survivors: A qualitative study. Current Oncology, 30(7), 6720–6733.

Markowitz, F. E., & Syverson, J. (2021). Race, gender, and homelessness stigma: Effects of perceived blameworthiness and dangerousness. Deviant Behavior, 42(7), 919–931.

Marques, A. S., Braga, A. F., Brito, Â., & Arantes, J. (2024). "Do I really need to ask?": Relationship between pornography and sexual consent. Sexuality & Culture, 1–22.

Matthews, P., Poyner, C., & Kjellgren, R. (2019). Lesbian, gay, bisexual, transgender and queer experiences of homelessness and identity: Insecurity and home (o) normativity. International Journal of Housing Policy, 19(2), 232–253.

May, J. (2015). Racial vibrations, masculine performances: Experiences of homelessness among young men of colour in the Greater Toronto Area. Gender, Place & Culture, 22(3), 405–421.

McCall, T. (2024). Making the renaissance man: Masculinity in the courts of renaissance Italy. Reaktion books.

McCann, E., & Brown, M. (2019). Homelessness among youth who identify as LGBTQ+: A systematic review. Journal of Clinical Nursing, 28(11–12), 2061–2072.

McCarthy, L., & Parr, S. (2022). Is LGBT homelessness different? Reviewing the relationship between LGBT identity and homelessness. Housing Studies, 1–19.

McKee, A., Dawson, A., & Kang, M. (2023). The criteria to identify pornography that can support healthy sexual development for young adults: Results of an international Delphi panel. International Journal of Sexual Health, 35(1), 1–12.

McKenzie, S. K., Collings, S., Jenkin, G., & River, J. (2018). Masculinity, social connectedness, and mental health: Men's diverse patterns of practice. American Journal of Men's Health, 12(5), 1247–1261.

McTigue, E. M., Schwippert, K., Uppstad, P. H., Lundetræ, K., & Solheim, O. J. (2021). Gender differences in early literacy: Boys' response to formal instruction. Journal of Educational Psychology, 113(4), 690.

Mellor, D., Fuller-Tyszkiewicz, M., McCabe, M. P., & Ricciardelli, L. A. (2010). Body image and self-esteem across age and gender: A short-term longitudinal study. Sex Roles, 63, 672–681.

Mergl, R., Koburger, N., Heinrichs, K., Székely, A., Tóth, M. D., Coyne, J., . . . & Hegerl, U. (2015). What are reasons for the large gender differences in the lethality of suicidal acts? An epidemiological analysis in four European countries. PLoS One, 10(7), e0129062.

Mestre-Bach, G., Villena-Moya, A., & Chiclana-Actis, C. (2024). Pornography use and violence: A systematic review of the last 20 years. Trauma, Violence, & Abuse, 25(2), 1088–1112.

Mfecane, S. (2018). Towards African-centred theories of masculinity. Social Dynamics, 44(2), 291–305.

Michalski, J. H. (2017). Status hierarchies and hegemonic masculinity: A general theory of prison violence. British Journal of Criminology, 57(1), 40–60.

Migliaccio, T. (2010). Men's friendships: Performances of masculinity. The Journal of Men's Studies, 17(3), 226–241.

Miller, E., Culyba, A. J., Paglisotti, T., Massof, M., Gao, Q., Ports, K. A., . . . & Jones, K. A. (2020). Male adolescents' gender attitudes and violence: Implications for youth violence prevention. American Journal of Preventive Medicine, 58(3), 396–406.

Mills, M. (2020). Teaching boys: Developing classroom practices that work. Routledge.

Miranda-Mendizabal, A., Castellví, P., Parés-Badell, O., Alayo, I., Almenara, J., Alonso, I., . . . & Alonso, J. (2019). Gender differences in suicidal behavior in adolescents and young adults: Systematic review and meta-analysis of longitudinal studies. International Journal of Public Health, 64, 265–283.

Mohammadi, B., Szycik, G. R., Te Wildt, B., Heldmann, M., Samii, A., & Münte, T. F. (2020). Structural brain changes in young males addicted to video-gaming. Brain and Cognition, 139, 105518.

Moreno-Agostino, D., Wu, Y. T., Daskalopoulou, C., Hasan, M. T., Huisman, M., & Prina, M. (2021). Global trends in the prevalence and incidence of depression: A systematic review and meta-analysis. Journal of Affective Disorders, 281, 235–243.

Morris, B. J., & Krieger, J. N. (2020a). The contrasting evidence concerning the effect of male circumcision on sexual function, sensation, and pleasure: A systematic review. Sexual Medicine, 8(4), 577–598.

Morris, B. J., & Krieger, J. N. (2020b). Non-therapeutic male circumcision. Paediatrics and Child Health, 30(3), 102–107.

Morris, B. J., Moreton, S., Bailis, S. A., Cox, G., & Krieger, J. N. (2022). Critical evaluation of contrasting evidence on whether male circumcision has adverse psychological effects: A systematic review. Journal of Evidence-Based Medicine, 15(2), 123–135.

Morris, B. J., Wamai, R. G., Henebeng, E. B., Tobian, A. A., Klausner, J. D., Banerjee, J., & Hankins, C. A. (2016). Estimation of country-specific and global prevalence of male circumcision. Population Health Metrics, 14, 1–13.

Moschion, J., & Johnson, G. (2019). Homelessness and incarceration: A reciprocal relationship? Journal of Quantitative Criminology, 35, 855–887.

Moyano, N., Sánchez-Fuentes, M. D. M., Parra, S. M., Gómez-Berrocal, C., Quílez-Robres, A., & Granados, R. (2023). Shall we establish sexual consent or would you feel weird? Sexual objectification and rape-supportive attitudes as predictors of how sex is negotiated in men and women. Sexuality & Culture, 27(5), 1679–1696.

Mshweshwe, L. (2020). Understanding domestic violence: Masculinity, culture, traditions. Heliyon, 6(10).

Muehlenhard, C. L., Humphreys, T. P., Jozkowski, K. N., & Peterson, Z. D. (2016). The complexities of sexual consent among college students: A conceptual and empirical review. The Journal of Sex Research, 53(4–5), 457–487.

Mullen, C., Whalley, B. J., Schifano, F., & Baker, J. S. (2020). Anabolic androgenic steroid abuse in the United Kingdom: An update. British Journal of Pharmacology, 177(10), 2180–2198.

Munoz, M., Crespo, M., & Pérez-Santos, E. (2005). Homelessness effects on men's and women's health. International Journal of Mental Health, 34(2), 47–61.

Munthe-Kaas, H. M., Berg, R. C., & Blaasvær, N. (2018). Effectiveness of interventions to reduce homelessness: A systematic review and meta-analysis. Campbell Systematic Reviews, 14(1), 1–281.

Muntoni, F., Wagner, J., & Retelsdorf, J. (2021). Beware of stereotypes: Are classmates' stereotypes associated with students' reading outcomes? Child Development, 92(1), 189–204.

Nadim, M., & Fladmoe, A. (2021). Silencing women? Gender and online harassment. Social Science Computer Review, 39(2), 245–258.

Nagata, J. M., Ganson, K. T., & Murray, S. B. (2020). Eating disorders in adolescent boys and young men: An update. Current Opinion in Pediatrics, 32(4), 476–481.

Najmi, A. H., Alhalafawy, W. S., & Zaki, M. Z. T. (2023). Developing a sustainable environment based on augmented reality to educate adolescents about the dangers of electronic gaming addiction. Sustainability, 15(4), 3185.

Nelson, B. S., Hildebrandt, T., & Wallisch, P. (2022). Anabolic – androgenic steroid use is associated with psychopathy, risk-taking, anger, and physical problems. Scientific Reports, 12(1), 9133.

Nimbi, F. M., Tripodi, F., Rossi, R., Navarro-Cremades, F., & Simonelli, C. (2020). Male sexual desire: An overview of biological, psychological, sexual, relational, and cultural factors influencing desire. Sexual Medicine Reviews, 8(1), 59–91.

Nonte, S., Hartwich, L., & Willems, A. S. (2018). Promoting reading attitudes of girls and boys: A new challenge for educational policy? Multi-group analyses across four European countries. Large-scale Assessments in Education, 6, 1–22.

Nowicki, G. P., Marchwinski, B. R., O'Flynn, J. L., Griffiths, S., & Rodgers, R. F. (2022). Body image and associated factors among sexual minority men: A systematic review. Body Image, 43, 154–169.

Obst, K. L., Oxlad, M., Due, C., & Middleton, P. (2021). Factors contributing to men's grief following pregnancy loss and neonatal death: Further development of an emerging model in an Australian sample. BMC Pregnancy and Childbirth, 21, 1–16.

O'Connor, P., Carvalho, T., Vabø, A., & Cardoso, S. (2015). Gender in higher education: A critical review. In The Palgrave international handbook of higher education policy and governance (pp. 569–584). Palgrave Macmillan London.

Ólafsdottir, K., & Kjaran, J. I. (2019). "Boys in power": Consent and gendered power dynamics in sex. Boyhood Studies, 12(1), 38–56.

Oliffe, J. L., Ferlatte, O., Ogrodniczuk, J. S., Seidler, Z. E., Kealy, D., & Rice, S. M. (2021). How to save a life: Vital clues from men who have attempted suicide. Qualitative Health Research, 31(3), 415–429.

Olsen, L. L., Oliffe, J. L., Brussoni, M., & Creighton, G. (2015). Fathers' views on their financial situations, father – child activities, and preventing child injuries. American Journal of Men's Health, 9(1), 15–25.

Orenstein, P. (2020). Boys & sex: Young men on hook-ups, love, porn, consent and navigating the new masculinity. Souvenir Press.

Oshana, A., Klimek, P., & Blashill, A. J. (2020). Minority stress and body dysmorphic disorder symptoms among sexual minority adolescents and adult men. Body Image, 34, 167–174.

O'Shaughnessy, B. R., & Michelle Greenwood, R. (2020). Empowering features and outcomes of homeless interventions: A systematic review and narrative synthesis. American Journal of Community Psychology, 66(1–2), 144–165.

Osserman, J. (2021). Circumcision on the couch: The cultural, psychological, and gendered dimensions of the world's oldest surgery. Bloomsbury Publishing USA.

Otten, D., Tibubos, A. N., Schomerus, G., Brähler, E., Binder, H., Kruse, J., . . . & Beutel, M. E. (2021). Similarities and differences of mental health in women and men: A systematic review of findings in three large German cohorts. Frontiers in Public Health, 9, 553071.

Pachankis, J. E., Sullivan, T. J., Feinstein, B. A., & Newcomb, M. E. (2018). Young adult gay and bisexual men's stigma experiences and mental health: An 8-year longitudinal study. Developmental Psychology, 54(7), 1381.

Pansu, P., Régner, I., Max, S., Colé, P., Nezlek, J. B., & Huguet, P. (2016). A burden for the boys: Evidence of stereotype threat in boys' reading performance. Journal of Experimental Social Psychology, 65, 26–30.

Parent, M. C., Gobble, T. D., & Rochlen, A. (2019). Social media behavior, toxic masculinity, and depression. Psychology of Men & Masculinities, 20(3), 277.

Parent, M. C., Hammer, J. H., Bradstreet, T. C., Schwartz, E. N., & Jobe, T. (2018). Men's mental health help-seeking behaviors: An intersectional analysis. American Journal of Men's Health, 12(1), 64–73.

Parkins, M., & Parkins, J. (2021). Gender representations in social media and formations of masculinity. Journal of Student Research, 10(1).

Pascoe, C. J. (2012). Dude, you're a fag: Masculinity and sexuality in high school. University of California Press.

Pascoe, G. J. (2015). A qualitative textual and comparative analysis of the representation of masculinity in the action and romantic comedy genres. Online Journal of Communication and Media Technologies, 5(3), 1–26.

Paymar, M. (2015). Violent no more: Helping men end domestic abuse. Turner Publishing Company.

Philaretou, A. G., & Allen, K. R. (2001). Reconstructing masculinity and sexuality. The Journal of Men's Studies, 9(3), 301–321.

Pinkett, M. (2023). Boys do cry: Improving boys' mental health and wellbeing in schools. Routledge.

Pinkett, M., & Roberts, M. (2019). Boys don't try? Rethinking masculinity in schools. Routledge.

Pirkis, J., Currier, D., Butterworth, P., Milner, A., Kavanagh, A., Tibble, H., . . . & Spittal, M. J. (2017). Socio-economic position and suicidal ideation in men. International Journal of Environmental Research and Public Health, 14(4), 365.

Pirkis, J., King, K., Rice, S., Seidler, Z., Leckning, B., Oliffe, J. L., . . . & Schlichthorst, M. (2023). Preventing suicide in boys and men. In Suicide risk assessment and prevention (pp. 483–494). Springer International Publishing.

Pirkis, J., Spittal, M. J., Keogh, L., Mousaferiadis, T., & Currier, D. (2017). Masculinity and suicidal thinking. Social Psychiatry and Psychiatric Epidemiology, 52, 319–327.

Plummer, D. (2016). One of the boys: Masculinity, homophobia, and modern manhood. Routledge.

Polak, K., Haug, N. A., Drachenberg, H. E., & Svikis, D. S. (2015). Gender considerations in addiction: Implications for treatment. Current Treatment Options in Psychiatry, 2, 326–338.

Pope Jr, H. G., Kanayama, G., Hudson, J. I., & Kaufman, M. J. (2021). Anabolic-androgenic steroids, violence, and crime: Two cases and literature review. The American Journal on Addictions, 30(5), 423–432.

Pope, N. D., Buchino, S., & Ascienzo, S. (2020). "Just like jail": Trauma experiences of older homeless men. Journal of Gerontological Social Work, 63(3), 143–161.

Prasetyaningtyas, S. W., & Prayogo, A. (2021, October). The effect of cyberbullying in multiplayer online gaming environments: Gamer perceptions. In 2021 International Conference on Informatics, Multimedia, Cyber and Information System (ICIMCIS) (pp. 244–249). IEEE.

Prohaska, A., & Gailey, J. A. (2010). Achieving masculinity through sexual predation: The case of hogging. Journal of Gender Studies, 19(1), 13–25.

Purwaningsih, E., & Nurmala, I. (2021). The impact of online game addiction on adolescent mental health: A systematic review and meta-analysis. Open Access Macedonian Journal of Medical Sciences (OAMJMS), 9(F), 260–274.

Raby, C., & Jones, F. (2016). Identifying risks for male street gang affiliation: A systematic review and narrative synthesis. The Journal of Forensic Psychiatry & Psychology, 27(5), 601–644.

Radcliffe, P., Gadd, D., Henderson, J., Love, B., Stephens-Lewis, D., Johnson, A., . . . & Gilchrist, G. (2021). What role does substance use play in intimate partner violence? A narrative analysis of in-depth interviews with men in substance use treatment and their current or former female partner. Journal of Interpersonal Violence, 36(21–22), 10285–10313.

Radtke, T., Apel, T., Schenkel, K., Keller, J., & von Lindern, E. (2022). Digital detox: An effective solution in the smartphone era? A systematic literature review. Mobile Media & Communication, 10(2), 190–215.

Raiden, A. B., & Räisänen, C. (2013). Striving to achieve it all: Men and work-family-life balance in Sweden and the UK. Construction Management and Economics, 31(8), 899–913.

Raifman, J., Charlton, B. M., Arrington-Sanders, R., Chan, P. A., Rusley, J., Mayer, K. H., . . . & McConnell, M. (2020). Sexual orientation and suicide attempt disparities among US adolescents: 2009–2017. Pediatrics, 145(3).

Ramirez, G., Fries, L., Gunderson, E., Schaeffer, M. W., Maloney, E. A., Beilock, S. L., & Levine, S. C. (2019). Reading anxiety: An early affective impediment to children's success in reading. Journal of Cognition and Development, 20(1), 15–34.

Rasmussen, M. L., Hjelmeland, H., & Dieserud, G. (2018). Barriers toward help-seeking among young men prior to suicide. Death Studies, 42(2), 96–103.

Reay, D., David, M. E., & Ball, S. J. (2005). Degrees of choice: Class, race, gender and higher education. Trentham books.

Reeves, R. V. (2022). Of boys and men: Why the modern male is struggling, why it matters, and what to do about it. Brookings Institution Press.

Reeves, R. V., & Smith, E. (2022). Boys left behind: Education gender gaps across the US. Brookings Institution. Retrieved from https://coilink.org/20.500.12592/xnf81v on 31 Aug 2024.

Reichel, D. (2017). Determinants of intimate partner violence in Europe: The role of socioeconomic status, inequality, and partner behavior. Journal of Interpersonal Violence, 32(12), 1853–1873.

Remster, B. (2021). Homelessness among formerly incarcerated men: Patterns and predictors. The ANNALS of the American Academy of Political and Social Science, 693(1), 141–157.

Retelsdorf, J., Schwartz, K., & Asbrock, F. (2015). "Michael can't read!" Teachers' gender stereotypes and boys' reading self-concept. Journal of Educational Psychology, 107(1), 186.

Rhead, R., MacManus, D., Jones, M., Greenberg, N., Fear, N. T., & Goodwin, L. (2022). Mental health disorders and alcohol misuse among UK military veterans and the general population: A comparison study. Psychological Medicine, 52(2), 292–302.

Rica, R., & Sepúlveda, A. R. (2024). Going deeper into eating and body image pathology in males: Prevalence of muscle dysmorphia and eating disorders in a university representative sample. European Eating Disorders Review, 32(2), 363–377.

Ricciardelli, R., Maier, K., & Hannah-Moffat, K. (2015). Strategic masculinities: Vulnerabilities, risk and the production of prison masculinities. Theoretical Criminology, 19(4), 491–513.

Rice, A., Kim, J. Y. C., Nguyen, C., Liu, W. M., Fall, K., & Galligan, P. (2017). Perceptions of masculinity and fatherhood among men experiencing homelessness. Psychological Services, 14(2), 257.

Rice, S. M., Purcell, R., & McGorry, P. D. (2018). Adolescent and young adult male mental health: Transforming system failures into proactive models of engagement. Journal of Adolescent Health, 62(3), S9–S17.

Richard, K., & Molloy, S. (2020). An examination of emerging adult military men: Masculinity and US military climate. Psychology of Men & Masculinities, 21(4), 686.

Richardson, C., Robb, K. A., & O'Connor, R. C. (2021). A systematic review of suicidal behaviour in men: A narrative synthesis of risk factors. Social Science & Medicine, 276, 113831.

Rivas-Rivero, E., & Bonilla-Algovia, E. (2022). Adverse childhood events and substance misuse in men who perpetrated intimate partner violence. International Journal of Offender Therapy and Comparative Criminology, 66(8), 876–895.

Roberts, M. (2021). The boy question: How to teach boys to succeed in school. Routledge.

Roberts, S. (2013). Boys will be boys . . . won't they? Change and continuities in contemporary young working-class masculinities. Sociology, 47(4), 671–686.

Robinson, J., Cox, G., Bailey, E., Hetrick, S., Rodrigues, M., Fisher, S., & Herrman, H. (2016). Social media and suicide prevention: A systematic review. Early Intervention in Psychiatry, 10(2), 103–121.

Robinson, S., & Anderson, E. (2022). Bromance: Male friendship, love and sport. Springer Nature.

Robinson, S., Anderson, E., & White, A. (2018). The bromance: Undergraduate male friendships and the expansion of contemporary homosocial boundaries. Sex Roles, 78(1), 94–106.

Rodriguez-Moreno, S., Vázquez, J. J., Roca, P., & Panadero, S. (2021). Differences in stressful life events between men and women experiencing homelessness. Journal of Community Psychology, 49(2), 375–389.

Roe, S. L. (2015). Examining the role of peer relationships in the lives of gay and bisexual adolescents. Children & Schools, 37(2), 117–124.

Romito, M., Salk, R. H., Roberts, S. R., Thoma, B. C., Levine, M. D., & Choukas-Bradley, S. (2021). Exploring transgender adolescents' body image concerns and disordered eating: Semi-structured interviews with nine gender minority youth. Body Image, 37, 50–62.

Roper, M. (2005). Between manliness and masculinity: The "war generation" and the psychology of fear in Britain, 1914–1950. Journal of British Studies, 44(2), 343–362.

Rothmann, J. (2022). Homosociality, Homohysteria and the gym. In Macho men in South African Gyms: The idealization of spornosexuality (pp. 117–153). Springer International Publishing.

Roza, T. H., Noronha, L. T., Shintani, A. O., Massuda, R., Lobato, M. I. R., Kessler, F. H. P., & Passos, I. C. (2024). Treatment approaches for problematic pornography use: A systematic review. Archives of Sexual Behavior, 53(2), 645–672.

Rudman, L. A., & Mescher, K. (2013). Penalizing men who request a family leave: Is flexibility stigma a femininity stigma? Journal of Social Issues, 69(2), 322–340.

Russell, S. T., & Fish, J. N. (2016). Mental health in lesbian, gay, bisexual, and transgender (LGBT) youth. Annual Review of Clinical Psychology, 12, 465–487.

Saiphoo, A. N., & Vahedi, Z. (2019). A meta-analytic review of the relationship between social media use and body image disturbance. Computers in Human Behavior, 101, 259–275.

Salahuddin, S., & Muazzam, A. (2019). Gaming addiction in adolescent boys. Clinical and Counselling Psychology Review, 1(2), 1–19.

Salifu, Y., Almack, K., & Caswell, G. (2023). "Out of the frying pan into the fire": A qualitative study of the impact on masculinity for men living with advanced prostate cancer. Palliative Care and Social Practice, 17, 26323524231176829.

Salvati, M., Passarelli, M., Chiorri, C., Baiocco, R., & Giacomantonio, M. (2021). Masculinity threat and implicit associations with feminine gay men: Sexual orientation, sexual stigma, and traditional masculinity. Psychology of Men & Masculinities, 22(4), 649.

Scarcelli, C. M. (2015). "It is disgusting, but . . .": Adolescent girls' relationship to internet pornography as gender performance. Porn Studies, 2(2–3), 237–249.

Scharrer, E., & Blackburn, G. (2018). Cultivating conceptions of masculinity: Television and perceptions of masculine gender role norms. Mass Communication and Society, 21(2), 149–177.

Scheibling, C. (2020). Doing fatherhood online: Men's parental identities, experiences, and ideologies on social media. Symbolic Interaction, 43(3), 472–492.

Schlichthorst, M., King, K., Reifels, L., Phelps, A., & Pirkis, J. (2019). Using social media networks to engage men in conversations on masculinity and suicide: Content analysis of man up Facebook campaign data. Social Media + Society, 5(4), 2056305119880019.

Schmidt, M., Taube, C. O., Heinrich, T., Vocks, S., & Hartmann, A. S. (2022). Body image disturbance and associated eating disorder and body dysmorphic disorder pathology in gay and heterosexual men: A systematic analyses of cognitive, affective, behavioral und perceptual aspects. PLoS One, 17(12), e0278558.

Scholes, L. (2019). Differences in attitudes towards reading and other school-related activities among boys and girls. Journal of Research in Reading, 42(3–4), 485–503.

Scholes, L., Mills, K. A., & Wallace, E. (2022). Boys' gaming identities and opportunities for learning. Learning, Media and Technology, 47(2), 163–178.

Scholes, L., Spina, N., & Comber, B. (2021). Disrupting the "boys don't read" discourse: Primary school boys who love reading fiction. British Educational Research Journal, 47(1), 163–180.

Schwabe, F., McElvany, N., & Trendtel, M. (2015). The school age gender gap in reading achievement: Examining the influences of item format and intrinsic reading motivation. Reading Research Quarterly, 50(2), 219–232.

Scoats, R., & Robinson, S. (2020). From stoicism to bromance: Millennial men's friendships. In The Palgrave handbook of masculinity and sport (pp. 379–392). Springer International Publishing.

Seidler, Z. E., Dawes, A. J., Rice, S. M., Oliffe, J. L., & Dhillon, H. M. (2016). The role of masculinity in men's help-seeking for depression: A systematic review. Clinical Psychology Review, 49, 106–118.

Seidler, Z. E., Rice, S. M., River, J., Oliffe, J. L., & Dhillon, H. M. (2018). Men's mental health services: The case for a masculinities model. The Journal of Men's Studies, 26(1), 92–104.

Setty, E. (2022). Educating teenage boys about consent: The law and affirmative consent in boys' socio-sexual cultures and subjectivities. Sex Roles, 87(9), 515–535.

Setyawati, R., Hartini, N., & Suryanto, S. (2020). The psychological impacts of internet pornography addiction on adolescents. Humaniora, 11(3), 235–244.

Shabanzadeh, D. M., Clausen, S., Maigaard, K., & Fode, M. (2021). Male circumcision complications – a systematic review, meta-analysis and meta-regression. Urology, 152, 25–34.

Sharp, P., Bottorff, J. L., Rice, S., Oliffe, J. L., Schulenkorf, N., Impellizzeri, F., & Caperchione, C. M. (2022). "People say men don't talk, well that's bullshit": A focus group study exploring challenges and opportunities for men's mental health promotion. PLoS One, 17(1), e0261997.

Shi, J., Potenza, M. N., & Turner, N. E. (2020). Commentary on: "The future of gaming disorder research and player protection: What role should the video gaming industry and researchers play?" International Journal of Mental Health and Addiction, 18, 791–799.

Shi, P., Yang, A., Zhao, Q., Chen, Z., Ren, X., & Dai, Q. (2021). A hypothesis of gender differences in self-reporting symptom of depression: Implications to solve under-diagnosis and under-treatment of depression in males. Frontiers in Psychiatry, 12, 589687.

Silvestri, M. (2017). Police culture and gender: Revisiting the "cult of masculinity". Policing: A Journal of Policy and Practice, 11(3), 289–300.

Sirola, A., Savela, N., Savolainen, I., Kaakinen, M., & Oksanen, A. (2021). The role of virtual communities in gambling and gaming behaviors: A systematic review. Journal of Gambling Studies, 37(1), 165–187.

Snapp, S. D., Watson, R. J., Russell, S. T., Diaz, R. M., & Ryan, C. (2015). Social support networks for LGBT young adults: Low cost strategies for positive adjustment. Family Relations, 64(3), 420–430.

Spector-Mersel, G., & Gilbar, O. (2021). From military masculinity toward hybrid masculinities: Constructing a new sense of manhood among veterans treated for PTSS. Men and Masculinities, 24(5), 862–883.

Spencer, C. M., Stith, S. M., & Cafferky, B. (2022). What puts individuals at risk for physical intimate partner violence perpetration? A meta-analysis examining risk markers for men and women. Trauma, Violence, & Abuse, 23(1), 36–51.

Spicer, B., Smith, D. I., Conroy, E., Flatau, P. R., & Burns, L. (2015). Mental illness and housing outcomes among a sample of homeless men in an Australian urban centre. Australian & New Zealand Journal of Psychiatry, 49(5), 471–480.

Star, J. (2021). Power, discourse, and subjectivity: Contextualizing steroid use among Two-Spirit gay, bi and queer men in Manitoba (Master's thesis).

Starr, C. R., & Zurbriggen, E. L. (2017). Sandra Bem's gender schema theory after 34 years: A review of its reach and impact. Sex Roles, 76, 566–578.

Steinmann, I., Strietholt, R., & Rosén, M. (2023). International reading gaps between boys and girls, 1970–2016. Comparative Education Review, 67(2), 298–330.

Steinþórsdóttir, F. S., & Pétursdóttir, G. M. (2022). To protect and serve while protecting privileges and serving male interests: Hegemonic masculinity and the sense of entitlement within the Icelandic police force. Policing and Society, 32(4), 489–503.

Stevens, C., Zhang, E., Cherkerzian, S., Chen, J. A., & Liu, C. H. (2020). Problematic internet use/computer gaming among US college students: Prevalence and correlates with mental health symptoms. Depression and Anxiety, 37(11), 1127–1136.

Stoet, G., & Geary, D. C. (2020). Gender differences in the pathways to higher education. Proceedings of the National Academy of Sciences, 117(25), 14073–14076.

Stovell, C., Collinson, D., Gatrell, C., & Radcliffe, L. (2017). Rethinking work-life balance and wellbeing: The perspectives of fathers. In The Routledge companion to wellbeing at work (pp. 221–234). Routledge.

Strier, R., & Perez-Vaisvidovsky, N. (2021). Intersectionality and fatherhood: Theorizing non-hegemonic fatherhoods. Journal of Family Theory & Review, 13(3), 334–346.

Studer, J., Baggio, S., Grazioli, V. S., Mohler-Kuo, M., Daeppen, J. B., & Gmel, G. (2016). Risky substance use and peer pressure in Swiss young men: Test of moderation effects. Drug and Alcohol Dependence, 168, 89–98.

Su, W., Han, X., Yu, H., Wu, Y., & Potenza, M. N. (2020). Do men become addicted to internet gaming and women to social media? A meta-analysis examining gender-related differences in specific internet addiction. Computers in Human Behavior, 113, 106480.

Sumter, S. R., Vandenbosch, L., & Ligtenberg, L. (2017). Love me Tinder: Untangling emerging adults' motivations for using the dating application Tinder. Telematics and Informatics, 34(1), 67–78.

Sun, C., Bridges, A., Johnson, J. A., & Ezzell, M. B. (2016). Pornography and the male sexual script: An analysis of consumption and sexual relations. Archives of Sexual Behavior, 45(4), 983–994.

Sundquist, K., Frank, G., & Sundquist, J. A. N. (2004). Urbanisation and incidence of psychosis and depression: Follow-up study of 4.4 million women and men in Sweden. The British Journal of Psychiatry, 184(4), 293–298.

Swann, C., Telenta, J., Draper, G., Liddle, S., Fogarty, A., Hurley, D., & Vella, S. (2018). Youth sport as a context for supporting mental health: Adolescent male perspectives. Psychology of Sport and Exercise, 35, 55–64.

Tan, T. (2016). Literature review on shifting fatherhood. Masculinities: A Journal of Identity and Culture, 6, 102–128.

Tasker, Y. (2012). Dumb movies for dumb people: Masculinity, the body, and the voice in contemporary action cinema. In Screening the male (pp. 230–244). Routledge.

Taylor, J. C., Bates, E. A., Colosi, A., & Creer, A. J. (2022). Barriers to men's help seeking for intimate partner violence. Journal of Interpersonal Violence, 37(19–20), NP18417–NP18444.

Taylor, K., & Gavey, N. (2020). Pornography addiction and the perimeters of acceptable pornography viewing. Sexualities, 23(5–6), 876–897.

Thomas, G. M., Lupton, D., & Pedersen, S. (2018). "The appy for a happy pappy": Expectant fatherhood and pregnancy apps. Journal of Gender Studies, 27(7), 759–770.

Thompson Jr, E. H., & Bennett, K. M. (2015). Measurement of masculinity ideologies: A (critical) review. Psychology of Men & Masculinity, 16(2), 115.

Thornborrow, T., Onwuegbusi, T., Mohamed, S., Boothroyd, L. G., & Tovée, M. J. (2020). Muscles and the media: A natural experiment across cultures in men's body image. Frontiers in Psychology, 11, 501704.

Thurman, W., Semwal, M., Moczygemba, L. R., & Hilbelink, M. (2021). Smartphone technology to empower people experiencing homelessness: Secondary analysis. Journal of Medical Internet Research, 23(9), e27787.

Tiggemann, M., & Anderberg, I. (2020). Muscles and bare chests on Instagram: The effect of Influencers' fashion and fitspiration images on men's body image. Body Image, 35, 237–244.

Timler, K., Brown, H., & Varcoe, C. (2019). Growing connection beyond prison walls: How a prison garden fosters rehabilitation and healing for incarcerated men. Journal of Offender Rehabilitation, 58(5), 444–463.

Timotheou, S., Miliou, O., Dimitriadis, Y., Sobrino, S. V., Giannoutsou, N., Cachia, R., . . . & Ioannou, A. (2023). Impacts of digital technologies on education and factors influencing schools' digital capacity and transformation: A literature review. Education and Information Technologies, 28(6), 6695–6726.

Todorovic, L., Huisman, M., & Ostafin, B. D. (2024). Targeting mechanisms for problematic pornography use interventions. Sexual Health & Compulsivity, 31(1), 1–28.

Tokunaga, R. S., Wright, P. J., & Vangeel, L. (2020). Is pornography consumption a risk factor for condomless sex? Human Communication Research, 46(2–3), 273–299.

Toombs, A. L., Lee, A., Guo, Z., Buls, J., Westbrook, A., Carr, I., . . . & LaPeter, M. (2022). "We're so much more than the in-game clan": Gaming Experiences and Group Management in Multi-Space Online Communities. Proceedings of the ACM on Human-Computer Interaction, 6(CSCW2), 1–29.

Tosh, J. (2005). Masculinities in an industrializing society: Britain, 1800–1914. Journal of British Studies, 44(2), 330–342.

Tran, A., Kaplan, J. A., Austin, S. B., Davison, K., Lopez, G., & Agénor, M. (2020). "It's all outward appearance-based attractions": A qualitative study of body image among a sample of young gay and bisexual men. Journal of Gay & Lesbian Mental Health, 24(3), 281–307.

Trekels, J., Vangeel, L., & Eggermont, S. (2017). Media ideals and other-sex peer norms among Belgian early adolescents: Equating self-worth with attractiveness. Journal of Children and Media, 11(4), 466–484.

Turnock, L. A. (2021). Rural gym spaces and masculine physical cultures in an "age of change": Rurality, masculinity, inequalities and harm in "the gym". Journal of Rural Studies, 86, 106–116.

Tye, M. C., & Sardi, L. M. (2023). Psychological, psychosocial, and psychosexual aspects of penile circumcision. International Journal of Impotence Research, 35(3), 242–248.

Tylka, T. L. (2015). No harm in looking, right? Men's pornography consumption, body image, and well-being. Psychology of Men & Masculinity, 16(1), 97.

Umamaheswar, J. (2022). "On the street, the only person you gotta bow down to is yourself": Masculinity, homelessness, and incarceration. Justice Quarterly, 39(2), 379–401.

Van Hek, M., Kraaykamp, G., & Pelzer, B. (2018). Do schools affect girls' and boys' reading performance differently? A multilevel study on the gendered effects of school resources and school practices. School Effectiveness and School Improvement, 29(1), 1–21.

Vera-Gray, F., McGlynn, C., Kureshi, I., & Butterby, K. (2021). Sexual violence as a sexual script in mainstream online pornography. The British Journal of Criminology, 61(5), 1243–1260.

Vergel, P., La parra-Casado, D., & Vives-Cases, C. (2024). Examining cybersexism in online gaming communities: A scoping review. Trauma, Violence, & Abuse, 25(2), 1201–1218.

Verniers, C., Bonnot, V., Darnon, C., Dompnier, B., & Martinot, D. (2015). How gender stereotypes of academic abilities contribute to the maintenance of gender hierarchy in higher education. In Gender and Social Hierarchies (pp. 26–38). Routledge.

Verrastro, V., Liga, F., Cuzzocrea, F., & Gugliandolo, M. C. (2020). Fear the Instagram: Beauty stereotypes, body image and Instagram use in a sample of male and female adolescents. QWERTY-Interdisciplinary Journal of Technology, Culture and Education, 15(1), 31–49.

Vinther, A. S. (2023). "The challenge is that steroids are so effective": A qualitative study of experts' views on strategies to prevent men's use of anabolic steroids. Contemporary Drug Problems, 50(1), 85–104.

Vogel, D. L., & Heath, P. J. (2016). Men, masculinities, and help-seeking patterns.

Waling, A. (2017). "We are so pumped full of shit by the media" Masculinity, magazines, and the lack of self-identification. Men and Masculinities, 20(4), 427–452.

Waling, A., James, A., & Fairchild, J. (2023). "I'm not going anywhere near that": Expert stakeholder challenges in working with boys and young men regarding sex and sexual consent. Critical Social Policy, 43(2), 234–256.

Wall, D., & Kristjanson, L. (2005). Men, culture and hegemonic masculinity: Understanding the experience of prostate cancer. Nursing Inquiry, 12(2), 87–97.

Walther, A., Breidenstein, J., & Miller, R. (2019). Association of testosterone treatment with alleviation of depressive symptoms in men: A systematic review and meta-analysis. JAMA Psychiatry, 76(1), 31–40.

Wang, L., Li, J., Chen, Y., Chai, X., Zhang, Y., Wang, Z., . . . & Gao, X. (2021). Gaming motivation and negative psychosocial outcomes in male adolescents: An individual-centered 1-year longitudinal study. Frontiers in Psychology, 12, 743273.

Ward, L. M., Epstein, M., Caruthers, A., & Merriwether, A. (2011). Men's media use, sexual cognitions, and sexual risk behavior: Testing a mediational model. Developmental Psychology, 47(2), 592.

Wegner, B. (2021). Raising feminist boys: How to talk with your child about gender, consent, and empathy. New Harbinger Publications.

Weiss, M. R., & Smith, A. L. (2002). Friendship quality in youth sport: Relationship to age, gender, and motivation variables. Journal of Sport and Exercise Psychology, 24(4), 420–437.

Whelan, G., & Brown, J. (2021). Pornography addiction: An exploration of the association between use, perceived addiction, erectile dysfunction, premature (early) ejaculation, and sexual satisfaction in males aged 18–44 years. The Journal of Sexual Medicine, 18(9), 1582–1591.

Whitley, R. (2018). Men's mental health: Beyond victim-blaming. The Canadian Journal of Psychiatry, 63(9), 577–580.

Widanaralalage, B. K., Hine, B. A., Murphy, A. D., & Murji, K. (2022). "I didn't feel i was a victim": A phenomenological analysis of the experiences of male-on-male survivors of rape and sexual abuse. Victims & Offenders, 17(8), 1147–1172.

Willis, M., Canan, S. N., Jozkowski, K. N., & Bridges, A. J. (2020). Sexual consent communication in best-selling pornography films: A content analysis. The Journal of Sex Research, 57(1), 52–63.

Wong, Y. J., Horn, A. J., & Chen, S. (2013). Perceived masculinity: The potential influence of race, racial essentialist beliefs, and stereotypes. Psychology of Men & Masculinity, 14(4), 452.

Wong, Y. J., Liu, T., & Klann, E. M. (2017). The intersection of race, ethnicity, and masculinities: Progress, problems, and prospects. In R. F. Levant & Y. J. Wong (Eds.), The psychology of men and masculinities (pp. 261–288). American Psychological Association. https://doi. org/10.1037/0000023-010

Wood, J. L., Kallis, C., & Coid, J. W. (2017). Differentiating gang members, gang affiliates, and violent men on their psychiatric morbidity and traumatic experiences. Psychiatry, 80(3), 221–235.

Wood, J. L., Kallis, C., & Coid, J. W. (2022). Gang members, gang affiliates, and violent men: Perpetration of social harms, violence-related beliefs, victim types, and locations. Journal of Interpersonal Violence, 37(7–8), NP3703–NP3727.

Wood, P., & Brownhill, S. (2018). "Absent fathers", and children's social and emotional learning: An exploration of the perceptions of "positive male role models" in the primary school sector. Gender and Education, 30, 172–186.

Woodford, M. S. (2012). Men, addiction, and intimacy: Strengthening recovery by fostering the emotional development of boys and men. Routledge.

Woodhall-Melnik, J., Dunn, J. R., Svenson, S., Patterson, C., & Matheson, F. I. (2018). Men's experiences of early life trauma and pathways into long-term homelessness. Child Abuse & Neglect, 80, 216–225.

Wright, D., & Brownhill, S. (2018). Men in early years settings: Building a mixed gender workforce (1st ed.). Jessica Kingsley Publishers.

Wright, P. J. (2022). Pornography consumption and condomless sex among emerging US adults: Results from six nationally representative surveys. Health Communication, 37(14), 1740–1747.

Wright, P. J., & Tokunaga, R. S. (2016). Men's objectifying media consumption, objectification of women, and attitudes supportive of violence against women. Archives of Sexual Behavior, 45, 955–964.

Wright, P. J., & Tokunaga, R. S. (2018). Women's perceptions of their male partners' pornography consumption and relational, sexual, self, and body satisfaction: Toward a theoretical model. Annals of the International Communication Association, 42(1), 55–73.

Wulff, H. (2022). Inter-racial friendship: Consuming youth styles, ethnicity and teenage femininity in South London. In Youth cultures (pp. 63–80). Routledge.

Xu, L. X., Wu, L. L., Geng, X. M., Wang, Z. L., Guo, X. Y., Song, K. R., . . . & Potenza, M. N. (2021). A review of psychological interventions for internet addiction. Psychiatry Research, 302, 114016.

Yager, Z., & McLean, S. (2020). Muscle building supplement use in Australian adolescent boys: Relationships with body image, weight lifting, and sports engagement. BMC Pediatrics, 20, 1–9.

Yousaf, O., Grunfeld, E. A., & Hunter, M. S. (2015). A systematic review of the factors associated with delays in medical and psychological help-seeking among men. Health Psychology Review, 9(2), 264–276.

Yu, J., McLellan, R., & Winter, L. (2021). Which boys and which girls are falling behind? Linking adolescents' gender role profiles to motivation, engagement, and achievement. Journal of Youth and Adolescence, 50(2), 336–352.

Yvonne, J. (2017). Men behind bars: "Doing" masculinity as an adaptation to imprisonment. In Crime, Criminal Justice and Masculinities (pp. 381–400). Routledge.

Zamorano, S., González-Sanguino, C., Sánchez-Iglesias, I., Sáiz, J., Salazar, M., Vaquero, C., . . . & Muñoz, M. (2022). The stigma of mental health, homelessness and intellectual disability, development of a national stigma survey with an intersectional gender perspective. International Journal of Clinical Trials, 9(4), 286–292.

Zendle, D., Cairns, P., Barnett, H., & McCall, C. (2020). Paying for loot boxes is linked to problem gambling, regardless of specific features like cash-out and pay-to-win. Computers in Human Behavior, 102, 181–191.

Zhouxiang, L. (2022). A history of competitive gaming. Routledge.

Zsolnay, I. (Ed.). (2016). Being a man: Negotiating ancient constructs of masculinity. Routledge.

Zuair, A. A., & Sopory, P. (2022). Effects of media health literacy school-based interventions on adolescents' body image concerns, eating concerns, and thin-internalization attitudes: A systematic review and meta-analysis. Health Communication, 37(1), 20–28.

Please also see https://xyonline.net/ for a huge collection of texts, articles, and organizations examining and intervening in issues affecting men and boys.

Other Key Texts

1. *Angry White Men: American Masculinity at the End of an Era,* by Michael Kimmel

    - Kimmel explores the rise of angry White male identity in the context of economic and social changes in America.

2. *Manhood in America: A Cultural History,* by Michael Kimmel

    - This book provides a comprehensive history of masculinity in America, detailing how perceptions of manhood have evolved over time.

3. *The Gendered Society*, by Michael Kimmel

    • Kimmel discusses gender inequality and the social structures that reinforce traditional gender roles.

4. *Guyland: The Perilous World Where Boys Become Men*, by Michael Kimmel

    • This book explores the period of life when boys transition to men, focusing on the social pressures and cultural norms they face.

5. *Men and Masculinities*, by Raewyn Connell

    • Connell provides a sociological perspective on masculinity, examining how it is constructed and maintained in society.

6. *Men and Masculinity: The Basics*, by Nigel Edley

    • Edley explores contemporary theories of masculinity, integrating sociological and psychological perspectives to understand the changing nature of male identity.

7. *The Descent of Man*, by Grayson Perry

    • Perry, an artist and commentator, discusses contemporary masculinity and its impacts on society.

8. *How to Be a Man*, by Robert Webb

    • Webb, an actor and comedian, explores the concept of masculinity, reflecting on his personal experiences and societal expectations.

9. *The Boy Crisis: Why Our Boys Are Struggling and What We Can Do About It*, by Warren Farrell and John Gray

    • This book examines the societal challenges boys face and offers solutions to help them thrive.

10. *Of Boys and Men: Why the Modern Male Is Struggling, Why It Matters, and What to Do about It*, by Richard Reeves

    • Reeves addresses the struggles faced by modern males, examining the reasons behind these challenges and proposing ways to help boys and men thrive.

11. *What About Men?* by Caitlin Moran

    • Moran explores the contemporary challenges faced by men, addressing topics such as masculinity, mental health, and societal expectations with her characteristic wit and insight.

12. *Real Boys: Rescuing Our Sons from the Myths of Boyhood*, by William Pollack

    • Pollack challenges common myths about boys and provides insights into the emotional lives of boys and young men.

13. *The Mask of Masculinity: How Men Can Embrace Vulnerability, Create Strong Relationships, and Live Their Fullest Lives*, by Lewis Howes

    • Howes addresses the emotional challenges men face and encourages vulnerability as a path to a more fulfilling life.

14. *For the Love of Men: A New Vision for Mindful Masculinity*, by Liz Plank

    • Plank explores how traditional masculinity harms men and society, proposing a more inclusive and emotionally healthy vision of manhood.

15. *Boys Adrift: The Five Factors Driving the Growing Epidemic of Unmotivated Boys and Underachieving Young Men*, by Leonard Sax

    • Sax examines the various factors contributing to boys' academic underachievement and social disconnection.

16. *The Will to Change: Men, Masculinity, and Love*, by Bell Hooks

    • This book examines how traditional masculinity affects men emotionally and explores ways to cultivate a more loving, supportive masculinity.

17. *Strong Mothers, Strong Sons: Lessons Mothers Need to Raise Extraordinary Men*, by Meg Meeker

    • Meeker provides advice for mothers on how to raise boys into strong, responsible men.

18. *Saving Our Sons: A New Path for Raising Healthy and Resilient Boys*, by Michael Gurian

    • Gurian offers practical advice for raising boys in today's complex world.

19. *Iron John: A Book About Men*, by Robert Bly

    • Bly uses myth and psychology to discuss the inner lives of men and the journey to mature masculinity.

INDEX

For Product Safety Concerns and Information please contact our EU
representative GPSR@taylorandfrancis.com
Taylor & Francis Verlag GmbH, Kaufingerstraße 24, 80331 München, Germany

www.ingramcontent.com/pod-product-compliance
Lightning Source LLC
Chambersburg PA
CBHW050623280326
41932CB00015B/2506

* 9 7 8 1 0 3 2 7 0 9 3 2 1 *